NATO ASI Series
Advanced Science Institutes Series

A series presenting the results of activities sponsored by the NATO Science Committee, which aims at the dissemination of advanced scientific and technological knowledge, with a view to strengthening links between scientific communities.

The Series is published by an international board of publishers in conjunction with the NATO Scientific Affairs Division

A Life Sciences	Plenum Publishing Corporation
B Physics	London and New York
C Mathematical and Physical Sciences	Kluwer Academic Publishers Dordrecht, Boston and London
D Behavioural and Social Sciences	
E Applied Sciences	
F Computer and Systems Sciences	Springer-Verlag Berlin Heidelberg New York
G Ecological Sciences	London Paris Tokyo Hong Kong
H Cell Biology	Barcelona Budapest
I Global Environmental Change	

NATO-PCO DATABASE

The electronic index to the NATO ASI Series provides full bibliographical references (with keywords and/or abstracts) to more than 30 000 contributions from international scientists published in all sections of the NATO ASI Series. Access to the NATO-PCO DATABASE compiled by the NATO Publication Coordination Office is possible in two ways:

- via online FILE 128 (NATO-PCO DATABASE) hosted by ESRIN, Via Galileo Galilei, I-00044 Frascati, Italy.

- via CD-ROM "NATO Science & Technology Disk" with user-friendly retrieval software in English, French and German (© WTV GmbH and DATAWARE Technologies Inc. 1992).

The CD-ROM can be ordered through any member of the Board of Publishers or through NATO-PCO, Overijse, Belgium.

The ASI Series F Books Published as a Result of
Activities of the Special Programme on
ADVANCED EDUCATIONAL TECHNOLOGY

This book contains the proceedings of a NATO Advanced Research Work-
shop held within the activities of the NATO Special Programme on Advanced
Educational Technology, running from 1988 to 1993 under the auspices of the
NATO Science Committee.

The volumes published so far in the Special Programme are as follows (further
details are given at the end of this volume):

Technology Education in School and Industry

Emerging Didactics
for Human Resource Development

Edited by

Dietrich Blandow

Eindhoven University of Technology
Department of Philosophy and Social Sciences
Postbus 513, HG 9.25, 5600 MB Eindhoven, The Netherlands

Michael J. Dyrenfurth

Technology & Industry Education
Department of Practical Arts & Vocational Technical Education
College of Education, University of Missouri-Columbia
105 London Hall, Columbia, MO 65211, USA

Springer-Verlag Berlin Heidelberg GmbH

Proceedings of the NATO Advanced Research Workshop on Advanced
Educational Technology in School-Industry Link Projects, held in Prague,
Czech Republic, and Poprad, Slovakia, August 15–22, 1993

CR Subject Classification (1991): K.3, H.4, J.6

ISBN 978-3-642-63393-5

Library of Congress Cataloging-in-Publication Data. Technology education in school and industry:
emerging didactics for human resource development/edited by Dietrich Blandow, Michael J. Dyrenfurth.
p. cm. – (NATO ASI series. Series F, Computer and systems sciences; vol. 135) "Proceedings of the
NATO Advanced Research Workshop on Advanced Educational Technology in School-Industry Link
Projects, held in Prague, Czech Republic, and Poprad, Slovakia, August 15-22, 1993" – T.p. verso.
Includes bibliographical references and index.
ISBN 978-3-642-63393-5   ISBN 978-3-642-57897-7 (eBook)
DOI 10.1007/978-3-642-57897-7
1. Technical education–Congresses. 2. Educational
technology–Congresses. 3. Industry and education–Congresses. I. Blandow, Dietrich, 1937- . II.
Dyrenfurth, Michael J. III. NATO Advanced Research Workshop on Advanced Educational Technology
in School-Industry Link Projects (1993: Prague, Czech Republic, and Poprad, Slovakia) IV. Series:
NATO ASI series. Series F, Computer and systems sciences; no. 135.   T62.T43   1994   607'.1–
dc20   94-36998

© Springer-Verlag Berlin Heidelberg 1994
Originally published by Springer-Verlag Berlin Heidelberg New York in 1994

Typesetting: Camera-ready by authors/editors
SPIN: 10130776   45/3140 – 5 4 3 2 1 0 – Printed on acid-free paper

Preface

The economic and social developments in the world continually pose new questions to both the social and physical sciences, to the state and to the economy. Currently, the social, natural, and technological fields are particularly impacted by these developments. The facilitation of scientific insights and the utilization of the assembled knowledge of millions of people in their daily work has evolved key questions about the very existence and continuation of society.

In a time where almost anything is technically possible, the means of advancing/facilitating (didactics) technological capabilities are being pursued with even more fervor than the actual hunt for new technological capabilities – at least by the most far-seeing nations. In comparison to natural resources, it is a nation's human resources and their combined capability that is infinite. The development of these capabilities was the impetus for this workshop.

To this challenge and process, new, hitherto unknown tasks and needs have emerged to energize the dynamic even further. Currently characterizing this search are key words and concepts that include interdisciplinarity, cognitive science, complexity, personal competence, synergistic competence, human resource development, technological literacy, school-industry links (partnerships), private practice partnerships, cognitive apprenticeship, reengineering education, concurrent education, hypermedia, meta-cognition, etc.

Much of the workshop's content involved the term didactics. It is nearly impossible to describe this term simply. Didactics involve the scientific discipline that focuses on structuring and organizing all learning situations including the constants and principles of teaching innovative thinking. In short, it is a scientific discipline about the principles and laws of teaching and it is closely connected with the structure of the subject being taught. These structures of the subjects and their didactic simplification for teaching purposes is a key function of didactics.

The ARW's dual foci were derived from the milieu described in the preceding paragraphs. These foci were:

1. Advanced technology in the individual disciplines and
2. Advanced educational technology in the field of didactics.

To ascertain the tendencies in didactics, as well as in the technical fields, the consequences of employing advanced technology for educational purposes brings forward also questions about advanced technology's role in education. These new questions in didactics are characterized by concepts such as think tanks, interactive teaching, multimedia, investigative orientation, structivism, constructivism, work didactics, problem solving, decision-making training, team teaching, and performance assessment. Such concepts represent new fields in the methodological explorations/research of future-oriented pedagogics.

The NATO Advanced Research Workshop in the Czech Republic and in Slovakia, conducted August 15–22, 1993, linked seamlessly to these developments. As suggested by its title, "Advanced Educational Technology in

School-Industry Link Projects", the workshop sought to identify elements in industrial training programs incorporating advanced educational technology that could be appropriately transferred to the secondary school environment. The second aim was to develop a model which blends contemporary educational pedagogy into the delivery of instruction relative to topics in advanced educational technology. The workshop's two main streams were: new didactic concepts for developing key qualifications through technology education programs using advanced educational technology and the correlation of advanced educational technology with innovative integrative situations in industrial practice. The target was to develop integrated learning situations suitable for secondary schools and teacher education, as well as for university-level technology, teacher education, and engineering programs. To this end, the workshop was structured and prepared as represented by this volume's outline.

Readers should be alert to the intertwined nature of the individual papers. Although each had to be assigned to one section or theme of the workshop, given the advanced level and research of the participants, their work invariably contained significant import for more than just a single theme. Hence, readers will find strands of interest threaded across the various sections and theme presentations.

Via formal paper sessions, group discussions, plenary feedback, and multiple personal interactions, the participants carried away new insights and capabilities that will take root in their research projects and that will invariably stimulate new questions themselves. In the group discussion summaries, for example, the reader will find the initial results of such insights synthesized from the interactions. In addition, the presented papers are provided. To make this volume manageable, most papers have been edited to some extent, therefore if readers wish for additional detail, they are encouraged to contact the presenters directly through the addresses provided in the List of Participants.

Acknowledgments

Undoubtedly for each NATO Advanced Research Workshop participant, the memories of their days in Prague and Poprad will long linger. Such persistence is due to the high standard of the academic exchange that was achieved as well as to the openness and warmth with which the participants accepted each others' ideas and perspectives. In addition, the effectiveness of the local organizers contributed significantly to the intellectual climate and hence to genuine understanding. The names of Katrin Langer, Detlef Wahl, Matthias Metzing, Jacub Serych, Thomas Sabol and others come to mind as colleagues who contributed much to the workshop's success. In addition, special thanks must also be extended to Professor Dr.-Ing. Sinay, Technical University of Kosice, Slovakia, as well as Ambassador Hacker, who leant their considerable stature to this venture.

Our appreciation also goes to NATO for making this event possible and to each participant and local organizer as well as – in particular – to WOCATE, the World Council of Associations for Technology Education. The latter, as evidenced by its effective coordination of this Advanced Research Workshop, demonstrated conclusively its capability to deliver world-class professional development experiences. Finally, our thanks go to the Springer publishing house for giving us the possibility for distributing and sharing the outcome of this most valuable workshop with colleagues all over the world.

June 1994

Erfurt   Dietrich Blandow
Columbia   Michael Dyrenfurth

Table of Contents

Official Opening and Welcome

Jozef Belak
Ministry of Economy of the Slovak Republic
Department for Technical Policy
Bratislava, Slovakia

Dear workshop participants,

Let me first bring you greetings from the Minister of Economy of the Slovak Republic with wishing success to your workshop. We highly appreciate the activity and the decision of the organizers of this meeting to organize a part of the workshop in the Slovak Republic.

The Slovak Republic, together with the Czech Republic is today the youngest country in the world. Both countries were established only on January 1, 1993. We appreciate most of all two facts in this, and that is:

– the split of the former Czechoslovak Federative Republic took place without any disputes, violence or fighting, without any shot,
– no national contradictions led to this split, neither rancour between the nations of the former federal republic, nor hostile tendencies of the national, political, or social groups of the population.

The split of the former state took place by an agreement and without violation.

The former Czechoslovak Republic was established in 1918 as a result of the World War I, from two related Slavic nations, Czechs and Slovaks, living before this in the Austro-Hungarian Monarchy. In connection with the ceasing of this Monarchy, by an agreement between the representatives of both Slavic nations, with the approval of the world great powers, the Czechoslovak Republic was established as a common state of Czechs and Slovaks. In that time this was a progressive and mutually advantageous solution. Regarding the fact, that the number of Czech nationals is approximately twice as high as the number of Slovak nationals, the Czech nation became a leading social power in the common state.

In the period between the two world wars, the Czechoslovak Republic as a whole achieved a significant position among developed industrial countries in Europe. This position was secured most of all by an extensive development of industrial production in the Czech Republic, where historically the conditions were more advantageous for it. These conditions were as an objective result of a different development of both parts of Czechoslovakia in the periods prior to the establishment of the common state. The Czech lands belonged till the ceasing of the Austro-Hungarian Monarchy into the Austrian part, and Slovakia into the Hungarian part of the monarchy. As a consequence of this, in a long term, there was historically different development and its consequences in both parts of the newly established state – the Czechoslovak Republic. The differences were adversely shown most of all in a lower industrial potential of Slovakia compared to the Czech lands, and also by a smaller extent of own national intelligence. These differences were not balanced during the 20-year of existence of the common state, till the beginning of the World War II. In the years of the World War II, both parts of Czechoslovakia were occupied by Hitler Germany, even when each part in a different way. These years were lost years for development of both parts of Czechoslovakia.

After the World War II, the common state – Czechoslovak Republic, was renewed. In a short time, it was politically reoriented to the camp of communist countries with the political and economic influence of the former Soviet Union, and by that it gained a new, for Czechoslovakia disadvantageous position. According to the military doctrine of the Soviet Union, Czechoslovakia was on the border of contact of so called socialist camp with the capitalist world, and as a "bumper" country of a possible encounter of military powers of both world camps, it was developed for purpose in a way, that is in its Western part, i.e. in Czech lands, the light and consumption industry was significantly developed, in the Eastern part – in Slovakia, further away from the line of contact, heavy and military industry was significantly developed, equipment for the rear components of the army, base for military airforce and for supply of armies, including education of military young people. By this orientation of the economic development of post-war Czechoslovakia, contradictions in the structure of industry was further deepening in both parts of Czechoslovakia.

After the change in political orientation of our country in 1989, and in connection with the decision on transformation of the centrally planned economic mechanism to a market-oriented mechanism, there was a significant difference between the economic situation of the Western part of Czechoslovakia – Czech lands and the Eastern part – Slovakia. Both parts, regarding their previous economic development, found themselves in a different position and different possibilities of their regional economies. Furthermore, in Slovakia a total ceasing of extensive military production was decided.

As a consequence of historical development and provisions after the trans-formation of the political orientation of Czechoslovakia, these differences in the regional economies were so obvious, that it was not possible to manage further development by a common economic policy resulting form possibilities of the economic state of the development in the Czech lands. As the Czech party did not agree with two regionally managed economies within the federation, both nations agreed on the ceasing of existence of the common state and on establishment of two new countries with their own economic policies – the Czech Republic and the Slovak Republic. Establishment of the new states took place on January 1, 1993.

Differentiated facilities of economy in both new republics require also different approach to the further development. In the Slovak Republic, most of all as a consequence of a very fast conversion of the military production and a stagnation of consumption of metallurgy products, there was a very fast decline of economy and a sharp increase of unemployment. Also the collapse of former Eastern block markets had an adverse impact, where most of the production of the Slovak industry was directed. The economic situation of the Slovak Republic, as a new state, is most burdened by costs associated with the necessity to build its own diplomatic and business missions abroad and seats of foreign missions at home, to urgently prepare staff for them, to build own state apparatus, all the executive components of the state, including defense and at the same time to restructure its industry for covering, if possible, all the common needs of economic and civil life of the state. Many of these activities, functions of the state, but also productions, were secured either by former bodies of federation, jointly for the whole state, or by organizations in the Czech Republic, which is today for us abroad.

The Slovak Republic is seeking ways out from this situation. The processes of the present building of the new state, transformation of the social, political and economic life, and the restructuring of the economy, which are taking place parallely with the staff professionally not prepared, in general, by its claims and requests is exceeding possibilities of the starting small new state. Therefore the transformation of the country to a prosperous market-oriented modern state, is complex, slow and we do not have sufficient money for that. All this is naturally reflected in the difficulties of the everyday life.

During this year, 1993, still continues a mitigation of negative tendencies provoked by transition to a new tax system, and by establishment of the new state, but also an adverse fact is, that the daily output of industrial production and unemployment are increasing. Declining output of industry is in total shown in the decline of gross domestic product. The use of gross domestic product increased mostly by final consumption of the state administration, provoked by securing the functions of newly-established state.

The rate of inflation for the first half year of 1993 is 12.1%, and the state budget deficit reached 14.8 bill. Sk. In the process of privatization the pace of ownership transformation has decreased, which we consider for an adverse development. The Slovak government executed provisions for increasing this pace in a so called second wave of privatization. The share of private ownership (without cooperative) makes now 27%. The highest share of the private ownership is in trade and services (84%), in construction (74%) and in the truck transport (47%).

The Slovak Republic is inhabited by 5.4 mill. inhabitants. The share of women makes 51.32%. The structure of economy is made of slightly more than 25 thousand economic entities and 283 thousand small businesses. There are 22 thousand private and cooperative firms.

Because of a slow process of industry restructuring, the volume of industrial output is still decreasing (in the first half year of 1993 less by 18% than in the first half year of 1992). In total, the expectation for the end of 1993 is, that the gross domestic product will be lower by 5% compared to 1992, and that the average unemployment will increase to 14%, which represents about 360 thousand unemployed persons in a productive age.

In spite of this we are assured, that we will be successful on the way we started, and that we will gradually create from this country a modern, economically prosperous state.

From this prospective we judge also the meaning of your today's event in our country. We appreciate the decision of WOCATE to organize a part of its workshop in Slovakia, and we are pleased to welcome all its participants to Slovakia.

The Ministry of Economy of SR is executing state administration over the development of nearly the whole industry (expect foodstuffs industry) in the Slovak Republic, at the same time is in charge of issues of the domestic and foreign trade and development of tourism. For all these areas is also in charge in the applied research and development, as well as preparation of staff in professional working professions of its resort. Moreover, the Ministry of Economy plays a role of the owner of extensive part of the industry till the privatization of the industry is finished. In this context, the Ministry of Economy realizes the importance of interconnection of the professional education in the technology education to an industrial practice. Therefore I support WOCATE's activity, as well as this workshop, but also future intentions of such working meetings, as an important part of the professional preparation of the future technical intelligence in our economy.

The Ministry of Economy is introducing its industrial policy approved by the government, in order to secure the process of industry transformation towards market economy. The industrial policy is setting tasks for development and modernization of production in more than 30 production industries. In connection with the industrial policy, also a technical policy is elaborated on the Ministry of Economy, which determines tasks of technical development necessary for fullfillment of industrial policy conclusions.

In determining the intention of the technical policy for the near future, the starting point is that the decline in production in individual industries of our economy has not taken the character of transformation yet, and did not provoke the establishment of effective economy. The present course of the transformation process has created the most advantageous reproduction conditions for industries of traditional heavy structures, which are a burden on our economy by a high raw material, energy and transport intensity, and by ecology impacts on environment.

These realities are also putting before the technical policy an exacting task of intention selection in a way, that it would create presumptions for dynamics recovery and growth efficiency of the Slovak economy, but also for the growth in consumption volume of households.

The strategy of the technical policy of the Ministry of Economy for the period of 3-5 years, is based on:

– revival of innovation activity within the existing economic entities, but mainly in establishment of small, technology-oriented firms, which would finalize scientific and technical knowledge into the final maturity and would gain customers for it,
– adjustment of technical activities, technical standards, and technical regulations to regulations and standards valid in EC,
– providing relevant performance of testing facilities in harmony with the European Community,
– applying principles of quality policy, as a starting point for need of complex protection of the customer. To use systems of customer protection in countries with developed market economy,
– providing developed international scientific and technical cooperation and involvement in research programs of the developed countries of EC.

Such a strategy is providing complex solution of mutually interconnected issues of technical policy for industries and creating a starting point for removal of technical obstacles in applying industrial production of Slovakia on the markets not only of developed countries of EC, but the whole world.

Within the approved strategic directions, scientific and technical projects are being elaborated and selected during this year, supporting especially acceleration of transfer of progressive technologies and recovery in innovation process in the industrial production.

Realization of these intentions requires unconditional participation of well prepared professional people and company managements. Therefore we consider our effort in seeking and providing modern education technologies with the focus on cooperation of schools with industry for a very suitable way in securing desired education of our present, but mainly future professional staff in industry, businessmen and managers.

From this point, I wish working success to your discussions, and to us, successful and early usability of workshop results in the economy practice. At the same time I want to assure you, that we would be pleased to welcome you also on future events of WOCATE in our country.

Rudolf Bauer
Mayor of Kosice
Kosice, Slovakia

Ladies and Gentlemen,

in spite of the fact that I am joining you only in the end of your workshop I am very glad that I am here. Thank you very much for your invitation.

I have been Mayor of the City of Kosice only since last January, but I would not be a good mayor if I did not use this occasion to tell you several words about our city.

Kosice is the metropolis of East Slovakia with about 1/4 million inhabitants with an exciting history. In the past Kosice was the meeting point of two cultures, those of the West and East. This is noticeable everywhere in the historical centre which attracts the attention of all the visitors and tourists. We take pride in St. Elizabeth's Cathedral, St. Michael's Chapel, Urban's Tower and other monuments. However, a real pearl is in the City Archives. It is the coat of arms which was granted to Kosice by the sovereign Louis the Great in 1369. It is the oldest granting of a coat of arms to a juristic person – a town in Europe. Until that time, coats of arms had only been granted to natural persons.

I hope that sometime in future you will have a chance to see what our forefathers left us. Then you will also find out that our university tradition stratches back to 1657 when the first university had been established. At present there are P. J. Safarik's University, the Technical University, the University of Veterinary Medicine and the Military College of Aviation. The Bratislava University of Economics and the Nitra College of Agriculture both have their branches in Kosice.

You are undoubtly aware that after November 1989 our priority number one has been to overcome the consequences of the previous regime, to change the old thinking and create a new consciousness etc. This is where the intellectual potential of these universities has to be used. From this point of view the issues you were dealing with at the conference are most significant and useful.

Ladies and gentlemen, I wish you every success in your work. Should you one day come to Kosice, you would be welcome.

1. Advanced Technology and Technology Education

Both advanced technology and technology education exist in the context of human resource development, and *that* context resides within economic, societal, and personal life. Currently, and for the foreseeable future, these contexts are significantly impacted by technology to yield both quantitative and qualitative effects and demands. The ARW stressed the situation, that learners – actually all individuals – need, seek, develop, and employ new capabilities to live with and control, rather than be controlled by, technology.

The workshop's participants overwhelmingly felt that the development of such capabilities was too important to leave to happenstance. It was stated that there exists a close, perhaps even causal, relationship between higher level capabilities of individuals (e.g., technological problem solving, literacy, analysis and synthesis) the structure and processes of didactical situations, and the effectiveness of society as a whole. The latter effectiveness must be seen in personal as well as technological and economic dimensions. Furthermore, the workshop participants clearly called for acknowledgment of the study of technical artifacts, technological processes, and human interaction with technology as a scientific subject.

Invariably, such interactions led to in-depth discussions about the existence of laws and principles of technology and their treatment as an interdisciplinary subject. In this volume's first part, the major conclusions included the new contexts' demand for a polyvalent arsenal of skills, including practical as well as intellectual ones, for new forms of learning enterprises and didactics, and for the development of the capability to use the living world around us for human as well as for technological purposes while maintaining a sustainable quality of life for humankind.

These conclusions were derived from an eclectic set of analyses presented by participants with perspectives ranging from Theuerkauf's intricate industry-rooted exploration of new didactical concepts to Duby's positing of reverse engineering from education-generated capabilities to the development of technical means. Focusing on didactics, Wild highlighted media and instructional application capabilities and their implications for practice in school-industry link projects. While the latter setting was employed to anchor his observation, in discussion Wild suggested these capabilities also extended to other learning settings.

Each workshop participant's vision was then stretched by McCormick's construction of a cognitive apprenticeship model for learning and its application as an approach to frame and support new learning situations for developing higher order capabilities. Such a provocative beginning, together with the impetus provided by Blandow's orientation and goal setting, theme presentations, and the interaction led by Liao, yielded energizing insights which spurred the participants' discussion and intensity of involvement.

Industry Productivity Improvement Techniques for Education: A Reverse Technology Transfer?

Jean-Jacques Duby
Union des Assurances de Paris
Tour Assur, CEDEX 14
Paris La Défense, F-92083, France

Abstract. Education productivity, expressed in units of students processed by educator, has been steadily decreasing since the late 1950s: education is facing the same productivity- and quality-crisis as many other labor-intensive industries have encountered and – in many cases – resolved. Can it benefit from their experiences and solutions? This paper will attempt to investigate how the education process could benefit from industry productivity and quality improvement techniques, e.g. computerisation, cultural incentives, and product and process specification methodology.

Keywords. Education, productivity, quality, computer-assisted learning, process control, organisational culture, Kaizen

1 Introduction

The productivity of the education system has been steadily decreasing for the past 35 years. The figures below show the ratio of students per teacher at the different education levels in the French public education system:

School year	1958 - 59	1968 - 69	1978 - 79	1988 - 89
Primary	30.1	27.2	22.2	19.5
Secondary	20.3	16.8	14.7	13.2
Higher	34.6	23.3	21.0	23.7

One could argue that with fewer students per teacher, the quality of the education process should improve. Indeed, the proportion of youngsters who exit the French education system without any diploma was halved between 1978 and 1989, but it is still above 13% or roughly 100 000 young adults every year. Other indicators show that, even if the situation has improved, it is far from satisfactory: more than 25% of elementary school pupils are late in their cursus; more than 50% of students have to repeat at least one grade during secondary school; and 11% of the French nationals below 26 cannot either read or write or be proficient in their native tongue according to a 1990 study by J. L. Borkowski[1]. Any production manager in a private company with such a poor record would be fired for incompetence...

As a consequence of this productivity decrease, combined with the evolution of student demography, the total number of persons employed in the education system, i.e., in teaching, administrative, and support functions, in public and private education, is growing steadily: in 1990, more than 7% of the active population in France worked for education, up from 6.1% in 1982. One should start questioning the social and economic affordability of such a trend if it were to be pursued.

Clearly, our education system has a productivity problem, combined with a quality problem. Those are the same problems enterprises have encountered for decades. The purpose of this paper is to show that education could benefit from the experiences and successes of the enterprise sector in increasing its productivity and quality, and adapt some of the enterprises techniques to improve its own throughput. The paper will consider firstly computerisation, secondly production methodology.

2 Computerisation in Education

Computerisation has been used extensively since the 1970s by the service sector to improve its productivity. The US Department of Commerce statistics shows that industries like finance, health and wholesale devote more than a third of their capital stock to information technology. Interestingly enough, one of the leading service industries in terms of IT share of capital stock is the educational sector, with a ratio of 63.5% in 1988, a dramatic increase from 7.4% in 1970. Of course, the educational sector in the US Department of Commerce classification, being restricted to private and mostly professional education, is not representative of the general education system although it may be closer to technology education. The hard fact remains that educational enterprises faced with productivity and quality problems in a competitive environment did find a solution in computerisation.

2.1 Objectives

Computer-assisted learning started to develop rapidly in the 1980s with the availability of personal computers (PC) and efficient data communication. As of today, actual implementation and practical use are concentrated in numerically marginal areas of education, like distant learning and professional training. In general education, maybe to a lesser extent in technical education, the use of computer remains local or experimental. Two reasons can be seen for this limited use:

– introduction of computers in the general education system was too much oriented towards teaching a new discipline, i.e., computer science, and not towards using computer tools. Yet, advances in hardware and software in "user friendliness" make it less and less necessary to master the discipline to use the tool, and more and more difficult to master enough of the discipline to be able to relate it to the tools.

– the use of computers in other disciplines than computer science has been limited to sporadic and superficial patches (e.g., exercises and pieces of courseware) over existing curricula, most of them restricted to mathematics and "hard" disciplines. Computer tools are not used permanently and pervasively in education, the way they are in other professional activities; they have not changed the way teachers perform their job, as they did for bank clerks, secretaries, or engineers.

To be efficient, i.e., to increase education productivity, education computerisation should be based on a dual objective:

Objective 1.   teach the use of standard IT tools, i.e., standard PC, standard software products, and relevant professional software when applicable.

Objective 2.   take a significant role in the teaching of *every* discipline.

Objective 1 needs of course be modulated according to the level and the specialisation of education: word processors should come first, then spreadsheets and data base managers, with CAD systems for technology students for instance. The main point being that, at the end of the education cycle, any student should be able to use standard IT tools like those he or she will use in his or her first professional years.

Objective 2 may look too ambitious, particularly when it comes to disciplines like philosophy or physical education. Obviously, computers will be used more extensively for teaching maths than history, but it is politically important that they will be also used in philosophy and in physical education: for instance, using statistical linguistic software to compare writings from different authors or visualisation models to explain technical gestures. Besides, *ad hoc* programs can be developed for specific disciplines, e.g., simulators to complement physics or chemistry experiments.

2.2 Consequences and Requirements

Computers will not replace teachers, but will allow them to teach more efficiently. In order to really gain efficiency however, teachers will need to change what they teach, and the way they teach. Such changes can be viewed as consequences of computerisation, but they are also requirements for an efficient computerisation.

Computerisation requires changes in the contents of curricula: hand held calculators have obsoleted manual arithmetic operations; with the multiplication of graphic calculators, it is increasingly difficult to justify spending hours of courses on function representation when it takes but a few seconds to see the curve of any function on the screen; and formal algebra will follow the same evolution... Computerisation of education raises the complex issue of transfer of competence from the human to the machine: to what extent should one teach the student to do what the machine can do ? Where should one draw the line between human competence and machine competence? It is not necessary to computerise education to answer these questions, but education computerisation should force answering them. It should also help measuring what minimum competence should be taught to enable the future IT user to keep control of and confidence in the machine results.

Computerisation also requires changes in the pedagogy. Advanced IT tools like Hypertext, logic programming, and natural language processing will allow transfer of part of the teacher competence to the machine. Here again, careful consideration should be given to determine what kind of competences should be transferred: explaining concepts, teaching facts, checking knowledge, exercising skills, correcting mistakes... Answers need be adapted to disciplines and curricula.

To conclude this part, one could say that the successful use of computers in education will depend less on the computer scientists, who have now developed powerful and easy to use tools, and more on education specialists in each discipline, who must know reconsider what they should teach and how they should teach it in a computerised environment.

3 Industry Productivity and Quality Improvement Techniques in Education

Manufacturing industry has been slower at computerisation than service industry, but it has been leading in the development of production methods and techniques aimed at productivity and, later, quality: mass production between WW I and WW II, "lean production"[2] and "total quality"[3] after WW II. While those techniques were designed for production processes, some of them are now used in services, like zero inventory or continuous flow supply in wholesale, but the large differences which exist between manufacturing and education in terms of materials and processes make them less readily usable in education. Technology education, which is favourable to links between school and industry and to the use of advanced technology and methodology, is probably the best education domain to start experimenting such industry techniques.

This part of the paper will propose some directions of research to investigate the use of industry productivity and quality improvement techniques in education. Those directions fall into three broad areas: organisation culture, product specification techniques, and process control techniques.

3.1 Developing a New Educational Culture

Sociologists, ethnologists and organisation consultants agree that the philosophy that animates an organisation is critical to its evolution and to the success of its endeavour. Components of an organisation culture are key to its efficiency, like clearly stated and commonly understood goals, shared beliefs or strong ethics. Most leading industrial corporations have developed strong corporate cultures aiming at quality, e.g., zero defect or customer satisfaction, and productivity, e.g., cost reduction or continuous process improvement. Some time ago, educators were inspired by the messianic culture they shared, as the French Third Republic school teachers were dubbed "Hussards de la République". Today, one hears more about the lowering of educators morale. Forging a strong positive culture in the education world should be key to its progresses, just as it is for enterprises.

One difficult point in establishing a "productive" educational culture will be that the education world culture must by essence be open to other cultures: the culture of everyday life, the technical culture, the different professional cultures. Conversely, the long time educational tradition to delegate maximum responsibility to the "direct worker", i.e., the teacher in his class, will represent a starting lead compared to manufacturing organisations based on mass production techniques, which must undergo complete structural overhauls to switch from old mass production, with no responsibility to the production line worker, to new lean production, with maximum responsibility to the production worker.

3.2 Product Specification Techniques

Defining course contents is as essential a task for education as defining a product for a company. Manufacturing industry has developed new methods to better ensure that its product meets customer needs and that every component that goes into it brings value to the user. The design of curricula and of course contents should benefit from using some of these industrial development techniques, as shown in the examples below.

– *Functional specification*: Industry distinguishes between functional specification – describing what the product should do – and internal specification – describing what the product is made of. The modern industry-wide trend is to shift effort from internal specification to functional specification. In the education world today, 99% of curriculum design goes into internal specification, e.g., should Thales theorem go into 7th or 8th grade? More functional specification should be as useful for education as it was for industry, e.g., what do we want an *n*th grader to know, to understand, to be able to do?

– *Value analysis*: Value analysis techniques were developed by industry to ensure that every component in a product and every step in a process contributes to the overall value of the product to the user. Likewise, it should be beneficial to define values for curricula items and for pedagogical steps. If it seems close to impossible, just consider that giving a usage value – not cost – to every single nut and bolt in a complex assembly probably looked as impossible to the first industry researchers who attempted it...

– *Customer test*: establishing links between the production system and the customer, and particularly ensuring feed-back from the user, have been major concerns for the industry. "Field testing" a curriculum or a pedagogy does raise serious practical and ethical problems due to the school year and grade structure of the education system, as students can hardly be considered as guinea pigs. On the other hand, changing a curriculum without any test, as it is done today, amounts to no less than holding an entire class age as guinea pigs...

3.3 Process Improvement Techniques

The education process – if a very long one – can benefit from the techniques in process design and process management that industry has developed to improve its productivity and its quality, as shown by the examples below.

– *Flexible work units*: education has traditionally a uniform work unit, i.e., the class period, characterised by a constant number of students taught during a constant lapse of time. On the shop floor, by contrast, machine cycle time and throughput are adjusted according to the nature and the complexity of the operation to be performed. Similarly, there are matters which need be taught only to a few students for a short duration at a time, while others can be taught efficiently to a group of a hundred or more over several hours. Fixed class size and period duration thus impact negatively both productivity and quality. Of course, flexible work units will create scheduling problems, but production industry has developed powerful algorithms to solve them.

– *Quality control*: when it comes to quality control, education is many years behind industry, as it still uses the old system of inspecting finished products for defects, i.e., in yearly exams or teachers deliberations. Modern quality control methods implemented by industry monitor continuously the whole production process, using such techniques as Statistical Process Control (SPC) – and computers. SPC will not do the job alone however: a strong quality culture is necessary (see Sect. 3.1). An established quality culture and common use of SPC measurement techniques could lead ultimately to a quality notation system for education establishments, analogous to the supplier notation systems developed by the automotive industry (e.g. Ford's Q1 or GM's SPEAR) ...

– *Continuous quality improvement*: considered key to Japan's competitive success, the "Kaizen" concept, meaning continuous improvement involving every part of the production organisation, is now being implemented by many large manufacturing and service enterprises. Kaizen is a combination of organisation culture, management practices, work practices, quality control, and productivity improvement techniques. In the recent past, Western organisations have more relied on quantum leap innovations to improve their production, while Pacific Rim countries trusted more continuous incremental improvements over the long term. As we are investigating the use of advanced education technology in technology education, it could be useful to hedge our bets and start injecting some Kaizen into education.

4 Conclusion

Computerisation and the use of other productivity and quality enhancement techniques developed by industry are two complementary ways to improve our education systems: quality and productivity control tools require computers, effective computerisation needs a change of culture, both will progress in the education world through a combination of quantum leap innovations and continuous incremental improvements. Technology education is the most favourable area and school-industry cooperation the most efficient way to make industry advances available to education: reversing the traditional current, Academia should benefit from a technology transfer from Industry.

It is a long term goal and, as Foch once said, "this strategy is a long term one, therefore let us start right away !".

References

1. Borkowski, J. L.: L'Illettrisme, Données Sociales, INSEE, Paris, 1990
2. Womack, J. P. et al.: The Machine that Changed the World, Macmillan, New York, 1990
3. Dixon, G., Swiler, J. (eds.): Total Quality Handbook, Lakewood Publications, Minneapolis, 1990

Learning Through Apprenticeship

Robert McCormick
The Open University
Centre for Technology Education
Walton Hall
Milton Keynes MK7 6AA, United Kingdom

Abstract. It is argued that cognitive apprenticeship is a powerful theoretical base to consider the teaching and learning of technology. This paper outlines this from the perspective of situated cognition, and considers its two important concepts of 'guided participation' and 'community of practice'. It goes on to examine what the technological community of practice is and how technology education can fulfil the requirements of cognitive apprenticeship. A major tension for education is the contrast in the culture of school with that of communities of practice. A case is made for helping to reduce that contrast by providing school-industry links founded upon the rationale of cognitive apprenticeship.

Keywords. Cognitive apprenticeship, situated cognition, guided participation, community of practice, technology education, educational technology, school-industry links

1 Introduction

Technology educators have spent much of the time in the last few years trying to define the nature of this area and to establish its place in the curriculum. Although arguments still continue as to its nature, it is time that we turn to the teaching and learning issues, a plea I made on an earlier occasion (McCormick, 1993a). This becomes more pressing as teachers in many parts of the world are faced with implementing new technology curricula. For them it is the teaching and learning issues that they have to wrestle with on a day to day basis, and there is evidence in some quarters of difficulties.[1] Technology educators no doubt operate with a variety of ideas and 'theories in action', but these are not always

---

[1] In the UK there is controversy about where the cause of the difficulties lies, but it is evident that teachers are having problems (Smithers and Robinson, 1992; HMI, 1992; McCormick, Hennessy and Murphy, 1993; Bierhoff and Prais, 1993).

well founded, as my colleagues and I have argued in relation to views on problem solving (Hennessy, McCormick and Murphy, 1993). We therefore need a sound theoretical base upon which to build teaching and learning activities. While research on the teaching and learning of technology is sparse, there exists considerable research in other areas that is relevant. In this paper I want to focus upon ideas that emanate from research on learning in a social context and in particular upon *cognitive apprenticeship*.

In the context of the theme of this conference there are some interesting connections that make cognitive apprenticeship relevant. Firstly, in the origins of technology education apprenticeship was the classic way skills were taught, and so it may be worthwhile to go back to these roots (at a time when many technology teachers think they have to abandon the past). Secondly, one of the thrusts of ideas on learning in context is that there should be closer a relationship between school and non-school activities. Those involved in technology education claim this closer relationship as one of their hallmarks, not always justifiably as I will show, and therefore technology activities have the potential to offer a unique learning environment. Thirdly, educational technology[2] has proved to be an interesting implementation for cognitive apprenticeship (e.g. Spensley, 1989) and, in the context of expert systems, a spur to consider cognition and the nature of knowledge.

In this paper I will therefore try to outline the theoretical base from which cognitive apprenticeship comes, and to relate this to technology education by exploring how it helps us to understand expert practice in design and engineering, and technology education in schools.

2 The Theoretical Base

Early theories of cognitive development focused on the intellectual processes of the individual child, drawing upon Piaget's research. Learning in context was a development from this and came to be known as *social cognition*. This approach built upon the work of Vygotsky who emphasised the interpersonal nature of cognitive growth.[3] The third phase of development has been the shift to *situated cognition*, which is concerned with cognition in a social *and* physical context (Butterworth, 1992). Not surprisingly there is an extensive literature on situated cognition,[4] but I will focus upon two main sources because each represents an emphasis that is worth highlighting.

---

[2]A different beast I have elsewhere examined in relation to technology education (McCormick, 1993b).

[3]Rogoff (1990) compares in detail the emphasis Piaget and Vygotsky each gave to the social context of learning.

[4]See Hennessy, 1993, for a review.

Rogoff (1990) is the first of these sources that I will consider, and her focus is upon the interpersonal nature of cognition. In recognising that cognitive processes "differ according to the domain of thinking and the specifics of the task context" (p. 6), she sees therefore the goal of the activity and its interpersonal and socio-cultural context as being important. Both the goals of the activity and the means of handling the problems are socially and culturally defined. She develops the metaphor of apprenticeship in thinking: children's active efforts to learn from observing and participating with peers and skilled partners. Guided participation, as she calls it, involves the use of routine problem-solving activity, tacit and explicit communication (verbal and non-verbal), a structure of successive activities that is supportive, and a transfer of responsibility to the learners as they gain in understanding. She reviews a considerable amount of evidence to show how children can learn from skilled adults and from more experienced peers, through joint participation in problem solving. Metacognitive support by helping regulate activities, discussing the next step, making suggestions and asking questions that reveal the overall strategy, are very important in procedural tasks such as planning. Interestingly, in the context of technological activities such as design, guided participation is not quite so successful with problem-solving activities that involve future events (e.g. planning), but it is crucial that the children participate in the joint thinking processes with the support of a *skilled* partner. When these processes are not spelt out children perform poorly.

Much of the research Rogoff draws on is with children, but the second source of work is grounded more in research with adults in everyday situations (e.g., dairies, supermarkets, and tailors).[5] This source (Brown, Collins and Duguid, 1989a) focuses upon the culture of learning.[6] Like Rogoff, they see an intimate connection between knowing and doing, such that situations "might be said to co-produce knowledge through activity." (p. 32)[7] Concepts are therefore "both situated and progressively developed through activity" (p. 33) and become like a set of tools. Understanding concepts through use entails understanding the culture within which they are used. Thus physicists and engineers use mathematical formulae differently. The important implication of this stance is that learning mathematics, science, technology or whatever, is a process of *enculturation*. This entering into the culture of a discipline or profession is the essence of learning,

---

[5]The idea of everyday activity is that it is routine, not just that it is what everybody does. Thus the everyday activity of an engineer or a shopper would be included.

[6]In fact I shall also cite the work of Jean Lave and her co-authors.

[7]This view rejects the distinction often made in the technology education literature between 'knowing that' and 'knowing how' (e.g. Cross, Naughton and Walker, 1986).

and if it is part of an increasing participation, then it is an apprenticeship.[8] A critical idea in engaging in what Lave and Wenger (1990) call a 'community of practice', is that activity is *authentic*. This means it is coherent, meaningful and purposeful within a social framework – the ordinary practices of the culture. Here we have the parallel with traditional apprenticeship, where the apprentice engages in increasing amounts with the everyday activity of, say, the factory. 'Learning the trade' means learning the norms and values, as well as the skills of the trade.

A second distinctive element that comes from this source (or rather from the literature it draws upon) is the understanding of everyday day activity carried out by practitioners and what has become known as 'just plain folks' (JPFs). Studies of weight watchers, milk loaders in a dairy, shoppers in a supermarket, and tailors, reveal a great deal about the active, flexible, and inventive strategies they use. Their mental processes are structured by the context, the activity, the tools and their interactions with others. Thus in routine everyday activity arithmetic is more structured by, than structures, shopping (for best buys). Significantly, JPFs can solve arithmetic problems with a very high success rate in the supermarket, compared to a mediocre performance in the equivalent problems set in school-like tests (Lave, 1988, pp. 55–61). In contrast to the algorithms for solving arithmetic problems that JPFs were taught at school, which they could not use effectively in the tests, their supermarket problem-solving strategies varied across the various settings (i.e. when choosing the best buy of particular products). Indeed they could transform or abandon a problem, and the problem and its resolution would merge. Rather than there being a posed problem (as in school-like tests) the on-going activity (e.g. shopping) shapes the action and the JPFs are constantly facing dilemmas that they resolve by solving problems, with no 'correct' solution and no solution that is entirely satisfactory (Lave, 1988, p. 139).

All this is in stark contrast to the school situation. Resnick (1987) has spelt out the differences between school and life outside in relation to cognition:

– individual cognition in school versus shared cognition outside
– pure 'thought' activities in school versus the manipulation of tools outside
– symbolic manipulation in school versus manipulations of objects and events outside
– generalised learning in school versus situation-specific competencies outside.[9]

---

[8]Much of this idea of apprenticeship and situated cognition was developed by Lave and Wenger (1990), who used the term 'legitimate peripheral participation' as a more general term than apprenticeship.

[9]The generalised learning does not transfer very well, as was illustrated in the case of arithmetic in the supermarket versus that in tests. Lave (1988, p. 68) refers to this as 'negative transfer'! In an earlier chapter (2) she reviews the classic transfer of learning literature in cognitive psychology and concludes that few experiments showed any transfer and at best very little. Resnick (1987) came to the same conclusion.

As noted earlier, the result is that students are taught formalised processes, for example in the form of algorithms to solve mathematics problems, or the design process to design and make something. The source of the difficulty for the school is that it denies the students the opportunity to engage in the community of practice, in other words they do not engage in authentic activities. Instead students participate in the school culture and pick up the cues that give purpose to, and success in, school activity: easy problems always come first at the end of textbook chapter, and they relate to that chapter; there should always be four alternative designs. These parts of the school culture are likely to be irrelevant outside and not generalisable.

Not surprisingly the view of culture and learning from situated cognition has not gone unchallenged (Palincsar, 1989; Wineburg, 1989; Sandberg and Wielinga, 1991), and two aspects are of particular importance here.[10] Firstly, an example of JPFs solving problems given by Brown, Collins and Duguid (1989a) was not thought to show inventiveness but rather ignorance. Had the problem solver been faced with a slightly different situation he would not have been able to solve the problem, whereas had he used the decontextualised knowledge of mathematics she could have done so in any situation.[11] Secondly, even given the significance of the idea of situated cognition, is it feasible to adopt wholesale a pedagogy in schools based upon enculturation to a variety of discipline cultures? The reply from Brown, Collins and Duguid (1989b) to some of their critics was, on the first point, to contrast abstraction (what is taught in school) with generalisation (being able to operate across a variety of situations. This they saw occurring through apprenticeship, working in variety of situations and reflecting upon the learning. They agreed with their critics on the second point, noting that there would have to be a compromise with authenticity. But they argued that it was not essential for students to be brought into contact with practitioners, rather that teachers needed to be inducted into the cultures. In fact in another article (Collins, Brown and Holum, 1991) they spelt out a complete pedagogy for cognitive apprenticeship, and I will deal with that in Section 5.1.

A third criticism was made by Palincsar (1989), who questioned the comparison of JPFs with practitioners (experts). Brown, Collins and Duguid (1989b), in reply, said the comparision of JPFs with practitioners was to show the similarity

---

[10]I am conscious that I do not consider the literature on general thinking skills, which contrasts in its approach to that of situated cognition. However, see Hennessy, McCormick and Murphy (1993) for some discussion of this literature.

[11]The example in question was of a weight watcher who had to make up a meal using cottage cheese, and the recipe called for three quarters of two-thirds of a cup of the cheese. Rather than perform a multiplication of fractions the weight watcher filled the cup to two thirds, tipped out the cheese onto a board, patted it into a circle then divided into four quarters, and used three of them! Those objecting to this solution wondered what would have happened had it been chocolate sauce, or if he had had to cater for a family of sixteen.

of thinking and the need for education to avoid just overlaying this thinking with artificial and unproductive tasks. Part of the weakness of their research base, is the relatively low level of practitioners they include.[12]

I have elaborated these theoretical approaches at length because, as I will show, they hed light on the situation in the communities of practice of technology and on the associated technology education.[13] These are the subject of the next two sections.

3 The Technological Community of Practice

Most of the communities of practice referred to in the literature on situated cognition cited above do not relate directly to those found in technology. In this section I want to see to what extent technology practitioners, in their everyday activity, exhibit the kind of problem-solving processes indicated in situated cognition. I shall then, in the next section, compare this with the situation of technological activity in the school classroom. I have already noted the tradition of apprenticeship that has existed in technology, and this has a long history in craft activity. It also has a history in technician and engineer training, although the latter has not always been successful. Technology is of course a diverse field with many communities of practice, and here I shall restrict myself to considering designers, including particular kinds such as engineering designers and architects.[14]

There have been an increasing number of studies of the work of designers, using a variety of techniques: general interviews of their approach to design; interviews that try to construct a retrospective account of a particular design activity; test problems where designers think out aloud while they solve them (protocol studies); ethnographic studies of designers working in their factories and studios. Only one of the studies referred to here drew on the literature of situated cognition (Davies and Castell, 1992), although one (Bucciarelli, 1988) was an ethnographic study in the style of Lave (1988). The main findings of these studies as they relate to the situated cognition literature are as follows.[15]

---

[12]For example, Lave and Wenger (1990) include studies of midwives, butchers, tailors, and naval quartermasters.

[13]The idea of cognitive apprenticeship has been applied to a number of areas, other than those in the original literature. For example: reading (Coles, 1990); aircraft technician training (Lajoie and Lesgold, 1989); a CAL version of supermarket purchasing (Pieters and de Bruijn, 1992); educational administrators (Prestine and LeGrand, 1991); trainee teachers learning about language in education (Bayer, 1990).

[14]Despite the fact that designers are a small percentage of those involved in technology, design is a major part of the UK school technology curriculum.

[15]I will not refer to the studies individually except where the point is unique or I quote from the study. The studies are: Bucciarelli, 1988; Culverhouse, Ball and Burton, 1992;

Absence of algorithms. Most of the studies reject the idea that the way designers work can be represented by an algorithm (such as define the problem/need, generate solutions, implement/model, evaluate). The only one that confirmed a model was one using a Hypercard system structured according to that model (Culverhouse, Ball and Burton, 1992).

Interaction between problem and solution. This interaction was characterised in the account of Darke's research, on the generator-conjecture-analysis approach to design, in Lawson (1990, pp. 33–35). In this approach the designer starts with an important aspect of the problem, develops a crude idea for a solution and then evaluates it to learn more about the problem. Schon (1988) observed a similar approach where architects had 'types' of designs in mind which they would try out to match with the situation. This allowed a dialogue with the situation "the type can function both to transform the situation and to be transformed by it ... a form of *seeing-* and *doing-as*, in which a designer both transforms a design situation and enriches the repertoire of types available to him (*sic*)." (p. 183) Schenk (1991) found designers used their drawings in this way to try out ideas to help them understand the problem.

Schon (1988) also identified rules that architects reasoned with (e.g., having control over movement in an entrance space). They would apply these until a difficulty arises, which would then trigger new design ideas. This is a form of dilemma resolution. Schon in an earlier study (Schon, 1984) recounted a dilemma of a student who was struggling with the conflict of a design which had little spatial organisation (like a 'spaghetti bowl') because he was reluctant to adopt a hierarchical one on ideological grounds. The student's realisation of that dilemma was a key to his resolution of it and his further progress with the design.

Object worlds. Bucciarelli (1988) uses this idea to show that in a company that makes X-ray equipment, the various participants in the design (e.g., mechanical engineer, electrical engineer, project manager) deal with different objects as part of the design process. Each of them sees the object (the X-ray equipment) differently, and uses different models, theories, tools and constraints in doing their design task. Schon (1988) uses a more abstract formulation of this idea in what he calls 'design worlds':

These are environments entered into and inhabited by designers when designing. They contain particular configurations of things, relations and qualities, and they act as *holding environments* for design knowledge. A designer's knowledge is not only in his ideas or actions, but in the things with which he deals. The objects of a design world are ...'things to think with' ....Designers *construct* their design worlds not only through shaping of materials but through interlocking processes of perception, cognition and notation. (Schon, 1988, pp. 182–3)

Darke, 1978 and Rowe, 1987 (cited in Lawson, 1990, pp. 33-6); Davies and Talbot, 1987; Davies and Castell, 1992; Eckersley, 1988; Schenk, 1991; Schon, 1984 and 1988; Waldron and Waldron, 1988.

I have quoted this at length because it reflects much of the language of the situated cognition literature cited in the last section. Similarly the example of physicist and engineers using mathematical formulae differently (Brown, Collins and Duguid, 1989a), is addressed directly by engineers who show specific examples of this (Monk, 1993). Such examples argue for seeing the cultural dimensions of engineering.

Design as a social process. At times these various participants work on their own, and at other times collaboratively, but as a whole the design process (of the X-ray equipment) is a social process, indeed the design as a whole only exists in a collective sense. As Schon (1988) says in a different context, the project cannot come to completion without their collective agreement.[16] Further, the organisation of the design process to some extent reflects the object, creating ambiguities and interface issues between the different sub-systems (of say an X-ray machine). The sub-cultures of the various participants also operate in the context of the particular culture of the company. Davies and Castell (1992), picking up from Lave (1988), stress the importance of being "aware of the social, educational and organisation factors which mediate design behaviour." (pp. 392)

As I noted above, Monk (1993) stresses the cultural dimension giving examples of: the way electronic engineers think about signals through different sets of notation is affected by language; colour understood through different theories covering different circumstances; and resistors values as manufactured affecting the circuit design which would be revised to use the standard components. He concludes "One way of looking at the education of an engineer is to see it as a cultural acclimatisation for a branch of engineering; that is the development of a fluency in a specialised language and its specialised traditions." A community of practice indeed!

It seems to me then, that technology as seen by at least some of its practitioners corresponds to the ideas of situated cognition set forth in the last section, particularly with regard to the idea of a 'culture of learning'. I hope to show in the next section how some of the ideas on learning that stem from both the Rogoff (1990) and Brown, Collins and Duguid (1989a) approaches, apply equally well to technology education, at least in some parts of the world.

4 Technology Education in Schools

In this section I want to examine both the potential and the practice of technology education in (secondary) schools in the light of the previous sections. The first examination will be a more general consideration of technology education of the

---

[16]Peter Medway in a study of architects used the term 'virtual building' to convey the idea that the many people involved in the process collectively 'hold' the building design; the drawings are not the design, nor are the costs, nor the planning application etc. (Seminar, The Open University, 23 June 1993).

kind found in British schools, and the second will draw upon a study that my colleagues and I have began into problem solving in technology education.[17] Although there are special issues associated with the particular implementation of technology and 'design and technology' in the UK, and with the introduction of such a national curriculum subject in the schools in England and Wales, there are sufficient general issues to warrant this focus in an international workshop such as this.

For my first examination I will consider the ideas inherent in the community of practice and guided participation, under the headings of: practical action, meaningful problems, the use of knowledge, and finally group learning. In particular I will reflect on the technology education classroom culture and its effect on cognitive apprenticeship, although some of this will also be part of the second part of my examination (Section 4.5).

4.1 Practical Action

Typically design and technology activities involve designing and making an artefact, such as a toy mechanism (by 12–13 year olds). Although a number of commentators have questioned the reliance upon 'design' as the major technological process (McCormick, 1990; Medway, 1992; Yoemans, 1992), this focus on 'design and make' does help to link thinking with action. The outcomes are expected to be physical outcomes, not investigations alone, nor reports on say energy issues; even 3-D models (especially cardboard ones) are frowned on. When thinking is combined with doing, using the physical modelling media (2-D and 3-D), thought and action can combine in the sort of way hoped for by those advocating cognitive apprenticeship. This is interestingly represented in a model of the design process by Kimbell and his colleagues (APU, 1991; also reproduced in McCormick, Murphy and Harrison, 1992, p. 61), which shows the interaction between mind and hand.

4.2 Meaningful Problems

The engaging in problems and situations that are relevant and meaningful to students is part of the rhetoric of this area of the curriculum. Teachers of technology have long recognised the importance of students tackling problems for which they have some stake in ('ownership of' in the jargon). Thus they may want

---

[17]The more general examination of technology education draws upon other publications we have produced (Hennessy, McCormick and Murphy, 1993; McCormick, 1994). The study the 'Problem Solving in Technology Education' research team is undertaking is funded by the UK Economic and Social Research Council (grant number R00023445).

students to design a toy for their baby brothers or sisters, or some child they know, or, alternatively to control the defining of the task through identifying a need or design opportunity. However, this only helps at a superficial level; it improves motivation. Nevertheless the active participation that might therefore result could be a basis for cognitive apprenticeship.

It does not, however, tackle the more difficult issue of making it meaningful in the same way as the problems they meet as part of their daily life. The design of the toy will still be a school activity and will only have meaning if students realise that school is all about such activities and that to succeed it is necessary to suspend normal operation and do what the teacher says. Neither will students ever attain the commitment to the task that, say, a toy designer, whose livelihood or company depends upon the design, will have. Creating this sense of meaning and reality is very difficult within the context of school, an issue I will return to later. Thus students are unlikely to be meeting authentic problems in the sense identified earlier.

4.3 The Use of Knowledge

One of the strengths of the technology curriculum is that there is a wide range of knowledge that could potentially be drawn upon in completing a design and make task. In this sense the activity can resemble everyday life in the way a science lesson cannot. In science an activity, practical or otherwise, is likely to be based upon the conceptual knowledge just taught, either as an application or illustration of it. A technology task may, on the other hand, involve a variety of scientific concepts (e.g., friction and levers in a mechanism) combined with knowledge of materials (e.g., likelihood of wear), and economics, to name but a few. These concepts can only be potentially relevant, and student activity in the technology classroom is just as likely to resemble JPFs in the supermarket in their use of science or mathematics concepts and procedures, as I will show later.[18]

One approach to help students to generalise their scientific (say) conceptual knowledge is to provide a context that will use it. In effect this is using the science to shape the activity,[19] but in doing so the technology activity is corrupted. This presents an insuperable curriculum planning task to ensure that meaningful technology tasks are undertaken, but which enable students to

---

[18]See McCormick (1993c) for a fuller discussion of the use of science in design activities.

[19]This is what Lave (1988, Chapter 5) calls 'structuring resources'. She discusses how shopping structures the mathematics used in supermarkets, and how those who want to investigate the mathematics of JPFs use scholastic type tests assuming that only mathematics is going on. In fact there is shopping, planning meals and making ends meet. Similarly in the technology classroom there is more than one thing going on.

generalise their scientific knowledge in the way expected by Brown, Collins and Duguid (1989a). The answer may be that we should not try, because, as Job (1992) notes, it may not matter what science they use they can still create a successful technological outcome. If we knew more about how practitioners, such as engineers, use scientific knowledge we may at least know whether it is worth the effort of trying. The albeit partial evidence from the last section (Bucciarelli, 1988), indicates that the various engineers keep to their own specialised parts of science, and hence they do not call upon a wide range, as and when needed. In some senses therefore they are perhaps JPFs in the areas they do not specialise in. However, we need more empirical work to avoid mere speculation.

4.4 Group Learning

A central feature of Rogoff's argument for guided participation was interpersonal participatory activity. She argues that for the development of skills and understanding, rather than qualitative shifts in perspective, social interaction with a skilled person is more effective than with a peer (Rogoff, 1990, p. 168). Thus in technological activity, which has a strong element of skills and procedural understanding, ordinary group learning may be problematic, particularly as I noted earlier, when undertaking the kind of tasks involving the future (e.g. planning). In such a case participation with a skilled person is important. That does not deny the role of group work in conceptual development, where argumentation can take place, or in learning about the collaborative activity that, as I showed earlier, is central to the community of practice of technology.

4.5 A Pilot Study of Technology Projects

In this section I want to examine some of the findings of this study to see what insight they give to cognitive apprenticeship as it does or could operate in the classroom.[20] This study involved observing and video-taping a group of four girls aged 13, over two related projects with the same teacher. The first project was a 3-week skills module which focused on (a) making patterns using various printing techniques and (b) constructing objects affected by wind (e.g. a mobile). The second project, designing and making a kite for a special occasion, lasted 8 weeks. The teacher involved was an art teacher working as part of a team trying to implement the National Curriculum for technology, which had at that time a strong 'process' orientation (DES, 1990).

This teacher was aware of the need to keep in mind all of the processes required by the National Curriculum. She had decided for the kite-making project to

---

[20]See McCormick, Hennessy and Murphy (1993) for a full account of this study.

emphasise the processes concerned with 'generating ideas' and 'evaluation', and the practical activity of using materials. She did not want the overall process to be seen as a rigid linear sequence (hence students were to "evaluate throughout"), but was concerned in addition to emphasise creativity. By this she meant encouraging the children to experiment with materials and to try out ideas without any preconceived notions of a final product. However, in students' minds the over-riding impression of the project, and of technology generally (both in and out of school), was essentially of 'making', and learning outcomes in design and technology lessons were described as skills related to making. The children appeared to be largely unaware of the design process. In an interview six months after the project the teacher expressed concern about the National Curriculum processes and felt some conflict between teaching the design process and encouraging learning in Art that she valued, i.e., creativity.[21] It is therefore unsurprising that students' perceptions would not include these processes.

This conflict in aims led to a lack of explicit treatment of the processes. The lessons over the eight weeks of the project followed the usual sequence of processes:

– defining a reason for a kite (a need)
– generating four designs
– modelling in 2-D and 3-D
– evaluating these models and modifying
– planning the making (using a full-scale 2-D drawing)
– making the kite
– evaluating and modifying the kite
– carrying out final evaluation

Despite this there was little reflection on the individual processes and no explicit discussion of the overall process. This was in part a deliberate pedagogic strategy on the teacher's part. In order to prevent the students becoming focused upon a final product prior to being creative with their initial ideas, she tended to 'reveal' the process implicitly as the class went through the various stages of the project. This reflected the belief that this stage of exploration was critical if students were to apply understanding of the materials to the product from an informed and experienced position. Hence creative experience of the materials was seen as pre-requisite to a good solution. Rather than being devalued by the teacher, the design process to an extent became secondary to other learning she considered more fundamental. But nevertheless the effect would almost certainly be that pupils were not being sufficiently reflective for them to be guided in this kind of procedural thinking.

---

[21] A profoundly difficult problem in the light of the recommendation from Brown, Collins and Duguid (1989b) of inducting teachers into the community of practice as one of the ways to avoid the need to bring (real) practitioners into contact with students.

As the research examined in Section 2 predicted, our pilot results also suggest that to assume that learners can use relevant bodies of knowledge from other contexts is unrealistic. Students frequently appeared not to have grasped concepts in such a way as to enable them to use them in a practical situation. For example, one student, in a conversation with the teacher about her scale drawing, revealed that not only did she not understand the distinction between the actual and scale length of a line, but that even when prompted by the teacher she could not work out the scale. The technology classroom had indeed become the 'supermarket' for the use of mathematics as taught in mathematics lessons.

This evidence, partial and tentative though it is, does not give us much confidence that technology education (as it is being implemented in England) recognises adequately the needs of students who are entering into a community of practice. Although we have not yet analysed our evidence in detail to see if the conditions for guided participation are present, our impression is that the teacher was unable to spend the time to support students in the ways suggested by Rogoff (1990).

5 Encouraging Cognitive Apprenticeship

In the paper by Resnick (1987), where she analysed the differences between school and the outside world, she gave two separate strands of advice with the main emphasis on education in the workplace. The two sources examined in Section 2, guided participation and enculturation into the community of practice, give principles to aid the changes to the school environment, and to make links with the world outside, respectively. The changes needed to the school environment present a problem for encouraging cognitive apprenticeship, as I have already noted, but there are some useful guidelines which I will consider in the case of technology education. However, in the context of this Advanced Research Workshop, the boundary between school and the outside world is perhaps the most significant consideration. I will deal with each of these (the school environment and the links with the outside world) in the next two sub-sections.

5.1 Inside the School

A good prescription already exists for encouraging cognitive apprenticeship within the school, in the form of a "Framework for designing learning environments" by the same group who put forward the case for this situated approach to learning. In an article with a telling subtitle ("making things visible") Collins, Brown and Holum (1991) outlined their framework based on a number of principles:

Content types of knowledge required for expertise
   Domain knowledge subject matter, specific concepts, facts and procedures
   Heuristic strategies generally applicable techniques for accomplishing tasks

Control strategies general approaches for directing one's solution process
Learning strategies knowledge about how to learn new concepts, facts, and procedures
Method ways to promote the development of expertise
   Modelling teacher performs a task so students can observe
   Coaching teacher observes and facilitates while students perform a task
   Scaffolding teacher provides support to help the student perform the task
   Articulation teacher encourages students to verbalise their knowledge and thinking
   Reflection teacher enables students to compare their performance with others
   Exploration teacher invites students to pose and solve their own problems
Sequencing keys to ordering learning activities
   Global before local skills focus on conceptualising the whole task before executing the parts
   Increasing complexity meaningful tasks gradually increasing in difficulty
   Increasing diversity practice in a variety of situations to emphasise broad application
Sociology social characteristics of learning environments
   Situated learning students learn in the context of working on realistic tasks
   Community of practice communication about different ways to accomplish meaningful tasks
   Intrinsic motivation students set personal goals to seek skills and solutions
   Co-operation students work together to accomplish their goals

I will consider those only those principles that have the most significance for technology education.

Content. *Domain knowledge* is the conceptual and procedural knowledge of technology, which must be learnt in real problem-solving contexts using expert practices. Thus, as argued elsewhere (Hennessy, McCormick and Murphy, 1993), using the design process mechanically as a series of stages will not reflect the kind of procedures indicated in Section 3. Rather the dilemma resolution implied by Schon (1988) is more appropriate.
   Heuristic strategies Given the range of tasks that students could potentially tackle, there may be no one set of 'tricks of the trade'. They may be small things like what to do when you are stuck for ideas, or where to look for certain kinds of guidance.
   Control strategies These are used to manage the task, including the managing of heuristic strategies. At a mundane level they will be project management strategies, something seldom dealt with explicitly, indeed by the way teachers structure projects and control the timing etc., they often prevent students from progressively developing these strategies.

Method. This set of principles is the most difficult to implement in the technology classroom because of the lack of time a teacher has for interaction with individual students. However, when interaction does occur it is important that elements of these methods are used. The temptation is to give the students a 'quick fix' to keep up their momentum, but contribute little to their development of expertise. Collaborative activity offers an alternative approach, but 'skilled' help may remain a problem.

Sequence. *Global before local skills* This is an intriguing principle for technology education! The example usually used to illustrate it is the fact that tailoring apprentices experience the whole process of garment making in reverse by being allowed to do the finishing task first, then the assembly (sewing) and finally the cutting out. They thus get an overview of the whole process first, before getting to the difficult cutting out stage. The parallel in technology education based on design-and-make tasks would be to get pupils to start with existing products and to consider how they might be improved. Alternatively use short tasks so that students can see the essential holism of the process. With longer tasks not all processes need be emphasised. It is essential, however, not to assume that using a chart of design process steps, sheets with titles of the steps, and design folders structured around such steps, will by themselves give students an understanding of the processes; the articulation and reflection under 'method' are important to support any such devices.

Increasing diversity and complexity These raise the issue of how knowledge is controlled and recalls the discussion in Section 4.3.

Sociology. Most of the principles here are better seen in the context of school-industry links, which I will consider next, through activities such as mini-enterprises and industrial simulations as possible contexts for creating the conditions for an effective learning environment.

5.2 Across the Boundary

The title of this sub-section emphasises my concern not just to see activities that encourage learning to take place outside of the school (as Resnick (1987) advocated), but to see a continuum of activities with the outside world being brought into school at one end, and the school taken out into the world, at the other. For a technology education, which is aimed at encouraging enculturation, the 'outside world' is best seen as industry – the main community of practice for technology. Of course this is not an uncontroversial view because it raises issues of the purposes of teaching technology in schools, that I have reviewed elsewhere (McCormick, 1992). I take the view that technology is a part of the culture which students must come to understand and participate in, and that, in keeping with the view of cognitive apprenticeship, this means that students should enter into the culture of the community of practice of technology. Such enculturation does not imply that they will become technologists and hence that we must give them a vocational education.[22]

It is in the lack of clarity of purposes of education that school-industry links often fail to deliver what is hoped of them. Those who support school-industry links are often motivated by the desire to promote positive views of industry on the part of students, usually with little success (McCormick, 1992). On the other hand there is often little concern for the impact of the links on the substantive learning that is the main function of the school. For example in the UK, the school inspectors have criticised mini-enterprise activities (where students set up and run a business for a limited period of time) for not being linked to the curriculum (HMI, 1990).[23] There is a consistent message in research on activities related to links between school and the world outside, that the best experience for students is when these activities are part of their mainstream active learning.[24] My plea would therefore be to see the entry into the community of practice of technology, as part of cognitive apprenticeship, as one contribution to improving the learning potential of links between school and industry. In addition to the principles in Section 5.1, I would argue for breaking down the barrier between school and industry by seeing technology learning activities as an integrated continuum from within to outside school.

At one end, within the school, would be efforts to *simulate* activity in the world outside. Part of this would be the creation of realism as indicated in Section 4.2. Such creation need not involve an industrial context being brought into school. But there can be no doubt that constructing a context of, say, a company or a design consultancy within which the design task is set, and relating it to a 'real' or at least tangible customer, can have an important effect in creating meaning in the whole activity. Setting the activity in the context of a company, with say specialised roles for individuals or groups, will do much for the kind of collaborative learning discussed in Section 4.4.

Some such activities will need to simulate companies as organisations and operations etc., where there may not be a design-and-make activity. Production simulations, for example, can give students an insight into, and understanding of, technological processes, and, although they are not 'real', they are first hand –

---

[22]There is in fact a more complex argument that could be made as to why cognitive apprenticeship makes simple distinctions between vocational and general education problematic, but this is not appropriate in the context of this paper.

[23]A recent guidance booklet on school-business links focused only on the general motivational effects of such links: "curriculum enrichment for students to improve motivation and raise standards" (Miller, 1993, p. 2).

[24] I have already mentioned this in relation to mini-enterprises (HMI, 1990). In the context of the UK Neighbourhood engineer scheme (where an engineer is associated with a school) the best experiences reported by students were when the engineers worked with them on projects either inside or outside school (Bridges *et al.*, 1991).

students experience the processes. (See for example, Jamieson, Miller and Watts, 1988.)

The next step along the continuum is to embed the design-and-make activity within a mini-enterprise activity. This helps to create authenticity by giving goals that resemble those of the community of practice in industry. This does not mean being a prisoner to the apparent goals of industry (e.g., a simple profit motive), and provides an opportunity to examine and be involved in other goals, for example community service.[25]

Next along the continuum is to involve students in first hand experiences of design-and-make activities, but enhancing the realism by seeking problems from industry. This can be in the form of getting applications from industry (e.g., testing and calibration - Butlin, 1988, p, 19), or specific tasks which industry finds unsuitable to solve (Clegg, Medway, Yoemans, 1987, pp. 51–2; Harrison, 1988, pp. 64–79). Elaborate programmes exist for specialist students of science or technology that involve an activity that exemplifies real industrial projects which are supported by higher education and industrial tutors (Wharton, undated).

Finally, there are work experience activities where students go out into industry and work within the community of practice, and here we are returning to the traditional apprenticeship model. Again this experience is most effective when it is related to activities in the school. HMI (1990) report favourably on a student who used work experience to do research on the market, and work on how to develop and produce a product he was making for his school project work.

6 Conclusion

I hope I have shown how the theory of cognitive apprenticeship provides a coherent underpinning for technology education and a sound rationale for school-industry links. It is of course a *theory*, well founded in empirical research, but not without its difficulties. In the context of technology education activities we have much to understand about the community of practice of technology. Not least is the fact that there are many such communities, and that representing them in a curriculum for all children is no easy task. There is also the associated problem of how teachers are to be help themselves to enter into the communities of practice, as many of them come from other, all be they related, communities.

Much also needs to be done to understand how guided participation could be implemented in the ordinary classroom, where at least twenty students are frequently carrying out a variety of complex practical activities. There are also special issues, one I have already noted, related to 'future-oriented' activities such as 'design' and 'planning'. In addition there is the fact that much of the research on

---

[25]HMI (1990) criticised schools for being too focused upon the simple profit motive, and encouraged the use of activities that provided something for the community to balance those aimed at market forces.

guided participation concerns children up to the end of primary education. This contrasts with the situated cognition work on adults, and, along with investigations on the communities of practice of technology, we need to consider how we deal with the education of older students. In this latter context, school-industry links have no doubt an important role to play.

References

1. Assessment of Performance Unit [APU]: The assessment of performance in design and technology. London: School Examinations and Assessment Council 1991

2. Bayer, A. S.: University students as apprentice thinkers. The Quarterly Newsletter of the Laboratory of Comparative Human Cognition. 12 (2), 64-70 (1990)

3. Bierhoff, H., Prais, S. J.: Britain's industrial skills and the school-teaching of practical subjects: comparisons with Germany, the Netherlands and Switzerland. National Institute Economic Review. 2/93 (1993)

4. Bridges, D. *et al..*: Neighbourhood Engineers: an evaluation. Norwich: University of East Anglia, School of Education 1991

5. Brown, J. S., Collins, A., Duguid, P.: Situated cognition and the culture of learning. Educational Researcher. 18 (1), 32-41 (1989a)

6. Brown, J. S., Collins, A., Duguid, P.: Debating the situation: a rejoinder to Palincsar and Wineburg. Educational Researcher. 18 (4), 10-12, 62 (1989b)

7. Bucciarelli, L. L.: An ethnographic perspective on engineering design. Design Studies. 9 (3), 159-168 (1988)

8. Butlin, C.: Applications-based science education, should we apply? Physics Education. 23, 17-23 (1988)

9. Butterworth, G.: Context and cognition in models of cognitive growth. In: P. Light, G. Butterworth (eds.) Context and cognition: ways of learning and knowing. (pp. 1-13) New York: Harvester Wheatsheaf 1992

10. Clegg, A., Medway, P., Yoemans, D.: Planning for Technology within the Curriculum. Units 1-2, ET887/897, Teaching and Learning Technology in Schools. Milton Keynes: The Open University Press 1987

11. Coles, M.: The 'real books' approach: is apprenticeship a weak analogy? Reading. 24 (2), 50-56 (1990)

12. Collins, A., Brown, J. S., Holum, A.: Cognitive apprenticeship: making things visible. American Educator. (Winter), 6-11, 38-46 (1991)

13. Cross, N., Naughton, J., Walker, D.: Design method and scientific method. In A. Cross, R. McCormick (eds.) Technology in schools. (pp. 19-33) Milton Keynes: Open University Press 1986

14. Culverhouse, P. F., Ball, L., Burton, C. J.: A tool for tracking engineering design in action. Design Studies. 13 (1), 54-70 (1992)

15. Darke, J.: The primary generator and the design process. In: W. E. Rogers, W. H. Ittelson (eds.) New directions in environmental design research. Proceedings of EDRA 9 (pp. 325-337). Washington: EDRA 1978

16. Davies, R., Talbot, R. J.: Experiencing ideas: identity, insight and the imago. Design Studies. 8 (1), 17-25 (1987)

17. Davies, S. P., Castell, A. M.: Contextualising design: narratives and rationalisation in empirical studies of software design. Design Studies. 13 (4), 379-392 (1992)

18. Department of Education and Science and the Welsh Office [DES]: Technology in the National Curriculum. London: HMSO 1990

19. Eckersley, M.: The form of design processes: a protocol analysis study. Design Studies, 9 (2), 86-94 (1988)

20. Harrison, M. K.: Technology in Schools: case studies. ET887/897, Module 4, Teaching and Learning Technology in Schools. Milton Keynes: The Open University Press 1988

21. Hennessy, S.: Situated Cognition and cognitive apprenticeship: implication for classroom learning. Studies in Science Education, 21 (in press) (1993)

22. Hennessy, S., McCormick, R., Murphy, P.: The myth of general problem-solving capability: design and technology as an example. Curriculum Journal. 4 (1), 74-89 (1993)

23. Her Majesty's Inspectorate of Schools [HMI]: Mini-enterprise in schools: some aspects of current practice 1988/1989. London: Department of Education and Science 1990

24. Her Majesty's Inspectorate of Schools [HMI]: Technology at Key Stages 1, 2 and 3. London: HMSO 1992

25. Jamieson, I., Miller, A., Watts, A. G.: Mirrors of work: work simulations in schools. Lewes: Falmer 1988

26. Lajoie, S. P., Lesgold, A.: Apprenticeship training in the workplace: computer-coached practice environment as new form of apprenticeship. Machine-Mediated Learning. 3, 7-28 (1989)

27. Lave, J.: Cognition in practice: mind, mathematics and culture in everyday life. Cambridge: Cambridge University Press 1988

28. Lave, J., Wenger, E.: Situated learning: legitimate peripheral participation. IRL Report No. IRL90-0013. Palo Alto, CA: Institute for Research on Learning 1990

29. Lawson, B.: How designers think. (2nd edition) Oxford: Butterworth Architecture 1990

30. McCormick, R.: Technology and National Curriculum: the creation of a 'subject' by committee? The Curriculum Journal. 1 (1), 39-51 (1990)

31. McCormick, R.: The evolution of current practice in technology education - part 1. Journal of Epsilon Pi Tau. 28 (2), 19-28 (1992)

32. McCormick, R.: The Evolution of current practice of technology education - part 2 Issues. Journal of Technology Studies. 29 (1) (forthcoming) 1993a

33. McCormick, R.: Integrating advanced educational technology into technology education. In: Gordon, A. (ed.) Integrating Advanced Educational Technology into Technology Education. Berlin: Springer-Verlag (forthcoming) 1993b

34. McCormick, R.: Design education and science: practical implications. In: M. J. de Vries, N. Cross, D. P. Grant (eds.) Design methodology and relationships with science. Dordrecht: Kluwer 1993c

35. McCormick, R.: Teaching and learning design. E885 PGCE Technology. Milton Keynes: The Open University (forthcoming) (1994)

36. McCormick, R., Hennessy, S., Murphy, P.: Problem-solving processes in technology education. Paper to International Technology Education Association 55th Annual Conference, Charlotte, North Carolina, April 1993

37. McCormick, R., Murphy, P., Harrison, M.: Teaching and Learning Technology. Wokingham, England: Addison-Wesley 1992

38. Medway, P.: Constructions of technology: reflections on a new subject. In: J. Beynon, H. Mackay (eds.) Technological literacy and the curriculum. (pp. 65-83) London: Falmer 1992

39. Miller, A.: Building effective school-business links. London: Westex Publications Centre (1992)

40. Monk, J.: The politics of engineering and the rituals of engineering education. Faculty of Technology Report No. SAG/1993/RR27/JM. Milton Keynes: The Open University 1993

41. Palincsar, A. S.: Less charted waters. Educational Researcher. 18 (4), 5-7 (1989)

42. Pieters, J. M., de Bruijn, H. F. M.: Learning environments for cognitive apprenticeship: from experience to expertise. In: P. A. M. Kommers, D. H. Jonassen, J. T. Mayes (eds.) Cognitive tools for learning. (pp. 241-248) Berlin: Springer-Verlag 1992

43. Prestine, N. A., LeGrand, B. F.: Cognitive learning theory and the preparation of educational administrators: implications for practice and policy. Educational Administration Quarterly. 27 (1), 61-89 (1991)

44. Resnick, L. B.: Learning in school and out. Educational Researcher. 16 (12), 13-20 (1987)

45. Rogoff, B.: Apprenticeship in Thinking: cognitive development in a social context. New York: Oxford University Press 1990

46. Rowe, P. G.: Design thinking. Cambridge, Mass: MIT Press 1987

47. Sandberg, J., Wielinga, B.: How situated is cognition? Paper to 12th International Conference of Artificial Intelligence, Sydney, 24-30 August 1991

48. Schenk, P.: The role of drawing in the graphic design process. Design Studies. 12 (3), 168-181 (1991)

49. Schon, D. A.: Problems, frames and perspectives on designing. Design Studies. 5 (3), 132-136 (1984)

50. Schon, D. A.: Designing: rules, types and worlds. Design Studies. 9 (3), 181-190 (1988)

51. Smithers, A., Robinson, P.: Technology in the National Curriculum: getting it right. London: Engineering Council 1992

52. Spensley, F.: Dominie: teaching and learning strategies. CAL Research Group Technical Report No. 74, Institute of Educational Technology. Milton Keynes: The Open University 1989

53. Waldron, M. B., Waldron, K. J.: A time sequence study of a complex mechanical system design. Design Studies. 9 (2), 95-106 (1988)

54. Wharton, M.: Hertfordshire Engineering Education Unit - the Sainsbury Trust Scheme - Progress Report October 1984 - May 1987. Hertford: Hertfordshire County Council (undated)

55. Wineburg, S. S.: Remembrance of theories past. Educational Researcher. 18 (4), 7-10 (1989)

56. Yoemans, D.: The creation of a subject by committee: comissions and commissions? The Curriculum Journal. 3 (1), 87-89 (1992)

New Didactical Concepts Through the Application of Flexible Learning Systems

Walter E. Theuerkauf
University of Hildesheim
Institut für Angewandte Elektrotechnik und Technikpädagogik
Kreuzstr. 8, D-31134 Hildesheim, Germany

Abstract. By means of the example of the outstanding key-qualification "Thinking and acting in systems", the necessity to translate modified concepts in learning processes is shown. Starting-points for the concretizing were represented by means of selected key-contents of automation technology within networked structures.

In this connection, the didactical concept integrates a flexible media-structure that may be formed for learning processes, and that is able to clarify integral labour-related processes, thus providing the group-controlled learning for resolving project tasks. The conception makes it possible to initiate the individual process of qualification by the learning group itself, as the requirements for professional, methodical and social qualifications result from the distribution of tasks within the group. Within the individual increase in knowledge in the field of the professional, methodical and social competences, the success of the group, the model production that is able to function, will not be possible. Additionally, auto-controlled learning processes for the individual further and continued education can be initiated on the basis of the individual evaluation of qualification.

Consequently, this didactical concept represents an attempt to prepare for the autonomous action of the collaborator within forms of organization that require a modified and wider competence-profile.

Keywords. Didactical concepts, key qualification, new learning processes, FLS (Flexible Learning Lab Systems)

1 Definition of the Problem

New didactical concepts for the structuring of learning processes are determined by the newly emerging competencies to be imparted. Additionally, every learning process irrespective of this level has to be considered from the pedagogical point of view as an integral process. Within this process the clients, the leader of the course and the supporting media system must have contemplary functions. In this context the competencies represent the aims in the learning process that must be legitimized. This was not undisputed from the scientific point of view. Previously the Federal Republic of Germany had set a frame in order to delimit clearly the general education from the vocational education. But, because of the different scientific positions the diverging views in discussion are characterized in both ways – hermeneutically and empirically.

The necessity for developing socially agreed aims for vocational education exists not only in the industrial nations but in all other countries as well. This results from the world-wide operations of enterprises with their production systems and efforts aiming at an internationally competitive quality level. The latter includes vocational training, further and continued education.

The competencies to be developed in professional and technical learning processes are called key-qualifications in the Federal Republic of Germany (cf. Mertens 1974). Apart from their validity in the field of vocational learning processes they may be also valid for a general technological education as well (cf. Theuerkauf, Weiner 1992).

Analogous general aims to define standards for basic competences can be found in the American literacy as so-called "Essential" or "Workplace skills" (cf. Carnevale and others, 1990, Dyrenfurth 1991). Even if there are differences in the expressions or in the character of the qualifications, it should be noted that they are similar. This similarity results from the fact that both concepts are based on empirical investigations. The concept of the key-qualifications is not derived from a "Herbartien" educational theory, but it is based on analyses in the field of labour educational theory and social research. Even if different methods are used in order to abstract the competencies to be imparted, one can see that identical or complementing results may arise, as for instance with regard to the transferability of the cognitive dimension or to the moral concepts of the affective dimension.

It is undisputed that the high degree of generalization of the key qualifications, as "The application of learning systems and systems for intellectual work" makes it more difficult to recognize and to examine the ultimate goal to be achieved by a student within a learning process (cf. Reets and others, 1990). Key-qualifications as components of "Technological Literacy" represent only categories and characteristics and consequently the basis for taxonomy graduations (cf. Foster, Perrault, 1986). These are overall goals that serve as a planning basis, as guide-lines and correction factors for the learning processes, rather than specific objectives.

The particular value of the concept of key-qualification consequently resides in the integral contemplation of the learning process that is to be structured and also evaluated. It guarantees in this way both, the linking of expert, methodical and social competence and the respective profile, thus leading equally to the mutual evaluation and accentuation of these components within the learning process.

To limit the learning process to only the imparting of key-qualifications, however, would mean to view it in an one-sided way. Qualifications with a performance that can be described are always connected with contents. Analogous to the key-qualifications key-contents or "Advanced Technologies/Workforce Trends" (cf. Barnes, Erekson 1991) may be defined or extrapolated by means of present and future constants of technical systems and processes. The distinction of new didactical concepts within a learning process aiming at a defined key-qualification therefore must inevitably integrate key-contents that are both, discipline-specific and overarching in character. Only on this basis can a plant-oriented didactical conception for the structuring of the learning process be developed.

Key-qualifications and key-contents form the basis for an individual further education and adaptation. Consequently, they serve as the pedagogical and psychological basis for planning. The range of the learning process is represented by the degree to which it has been concretized. From the breadth of range of these key-qualifications comes the question for the central qualifications that may be of particular relevance with regard to the demands for coping skills made by a plant on its workers.

2 Modification of Work Structures

Key-industries are involved in a process of restructuring as engendered by the new paradigms. For example, the Japanese realized this process under the title "Lean-Production". The process is characterized by its high degree of networking as well as by lower hierarchies that make it easier to control the increasing complexity of the enterprise structures. More and more process chain-oriented tasks consequently are resolved in a decentralized and autonomous way in order to enable the faster closing of flatter control systems in a shorter time.

The central paradigm of conventional mass production is characterized historically by the division of labour according to Taylor. This system made it possible to split complex work in a way to create tasks that can be learned easily by "semi-skilled" persons, or that can be performed by "skilled workers" with specialized knowledge. These divided production structures consequently lead to a separation into "intellectual and manual labour". This means the separation into planning and production functions. Mechanization, automation and computer technology are regarded as representation stages of development for modern technology. They have developed the technically oriented system for the division of labour and have led to more and more perfect solutions for partial tasks. This starting-point of the division of labour with its emphasis on a centralist and consequently "split-off" planning, however, reaches its organizational and economic limits soon, particularly when it is desired to produce a greater variety of products and only a smaller number of pieces are to be fabricated. Similar limits are reached as a consequence of the flatter hierarchies – more flexible production systems for the realization of the orders are of increasing importance.

The work structures observed during the investigations of production facilities having a high degree of automation (cf. Dostal et al. 1982; Lutz and Schultz-Wild 1982; Sonntag and Wöcherl 1985) demonstrate in a conclusive way that a general system performance can be achieved when the work teams were qualified on an uniform level (Figure 1). In comparison with the traditional work structures the most crucial modification consists of a reduction of the division of work and this occurs in three key ways:

– the hierarchical division of work within a production process is canceled (i.e., the division of labour existing between an unskilled worker, the operator, the stand-in, the tool setter and the foreman/system driver, eventually).
– the professional division of work between the different production methods (particularly between turning and milling) is reduced or completely canceled, and
– the functional division of labour between the production, the preceding and the following operations is reduced (cf. Schultz-Wild 1985) as the routing, the presetting of tools, the safeguarding of quality.

A further structuring principle for flexible production is derived from teamwork where all the tasks that come up are not allocated to the different workers automatically, but they are taken over by the group in their entirety in order to be assigned according to the specific labour situation. (Task-Rotation).

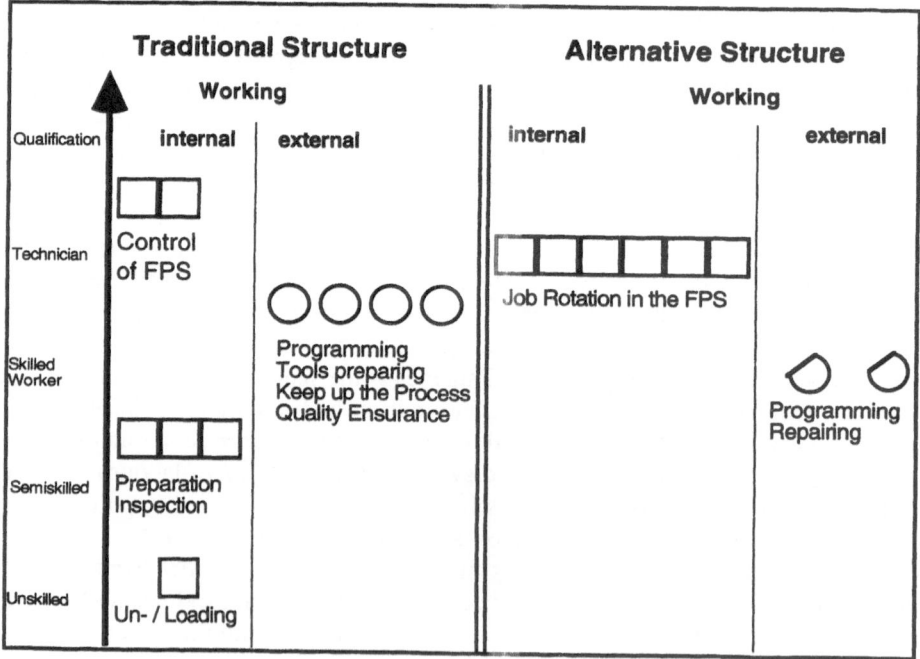

Fig. 1 Traditional and alternative structures of working (Martin 1985, p. 23)

Because of the changed organization of work and the allocation of competence and responsibility as a consequence of the modified structure of enterprises the demand for a total consideration of the plant processes arises. It demands, on the one hand an expert-competent, discipline-oriented action, and on the other hand a general understanding. The volume of orders given from outside and as it is seen from the micro-view of a production cell, must be included therefore in the macro-view of the given frame of objectives of an enterprise. With the available complex structures, this requires a "system-theoretical thinking and acting" in order to satisfy the demands for an expert-competent and general understanding and the classification of processes within networked structures of enterprises.

Systems and process analysis make it possible to cope with the complex of networked systems by means of the reduction of functional connections and the description of the interactive networked exchange of information. The use of systems theory as support for actions consequently represents a methodical aid in the learning processes of technical education and training. Only by means of this aid will it be possible to get access to technical systems and to their parameters. Furthermore, this access must not only be limited by a technically oriented point of view.

In this context, acting and thinking in systems represents one of the out-standing key-qualifications in the field of vocational training. The understanding of systems thus can be described as the ability to structure functions that are networked in both, an easy and a complicated way. They link, on the one hand, technological, planning and organizational systems, and on the other hand the algorithmizing of control functions and their chronological dimensions within a course of processes that are defined by the limits of the system.

The qualification "Thinking and acting in systems" requires further detailed qualifications. For instance, "Thinking in functional blocks", "Abstraction of functions", "Organizing of functions according to chronological order", "Thinking with regard to the future" etc.

Closely connected to the key-qualification "Thinking and acting in systems", is the use of systemics and process analysis and synthesis as a methodical tool. It is not limited to the analysis of technical linking in systems, but it also refers to the synthesis and to the structuring of technical, sociotechnical and human-centralized systems and their process development.

3 Model Configuration for the Imparting of System-Competence

The development of the key-qualification "Thinking and acting in systems" requires complex networked media configurations with such a high degree of adaptability that they make it possible to initiate learning processes adequate to the work place.

In order to realise system structures that are able to link the flows of information and material as key-contents of learning processes for automation technology, a Flexible Learning Lab System (FLS) was developed and elaborated. By using the FLS as an open system, it is possible to reproduce in the laboratory flexible automation structures of production processes using industry-oriented means, and also to realize the networking of partial and complete automation in a product-oriented way (cf. Theuerkauf, Weiner 1993).

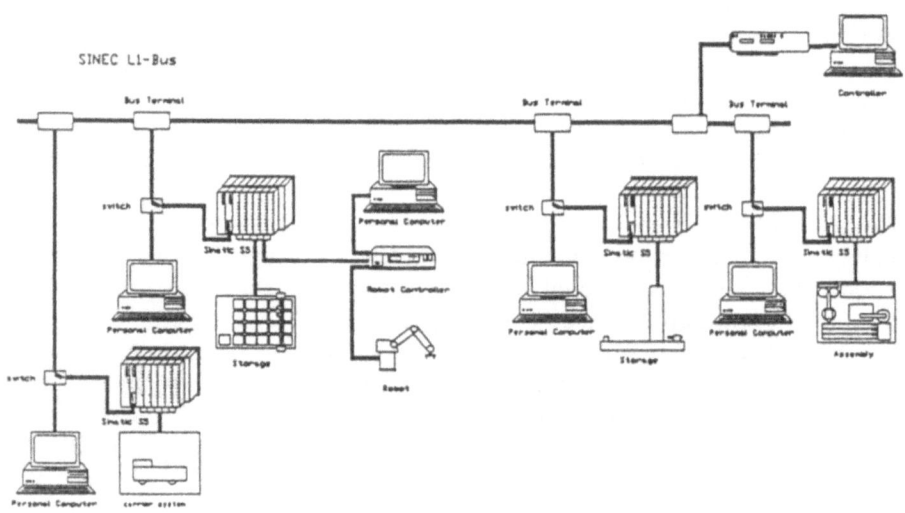

Fig. 2 Network of the Flexible Laboratory System

From the system-theoretical point of view the different places of learning represent partial systems of a FLS configuration to be generated. In accordance with their objectives, these link elementary operations of production systems as "transporting", "processing", "accumulating", "storing", etc. Via a bus-system, these partial systems represent the networking of laboratory experiments. Production control, as embedded in a production planning system (PPS), illustrates clearly the process character of the system of the model-like production. Thus the media configuration corresponds structurally to the reduced workshop production that has to realize a given quantity of orders.

The development of the media configuration was guided by the nature of flexible computer-integrated plant systems. The networking is determined by vertical and horizontal flows of information that have effects on material/product flows. The communication is characterized by data structures on different levels of the FLS and the partial systems are linked based on their differing degrees of networking.

This concept allows both, a macro-view of production planning and a micro-view of the representation of a production spectrum. In this connection, the macro-view includes the whole enterprise, while the micro-view represents only a processing centre.

Consequently, the reproduction of micro- and macro-systems within a flexible media-configuration allows the imparting of subject-specific technologies on the one hand, and of logistical, controller contents on the other hand.

4 Imparting Systems Competence with the FLS

Systems competence and the other key qualifications have to be imparted within one teaching process. The following illustrates the possibilities the FLS offers for this.

Apart from the media to be used, the question also is as to what teaching method is best suited to impart key qualifications, particularly the ability to think and act within systems. This would include project-related work and learning. (Rectz 1990). Such methodologies place theory and practice into a relationship and thereby stimulate comprehensive thinking and group communication.

When the aim is to encourage system-dominated competence to act, after expert competence the competencies to be developed, are methodical and social competence. To develop methodical competence, particular methods of problem solution, which include systems analysis and synthesis, have to be applied for different learning situations in the plant (vgl. Theuerkauf, Weiner 1992 b).

To develop problem solving competence and the capacity for teamwork, the activity guide method appears to be suitable. It allows the participants to achieve the aims of the course in a step-by-step approach.

To develop social competence, learning phases have to be provided for where the individual works in differently composed groups to achieve a common aim within networked systems. Performance motivation of individuals within the group can be encouraged by communicating the message that only with mutual assistance and the exchange of interface parameters can the task be solved.

Starting from a central problem or task, all the students worked to develop a concept for solving problem. Individual part problems were developed together and then delegated for solution to the small groups formed at this stage. The concept includes phases of reflection and exchange of experience encountered during the small group work. It also provides for the acquisition of expert competence by learning units, e.g., for CNC technology, robot technology, programmable controller technology and aspects of networking. The procedures developed in the theoretical sessions are verified as to their suitability by dealing with the model, and they are practiced until mastered. The development of social competence is accounted for working in various group configurations. A joint project phase for presentation of the results achieved completes the concept.

5 System Competence as a Basis for Trouble Shooting

Quality is a decisive factor in efficient production. Among other reasons, we teach this to ensure that plant stoppages caused by malfunctions are reduced to a minimum. For producers integrated into the Kanban or Just-in-Time principle, short malfunction reaction times in the networked partial production processes are a must.

If systems competence means the ability of putting networked production systems into operation and maintaining trouble-free operation, the ability to diagnose, localise and eliminate malfunctions in networked structures has to be developed as an enabling qualification.

Different strategies can be followed for fault diagnosis. Most efficient are strategies that are both system and detail-dominated. Here, differential action patterns are independent of the individual competence. Competence development aims at the ability to systematically expand system boundaries on the basis of the acquired know how.

The occurance of a fault always goes along with the malfunction of at least one plant component. To be able to trace the cause of the trouble in a complex production plant, different trouble shooting strategies are available. Serving as a foundation for these strategies are hierarchies that are based on an analysis of the specific functions of the plant. Suitable analysis methods are the fault tree analysis (German DIN Standard 25.424), the incident sequence analysis (DIN 25.419), and the failure-effect analysis (DIN 25.448).

With the aid of the established hierarchies, and the trouble shooting strategies derived from these hierarchies, it is possible to determine the cause of the malfunction. For this purpose, a large number of steps may be required.

The cause of a plant stoppage may be determined through branched linking of the functional elements. As subsets of possible faults, the different intermediate conditions have to be identified through deduction of the logic operations. Only then can the cause be definitely determined.

The considerations with respect to error logic demonstrate that there need not necessarily be an immediate connection between the effect of a fault (e.g., parts transport interrupted) and the cause (e.g., driving motor defective). The fault tree, which shows all the logic functional operations, reveals the multitude of possible causes of a malfunction and thus the complexity of the trouble shooting process.

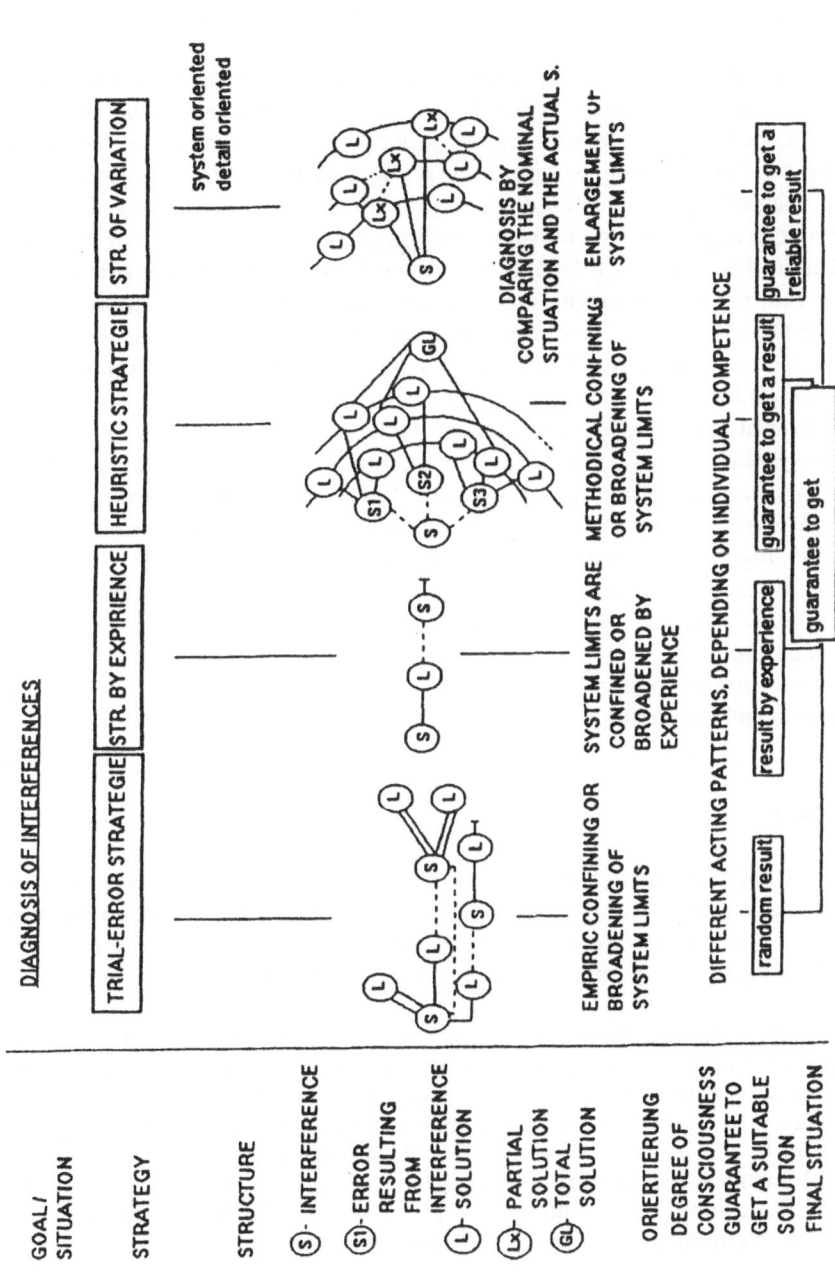

Fig. 3 Strategies of trouble shooting

The fault tree also shows the grading of the cause/effect chains. The apparent defect of the driving motor can again be attributable to a number of errors, which can be of a mechanical or electrical nature or be found in the program. A presentation, which may not be entirely accurate in the logic operations and evaluations, but which is highly practical is the cause/effect diagram.

A fault in a computer-controlled production system is not always a sudden event. Often faults can be addressed by preventive measures. When starting from this premise, it is possible to integrate quality losses as an effect of malfunctions into trouble management. When seeking high product quality and plant availability, trouble management involves an ongoing link to the plant operations. To know the design behaviour of the plant is an essential prerequisite of trouble prevention. (Total Quality Management). Quality assurance is always linked to the tracing of causes of faults. Only when the causes have positively been determined can a decision be taken as to the type of corrective measures so as to preclude, or reduce, the recurrance of the fault. While solving such problems, it is important to maintain a high level of technical safety and plant reliability.

Application of such graded and classified fault analyses to the flexible teaching laboratory system enables future plant supervisors to acquire diagnostic strategies that can be translated into real systems. Another advantage that learning from a model plant offers, is the possibility of variation, also of the complexity, of the fault diagnosing and elimination procedure. This can be achieved by fixing and combining elementary causes of malfunctions as required. Generation of the different malfunctions and their realistic characterization necessitates predetermination.

Fault generation through a software provides fault input routines. It supports fault statistics and evaluation of the performance of future plant supervisors.

6 Summary

By means of the example of this selected key-qualification, "Thinking and acting in systems", this report has shown the necessity to address new concepts via new learning processes. Starting-points for the implementation were represented by means of selected key-contents of automation technology within networked structures.

The didactical concept integrates in this connection, a flexible media-structure that may be formed for learning processes, and that is able to clarify integral labour-related processes, thus providing group-controlled learning for resolving project tasks. The concept makes it possible to initiate the individual process of qualification by the learning group itself and the requirements for professional, methodical and social qualification result from the distribution of tasks within the group. Without such individual increases in knowledge in the field of the professional, methodical and social competencies, the success of the group, as

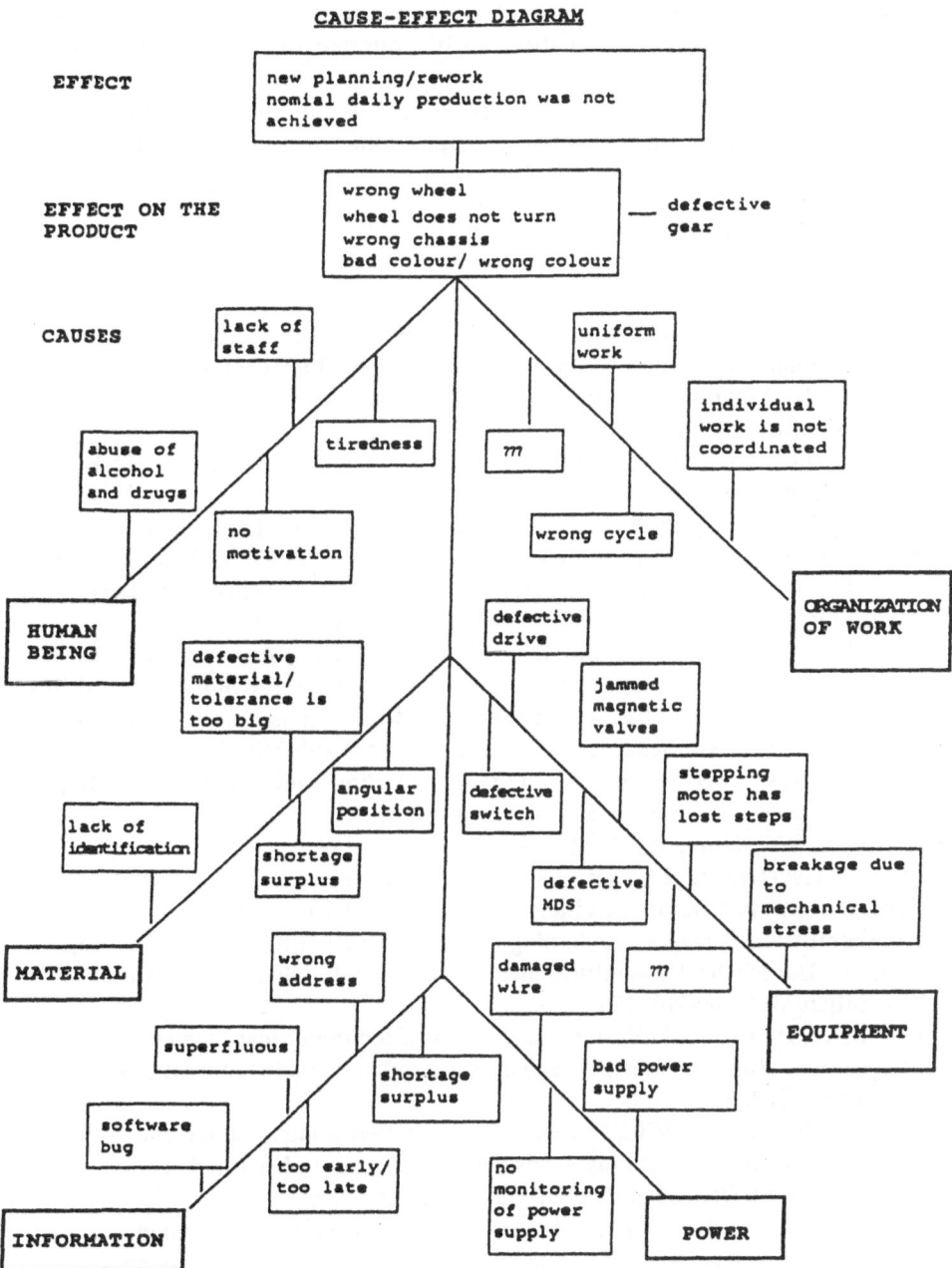

Fig. 4 Cause/effect diagram for the FLS

seen by a functioning production model, will not be possible. Additionally, note that the FLS enables auto-controlled learning processes for individual, further and continued education, and that this can be initiated on the basis of individual evaluations of qualification.

Consequently, this didactical concept represents an attempt to prepare for the autonomous acting of all personnel within forms of organization that require a modified and wider competence-profile.

References

1. Barnes, James L., Erekson, Thomas L.: Labor, private sector, and governmental perspectives on technological literacy. In: Technological Literacy. (ed.): Michael Dyrenfurth, Michael R. Kozak. Glencoe Division, Macmillan/McGraw-Hill P.94-118 (1991)
2. Carnevale, Anthony P., Gainer, Leila J., Meltzer, Ann S.: Workplace Basics-The Essential Skills Employers Want- San Francisco 1990
3. DIN 25 419. Ereignisablaufanalyse. Verfahren, graphische Symbole und Auswertung. Hrsg.: Deutscher Normenausschuß. Berlin, Köln: Beuth-Vlg. 1985
4. DIN 25 424 Teil 1. Fehlerbaumanalyse. Methode und Bildzeichen. Hrsg.: Deutscher Normenausschuß. Berlin, Köln: Beuth-Vlg. 1981
5. DIN 25 424 Teil 2. Fehlerbaumanalyse. Verfahren zur Auswertung eines Fehlerbaumes. Hrsg.: Deutscher Normenausschuß. Berlin, Köln: Beuth-Vlg. 1990
6. DIN 25 448. Ausfalleffektanalyse (Fehler-Möglichkeits- und Einfluß-Analyse). Hrsg.: Deutscher Normenausschuß. Berlin, Köln: Beuth-Vlg. 1990
7. DIN 40 150. Begriffe zur Ordnung von Funktions- und Baueinheiten. Hrsg.: Deutscher Normenausschuß. Berlin, Köln: Beuth-Vlg. 1979
8. Dostal, W., Kamp, W.-W., Lahner, M., Seesle, W.-P.: Flexible Fertigungssysteme und Arbeitsplatzstrukturen. In: Mitteilungen aus der Arbeitsmarkt- und Berufsforschung 15 2, S. 182-191 (1982)
9. Dyrenfurth, Michael J.: Technological literacy synthesized. In: Technological Literacy. Ed: Michael Dyrenfurth, Michael R. Kozak. Glencoe Division, Macmillan/McGraw-Hill 1991
10. Foster, P., Perreault, R.: Characteristics of technological literacy: Perspectives from the industrial and educational sectors. In: Journal of Epsilon Pi Tau, 12 (1) (1986)
11. Lutz, B., Schultz-Wild, R. (eds.): Flexible Fertigungssysteme und Personalwirtschaft - Erfahrungen aus Frankreich, Japan, USA und der Bundesrepublik Deutschland. Frankfurt: Campus 1982
12. Reetz, Lothar, Reitmann, Thomas (eds.): Schlüsselqualifikationen. Dokumentation des Symposions in Hamburg "Schlüsselqualifikationen - Fachwissen in der Krise". Hamburg: Feldhaus 1990

13. Sonntag, Karlheinz, Wöcherl, H.: Qualifikationsanforderungen im Flexiblen Fertigungssystem. Forschungsbericht über den arbeitspsychologischen Untersuchungsteil des BMBW/BIBB-Projektes D 0560.00. Kassel. 1985
14. Theuerkauf, Walter E., Weiner, Andreas: Key qualifications as an ability for a technical education. International Conference on Technological Education. Weimar, Germany 1992
15. Theuerkauf, Walter E., Weiner, Andreas: Network teaching of key qualifications as instanced by the Flexible Learning Lab System (FLS). In: Rauner, Felix (ed.): Qualification for Computer Integrated Manufacturing. Berlin, New York: Springer 1992b.

2. Aspects of Identifying Key Competencies

Tolerance, the ability to work in a team, the ability to reach compromises, to acknowledge social responsibility, to demonstrate acceptance are among the new competencies individuals require to interact effectively with technology and to work efficiently. Part 2's sessions directed participants to consider the results of research that identified key qualifications, not only for factories or companies, but also for education at all levels. These sessions drew attention to both the process of identifying the new concepts needed and the actual competencies yielded by such procedures. The session's presenters identified thinking in systems, being able to structure a problem in time and hierarchy and formulating the contradictions and compromises as examples of new capabilities that are not yet adequately acknowledged by technology and general educators alike. All participants stressed that technology has itself become a driving source for our development of human resources.

Initially the discussion evolving from Part 2's presentations centered on how the new key competencies will be identified. But soon they extended to address the possibilities for identifying and measuring an individual's performance and the generation of appropriate standards/criteria. With respect to testing and assessment, the participants pointed out the contrast between the trend, in national testing systems, to move increasingly towards itemized, criterion referenced systems while the need was actually to move to more judgmental and holistic approaches. Given the increasing pressures for accountability in many countries it was agreed that it was important to develop systematic indicators of student achievement and capability. The need for a benchmark capability was also pointed out.

The group's discussion base was enriched by Halliday's compassionate call for the extension of our focus from education systems to comprehensive, inclusive learning communities. Fisher explored the key competencies called for by our new world and Kunz used the example of the Skoda car company to discuss the didactics necessary to develop those competencies.

Identifying Key Competencies in Specific Occupational Sectors for Incorporation into Vocational Training Programmes

Kenneth L. Fisher
Bolton Institute of Higher Education
Chadwick Street
Bolton BL2 1JW, United Kingdom

Abstract. This paper focuses upon strategies for elucidating key competencies for inclusion in vocational education and training programmes.

Job analysis – as a technique through which job-related key competencies can be highlighted – is critically explored. From the exploration, Hierarchical Job Analysis and Hierarchical Task Analysis are presented as viable and powerful analytical techniques for training programme developers. A case is cited where these techniques have been used with considerable success and the point is made that they can be applied to any job undergoing analysis for training purposes (*inter alia*).

Keywords. Vocational education, job analysis, sector-based National Qualifications, key competencies

1 Background

'A New Training Initiative' was introduced in Britain in 1981 following the collapse of the measures associated with the 1964 Industrial Training Act. It called for a massive overhaul of vocational education and training (VET) and the introduction of a training infrastructure that would help combat the paradoxical situation of rising unemployment and a growing skills' shortage.

It was asserted that vocational training could not be detached from the world of work if Britain – through the efforts of the workforce – is to remain buoyant in increasingly competitive world markets. Educationally-driven training and knowledge-based examinations had done little, if anything, to develop the vocational competencies which employees and potential employees need, so the critics contended. They argued cogently and convincingly that the spotlight should be on what is required to attain employable competency in specific occupational roles in defined employment sectors, and for vocational qualifications to be more closely attuned to work-relevant practices. Indeed, both 'A New Training Initiative' – and the subsequent 'Review of Vocational Qualifications' (MSC/DES, 1986) criticised the barriers and constraints that not only prevented access to training but which denied people access to qualifications. Among the inhibiting factors cited were time-served apprenticeships, age limits, and the need to follow prescribed programmes of study.

Outside formal apprenticeships, work experience has hardly ever been acknowledged as a major contributor to assessable occupational competence and for far too long there has been a preoccupation with training inputs rather than with performance outcomes. In Britain the situation was destined to change.

2 Job Analysis: An Overview

It may not be surprising that jobs have not been analysed as a precursor to the design, development and delivery of training programmes when one realises the attendant dilemmas about appropriateness of analytical techniques for training purposes.

One of the primary causes for that decline seems to have been a lack of understanding of job analysis as a powerful investigatory technique that has many applications in addition to "wage and salary administration" (Ghorpade and Atchison, 1980). Prien and Ronan (1971) refer to "traditional work measurement systems" that are expressly concerned with maximising the efficiency of the "economic system" as the primary focus of job analysis. The sinister implications are apparent. This is particularly regrettable and extremely restrictive because job-related information is required for many purposes, including personnel selection, personnel appraisal and job design – in addition to the invaluable contribution it makes to the identification of key competences on which to develop training programmes.

Secondly, McCormick (1976) refers to the dismal and uninspired background that informed early attempts at job analysis. In condemning these attempts as floundering, confused and largely directionless, he targets his sharpest criticism at the methodology that was applied to obtain the required information. (This, incidentally, is a recurring difficulty and one that is still frequently referred to [see, for example, Prien and Ronan, 1971; Sturm, 1979; Ash and Levine, 1980]). According to McCormick the methods revolved around narrative descriptions of job activities by analysts who observed jobs in progress and interviewed job-holders.

Such techniques are stigmatised as cumbersome and inadequate. Similarly, McCormick, Jeanneret and Mecham (1972) endorse and elaborate upon these methodological problems which appear to present genuine handicaps. They refer specifically to the fact that:

"... conventional job analysis procedures ... tend to be more 'qualitative' than 'quantitative' in form. Qualitative job information is characterized by typically narrative, essay descriptions in the case of some types of job information (especially job content) or qualitative statements about other aspects of jobs (such as working conditions, context, personnel requirements, etc)." (McCormick, Jeanneret and Mecham, 1972, p. 347)

Ghorpade and Atchison (1980) are similarly critical of data gathering methods which, apparently, consisted of observation and time-and-motion studies which one might have expected if job analysis is restricted to the measurement of work. They assert that job analysis is a "technique bound" process and, therefore, greatly hindered and seriously restricted in its applications.

So far as Britain is concerned Patrick and Moore (1985) and Pearn and Kandola (1988) justify the "resurgence of interest" on the basis of a need to analyse jobs as a result of rapid technological developments in industry and commerce. Not only is there a pressing and urgent need to analyse jobs:

"... more precisely but by methods which produce information which can be quantified and compared for different jobs." (Patrick and Moore, 1985, p. 149)

Training may be implied, but there are, unfortunately, no specific references.

Although stressing the need to obtain *accurate, representative and meaningful data*, Ghorpade and Atchison (1980) regretfully concede that all too often job analysis is an ad hoc, haphazard activity, rather than a continual, systematic and purposeful process.

3 Possible Analytic Techniques for the Identification of Key Competencies a Critical Overview

In a project in 1988, Miller et al. (1988) –– when selecting an analytical technique for their work-based learning project – assessed the analytical potential of Dacum, Delphi, Critical Incident and Behavioural Events which, like Functional Analysis (which is used to develop National Vocational Qualifications), are not based on "simple task skills". In their report they extol the scope these techniques provide for considering "the more nebulous areas of competence".

Unfortunately, Delphi and Dacum – in common with Functional Analysis suffer from heavy reliance on panels of experts (see Dalkey, 1969; Jones, 1973 – quoted by Miller et al., 1988). Wolf (1990), corroborates this in noting that Functional Analysis:

"... is closest to Dacum and Delphi, both of which involve brainstorming and consensus building by groups of experts. (Wolf, 1990, p. 37)

Finch and Crunkilton (1984) add further derogatory remarks. Dacum is an imprecise technique and little better than introspection, while Delphi focuses more on the future of a particular occupational area and is (like all future-orientated techniques) prone to speculation and prediction.

Along with Delphi and Dacum, the Critical Incident technique seeks to define the components that contribute to broadly-defined work-based competence. Although it is said that the strategy is objective and popular with competency-based trainers, because the grouping of incidents into clusters relies on subjective opinion, its objectivity is somewhat diminished.

The Behavioural Events approach is an adaptation of Critical Incident, to which it has a close resemblance. While the latter is concerned mainly with the incidents, not with the people recounting them, the former is concerned with people and with the behaviours, skills and characteristics that distinguish levels of performance and the separation of "star performers" from "average performers". The pre-occupation is with personal attributes, not with situational demands, resources or constraints that inhibit or facilitate competence and performance. In this respect, "star" and "average performers" have to be identified and questions concerning the criteria on which the selection is made undermine the validity of the technique (Miller et al., 1988).

Such comments have great potential for damaging the credibility of Functional Analysis in addition to injuring the plausibility of Delphi, Dacum, Critical Incident and the Behavioural Events technique.

4 Task Analysis: An Ambivalent Perspective

Miller et al. (1988) note that Delphi, Dacum, Critical Incident and Behavioural Events were developed for generating curricula in education and they have, consequently, been favoured more by educationalists than by industrialists. On the other hand, Task Analysis has been commonly used within industry and it is associated with industrial, rather than educational, analyses. However, it is conducted:

"... at the level of jobs (and) really requires that the analyst be experienced in the occupational sector under consideration." (Miller et al., 1988, pp. 82–83)

Task analysis is castigated by Miller et al. (1988) as time-consuming and restricted to the identification of sector-specific tasks and "simple task skills". Similarly, Mansfield (1989a) is highly critical of task analysis for its tendency to measure and atomise work activities either for work measurement or for skills' training. He regards it as a wholly inappropriate technique for developing National Vocational Qualifications which, he says, are based on work role expectations and on a broad concept of competence.

After all, task analysis has been widely used over a long period – as Miller et al. (1988) have to agree (maybe somewhat reluctantly). What they, like Annett (1987), could stress is that it is a generic concept that needs to be unpacked, rather than discarded, for the packing conceals a wide array of applications such as job analysis, skills' analysis, content analysis, procedural analysis – to name but four (see Piso, 1981; Stammers and Astley, 1987). As a result of task analysis it is possible to obtain:

"... a detailed description of the functional actions which constitute the practice of that vocation. The activities observed and the reported areas of applied knowledge relating to the activities could then be arranged into a logical sequence to form the basis of an accreditation system." (Miller et al., 1988, pp. 102–103)

Patrick (1980) notes that job analysis, which is carried out for training purposes, emphasises:

"... the use of task-oriented data which is necessary to determine accurately the content of training." (Patrick, 1980, p. 57)

To support his assertion he says Smith (1964) describes how a job can be broken down into a series of tasks and sub-tasks, Christal (1974) finds an inventory of tasks useful in describing a job, while a review by Wheaton et al (1976) reveals that job analysis in training contexts begins by deriving task-oriented data.

The later comments by Miller et al. (1988) about the failure of task analysis to yield performance criteria and details of *how* a task is performed (in addition to *what* is performed) illustrate an imperfect understanding of task analysis and its potential. Additionally, throughout the commentaries on job analysis, a lot is said about gathering the data: little, or nothing, is said about analysing that data by exploiting the potential of high-speed computing facilities (see, for instance, Miller et al., 1988; Mansfield, 1989a and 1989b; Mitchell, 1989).

5 Task-Based Approaches to the Identification of Key Competencies in Specific Occupations

It should be stressed (in common with Patrick [1980]) that a task-approach, or activities-approach, to job analysis provides a dependable foundation for the development of work-related training programmes. This has been acknowledged on innumerable occasions (see, for instance, Blank, 1982; RSA, 1986; Black, 1990). As Blank (1982) says:

"Describing the competent worker ... involves identifying and listing the ... tasks the competent worker actually performs and is paid for on the job. ... Identifying the tasks actually performed by workers on the job is essential if we want to develop a training program that will help trainees acquire the tasks that will make them successful workers." (Blank, 1982, p. 65)

To illustrate his point, Blank presents what he calls a "closed loop" which consists of three interrelated segments, as the diagram below illustrates.

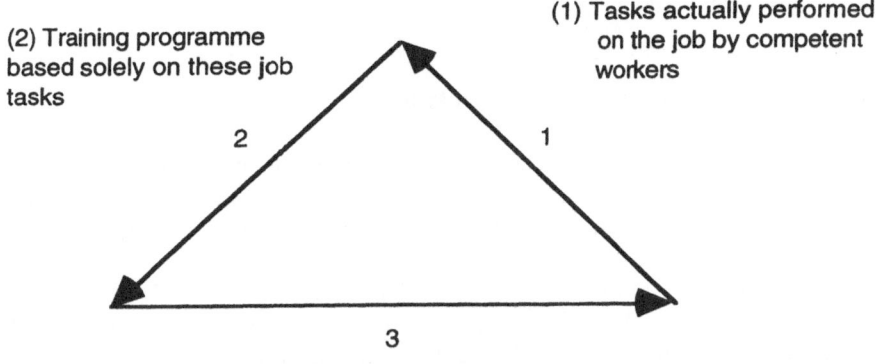

(2) Training programme
based solely on these job
tasks

(1) Tasks actually performed
on the job by competent
workers

2

1

3

(3) Programme graduates master
these job tasks and enter the
occupation as competent workers

Fig.1 Relationship among job competencies, training program and competent trainees (Blank, 1982, p. 65)

Blank (1982) further notes that if training programmes are based:

"... on anything *other* than valid job tasks ... we may break this closed loop, and we cannot be sure if students are mastering the tasks actually needed on the job." (Blank, 1982, p. 66)

The message is clear for providers of vocational education and training. In order to ensure the relevance of VET, it is fundamentally necessary to analyse, or break down, jobs into tasks to provide a focus for training and to enable trainees to develop key competencies. In stressing that the 'task base' provides a dependable foundation for the construction of training programmes, it can be argued that *all* jobs are task- or activity-based. Even in the absence of a 'tangible product' a carefully-selected analytical technique should be capable of yielding insightful data that can be used as a basis for structuring work-related training programmes.

While RSA (1986) acknowledges that it is easier in some 'areas' than others to identify tangible outcomes (contrasting clerical work with distributive studies), it nevertheless, realistically, points to the benefits of "clearly-defined clusters (or modules) of tasks" as a basis for work-related, competency-based, learning programmes.

To go beyond the identification of work-related tasks in the pursuit of occupationally-specific activities, one is in danger of stifling individual creativity and dehumanising workers. As Hall and Jones (1976) note, a competent worker has an individual personal style of working, of managing work, of interacting with others and in responding to the ongoing nature of the job. While they stress that "total performance" is indicative of competence, they equally forcibly emphasise the need for individuals to be encouraged to develop their own unique blends of "personal style".

6 Task Description and Task Analysis

The writer of this paper found little encouragement in many of the published techniques for analysing jobs to identify key competencies for inclusion in vocational training programmes. However, renewed inspiration was obtained from Gagne's (1965) approach.

Gagne distinguishes between analytical techniques on the basis of projected outcomes. For him, the key determinant is the communicative purpose of the analytical process which manifests itself in the depth or penetration of the analysis. More particularly:

"Describing a human task for purposes of classifying a job ... requires a different approach than does describing a task in order to reveal what is necessary for its learning. ... The problem of choosing a degree of specificity for the description of human tasks has been a puzzling one. It appears to be best solved by considering the communication purpose of the description. That is to say, the degree of specificity of description should be determined by consideration of the question, What is being communicated to whom?" (Gagne 1965, p. 258)

Allied to the communicative purpose of the analysis is the point at which the analysis begins. In the case of job-task analysis a suitable starting point is the job title, whereas in the case of learning-tasks for instructional purposes, the analysis begins with the task.

In addition to using job-task descriptors as indicators of key competencies and bases for vocational training programme content, they may be used, for example, to formulate job descriptions, to describe jobs to potential employees, and to classify jobs within career hierarchies. From the point of view of the learner, job-task descriptions represent terminal learning outcomes – or competencies – that they should be able to demonstrate at some pre-determined future time (Gagne, 1962; Mager, 1962; Miller, 1963; Gagne, 1965). As Gagne (1965) says, the description of tasks as learning outcomes has been the focus of much writing –– with a long history. He quotes Mager (1962), Popham and Baker (1970) and Bloom, Hastings and Madaus (1971) in corroboration.

The training implications are clearly apparent from Gagne's (1965) work. At the level of job-task description, job-tasks are identified and they form the content of training programmes. Further analysis of these activities to reveal their sub-tasks, or operations, then forms the basis for instructional processes and performance criteria. Cunningham and Duncan (1967) neatly summarise the distinction on the basis of training content and instructional techniques. As they say, job-task descriptions specify terminal performance of trainees and, thus, the *content* of training programmes, whereas learning strategies and training methods are the concern of learning-task analyses which seek to identify and classify performance components in behavioural terms.

7 The Emergence of Hierarchical Task Analysis and Hierarchical Job Analysis

There are many forms of Task Analysis, as Annett (1987) implied when he referred to the generic nature of the Task Analysis concept (see Miller, 1963; McCormick, 1979; Drury, 1983). Each form has the common purpose of breaking down work activities as objectively as possible in terms of identifiable units or activities. McCormick (1979) also refers to analysis and description at "task level" and to the identification of tasks inherent in jobs – *key competencies* – and to the further analysis of those tasks to reveal more specific "actions or activities" on which the *instructional process* is developed.

In response to the question of analytical penetration, Annett and Duncan (1970), Annett, Duncan, Stammers and Gray (1971) and Shepherd (1985) – in their development and application of *Hierarchical Task Analysis* (HTA) – say that on different occasions different levels, or degrees, of analysis are appropriate. To predetermine an invariant number of levels may prejudice the quality and utility of the analysis, they argue. As Duncan (1974) illustrates:

"... describing the duties of a hall porter might entail no more detail than the statements that he must, for example, call taxis, take up and bring down luggage, ... but in *cordon bleu* cooking, many of the steps in preparing the dish may require extensive redescription of the various sub-routines involved ... ." (Duncan, 1974, p. 283)

He notes that the level of description is governed to a large extent by the task and the trainee who is to perform it. However, in HTA the analytical levels — while flexible – are guided by a formula which relates error probability (P) to the cost of an error (C). It is conceivable that when describing and redescribing an activity or task for instructional purposes, the redescription could – in principle — be continued ad infinitum. However, the so-called 'P x C rule' devised by Annett and his colleagues – and uniquely associated with HTA – states that further redescription or analysis of a task is unnecessary where the probability of inadequate performance (P) and the cost of inadequate performance (C) of a particular sub-task is acceptable to the person requesting the analysis – which is usually zero. This gives rise to the 'P x C = 0' rule.

Specific reference has been made to the work of Annett and his colleagues because of their unique contribution to analysing tasks through the systematic development of a hierarchy. As Shepherd (1987) remarks, while the technique was greeted with considerable enthusiasm initially, it still has considerable potential for extended use as the writer of this paper can confirm.

As indicated earlier, the literature is replete with accounts and examples of techniques that are extremely complex (see McCormick, Jeanneret and Mecham, 1972), rather dated (see Thomas, 1952) or lacking in completeness (see Flanagan, 1954). Additionally, most of the published techniques superimpose predefined and rigid analytical structures on to jobs in a mechanistic and inflexible manner, thereby having the potential to distort the true nature of the jobs under scrutiny (Youngman et al, 1978). By contrast, the method of Annett and Duncan (1967a, 1967b, and 1970) and Annett, Duncan, Stammers and Gray, (1971), although (apparently) not used as a job analysis technique, has considerable potential for:

– Highlighting the key competencies for work-related training programmes, and
– Further analysing or redescribing the key competencies in order to highlight
  instructional processes and performance criteria.

As an analytical technique HTA is logical, flexible and relatively uncomplicated - and one that could be used to analyse jobs in any occupational sector. Despite its viability and power, Annett (1987) modestly remarks that:

"... it's not very clever really. What it is is a systematic way of working down and gradually unpacking contents." (Annett, 1987 Personal Interview)

When used to identify key competencies inherent in jobs, the technique is referred to as 'Hierarchical Job Analysis' (HJA) ('Hierarchical Task Analysis' being reserved for the further analysis of identified competencies for instructional purposes). Potential users of HJA may need to be convinced of its utility and answers to questions similar to the following may be required:

– Is HJA rigorous enough to reveal job components/activities?
– Will the technique cause minimum disruption to ongoing job activities?
– How many jobs will have to be analysed before all the components/activities
  emerge and how valid will the components/activities be when obtained and
  subsequently analysed?
– Who will supply the information?
– How will the data be analysed and how will job functions and job structures be
  determined? (See "A Case in Point" cited later)

8 Hierarchical Job Analysis: A Participative Approach

Research carried out (inter alia) by Wernimont and Campbell (1968), Christal (1970) and Youngman (1975) points strongly:

"... towards the need for an operational basis for training." (Youngman, 1975, p. 73)

In simple terms Youngman (1975) interpreted this as a need to:

"... examine what *is actually done*, not what ideally *ought* to be done, or what someone in authority *thinks* is done." (Youngman, 1975, p. 73)

Gael (1983), in his practical guide to assessing work activities, also corroborates the importance of obtaining:

"Information about the work itself ... directly from those employees best informed about current job content ..." (Gael, 1983, p. 12)

Such a philosophy provided the basic guidance for the job analytic aspects of the investigatory process outlined in the section 'A Case in Point'. The jobs, tasks and activities that the employees carried out were of major significance throughout the analytical process and the involvement of these people was essential.

It may be somewhat platitudinous to say that if one wishes to capture the day-to-day activities inherent in any jobs it is essential to consult the people who are carrying out those activities. They have first-hand experiences and are (almost always) in a far stronger position to analyse jobs in terms of their constituent activities than are, say, managers or supervisors – who might have a very broad overview of the jobs but difficulty in delineating the *specific* functions and associated activities.

9 A Case in Point

To illustrate the use of HJA as a powerful analytical technique for revealing job-related key competencies as a basis for training programme design, one can cite the case of programme design undertaken in the financial services sector (which the writer of the paper undertook). All jobs (with the exception of Branch Managers' jobs) in the branch offices of a major Building Society were rigorously analysed and training programmes could be compiled on the basis of the investigation undertaken.

Fundamentally, the research consisted of a number of well-defined, if interrelated, stages:

– Researcher familiarisation with the Building Society and its modus operandi, including semi-structured interviews with a sample of Branch Managers (N = 12)
– Job analysis interviews with all categories of branch office staff (N = 60) in twenty five branches

The whole ethos guiding the analysis of branch-based jobs was identical to Kosidlak's (1987) philosophy:

– Job holders are 'experts' and better able than anyone else to describe/define/analyse their jobs
– *Any* job can be effectively and sufficiently analysed in terms of the tasks that the worker performs, providing a penetrating analytical technique is used

– *All* tasks have direct implications for the knowledge, skills and attitudes that workers must have in order to perform the tasks correctly

– Reviewing, refining and sharpening the presentation of job-related activities (through further work in branch offices and head office)
– Developing and piloting a branch office staff questionnaire (in head office, branch offices and regional offices)
– Questionnaire survey to all branch office staff (with the exception of Branch Managers). Objective analysis of data using two computer programs ('Answers' and SPSS^X). The job activities were subjected to cluster analysis (SPSS^X).
– Interviewing new members of staff (N = 6) during their first week of employment in Society branches, and a follow-up visit to three of them at the endof three months.

Analysis of the data revealed twelve functional clusters of activities (undertaken in various combinations by different staff categories), and summarised below. (It should be mentioned that the cluster titles were attributed on the basis of the activities that were aggregated in each cluster.)

Cluster Number	Cluster Title
1	Counter-Based Activities
2	Mortgage-Related Advice and Administration
3	Supervisory Activities
4	Micro-Computer Applications
5	Advisory: Investment Accounts and Cheque Account Services
6	Advisory: Financial Planning
7	Control and Development of Branch Office
8	Security Control
9	Answering Mortgage-Related Queries
10	Mortgage-Related Administration
11	Maintaining Registers, Returns and Associated Activities
12	General Administration

On the basis of the twelve functional activity clusters of key competencies, it was possible to 'map' job profiles for each branch-based job title. The following profiles are illustrative:

JOB TITLES	COMMON CLUSTERS	JOB-SPECIFIC CLUSTERS
Cashier/Clerk	1 5 8 9 12	–
Cashier/Clerk/Typist	1 5 8 9 12	4 10
Cashier/Clerk/Audio Typist	1 5 8 9 12	4 10 11
Cashier/Clerk/Shorthand Typist	1 5 8 9 12	2 3 4 10 11
Assistant Branch Manager	1 5 8 9 12	2 3 4 6 7 10 11
Branch Representative	1 5 8 9 12	2 3 4 6 7 10 11
Chief Clerk	1 5 8 9 12	2 3 4 6 7 10 11
Senior Clerk	1 5 8 9 12	2 3 4 7 10 11

Thus, the clusters of key competencies form an indispensable basis for exploring jobs, for re-distributing job-related functions between employees, for simplifying job structures, for re-writing job descriptions, and for structuring programmes of work-related training and assessment for all employees.

10 Discussion

Training programmes designed from HJA outcomes are job specific and, ipso facto, of great significance to employers and employees. It is somewhat platitudinous to reiterate that if employers are expected to sponsor training they have to be assured that the knowledge, skills, understanding and qualifications relate directly to their organisational needs.

This 'case' challenges a whole array of assumptions, among which are

– The validity of current vocational training programmes which are not developed from data obtained through rigorous job analysis
– The representativeness of vocational qualifications
– The British VET infrastructure

It is pertinent to reiterate Blank's (1982) insistence that vocational training programmes:

"... should be based on the actual activities performed on the job for which the worker is paid." (Blank, 1982, p. 60)

Consequently, the new British infrastructure for VET may be of limited value. A suggested alternative infrastructure is suggested and this begins at the level of local jobs. Job-specific training in isolation, however, is insufficient. There is a need for a coherent VET infrastructure that acknowledges the critical importance of local work structures as foundations for developing job-relevant training programmes, an infrastructure that can accommodate those programmes within an internationally-recognised framework established within the European

Community. Indeed, as 'Employment for the 1990s' (HMSO, 1988) explicitly recognises:

"Our competitive success depends upon training and developing our ... workforce to international standards." (HMSO, 1988, p. 48)

Such an alternative infrastructure would be encapsulated by:

– European legislative provision
– A credit accumulation and transfer scheme that is under the control of a
   functional Committee, under the auspices of the European Commission, whose
   powers would be discharged through European Sector-Specific Regulatory
   Boards

The alternative infrastructure would put the emphasis, first and foremost, on training that is:

Employer-led and responsive to the needs of employees and employer-organisations
– Based essentially on job-related practices
– Flexible and responsive, not rigid and bureaucratic
– Enforceable by law

Employers and employees, under the auspices of European Sector-Specific Regulatory Boards (ESSRBs) negotiate Work-Related Learning Agreements (WRLAs) which specify:

– Job-based practical experience
– Validated in-house training courses
– Validated externally-provided courses

Practical job-based experience, and in-house and external training programmes would be given 'levels' and credit-ratings, to co-ordinate with recognised awards. It is proposed that the WRLAs will be negotiated within a European Credit Accumulation and Transfer Scheme Framework (ECATS), the overall principles and regulations being determined by a European Committee for VET Credit Accumulation and Transfer Scheme (ECCATS). It is envisaged that the VET infrastructure will be headed by a European Council for the Approval and Accreditation of Work-Related Learning, thus operationalising the idealised notion of employee mobility between European States. (See Appendix 6)

References

1. Annett, J.: A Critical Appraisal of Hierarchical Task Analysis. A personal interview. February 1987, University of Warwick 1987
2. Annett, J., Duncan, K. D.: Describing Non-Repetitive Tasks for Training Purposes. In: Journal of Occupational Psychology, 41, 203-21 (1967a)

3. Annett, J., Duncan, K. D.: Task Analysis and Training Design. In: Journal of Occupational Psychology, 41, 211-223 (1967b)

4. Annett, J., Duncan, K. D.: Breaking down the Task. In: Personnel Management. May 1970, 32-34 (1970)

5. Annett, J., Duncan, K. D., Stammers, R. B., Gray, K. J.: Task Analysis Training Information Paper No 6 London, HMSO 1971

6. Argent Computer Services: Answers Manual Borehamwood, Argent Computer Services 1987

7. Ash, R. A., Levine, E. L.: A Framework for Evaluating Job Analysis Methods. In: Personnel. November/December 1980, 53-59 (1980)

8. Bass, B. M., Vaughan, J. A.: Training in Industry: The Management of Learning. London, Tavistock Publications Limited 1966

9. Black, H.: Meeting the Technical Requirements for Local Assessment of Underpinning Knowledge and Understanding. In: Black, H., Wolf, A. (eds.) Knowledge and Competence: Current Issues in Training and Education. Sheffield, Training Agency/Careers and Occupational Information Centre, 50-55 (1990)

10. Blank, W. E.: Handbook for Developing Competency-Based Training Programs. Englewood Cliffs, Prentice-Hall Inc 1982

11. Bouchardt, T. J.: Field Research Methods: Interviewing, Questionnaires, Participant Observation, Systematic Observation, Unobtrusive Measures. In: Dunnette, M. D. (ed.) Handbook of Industrial and Organisation Psychology. Chicago, Rand McNally 1976

11. Christal, R. E.: Implications of Airforce Occupational Research for Curriculum Development In: Smith, B. B., Moss, J. Process and Techniques of Curriculum Development. Minneapolis, University of Minnesota 1970

12. Cunningham, D. J., Duncan, K. D.: Describing Non-Repetitive Tasks for Training Purposes. In: Journal of Occupational Psychology, 41, 1967, 203-210 (1967)

13. Davidson, J.: Outdoor Recreation Surveys: The Design and Use of Questionnaires for Site Surveys. Cheltenham, Countryside Commission 1970

14. Drury, C. G.: Task Analysis Methods in Industry. In: Applied Ergonomics, 14/1, March 1983, 19-28 (1983)

15. Duncan, K. D.: Analytical Techniques in Training Design In: Edwards, E., Lees, F. P. (eds.) The Human Operator. In: Process Control London, Taylor and Francis, 283-319 (1974)

16. Finch, C. R., Crunkilton, J. R.: Curriculum Development in Vocational and Technical Education: Planning, Content and Implementation. London, Allyn and Bacon Inc 1984

17. Flanagan, J. C.: The Critical Incident Technique Psychological Bulletin, 51/4, July 1954, 327-358 (1954)

18. French, W. L.: The Personnel Management Process: Human Resources Administration and Development. Boston, The Houghton Mifflin Company 1982

19. Gael, S.: Job Activities: A Guide to Assessing Work Activities. London, Jossey-Bass Publishers 1983

20. Gagné, R. M. (ed.): Psychological Principles in System Development. New York, Holt, Rinehart and Winston 1962

21. Gagné, R. M.: The Conditions of Learning. London, Holt, Rinehart and Winston 1965

22. Gealy, N.: Writing Performance Criteria is not Easy. In: Competence and Assessment. Special Issue 1, December 1989, Sheffield, Training Agency, 17-19 (1989)

23. Ghorpade, J., Atchisaon, T. J.: The Concept of Job Analysis. In: Public Personnel Management, 9/3, 134-144 (1980)

24. Goldstein, I. L.: Training in Organisations: Needs Assessment, Development, and Evaluation. Belmont, California, Wadsworth Inc. 1986

25. Hall, G. E., Jones, H. L.: Competency-Based Education: A Process for the Improvement of Education. Englewood Cliffs, Prentice-Hall Inc. 1976

26. HMSO: White Paper: Employment for the 1990s. London, HMSO, CM 540 (1988)

27. Hoinville, G., Jowell,R. and Associates: Survey Research Practice. London, Heinemann 1978

28. Industrial Training Act, 1964, London, HMSO C16 (1964)

29. Jones, J. J. Jr., DeCotiis, T. A.: Job Analysis: National Survey Findings In: Personnel Journal. October 1969, 805-817 (1969)

30. Kosidlak, J. G.: DACUM: An Alternative Job Analysis Tool In: Personnel. 64/3, March 1987, 14-21 (1987)

31. Levine, E. L.: Everything You Always Wanted to Know About Job Analysis. Florida, Mariner Publishing Company Inc. 1983

32. McCormick, E. J.: Job and Task Analysis In: Dunette M D (ed.) Handbook of Industrial and Organisational Psychology Chicago, Rand McNally 1976

33. McCormick, E. J.: Job Analysis: Methods and Applications. Amacom 1979

34. McCormick, E. J., Jeanneret, P. R., Mecham, R. C.: A Study of Job Characteristics and Job Dimensions as Based on the Position Analysis Questionnaire (PAQ). In: Journal of Applied Psychology Monograph. 56/4, 347-368 (1972)

35. McGehee, W., Thayer, P. W.: Training in Business and Industry. London, John Wiley and Sons 1961

36. Mager, R. F.: Preparing Objectives for Instruction. Belmont, Fearon Press 1962

37. Mansfield, B.: Competence and Standards. In: Burke, J. W. (ed.) Competency Based Education and Training London, The Falmer Press, 26-38 (1989a)

38. Mansfield, B.: Functional Analysis - A Personal Approach. In: Competence and Assessment. Special Issue 1, 1989, Sheffield, Training Agency, 5-10 (1989b)

39. Miller, C., Hoggan, J., Pringle, S., West, G.: Credit Where Credit's Due Glasgow, Scottish Vocational Education Council 1988

40. Miller, R. B.: Task Description and Analysis. In: Gagné, R. M. (ed.) Psychological Principles in System Development New York, Holt, Rinehart and Winston 1963

41. Mitchell, L.: The Definition of Standards and their Assessment In: Burke, J. W. (ed.) Competency Based Education and Training. London, The Falmer Press, 54-64 (1989)

42. MSC : A New Training Initiative. Sheffield, Manpower Services Commission 1981a

43. MSC : A New Training Initiative: An Agenda for Action. Sheffield, Manpower Services Commission 1981b

44. MSC/DES: Review of Vocational Qualifications in England and Wales. Sheffield, Manpower Services Commission/London, Department of Education and Science 1986

45. Mumford, E.: Designing Secretaries. Manchester, Manchester Business School 1983

46. Mumford, E., Henshall, D.: A Participative Approach to Computer Systems Design. Manchester, Manchester Business School 1983

47. Nadler, L.: Designing Training Programs: The Critical Events Model. London, Addison-Wesley Publishing Company 1982

48. Patrick, J.: Job Analysis, Training and Transferability: Some Theoretical and Practical Issues. In: Duncan, D., Gruneberg, M. M., Wallis, D. (eds.) Changes in Working Life. Chichester, John Wiley, 55-70 (1980)

49. Patrick, J., Moore, A. K.: Development and Reliability of a Job Analysis Technique In: Journal of Occupational Psychology. 58/2, 149-158 (1985)

50. Pearn, M., Kandola, R.: Job Analysis: A Practical Guide for Managers. London, Institute of Personnel Management 1988

51. Piso, E.: Task Analysis for Process-Control Tasks: The Method of Annett et al Applied. In: Journal of Occupational Psychology. 54, 247-254 (1981)

52. Prien, E. P., Ronan, W. W.: Job Analysis: A Review of Research Findings: In: Personnel Psychology. 24, 371-396 (1971)

53. RSA: Assessing Work-Based Learning: A Summary of the RSA/MSC Core Certification Project. Sheffield, Manpower Services Commission/ London, Royal Society of Arts Examinations Board 1986

54. Shepherd, A.: Hierarchical Task Analysis and Training Decisions. In: Programmed Learning and Educational Technology. 22, 162-176 (1985)

55. Shepherd, A.: An Expert's Experience of HTA. A Personal Interview. February 1987, Loughborough University of Technology SPSS (1988) SPSS[X] User's Guide. Chicago, SPSS Inc. (1987)

56. Stammers, R. B., Astley, J. A.: Hierarchical Task Analysis: Twenty Years On'. In: Megaw, E. D. (ed.) Contemporary Ergonomics. London, Taylor and Francis, 135-139 (1987)

57. Sturm, R. D.: Mass Validation of Job Analysis In: Public Personnel Management. September/October 1979, 277-281 (1979)

58. Thomas, L. L.: A Cluster Analysis of Office Operations In: Journal of Applied Psychology. 36, 238-242 (1952)

59. US Department of Labor: Handbook for Analysing Jobs. US Department of Labor 1972

60. Wernimont, P. F., Campbell, J. P.: Signs, Samples, and Criteria In: Journal of Applied Psychology. 52/5,372-376 (1968)

61. Wheaton, G. R., Rose, A. M., Fingbroman, P. W., Korotkin, A. L., Holding, D. H.: Evaluation of the Effectiveness of Training Devices. Literature Review and Preliminary Model Research Memorandum 76-6. US Army Research. Institute for the Behavioral and Social Sciences 1976

62. Willett, J., Hemann, G.: Which Occupational Analysis Technique: Critical Incident, DACUM, and/or Information Search? In: The Vocational Aspect of Education. December 1989, XLI/110, 79-88 (1989)

63. Wolf, A.: Unwrapping Knowledge and Understanding from Standards of Competence In: Black, H., Wolf, A. (eds.) (1990) Knowledge and Competence: Current Issues in Training and Education. Sheffield, Training Agency/Careers and Occupational Information Centre. 31-38 (1990)

64. Wright, P. M., Wexley, K. N.: How to Choose the Kind of Job Analysis You Really Need In: Personnel. 62/5, 51-55 (1985)

65. Youngman, M. B.: Structuring Work for Training Purposes In: The Vocational Aspect of Education. Autumn 1975, XXVII/68, 77-86 (1975)

66. Youngman, M. B., Oxtoby, R., Monk, J. D., Heywood, J.: Analysing Jobs. Farnborough, Gower Press (1978)

Appendices

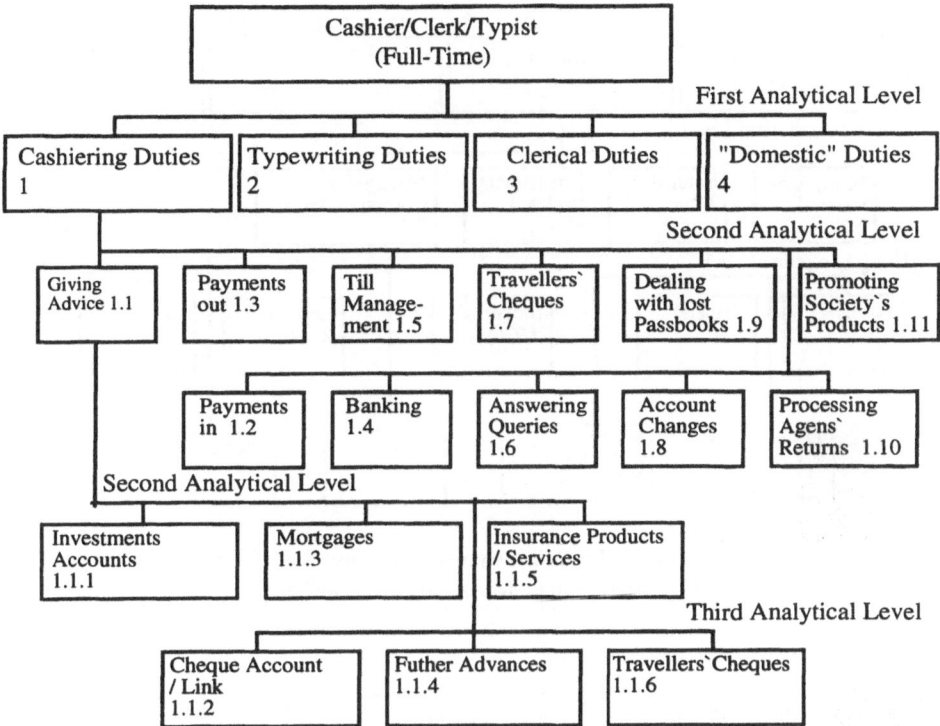

Fig. 2 Disaggretion of a cashier/clerk/typist's job-demonstrating the analytical penetration of Hierarchical Job Analysis

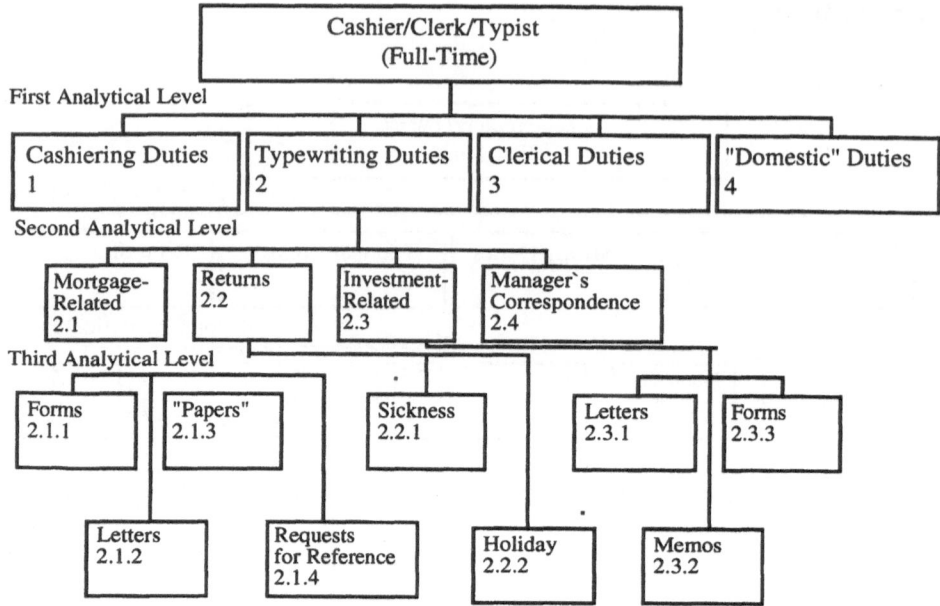

Fig. 3 Disaggretion of a cashier/clerk/typist's job-demonstrating the analytical penetration of Hierarchical Job Analysis (continued)

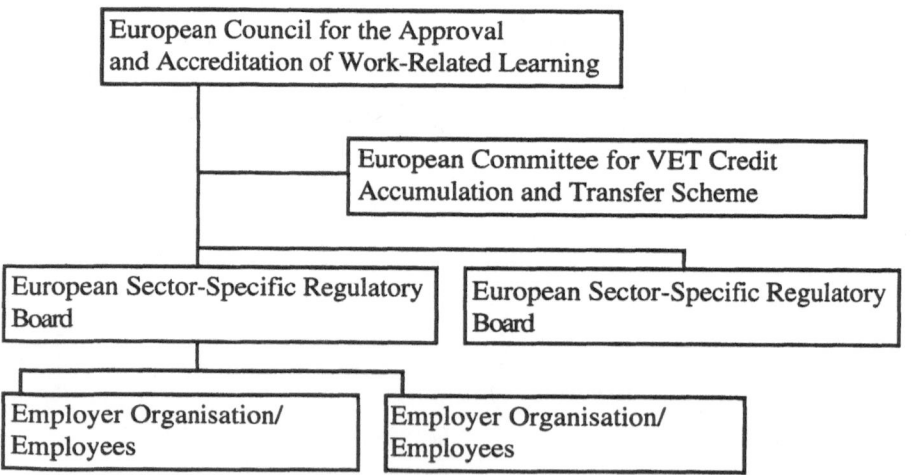

Fig. 4 Structural essentials of a proposed alternative infrastructure

CLUSTER 1: Counter-Based Activities

Identifying Numbers and Activities
32   Processing Transactions - Investments, withdrawals, etc
34   Processing Transactions - Travellers' cheques
36   Changing 'static' details on accounts
37   Opening new investment accounts
38   Closing investment accounts
39   Dealing with lost passbooks
40   Issuing continuation passbooks
41   Verifying entries/balances in passbooks
43   Banking - preparing own banking
47   Promoting Society's products 'over the counter'
48   Answering queries: Investment accounts (non-Cheque Account)
49   Answering queries: Cheque Account + Link facilities
50   Answering queries: Cheque Account-related - cheque book/card
54   Answering queries: Cheque Account-related - standing orders/direct debits
55   Answering queries: Cheque Account-related - salaries and wages
75   Answering queries: Travellers' cheques
78   Processing transactions through counter computer terminal
80   Using counter computer terminal for investment-related enquiries
81   Using counter computer terminal for mortgage-related enquiries
      (N=19 activities)

CLUSTER 2: Mortgage-Related Advice And Administration

Identifying Numbers and Activities
59   Answering queries: Secondary secured lending
60   Answering queries: Regulated loans
63   Answering queries: Pension-linked mortgages
67   Answering queries: Life assurance for protection
88   Conducting a full Mortgage interview
97   In-depth advice: New mortgages
98   In-depth advice: Re-mortgages
99   In-depth advice: Further advances
100   In-depth advice: Secondary secured lending
101   In-depth advice: Regulated loans
102   In-depth advice: Endowment mortgages
103   In-depth advice: Repayment mortgages
104   In-depth advice: Pension-linked mortgages
108   In-depth advice: Life assurance for protection
112   In-depth advice: TipTop Sure insurance

113   In-depth advice: Mortgage Protection insurance
114   In-depth advice: Accident, sickness and unemployment insurance
119   Interviewing borrowers in arrears (in Branch)
126   Compiling returns: Mortgage Quota Return
127   Compiling returns: Mortgage Statistics Return
139   Entries in 'special' registers: Endowment Commission
140   Entries in 'special' registers: Mortgage Applications
141   Entries in 'special' registers: Mortgage Quota
143   Operating Valuation Fees Register
145   Reviewing arrears cases (excluding interviewing)
146   Reviewing new mortgages to prevent arrears (N = 26 activities)

CLUSTER 3: Supervisory Activities

Identifying Numbers and Activities
163   Acquainting existing staff with new procedures
164   Acquainting existing staff with new products
165   Allocating work to Branch Office staff
166   Authorising withdrawals over specified limits
168   Balancing Valuation Fees Book
171   Checking Valuation Fees Book
173   Checking accuracy of staff's work
175   Checking Cash Withdrawals Over £500 Register
180   Checking Endowment Commissions Register
182   Checking Manual Input Form Register
183   Checking Mortgage Applications Register
184   Checking Mortgage Quota Register
192   Checking Valuation Fees Register
193   Checking Head Office input of Computer Transactions Report
195   Managing Branch Office
196   Monitoring/replenishing Branch cash
197   Monitoring progress of mortgage applications
198   Monitoring workflow of Branch staff
199   Prioritising Branch clerical work
201   Supervising Branch Office staff
202   Supervision of counter staffing levels
203   Training new Branch Office staff
212   General Branch Office maintenance (N = 23 activities)

CLUSTER 4: Micro-Computer Applications

Identifying Numbers and Activities
83   Using personal computer for accessing electronic notice board
84   Using personal computer for obtaining insurance quotes
85   Using personal computer for receiving electronic mail
86   Using personal computer for sending electronic mail
87   Using personal computer for word/text processing
159 Using personal computer to receive electronic mail
160 Using personal computer to send electronic mail
161 Using personal computer for word processing (N=8 activities)

CLUSTER 5: Advisory: Investment Accounts And Cheque Account Services

Identifying Numbers and Activities
89   In-depth interviews: Investment accounts
90   In-depth interviews: Cheque Account + Link facilities
91   In-depth advice: Cheque Account cheque book/cheque card
95   In-depth advice: Cheque Account standing orders/direct debits
96   In-depth advice: Cheque Account salaries/wages payments (N = 5 activities)

CLUSTER 6: Advisory: Financial Planning

Identifying Numbers and Activities
64   Answering queries: Executive pension plans
65   Answering queries: With-profit pension plans
66   Answering queries: Unit-linked pension plans
68   Answering queries: Life assurance for savings
69   Answering queries: Life assurance for investment
70   Answering queries: Life assurance for tax planning
76   Answering queries: Building society-related legal issues
105 In-depth advice: Executive pension plans
106 In-depth advice: With-profit pension plans
107 In-depth advice: Unit-linked pension plans
108 In-depth advice: Life assurance for protection
109 In-depth advice: Life assurance for savings
110 In-depth advice: Life assurance for investment
111 In-depth advice: Life assurance for tax planning
117 In-depth advice: Building Society-related legal matters
118 In-depth advice: Building Society-related tax matters
119 Interviewing borrowers in arrears (in Branch) (N = 17 activities)

CLUSTER 7: Control And Development Of Branch Office

Identifying Numbers and Activities
124   Compiling returns: Cash Withdrawals £500+
125   Compiling returns: Manager's Monthly Report
128   Compiling returns: Part-time Staff Return
130   Compiling returns: Share at Notice Return
142   Entries in 'special' registers: Registered/Recorded Incoming Post
152   Dictating letters on audio for transcription
154   Giving dictation to shorthandwriter
160   Using pc to send electronic mail
170   Checking petty cash book
174   Checking entries in ATM Register
175   Checking Cash Withdrawals Over £500 Register
176   Checking Change of Static Details Register
178   Checking Cheques Presented for Special Clearance Register
200   'Spot' checking tills
204   Visiting agencies (replenishing cash/checking)
206   Ensuring Branch Office complies with HASAWA
207   Ensuring Branch Office complies with OSRPA
208   Maintaining Office in safe/secure state
209   Checking fire alarms
210   Checking fire extinguishers
212   General Branch Office maintenance
216   Inspecting tenanted accommodation
217   Cleaning and checking ATM
221   Checking burglar alarm bells
222   Checking security cameras
223   Checking security in relation to ATM
227   Attending local events/functions
228   Entertaining local 'contacts'
229   Organising Branch-based competitions
230   Making 'outside' professional visits
231   Visiting schools/colleges
232   Assisting with developmental administration (N = 32 activities)

CLUSTER 8: Security Control

Identifying Numbers and Activities
35   Processing Transactions - Valuation fees
42   Checking for Computer messages each day
44   Banking - preparing 'corporate' banking
45   Banking - taking prepared banking to bank

46   Banking - cashing cheque at bank for Branch cash
79   Reload and recovery of counter computer terminal
129   Compiling returns: Petty Cash Return
133   Compiling returns: Travellers' Cheques Commission Returns
135   Keeping Branch manuals up-to-date
136   Maintng daily summary of Branch investments/withdrawals
138   Entries in 'special' registers: Audit Travellers' Cheques
144   Operating Petty Cash Book
167   Balancing Petty Cash Book
177   Checking Cheque Books Register
179   Checking Continuation Passbooks Register
181   Checking Keys Register
182   Checking Manual Input Form Register
185   Checking New Investment Accounts Register
186   Checking New Passbooks Register
187   Checking Receipt Pads Register
189   Checking Retained Passbooks Register
190   Checking Till Transfer Register
191   Checking Travellers' Cheques Register
193   Checking HO input of Computer transactions report
205   Weekly settlement of Travellers' Cheques commission
213   Organising/arranging Branch Office window displays
214   Ensuring notices/posters are up-to-date and seen
218   Allowing access to non-Branch staff
219   Responsibility for keys to Branch Office
220   Responsibility for keys to safe
225   Taking responsibility for all cash in Branch
226   Maintaining eye-wash solution/bottles (N = 32 activities)

CLUSTER 9: Answering Mortgage-Related Queries

Identifying Numbers and Activities
56   Answering queries: New mortgages
57   Answering queries: Re-mortgages
58   Answering queries: Further advances
61   Answering queries: Endowment mortgages
62   Answering queries: Repayment mortgages (N=5 activities)

CLUSTER 10: Mortgage-Related Administration

Identifying Numbers and Activities
71   Answering queries: TipTop Sure insurance
72   Answering queries: Mortgage Protection insurance
73   Answering queries: Accident, sickness and unemployment insurance
83   Using personal computer for accessing electronic notice board
84   Using personal computer for obtaining insurance quotes
85   Using personal computer for receiving electronic mail
139   Entries in 'special' registers: Endowment Commission
140   Entries in 'special' registers: Mortgage Applications
141   Entries in 'special' registers: Mortgage Quota
143   Operating Valuation Fees Register
159   Using personal computer to receive electronic mail
168   Balancing Valuation Fees Book
192   Checking Valuation Fees Register (N = 13 activities)

CLUSTER 11: Maintaining Registers, Returns and Associated Activities

Identifying Numbers and Activities
124   Compiling returns: Cash Withdrawals £500+
125   Compiling returns: Manager's Monthly Report
126   Compiling returns: Mortgage Quota Return
127   Compiling returns: Mortgage Statistics Return
128   Compiling returns: Part-time Staff Return
130   Compiling returns: Share at Notice Return
131   Compiling returns: Staff Overtime Return
132   Compiling returns: Staff Sickness Return
142   Entries in 'special' registers: Registered/Recorded Incoming Post
145   Reviewing arrears cases (excluding interviewing)
146   Reviewing new mortgages to prevent arrears
156   Composing/drafting for 'processing' by others
174   Checking entries in ATM register
176   Checking Change of Static Details Register
178   Checking Cheques Presented for Special Clearance Register
188   Checking Registered/Recorded Incoming Post Register
193   Checking Head Office input of Computer transactions report
       (N = 17 activities)

CLUSTER 12: General Administration

Identifying Numbers and Activities
122   Answering/making telephone calls
134   Filing
137   Making entries in 'general' registers
148   Processing outgoing mail/maintaining Post Book
149   Purchasing stamps from Post Office
150   Stamping brochures/leaflets with Branch Office stamp
151   Stationery stocktaking/ordering new stock
162   Making tea and/or coffee
169   Balancing Post Book
194   Making appointments in diary for Manager/Branch
211   Keeping Branch Office tidy
215   Keeping publicity brochures/leaflts up-to-date and available
224   Dealing with transfer of cash between cashiers (N = 13 activities)

Inclusion of Students with Significant Learning Difficulties

Anne Halliday
Psychology Department
St Michael's House, Dublin, Ireland

Abstract. This paper describes the history of people with learning difficulties (mental handicap) and the consequences of that history in terms of exclusion from regular educational systems and the opportunities available for participation in a wide range of curricular experiences in those systems. The paper also describes instructional strategies which have been researched within the last twenty years and which attempted to enhance the inclusion of students with learning difficulties in regular learning situations and queries the possibility of the application of these strategies to facilitate the participation of students with learning difficulties in technological education.

Keywords. Learning difficulties, inclusion, instructional strategies, technological science

Introduction

The purpose of this paper is to highlight and discuss the events which led to a significant percentage of the population in the western world being excluded from regular education systems because of difficulties learning and inadequate adaptation to their environments. The current trend to re-integrate them into regular systems highlights for educators the lack of knowledge in how best to facilitate learning in a wide range of subject areas for those students who have significant learning difficulties. Significant learning difficulties, also described as mental handicap or mental retardation, signify difficulties in a range of cognitive processes which inhibit learning.

The inclusion of students with learning difficulties within regular schools is a relatively recent phenomenon. Because of the history of segregated education services, restricted curricula based on deficit models of learning have not promoted approaches to teaching a wider curriculum. With increasing inclusion of such students in regular classes, teaching strategies are becoming available which should enhance the learning of all students.

1 History of Disability

1.1   To understand why the issue of including people with learning difficulties within ordinary school systems is so controversial at this end of the twentieth century requires some knowledge of the history of disability and the influences which led to the development of alternative models of service. Whilst this history is rather sketchy prior to the nineteenth century [1] it is clear that the major influences came from the worlds of religion, mythology, science, technology, medicine, education and psychology.

In the Christian world, the notion that "idiots" are a consequence of the evils of mankind , a punishment for the fall of Adam and other sins was a recurrent theme particularly in the writings of St Augustine [2]. Martin Luther saw the presence of "abnormal" children as a punishment for the sins of individual parents, rather than those of mankind in general. According to Luther, parents produced these children because of sexual intercourse between woman and devil, not fearing God, thinking bad thoughts or cursing their offspring [3]. He also associated "abnormal" children with animality, describing them as "lumps of flesh, with no soul". The two themes of punishment by God and "animality" were to recur through the following centuries until relatively recent times. Against that background, the writings of Paracelsus, a 16th century Swiss physician, had little or no effect [4]. His idea that fools are not only equal to other people in God's eyes but even superior is also found in other countries eg Ireland where a person, in any way "abnormal", was described in the Brehon code of laws as a 'duine le dia" (a person with God) and protected by law [5]. Unlike Augustine and Luther, Paracelsus did not blame parents for producing "abnormal" children. In his writings he suggests that there is nothing wrong with the material supplied by parents but that during the process of pregnancy, something goes wrong, comparing the process to inept carving of wood by apprentice carvers. This was the first recorded notion of what was later described as "congenital idiocy '.

The world of mythology prior to and during the Middle Ages contributed many myths about children who were in any way peculiar or deformed. The most common myth was that of the "changeling" child whose existence was explained by Thomas Willis thus : "fairies stole a mother's child from its cradle, and in its place laid a changeling with a big head and staring eyes who wanted to do nothing but eat and drink" [6]. This belief is evident in all kinds of folklore and indeed in literature e.g., W. B. Yeats' "Stolen Child" [7]. Changelings came from the non-human world of demons and elves and were treated well in the hope that good treatment would be given the stolen child. Having a child stolen was beyond the control of parents and indeed was considered a fate which could befall any family. The Christian version of this mythological exchange suggested that the devil had stolen the human child and substituted himself for it. This idea was espoused by Martin Luther [8] who described changelings as "more obnoxious than ten children with their crapping, eating and screaming" and indeed recommended killing them. This concept of the 'changeling" child combined with the suggestion of a woman having intercourse with the devil led to the notion, in Europe, of a woman who gave birth to a child with a deformity as being a witch [9].

The first indication of deformity being explained in a scientific manner was seen in the sixteenth century writings on the link between cretinism, goitre and the drinking water in parts of Switzerland [10]. Whilst travellers to this country wrote of deformed appearances and questioned the human nature of these people, the Swiss valley inhabitants regarded people with cretinism as being from heaven and treated them with care and respect [11]. The possibility of the obvious endemic and environmental nature of cretinism lessened the tendency to blame and led to acceptance and respect for people with cretinism. This clear example of environmental causation of "idiocy" did not have any significant effect on how disability was viewed as is evident in the emphasis over centuries on organic or hereditary causes. Indeed, the established links, in this century, between eg lead and disability and diet and disability have made little impact on the perception of disability or on further exploration of environmental involvement in disability.

Medical science also played a formative role in the explanation of disability in the seventeenth century. The English physician, Willis, was one of the first people to propose a theory of degeneration to explain disability. In an attempt to explain how intelligent parents could produce "fools", he suggested that apart from accidents at birth, parents may have supplied defective material for reproduction [12]. He also suggested that the size and texture of the brain may at times be abnormal and that "stupidity" may result from brain impairment. Whilst this suggestion initiated a new line of enquiry, Willis attributed the causes of impairment to parents who focus unduly on intellectual pursuits or who may have endured "somatic insults" through intemperance, effeminacy, luxury or extreme youth or age. Willis also believed that "stupidity" could not be cured but could be alleviated by physicians and educators.

1.2 Nineteenth Century

The major influences, in the field of disability, in this century came from the fields of education, social reform, psychiatry, genetics and industry/technology. Seguin, the most influential of educators, following on the work of Itard advocated that "idiots' participate in the benefit of education and thus ameliorate their condition [13]. Whilst stressing the humanity of "idiots', Seguin did not dismiss the possibility of their not being fully human and saw the purpose of education as lifting them from their near animal state " There is not one of any age who may not be made more of a man and less of a brute by patience and kindness directed by energy and skill" [14]. This concept was also advocated by a leading American humanitarian reformer, Howe [15], who in addition to seeing "idiocy" as a "social evil' attributed blame to parents, specifically to their sexual behaviour.

Despite the notions described above, Seguin was a major influence in the development of educational methods emphasising sensory and bodily functions, the need for structured learning situations with carefully analysed lesson plans. The roles of play, imitation, repetition and reward for learning were described and served as a foundation for teaching approaches which are still current in mainstream education. Indeed, this period was interesting in that the responsibility for success in learning lay with teachers. However, the belief that the humanity of "idiots" was dependent on their possible improvement through education underpinned the education provisions.

The provision of educational services for "idiots' through the establishment of asylums was initially organised to take them out of their solitude and the perceived need to be with those "who are like itself" [16]. These asylums were seen as instruments of social change, reforming agencies. With a widening definition of "idiocy" the size and populations of asylums increased, contrary to the advice of Seguin. In addition the expected improvements and consequent return to communities of the population of the asylums did not materialise. Large institutions led to regimentation of peoples' lives, denial of their individuality and lack of personal privacy. Management of asylums was given to people with medical training which ultimately changed the orientation from an educational one to one of control through medication. The Industrial Revolution was perhaps the greatest catalyst in highlighting the number of dependent children and adults within communities. The move towards centralised or urban based factories and the demands of this type of work resulted in the disintegration of community and family life. For many people, "idiots"and "feeble-minded" who may have been integrated into slower, self-determined, flexible ways of working in local communities were left without occupation, support or supervision hence necessitating being sent to asylums. The attribution to idiots of blame for crimes, especially those of a sexual nature, within a community led to widespread institutionalisation.

The asylums afforded an opportunity for the systematic study of different types and causes of idiocy at a time of great interest in genetics, the theories of Darwin [17] and Galton [18] and the supremacy of races as experienced through colonialism. Concurrent with these simplistic perceptions of genetic operations compulsory education had also revealed wide differences in scholastic ability leading to the founding of Galton's Eugenics Society and to the widespread belief that the higher breeding rates of the "least fit' would lead to national degeneracy. Anthropological studies at this time focused on the evolutionary order of various tribes and races and led to descriptions of idiots as Negroid, Grecian, Egyptian and American Indian. The clearest example of this racist classification is that of Langdon-Down [19] who identified one distinct sub-group of idiots as Mongolian and suggested that their ethnic features were a result of degeneration. These beliefs led to the founding in 1896 of the National Association for the Care and Control of the Feeble Minded who campaigned for the lifetime segregation of defectives and on the issue of "discouraging parenthood in feeble-minded and other degenerate types". This resulted in the Mental Deficiency Act of 1913 which introduced compulsory certification for people admitted to institutions as mentally defective and to the establishment of a separate and unified service which excluded "mental defective " people from the general education and welfare systems. This system was used as a model in most of the Western world.

1.3 Twentieth Century

The first half of this century is characterised by the development of instruments to measure intelligence which introduced the concept of "fixed intelligence", the predictability of educational outcomes, the description and classification of people in terms of IQ and the intense investigation of cognitive functions eg memory, in laboratory situations. The fields of medicine and education also investigated aspects of "inmates" lives with a particular focus on deficits. This focus on the individual as opposed to an interactive environmental one led to the adoption of a medical model of disability which viewed handicapping conditions as residing inside the individual and assumed that different causes suggest different treatments [20]. People who were mentally defective should be carefully diagnosed and then classified and treated according to the presumed cause of their condition.

This clinical focus of medicine and psychology has led to models of educational services which Stubbins [21] described as being based on a philosophy of functional limitations. This emphasis suggests that solutions may be found by surmounting those limitations but totally ignores the functional skills of the diagnosed people. In addition the focus on structured programmes to "prepare" students for life continues to run contrary to research on learning which states that when students spend their time and energy learning content that is directly related to the goals of instruction, they learn it [22]. It also set in train a system of training for personnel and educational programming focusing on deficits with little or no attention paid to environmental or social issues [23]. This philosophy, then, has played a major role in shaping the deficit image of disability within society.

Educational services, in the latter half of this century reflect a move towards integration of persons with "mental handicap" or learning difficulties into services within their communities. These range from institutionalised residential settings through segregated settings within the community to full inclusion within an age appropriate mainstream school. With the exception of the latter placement, services are organised on the basis of levels of diagnosed deficits.

The movement towards educating children with a mental handicap or learning difficulties within regular class settings was inspired by the Civil Rights movement in United States in the 1960s and further strengthened by the philosophies of Wolfensberger [24], Illich and McKnight. These philosophies focus on the rights of people with disabilities to lead as normal a life as possible within their community. In some countries this has led to legislation which confirms those rights. However, the pattern of educational arrangements emerging from this type of legislation is uneven.

2 Current Education Models

2.1   Various authors have described the range of services referred to in the previous section in terms of a "continuum" of placements [25] or a "cascade' model of services [26]. These models are based on the notion of the least restrictive environment and the proposal that students with disabilities would move to a less restrictive placement when ready. These models, do not include mixed ability classes and "tracking" for post-primary pupils. The following figure outlines the range of education settings available which, with the exception of the final two arrangements, segregate students on the basis of deficits.

Table 1

❏   Residential placement and residential school ;
❏   Residential placement and day school;
❏   Segregated day school, full time;
❏   Segregated day school and sessions in local regular school;
❏   Special class placement in regular school, full time;
❏   Special class base with some sessions in regular class;
❏   Regular class placement and withdrawal for extra help
❏   Regular class placement with help supplied in class

2.2 Outcomes of Segregated Arrangements

It is now acknowledged that separate systems continue because of specific political, professional and educational rationales that work to maintain the current organisation despite the growing evidence that the educational rationale for separate education at any level does not hold true [27]. Brown [28], and other authors have indicated that anything that can be taught in separate systems to students with severe learning difficulties can also be taught within regular class settings. Leinhardt [29] suggests that specific instructional treatments tend not to vary across settings and that effective strategies are effective in any setting. However, the level of goals set for special students are frequently lowered in comparison with those of children in regular classes because of reduced potential and lowered expectations of administrators and educators [30]. This results in a greater emphasis on vocational and social skills in special rather than in regular classes. The evidence on the outcomes of "streaming" or "tracking", particularly at post-primary (High School) level suggests that bright students rarely benefit from streamed situations and may well benefit from heterogeneous situations [31]; that students placed in low ability classes do not succeed academically, are less successful in terms of employment [32], have lowered self-esteem and negative attitudes towards school [33, 34] and that the initial differences between high and low ability students widens with this type of placement [35].

The consequences of segregated education for adult life has been described by Brown [36] who points out that students who are educated in such settings are more likely to spend their adult working, social and residential lives in segregated settings also. The "climate of fear" created by the practice of segregation particularly among those students who may be vulnerable academically, has been described by Granger [37]. In addition, students grow up not knowing how to communicate with peers who have a disability [38]. Indeed, the message given by this practice to future citizens is that disability is all-defining.

2.3 Alternative Models

Models which include all students within the regular class settings are generally described as Unitary systems in which the class or subject teacher is responsible for all of the children, but may have the support of a resource or special education teacher where necessary. Most unitary systems operate on the basis of evidence on effective learning [39] diminution of prejudice [40] and cost effectiveness. One specific system i.e. Inclusive Schools system is particularly interested in the concept of community and the role of schools in building community. This type of system besides requiring "excellence and equity in education" stress the necessity for every member of a community to be included and the consequent loss to a community by the exclusion of any member [41]. Inclusive Schools are described as reflecting communities which require and accept diversity and look at participation or contribution rather than labelling deviant members.

Unitary systems require a fundamental change in the way people who are "different" are viewed, in the way education is organised and how the purpose of education is perceived. These systems tend to focus on use of abilities towards learning and thus target interventions based on the type of educational support needed by students thereby labelling instruction and not children [42]. Instructional methods include concepts, e.g., "adapted learning environments" [43], peer tutoring, tutoring and co-operative learning strategies [44].

Whilst unitary or inclusive models are relatively new, research findings are indicating that "the integrated model (was) a viable alternative service delivery model for students with learning disabilities as the results are virtually indistinguishable from those of separate programmes". Any significant differences found supported the integrated model [45]. Positive outcomes have been noted for non-disabled students in unitary systems [46]. Unpublished reports from recently established inclusive systems indicate that the "drop-out" rate for students has decreased in schools within these systems and attribute this change to "students feeling part of the school and not being judged on academic performance alone".

3 Possible Instructional Strategies

Because the inclusion of disabled children within regular classes is a relatively new phenomenon research on instructional strategies within that context is limited. The complex nature of learning and the variety of individual learning styles of students with or without disabilities will need to be accounted for in any research on instructional strategies. In addition the variables of teachers and curriculum content will further complicate the issue. Ultimately, what we may be looking for are indications of what might facilitate learning for all students within regular classes. In the next section, I will outline the various structures and strategies which are known to facilitate learning and possible implications for students with learning difficulties.

3.1 Whole Class Approach

Perhaps the most traditional method of structuring instruction is the whole class model which when referred to in the context of learning difficulties brings up the issue of class size. The general assumption that reduction of class size automatically leads to more effective learning does not hold up in research. Clearly, reduction in class size may make the experience of teaching and learning more pleasurable. However, the data available from research is quite mixed.

In a summary of the literature by Glass [47] class size was seen to "matter" if size went below 15 or above 40. In the case of smaller classes. It was noted that the student received more of the teacher's instructional focus and time, waited for shorter periods for feedback or answers to queries. However, other authors remind us that reduction in class size will have no significant effect if teachers do not change their style of instruction to suit smaller classes. It is also interesting to note that some studies indicate that having an "instructional aide" in the classroom can be associated with lowered levels of achievement [48]. Overall, it would seem that the rule should be to have as small a class as is practicable, staffed by a fully qualified teacher and that variables such as curriculum content and instructional strategies are taken into account.

In relation to the effectiveness of whole classes it is common to have subjects such as gym, art, music and social studies and sometimes spellings and maths taught to the whole class. The literature will suggest that whole class lessons have a particular rhythm and flow to them [49], starting with some type of transitional behaviour and goal setting, moving into a presentation of some type and then to student rehearsal or practice. During the early stages of these rehearsals, the expert teacher gives quite an amount of corrective feedback. Whole group instruction works well if the teacher gives clear presentation or explanations, constructs an "elegant tryout and has ways of tutoring both the faster and slower students". Besides being efficient, this allows teachers to have a maximal focus on content, guiding practice, tutorials and constructing examples. In addition, each child has the rest of the class as helpers and models as well as the teacher.

4 Group Teaching

Grouping as a method of instruction is evident in a wide range of schools, particularly in the United Kingdom and Ireland. The composition and construction of groups varies, e.g., the composition varies from strict differentiation by ability to personal choice. The HMI survey [50] indicated that most teachers grouped children for some aspects of their work; mathematics, reading and writing were the most common subjects. Mixed ability groups, based on friendships were more frequently used for science, arts music and recreation.

Leinhardt [51] comments on the difficulties inherent in some small groups, e.g., reduction in time for direct teacher contact and may very well lower achievement levels of groups without high achieving students. However, small group instruction seems to be effective when (a) group size is determined by who fits rather than by some arbitrarily convenient number; (b) there are different groups formed for different subjects; (c) change of membership when necessary; (d) groups are formed based on specific skills within subjects; (e) membership is determined by instructionally based assessment, not standardised tests and (f) small-group and whole-group instruction is interspersed. Some evidence exists indicating that under specific conditions, small groups are particularly good instructional approach for reading. However, small groups can become rigid subtracks getting significantly less instruction than higher ability groups and spending significantly more time on organising for teaching/learning than actually teaching or learning [52]. In relation to teaching mathematics, small group arrangements can be problematic because of the amount of unsupervised seatwork whilst in whole class instruction most of the time is accounted for in direct teaching with very little seatwork time [53].

4.1 Co-operative Learning Groups

Co-operation is an important part of group life with benefits extending to quality work with others on shared tasks to its perceived function as the cornerstone of modern democracy. In the classroom, co-operation is both a skill necessary for the accomplishment of learning activities and a general norm to be learned. Cooperative learning methods were designed to facilitate social interaction and learning in classroom settings and to reduce dependency on the class teacher. The initial impetus for this movement came from Deutsch [54] and has been continued by education researchers in the United States and Israel where research projects attempted to link theory with practice by devising experimental studies in classrooms. Researchers also visualised that cooperative teaching strategies would provide teachers with techniques for daily instruction in standard curriculum rather than requiring schools to add these methods as extracurricular experiences. Group research in the United Kingdom has been limited to observational studies on the nature of groups.

Research on Cooperative learning projects, overall, indicates that student achievement is at least as high if not higher in traditional class subjects than when taught in traditional whole class settings. Cooperative learning situations also promote positive interpersonal relations particularly between multi racial groups and students of mixed ability and also foster higher self-esteem in students. Recent analyses suggest that the benefits of cooperative learning strategies hold for students at all ages, across all subjects and a wide range of tasks such as those involving motor decoding, retention and problem solving skills [55].

4.2 Types of Groups

The most commonly used cooperative learning methods can be categorised on the basis of the type of reward and task structures which are employed to motivate co-operation. Slavin [56] offers a summary of these methods, shown in Table 2.

The above techniques are described in detail by Cohen [57], Kagan [58] and Slavin [59]. The following is a brief outline of the techniques.

Table 2   Categories of Cooperative Learning Methods

	Group Rewards Contingent on Individual Performance	No Group Reward Not Contingent
Group study - no task specialisation	Student Team Learning TGT STAD TAI	Learning Together
Task Specialisation	Jigsaw 2	Jigsaw Group Investigation

1. Learning Together [60]   This technique involves students in small 4/5 member heterogeneous groups working collectively to complete a single worksheet. Students help each other learn the required material and praised for the level of co-operation and the quality of the competed task. Group rewards are not always offered and members of the group are encouraged to assess their functioning as a group. This technique does not involve competition with other groups hence its being described by some commentators as "pure co-operation".

These methods have been studied by the authors, Johnsons and their colleagues in a variety of classroom situations involving mixed ethnic and "mainstreamed" children. According to the authors, outcomes such as high achievement and positive interpersonal relationships occur because the techniques enhance students' cognitive processing, peer support and encouragement, self-esteem and time on-task.

2. Jigsaw [61]   This technique also involves students working in small study groups. The task or academic material is broken into small sections and each group member is assigned one segment to study. Students then meet with a member from another group who has been assigned that portion of the task and discuss the material together. The students then return to their original groups and teach the material to the remainder of the group. In that way, all of the material is learned by all of the students. Students may or may not be tested on the materials.

Positive outcomes of this technique are noted in the areas of students liking for their groups and school and self-esteem. These effects have been attributed to students' involvement in learning and helping each other.

3. Group Investigation [62]   This technique includes some of the strategies involved in the Jigsaw techniques but gives a substantial level of responsibility and freedom to the students. The group are responsible for division of tasks, organisation of work, collection of information and communication of same within the group. Groups choose their topics and work methods. Peer tutoring and other helping behaviours occur spontaneously. Evaluation of each group's contribution is carried out by the teacher and the students.

This technique is reported as increasing student achievement, prosocial behaviour and school attitudes.

4. Student Team Learning [63] techniques involve the completion of tasks in heterogeneous groups. Several versions of this type of learning activity technique have been developed.

– Student Teams Achievement Division (STAD)   In this technique the teacher presents, generally in lecture/discussion form, material to be learned. Groups of a heterogeneous nature study jointly and prepare each other for quizzes on the material. Points are awarded to the groups based on each individuals past performance. Groups are ranked and the winning group and individual contributors are recognised in a school newsletter.

– Teams-Games-Tournament (TG)   Teacher assigned worksheets are given to students to master material. Students earn group points by competing with students from other teams. competitors are matched on the basis of previous "tournaments' so that winners play winners and losers play losers. As with STAD, winners are recognised in weekly newsletters.

– Team Assisted Individualisation (TAI)   Using this technique students may work on different materials. Each student is placed at a specific level on a programmed mathematics series following diagnostic assessment. Students proceed through the series, helped by one of their group mates. Each student completes a mastery test before beginning the next unit of the series. Students' test scores and their weekly progress contribute to the team scores. Students administer and score the mastery tests leaving the teacher free for individual tutoring.

Slavin considers group rewards and individual accountability to be the essential elements of Student Team learning. He suggests that group rewards based on students' learning foster peer tutoring, high achievement, interpersonal relations and prosocial behaviour.

4.3 Outcomes of Cooperative Learning Methods

Slavin (64] reviewed the available research in this area using what is called best evidence synthesis procedures. Essentially the review confirms that cooperative learning can be an effective means of increasing student achievement but only if the method incorporates group goals and individual accountability. Some difference of effect is evident in outcomes when measured on standardised tests, however the effect of cooperative methods are still significant when standardised measures are used. The positive outcomes in areas of race relations [65], acceptance of students with learning difficulties increased self-concept and other social variables in addition to academic achievements are impressive given that the techniques can be applied with little cost.

4.4 Processes Underlying Cooperative Groups

To appreciate the widest possible range of application of these teaching approaches an understanding of the underlying processes would be helpful. In addition, knowing the processes should facilitate development of further approaches particularly in relation to students with complex learning difficulties. Whilst the available research on these methods does not seem to focus on the above issue Johnson and Johnson [66] outline several potential factors:

– *Reasoning strategies.* The above authors suggest that cooperative learning methods may promote the development and use of higher order thought processes.

– *Constructive controversy.* In heterogeneous groups reconciling varied opinions en route to solutions should foster problem solving skills through requirements such as information searching skills and taking perspectives.

– *Cognitive processing.* Cooperative methods require oral rehearsal for information, particularly for task related explanations.

– *Peer support and involvement in learning.* Increased friendship, acceptance and cognitive processing skills are likely outcomes of students helping each other.

– *Group Processing.* Through constant re-appraisal of actions, it is likely that collaborative problem solving would be improved.

In addition to the above, Sharan [67] suggests that some of the methods enhance imagination, judgement and evaluative skills. Other authors suggest that peer pressure increases time on task. Further research should evaluate the role of motivation in the above techniques. More specific research is required on the role of peer interaction, students' cognitive processes and instructional analysis.

5 Individual Tutoring

Whilst most forms of teaching allow for individual teaching time, the needs of students with significant learning difficulties may be such that adequate time is not available. With limited resources, needs for individual tutoring are being met by alternative "teaching" resources generally in the shape of peer tutoring.

Peer tutoring was pioneered in the late 18th and early 19th century by Andrew Bell and Joseph Lancaster. It has been revived again, particularly in the United States where 41 out of 50 states were found to be using tutoring [68]. In the United Kingdom teachers have made informal arrangements in and out of class to have older and more advanced pupils help younger or more vulnerable students. Peer tutoring can also include students being tutored by adults from the community [69] or university students [70] tutor in elementary or second level schools.

Peer tutoring is organised instruction given to students under the guidance of a class teacher. It differs from the informal unstructured peer support/help involved in cooperative learning situations.

5.1 Peer Tutoring and Disability

Most of the research on peer tutoring identifies social and academic benefits as outcomes of this type of tutoring. Studies indicate that children with significant learning difficulties benefit academically from tutoring by students with and without learning difficulties [71]. Research also indicates that negative attitudes towards students who have moderate or severe learning difficulties can be changed in a positive direction during the course of a seven week period of peer tutoring [72].

Students with learning difficulties or other forms of disability have also been used as tutors with younger or same age non-disabled peers in areas of skills. One interesting series of research [73] evaluated a project where students described as "educable mentally retarded, learning disabled and behaviourally disordered" have functioned as tutors of sign language. One side effect of this project was increased academic gains for the tutors as well as the tutees. In a meta-analysis of available research documenting the effectiveness of disabled students as tutors of other students, Cooke [74] concluded that tutoring is a viable and potentially powerful instructional intervention for special education and the learning disabled, behaviourally disordered and students with learning difficulties, in addition to gaining as tutees, can function effectively as tutors in academic areas.

6 Technological Education

Technology has facilitated access to education for people with disabilities in devising items, e.g., motorised wheelchairs, speech synthesisers, speech autocuers, the Kurzweil reading machine and the microcomputer-controlled interactive videodisc system designed to teach skills such as time telling, etc., to students with learning difficulties [75]. However, despite these developments very few studies report involvement of students with learning difficulties in technological education.

Preparing this paper, a literature search highlighted studies involving students with learning difficulties in science curriculum. The research available highlights the applicability of science education as a desirable goal for such students. Recently, the National Science Foundation has targeted individuals with disabilities as a priority for science education [76]. In fact science has been considered one of the most valuable subjects that can be taught to students with disabilities because of the following benefits: (a) expanding experiential background for students who have limited experiences; (b) skills and knowledge important for adult life; (c) using concrete hands-on activities and (d) developing problem solving and reasoning skills. Research also highlights the efficacy of instructional strategies, e.g., study skills training, structure of instruction, text adaptations and modifications such as picture and label additions, mnemonic strategies and elaborative techniques such as guided enquiry.

Mastropierri and Scruggs [77] located eleven reports that investigated the effects of activities oriented science curricula with students with learning difficulties, including those described as moderately handicapped. Most of the studies used activity oriented approaches which were reported to increase the abilities of the students to observe, communicate and predict. Adapted structured programmes were generally used in conjunction with problem solving approaches. Perhaps the lessons learned in relation to science teaching might be transferable to the world of technological education given that the world of technology, in the shape of computers, is available to and usable by people with significant learning difficulties.

7 Conclusion

Research in the earlier part of this century focused on the specific cognitive deficits of persons with learning difficulties whilst research at this end of the century is focusing on instructional strategies to extend the field of learning for these persons. Inclusion of these students within the regular school systems facilitates access to expanded curricula, a wide range of teaching strategies and learning situations. Research on student participation in science curricula raises the question of the extent to which these same students could participate in technological education and perhaps in the world of technology as adults. Perhaps their inclusion in technological education will promote further development in the field of technology to facilitate full inclusion in all aspects of life.

Acknowledgements

The author wishes to acknowledge the help of the following people:

Siobhan Cotter, Training Department, St. Michael's House, Dublin;
Kevin Coyle, Head of Training Department, St. Michael's House, Dublin;
Tony Grealy, Psychology Department, St. Michael's House, Dublin;
David Price, FAS Training Centre, Cabra, Dublin;
Mary Rohan, Education Research Centre, Drumcondra, Dublin;
Margaret Spelman, Psychology Department, St. Michael's House, Dublin.

References

1. Ryan, J., Thomas, F.: The Politics of Mental Handicap. Revised Edition. London. Free Association Books 1987
2. St. Augustine: Migne Patrologia Latina
3. Grimm, quoted in C. Haffter: The changeling: history and psychodynamics of attitudes to handicapped children in European folklore, Journal of the History of Behavioural Sciences 4 (1968)
4. Paracelsus: De Generatione Stultorum (11567), translated by Cranefield, P. and Federn, W. as The begetting of fools, Bulletin of the History of Medicine 41 (1967)
5. Robbins, J.: Fools and Mad. IPA Press, Dublin
6. Grimm, from C. Haffter: The changeling: history and psychodynamics of attitudes to handicapped children in European folklore, Journal of the History of Behavioural Sciences 4 (1968)
7. Yeats. WB.: The Stolen Child. Oxford Book of Irish Verse. Oxford Press 1963
8. as in 6
9. as in 6
10. Cranefield, P.: The Discovery of Cretinism, Bulletin of the History of Medicine 35 (1961)
11. Coxe, W.: Annual Register 1779
12. Cranefield, P.: A seventeenth century view if mental deficiency and schizophrenia. Thomas Willis on stupidity and foolishness. Bulletin of the History of Medicine 35 (1961)
13. Seguin, E.: Traitement moral, hygiene et education des idiots, et des autres enfants arrieres. Balliere Tindall 1846
14. ibid.
15. Howe, S.: The Causes of Idiocy. Maclachlan & Stewart 1848
16. Idiot Asylums, Edinburgh Review 22 (1865)
17. Darwin, C.: The Origin of the Species. London. John Murray 1857
18. Galton, F.: Hereditary Genius. London. Macmillan 1869

19. Langdon Down, J.: Observations on an ethnic classification of idiots. Clinical Lectures and Reports of the London Hospital, e, 259-62 (1866)

20. Stubbins, J.: The Clinical Attitude in Rehabilitation; a cross cultural view. New York. World Rehabilitation Fund 1982

21. ibid.

22. Carter, L. F.: The Sustaining Effects Study of Compensatory and Elementary Education. Educational Researcher 13 (7), 4-13 (1984)

23. Cooley, W. W., Leinhardt, G.: The Instructional Dimensions Study. Educational Leadership 2 (1), 7-25 (1980)

24. Hall, J.: Segregation by another name? Special Children 1992

25. Reynolds, M.: A Framework for considering some special issues in special education. Exceptional Children 28, 367-70 (1962)

26. Deno, E.: Special Education as Developmental Capital, Exceptional Children 37, 229-370 (1970)

27. Leinhardt, G.: Case studies of accademic mainstreaming. Pater presented at the annual meeting of the American Educational Research Association. New York 1982

28. Brown, L., Ford, A., Nisbet, J., Sweet, M., Donnilhan, A., Grunewald, L.: Opportunities available when slow learning students attend age appropriate regular schools. Journal of the Association for the Severely Handicapped 8 (1). 16-24 (1983)

29. as in 27

30. ibid.

31. Slavin, R. E.: Cooperative Learning. New York. Longman 1982

32. Stern, D., Hoachlander, E. G., Dhy, S., Benson, C.: One million hours a day: Vocational education in California public secondary schools. Report to the Californian Policy Seminar. Berkely, Ca. University of California School of Education 1985

33. Nolands, T. K.: The effects of ability grouping: A meta-analysis of research finding. Unpublished doctoral dissertation. University of Colorado. Boulder 1985

34. Madden, N., Slavin, R. E.: Mainstream students with mild handicaps. Academic and social outcomes. Review of Educational Research 53, 519-569 (1983)

35. Calfee, R. C., Brown, R.: Grouping students for instruction. In: D. L. Duke (ed.) Classroom Management. Seventy- eighth yearbook of the National Society for the Study of Education. Chicago. University of Chicago Press 1979

36. Brown, L., Rogan, P., Shiraga, B.: A vocational follow-up evaluation of the 1984-1986 Madison Metropolitan School District graduates with severe intellectual disabilities. A Research Monograph of the Association for Persons with Severe Handicaps 2 (2) (1987)

37. Granger, L., Grangeer, B.: The Magic Feather. New York. E. P. Dutton 1986

38. Reaction of the General Public to Physically Disabled and Mentally Handicapped and Ill People; MRBI Opinion Poll, Dublin; Health Education Bureau 1981

39. Algozzine, B., Maheady, L.: When all else fails, teach! Exceptional Children 32,11-22 (1985)
40. Mehta, V.: Personal History. New Yorker 1984
41. Flynn, G.: In a paper given to the Psychological Society of Ireland, Dublin October 1991
42. Leinhardt, G., Bickel, W.: Instruction's the Thing Wherein to Catch the Mind that Falls Behind. In: School and Classroom Organisation. Edited by R. E. Slavin, Hillsdale, New Jersey. Lawrence Erlbaum Associates 1989
43. Wang, M., Reynolds, M., Walberg, H.: Preparing the second system for students with special needs. Wingspread Conference on Special needs Proceedings. 1987
44. Slavin, R.: Cooperative learning and cooperative schools. Educational Leadership 45 (3), 7-13 (1987)
45. Affleck, J., Madge, S., Adams, Lowenbraum, S.: Integrated classrooms versus resource model: Academic viability and effectiveness. Exceptional Children (5494), 339-348 (1988)
46. Lawless, S.: Inclusion. Learning Together, Swansea. Open Eye Publication 3 (1992)
47. Glaser, R.: (ed.) Advances in instructional psychology. (Vol.2). Hillsdale, New Jersey. Lawrence Erlbaum Associates 1982
48. Scheutz, P.: The instructional effectiveness of classroom aides. Unpublished manuscript, University of Pittsburgh 1980
49. Leinhardt, G., Greeno, J.: The cognitive skills of teaching. Journal of Educational Psychology. 78 (2) 78-95 (1982)
50. H. M. I. Education. London HMSO 1982.
51. Leinhardt, G., Seewald, A. M.: Overlap: what's tested, what's taught? Journal of Educational Measurement 18 (3) 171-177 (1951)
52. Leinhardt, G.: Case studies of academic mainstreaming. Paper presented at the annual meeting of the American Educational Research Association. New York 1982
53. Leinhardt, G., Greeno, J.: The cooperative skill of teaching. Journal of Educational Psychology 7 (2) 75-95 (1986)
54. Deutsch, M.: A Theory of Co-operation and Competition. Human Relations (1949)
55. Slavin, R. E.: When does cooperative learning increase student achievement? Psychological Bulletin 1983
56. Slavin, R. E.: Cooperative Learning. New York. Longman 1983
57. Cohen, E.: Designing groupwork. Strategies for the heterogeneous classroom. New York. Teachers' College Press (1986)
58. Kagan, S.: Dimensions of cooperative classroom structures. In: R. Slavin, S. Sharn, S. Kagan, R. Hertz-Lazarowitz, C. Webb, R. Schmuck (eds.) Learning to co-operate, co-operating to learn. New York. Plenum Press 1985

59. Slavin, R. E.: An introduction to cooperative learning research. In: R. Slavin, S. Sharn, S. Kagan, R. Hertz-Lazarowitz, C. Webb, R. Schmuck (eds.) Learning to co-operate, cooperating to learn. New York. Plenum Press 1985

60. Johnson, D., Johnson, R.: Learning together and alone. Englewood Cliffs, Prentice Hall 1975

61. Aronson, E., Blaney, N., Stephan, C., Sikes, J., Snapp, M.:. The Jigsaw Classroom. Beverly Hills, Ca., Sage 1978

62. Sharan S., Sharan Y.: Small-group teaching. Englewood Cliffs. New Jersey. Educational Technology Publications 1976

63. Slavin, R. E.: Cooperative Learning. New York. Longman 1983

64. Slavin, R. E.: Cooperative learning and student achievement. In School and Classroom Organisation. Edited by Robert E. Slavin. Hillsdale, New Jersey, Lawrence Erlbaum Associates 1989

65. as in 60

66. Johnson, S., Johnson, D.: Effects of cooperative, competitive and individualistic learning experience on social development. Exceptional Children 1983

67. Sharan, S., Herta-Lazarowitz, R., Ackerman, Z.: Academic achievement of elementary school children in small-group versus whole-class instruction. Journal of Experimental Education 48, 128-129 (1980)

68. Smith, P. K., Tutoring: A National Perspective. ERIC. No ED 228 722, (1983)

69. Goodlad, S., Hirst, B.: Peer Tutoring. London. Kogan Page 1989

70. ibid.

71. ibid.

72. Fenrick, N. J., Peterson, T. K.: Developing positive changes in attitudes towards moderately/severely handicapped students through a peer tutoring project. Education and Training of the Mentally Retarded 19, 2, 83-90 1984)

73. Osguthorpe, R. T.: Handicapped Children as Tutors. 83-84. Final Report, Pravo, Utah, Brigham Young University 1975

74. Cooke, S. B.: Handicapped students as tutors. Journal of Special Education 19, 4, 483-492 (1986)

75. Cavalier, A.: The Application of Technology in the Classroom and Workplace: Unvoiced Premises & Ethical Issues. In: Images of the Disabled, Disabling Images; edited by A. Gartner, T. Joe. New York. Praeger 1987

76. Beherman, J.: Science foundation to seek persons with disabilities for science careers. Indiana Counterpart. 11 (3) 1-6 (1991)

77. Mastropierri, M. D., Scruggs, T. E.: Science for Students with Disabilities. Review of Educational Research, Vol. 62, 4, 377-411 (1992)

Didactical Concepts for Developing Key Qualifications

Peter Kunz
Skoda Car Plant
Human Resources / ZPK
Mlada Boleslav, 293 60, Czech Republic

Abstract. Skoda is going through a tremendous transformation process. In joint venture with VW Skoda is developing into a modern and competitive car company. By introduction of new technologies, new kinds of work organisation and modern personnel management the esssential steps to the "new Skoda" have been taken. Efficient project management and fast know-how transfer out of the VW group are accelerating the speed of the process of change.

By example of core projects on creating a Skoda management culture it is shown how the key processes in the company are initiated, controlled and stabilized.

Keywords. Joint venture, new technologies, work organisation, personnel and project management

1 Introduction

From the slow lane to the passing lane - a proverb, which sounds very daring, as SKODA is a car company of eastern origin just started learning to walk in the so called free market economy.

SKODA wants to be a serious competitor, i.e., a continental player on the European car market. The future of SKODA depends on achieving this ambitious goal. Because just those crowned with success will be able to survive in the increasingly competitive car market, those who have not reached success will disappear soon. Only companies having a qualified, motivated staff and offering a range of attractive high quality products at low costs and providing extensive services will be successful.

2 Where Is SKODA Coming From?

Before the political changes 1989 SKODA was the model of a state-owned enterprise. All important company decisions were subject to state planning. The quantitative accomplishment of the state plans had an absolute priority over the entrepreneurial decisions. The company's organization corresponded with the socialist structure and was organized centrally and autocratically. Due to this, the top management was organized in a strictly hierarchially way.

The purchase and selling prices were not subject to the laws of supply and demand, but were regulated by the state. The volume of investment and production was controlled by the state, although SKODA itself was allowed to create and develop its production and work processes. A large reserve of raw materials were stored to be relatively independent of those materials received by suppliers.

Compared with other eastern European car manufacturers SKODA was "the one-eyed king in the country of the blind", that means relating to Eastern European conditions SKODA was a company in good order, but unable to stand up to international competition in the free market economy.

3 Where Is SKODA Now?

SKODA-Volkswagen joint venture started in April 1991. Today VW holds 31% of shares and is responsible for SKODA's management. In spring 1995 the share of stock will be increased to 70%. The remaining shares will be transferred to Czech citizens through Czech privatization funds.

At present 3 different types of cars are being produced in 3 plants throughout the Czech Republic. SKODA car models are ranged between Polo and Golf and their names are: SKODA-Favorit, SKODA-Forman /a combi version of Favorit/ and SKODA-Pick-up.

– In 1993 about 17.000 employees are producing 220.000 cars;
– 80% of suppliers are from the Czech Republic and Slovakia,
– 35% of the cars are marketed in the Czech Republic and Slovakia,
– 21% in Central/Eastern Europe and 43% in Western Europe/Overseas.
– The markets SKODA is present on are changing rapidly.

Hereditary markets are suddenly vanishing /, e.g., former Yugoslavia, the former Soviet Union/ but new markets are being conquered/, e.g., Israel and the threshold countries of the Far East/.

The strengths of SKODA are:

– a long and historically successful tradition of the trade mark SKODA, one of the oldest car producers in the world;

– the pioneer spirit which helped the employees of SKODA in the past as well as today to design very creative and original solutions within a difficult environment. The very strict social and political system of the past needed a high degree of improvisational talent and flexibility to be able to work at all.;

– a high level of basic qualification comparable with that of the western industry countries;

– the ability to learn is exhibited shown by many of its employees. They are keen on learning and open to new and modern things. They are able to learn foreign languages in a relatively short time;

– many employees have a very strong readiness for change. The old system broke down and the traditional effective mechanisms are steadily loosing their impact. In todays society new values and standards are being established. There is a search for a new identitiy and new affiliations with diverse cultural groups and organizations.

The drawbacks of SKODA are:

– not only partly old technologies but also underdeveloped work processes;
– a striking lack of basic economic knowledge;
– a very low distinction of management abilities especially from the point of setting goals/delegation, initiative and willingness to responsibility, strategic and process oriented thinking. There is also a lack of professional knowledge in financial controlling, marketing, purchasing and personnel management;
– individual specialization is dominant, teamwork is not wide-spread;
– the "old boys' network" still exists partially and absorbs dynamics of change or even works counterproductive.

4 Where Is SKODA Going To?

SKODA's primary objective is to become a continental player, to belong to the top of the European competition. SKODA is creating a new, dynamic and powerful identity by means of an extensive cultural-change-process. By doing so SKODA will join the success of the past before the iron curtain was built up. In this respect, it is important to keep the independence of the trade mark SKODA and to provide it with a new powerful force through the image of VW as well as a wide range of new products.

The competitiveness of SKODA will be increased by dramatically raising its production. While actualizing products and modernizing the production, the number of products to be built will be increased from 220.000 in the present to 460.000 by 1996.

Further core processes on the roadchange are:

– implementation of Lean Production and Total Quality Management;
– up-to-date technologies and new types of work organization;
– and internal as well as external customer orientation.

The transformation of SKODA will be enhanced by means of well-aimed on the job training, project management and know-how transfer from the Volkswagen Group.

5 Skoda's Own Way and Its Speed of Change

The most decisive competitor in SKODA's process of change is time and in its level of employees, motivation among them and establishing the most appropriate corporate culture.

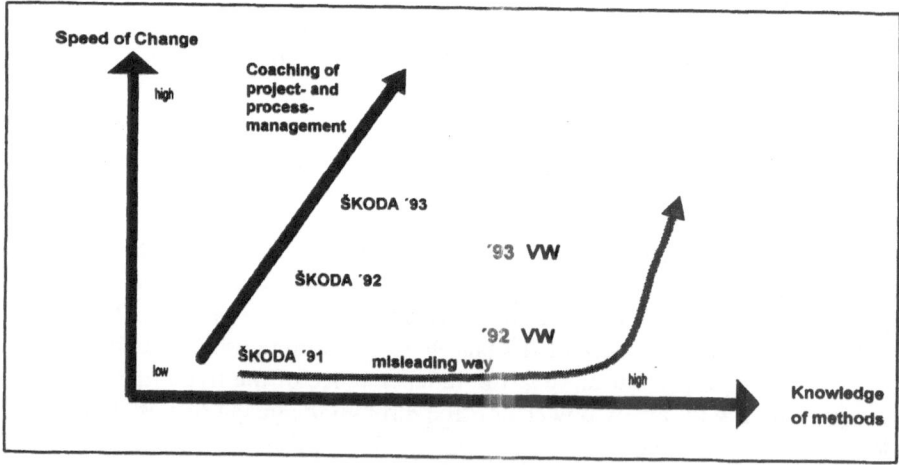

Fig. 1 SKODA's own way

It would be easy to copy the already proven methods and processes used by VW in the past and apply them directly to SKODA. This would be a misleading way.

– The proven methods and processes of the past are often no longer a key to success in the present. Today, Volkswagen fights for its own survival and is undergoing a crucial process of change. The knowledge of methodology is very high at VW, but the speed of change is very low. VW is in danger of falling behind the Japanese car manufacturing industry.

– The automotive industry is moving towards a quickly changing environment. A lack of time can not be compensated by conventional methods. In adapting VW's methodology SKODA would limp behind VW and never be able to keep pace with its competitors.

– Many of the methods of work and organization in the western automotive industry are very complex and require a deep professional knowledge, which cannot be aquired in a short period of time on a broad level under the SKODA-specific conditions.

– A direct transfer of know how on a 1:1 basis would not consider the unique origins and the present state of SKODA in the Czech Republic and would ignore or even destroy the fruitful attempts of the past. A strong passive resistance among local employees defending their cultural identity against the foreign joint venture partners would have to be taken into account.

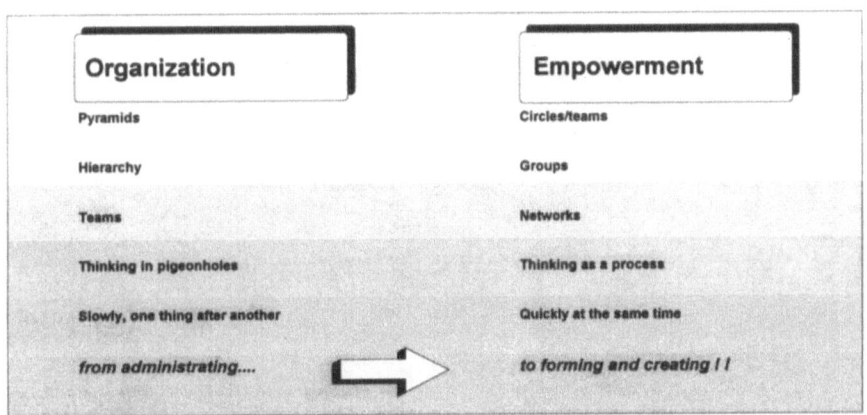

Fig. 2 Empowerment instead of organization

Therefore, SKODA tries to increase the speed of change dramatically and to find its own way to success. Methods and processes of VW are adopted by SKODA in a constructive and critical way. Core projects and key processes are defined and described. Volkswagen expatriates initiate and accompany the transformation process as coaches. They foster empowerment instead of organization. SKODA employees develop and grow from administrators to creators.

6 Change to Modern Personnel Management by Means of Project Control

The conventional way of transferring know how into a company with a lack of local professional knowledge is as follows: At the beginning, foreign managers will be installed into key positions. Further key functions are filled by local and foreign management tandem teams.

SKODA's Human Resources Division secures the qualification of Czech managers by efficient project management and coaching. Most of the local managers have been performing their functions since the start of the joint venture and are coached by a team of three project managers from the Volkswagen Group. Initiation and follow-up of changes take place throughout projects.

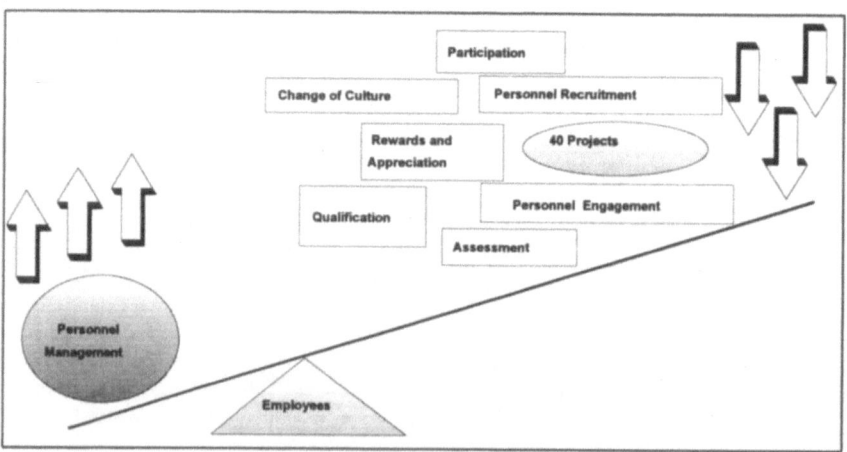

Fig. 3 Change to modern personnel management by means of project control

At the beginning of the joint venture about 40 core projects were defined at Human Resources in a common process. Since then 20 of them have been finished and 15 new ones have been started based on SKODA's necessity of change.

Currently all projects are led by Czech managers who are, according to their personnel progress, accompanied and supported by a member of the German project team.

6.1 Coaching in the Process of Change

Teambuilding in the departments and project groups is the beginning of all important steps in the process of change and lead to the identification of people who are intricately involved. A clear agreement on goals and objective monitoring lead to individual responsibility and clarity of objectives.

The announcement of changes and the communication of all essential steps are highly crucial to the success of the projects. Management and staff need to feel that they are involved. There is a quick feedback to success. Performance and results are rewarded.

The coach takes care of process reflection, adaptation of the course, fine tuning, creation of interfaces and synergy to other projects.

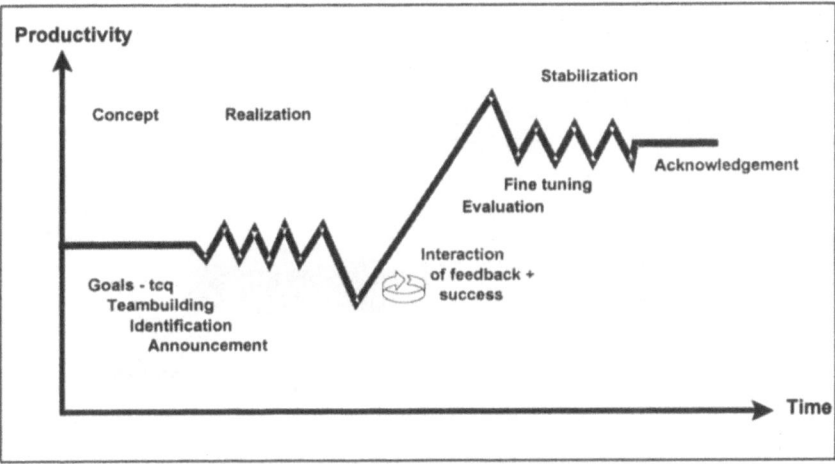

Fig. 4 Coaching in the process of change

The speed of change at SKODA is increased tremendously by inflaming many area conflagrations, the simultaneous managing of several projects. Fears and scepticism, which absorb a lot of energy and take much time, are diminished by the active and situative 'need to act'. Negative scenarios of thinking can hardly be counterproductive, as the current situation forces people to act and to act anew. This kind of action inevitably causes faults, which are corrected by competent coaching.

6.2 Creation of a New Management Culture at Skoda

The creation of a new management culture is exemplary for project management at SKODA. There are 1 - 2 annual management meetings in order to provide all managers with current information from the VW-Group and SKODA. Additionally, room is given for the exchange of experience and work on topics of fundamental importance.

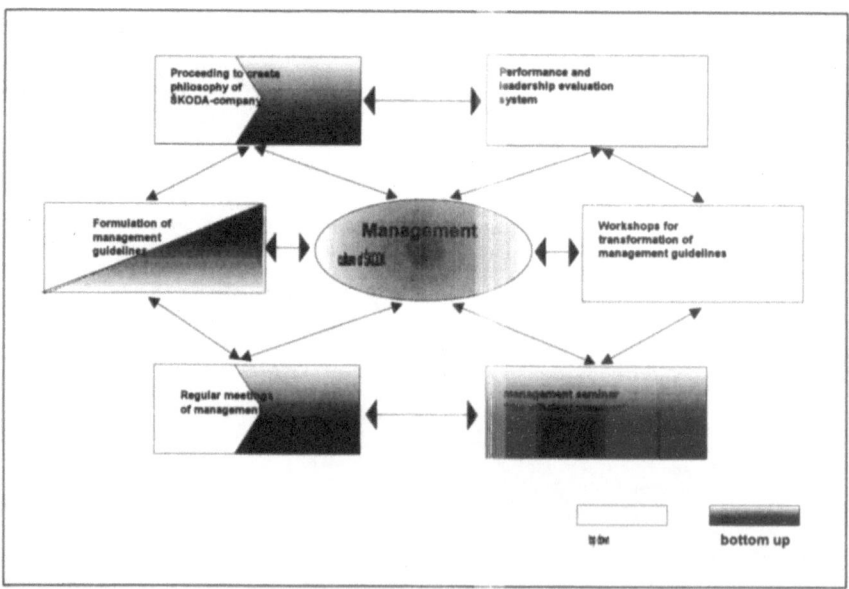

Fig. 5 Creation of a new management culture

On the occasion of the first management meeting the first milestone for the management guidelines was built, subsequently revised by a cross cultural editorial team and finally agreed to by the management.

These guidelines were used as well for the first SKODA leadership seminar which all SKODA managers took part in from January to April this year, and for the respective seminar for supervisors. A series of reports in the company newspaper were started in order to communicate the management guidelines to all employees.

At the same time workshops were initiated in the divisions, beginning with the board members, and the reset hierarchical level, top down in cascades, to the heads of departments. There the guidelines were used to mirror the state of the art regarding leadership and cooperation of the participants.

The Mission Statement of SKODA describes the dynamic vision of the future years. Many people created it in several workshops and editorial meetings, led by the spirit: 'SKODA -success through innovation and tradition'.

A management performance system consequently rewarding results and pointing out needs of personnel development for managers and staff is introduced presently.

Strategic corporate objectives and the management guidelines are essential parts of the system.

This bunch of projects is a network creating a SKODA management culture. Each project is synergetic to the others and is pushing the whole process of change to success.

7 Final Conclusion

SKODA, supported by Volkswagen, has a rapid pace in todays modern time. The achieved results of project management and the relatively good financial situation of the company clearly show that we are on the right road to success. SKODA has become one of the most important east-west joint ventures. Thereby, SKODA has become a model for the economic development in the Czech Republic and contributes significantly to the integration of Europe.

3. Advanced Technology Self-Learning Tools

The importance of a focus on adults and workers is that it rapidly accelerates the expansion of technology education to all age groups, and its manifestation in both in- and out-of-school forms. The concept of lifelong learning leads to the new dimension of work – didactic and environmentally integrated learning activities. The ARW participants noted that the urgent need for strategies to guide the teaching of technology education is directly related to technological change and to the ethics and social content of technology.

The papers in this part include Dyrenfurth's analysis of educational technology's fundamental implications and systems for learning. This focus on the impacts on the individual is extended to the attitudinal domain by Kath. Szücs then stresses the social and human needs that result from increased self-learning capabilities.

The participants also called for clarification of the laws and structures of technology as well as for the laws that explain the evolution of technology using systems concepts. The result would be usable in areas as diverse as agriculture and production in space and from basic metal working up to laser measurement. The main goal for lifelong learning that emerged was that the people are able to formulate views and solutions according to the individual–environment interface, that they are able to structure problems, that they are able to access, process, and generate information, and that they have a personal future-oriented view that systematically explains what is (and should be) happening in society and to themselves.

To such new goals, the participants fitted didactical concepts for lifelong learning. During their discussions associated with this part, the participants asserted loudly that dialogue and investigation of these fields needs to be strengthened.

The DNA of Advanced Educational Technology

Michael J. Dyrenfurth
University of Missouri
College of Education,
Department of Practical Arts & Vocational-Technical Education
105 London Hall, Columbia, Missouri 65211, USA

Abstract. DNA stands for **Dynamic, Nature** and **Application.** The dynamic interface between the existing evolution of advanced educational technology (AET) and human resource development in technological arenas is described using twelve dimensions to characterize AET and using Dyrenfurth's (1991) model for technological literacy. The latter posits seven key vectors essential to technological capability. The construct of AET is depicted using twelve major dimensions: Users, Duration, Genre, Function, Domain, Span, Purpose, Complexity, Impact, Order, Mode, Senses. Each of these dimensions is defined in terms of individual characteristics. Speculative projections, based on the models of AET and Technological literacy, and situated within the context of technological human resource development both in school and industry, are generated to demonstrate AET's emerging and promising applications.

Keywords. Advanced educational technology, technology education, instructional technology, technological literacy, key qualifications, school-industry links, future

The crux of this paper is speculation, rampant speculation. I don't know where, or to what, this analysis will lead, but I know why I am pursuing this thrust. Like many professionals engaged with education and technology, I have a significant need to make more sense of, i.e., to better understand, the dynamic interface between the existing evolution of advanced educational technology (AET) and the challenges of human resource development in technological dimensions.

Accordingly, as I explored the cascade of exciting, daunting, shallow, perceptive, huckstering and revealing articles about AET, the need for a rubric to organize it became ever more compelling. Combined with the analysis resulting from my reductionist side, this need forced me into a speculative mode, and it is the result of that speculation that I share with you today. More specifically, this will also reveal the meaning of the title acronym, i.e., DNA.

DNA, as used in this context is intended as an analogy to the mysterious key to the biological world that genetic scientists have provided us. Of course, I am not so presumptuous to think that my version of DNA is anywhere as systematic or explanatory as the empirically-based original. In fact, my DNA is purely speculative, but I do hope that it will help readers reach higher levels of understanding of AET and its applications.

Well then, what is AET's DNA? Consider it as the rudimentary beginning of a taxonomy to explain, i.e., to make sense of, the multi-faceted nature of AET. As such, DNA stands for Dynamic, Nature and Application of AET. There are twelve major dimensions of this construct:

- Users	- Duration	- Genre	- Function
- Domain	- Span	- Purpose	- Complexity
- Impact	- Order	- Mode	- Senses

The meaning of each of these dimensions is presented in Table 1.

These dimensions, in turn, each have a structure and/or constituents of their own. These constituents are presented in Table 2. Using the conventional descriptive algorithm of Who, What, Why, When, Where, and How; yields two "who" dimensions, one "what" dimension, five "how" dimensions, one "where" dimension and two "when" dimensions that combine to characterize each AET and our profession's use of it. Certainly this is not a simple or elegant analysis, but this is because it is a first stage and because AET itself involves far more than mere hardware.

The need for a rubric to characterize AET becomes abundantly clear when one scans, even on a cursory basis, the landscape of AET. For example, the landscape provided in Table 3 is nowhere complete, but even so, it is close to overwhelming in terms of its potential, and unfathomable in terms of its possible interactions with technology education.

Table 1 AET's DNA Dimension and their meanings

Users	The type of individual making use of the AET
Function	What the user does with, or via, the AET
Purpose	Why the user is employing the AET
Order	The extent to which the user employs the AET
Duration	The length of time that the user employs the AET

Domain	The user's target(s) or behavior impact arenas using the APA's taxonomy of educational outcomes (circa 1956)
Complexity	The number of senses directly and significantly involved by the user's interaction with the AET
Mode	The audience characteristic of the AET and its use
Genre	The nature of the entities that the AET's is linking or interacting with
Span	The distance between, and coalescence of, the entities being linked by the AET.
Impact	The extent to which the AET affects or controls the entities employing it. This dimension is based on Dale's cone of experience (circa 1960)
Senses	The pathways to cognizance which are used by the AET involved

1 On Technological Literacy

Technological literacy, as the primary outcome of formal schooling and informal (e.g., self taught) technology education is one of these three focuses. The purpose of this paper is not to serve as a treatise on technological literacy but rather to address the interaction of the three chief focuses that frame this NATO-funded Advanced Research Workshop.

Therefore, to expedite matters, I will only refer to the most current comprehensive synthesis of technological literacy as presented in Dyrenfurth & Kozak's, 1991 Council on Technology Teacher Education yearbook. This synthesis presents the model for technological literacy shown in Figure 1 and then various subsequent papers and presentations detailed the competencies that actually comprise the constituents of technological literacy. An overview of these competencies is provided in Table 4.

Table 2 The DNA of AET

Users(who)	Functions(what)	Senses(how)
• Learners • Teachers • Librarians • Administrators • BIL Personnel • Inservice Providers • Support Staff • Government Staff	• Accessing information • Analyzing information • Coding/classifying information • Searching/finding information • Exploring information • Developing information • Reducing information • Synthesizing information • Moving information • Storing information • e.g., see guidelines matrix of thinking skills (Table 5)	• Sight • Sound • Smell • Touch • Taste • Position • Velocity
Genre(who) • Human to human • Machine to human • Machine to machine	Order(when) • Intermittent • Steady • Recurring	Mode(how) • Individual • Small group • Large group • Mass Audience
Purpose(why) • Infinite number of reasons, e.g., • Learning • Entertainment • Relaxation • Stimulation • Safety	Duration(when) • Intermittent • Short • Sustained • Long • Ongoing	Complexity (how) • One sense • Two senses • Three senses • Four senses • Five senses • Six senses • Seven senses
	Span(where) • Internal • Local • Distant (direct) • Remote • Distributed	Impact Level(how) • Innocuous • Mild • Moderate • Strong • Intense • Unbearable
		Domain(how) • Cognitive • Affective • Sensori-motor

Table 3 A Cursory Landscape of AET

Optical disks	DAT, Digital Audio Tape
Digital video	Digital sound
Distributed video	Satellite communication
Digital telephone networks	Local distribution networks
Direct broadcast satellite	Pen/notebook computers
Storage technology	Human interface technology
Video disk	Interactive video
Teletext & videotext	Electronic/tele-conferencing
Encryption	Advanced generation software
Interactive cable systems	Voice recognition
Scanning & OCR	Client/server systems
Animation	Simulation & modeling
CD-I	Packet networks
Next generation networks	Entity/relationship modeling
LANS & WANS	Data warehousing
Learning environments	Adaptive testing
Device independent graphics	Virtual reality
Machine vision	High definition television
Voice synthesis	Voice recognition
Fiber optics	Human/computer symbiosis
Implant/sensor technology	Embedded training
Expert systems	CAI (computer-assisted instruction)
Integrated software	Electronic mail
Facsimile technology	High level authoring systems
Hypertext/media	Integrated/seamless multi-media
Groupware & middleware	Distributed information systems
Gopher & gopherspace	Graphic user interface
Cognitive mapping	Electronic white/black boards
Remote sensing	...

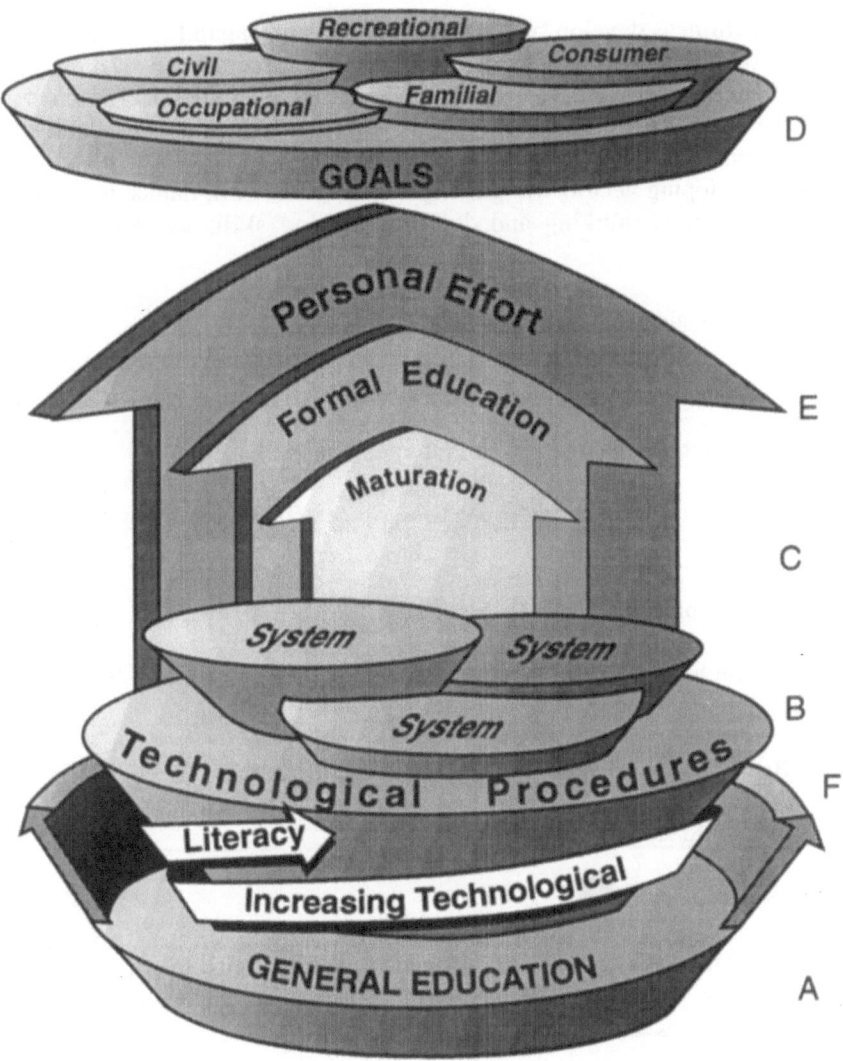

Fig.1 Model for technological literacy

Model notes: The illustration represents technological literacy as a construct consisting of seven vectors infused throughout a set of five [letter-designated] components. These vectors emanate from a base of basic skills and general education [A]. On this base is built a vector of technological procedures [B], i.e., generalized ways of interacting with technology. Beginning inside these technological procedures, but quickly emerging from them, is a vector representing technological capability [C] in one or more subsystems of technology. Humans develop such understandings and capability to move towards goals represented in the model by disks [D] and the force necessary to propel such movement derives from energy such as depicted by the model's arrows [E]. Finally, the actual technological literacy achieved is represented by the upwardly spiraling arrow [F]. Permeating components A, B, and C of the model are upwardly developing vectors designating constructive work habits, teamwork and interpersonal skills, thinking and decision making skills as well as life long learning skills.

Table 4 Technological literacy competency vectors

1.	Constructive work habits, values, attitudes
2.	Teamwork, collaboration and interpersonal skills
3.	Critical thinking, decision making, processing and monitoring skills
4.	Technological capabilities
5.	Technological procedures (generalizable), problem-solving & design
6.	Basic functional skills (reading, writing, arithmetic...)
7.	Ability to learn, adaptability

2 On BIL (Business, Industry, Labor) Links with School

Clearly there is much that BIL can offer school, and through them, society. Among the resources and services that BIL can share are:

− A close connection to the real world of economics, careers, technology and the consequences of varying degrees of capability.
− Contemporary technological resources and the leading/bleeding edge of their evolution as well as the productive, money-making side of their application.
− Insights into the career development and maturation process.
− Shared facilities and expertise.

In the author's more cynical moments the belief that self interest is everyone's primary motive for action rises to the fore. Even if this were false, it is important

Gubbins' Matrix of Thinking Skills	
I. Problem Solving	IV. Divergent Thinking Skills
A. Identifying general problem	A. Listing attributes of objects/
B. Clarifying problem	situation
C. Formulating hypothesis	B. Generating multiple ideas
D. Formulating appropriate	(fluency)
questions	C. Generating different ideas
E. Generating related ideas	(flexibility)
F. Formulating alternative	D. Generating unique ideas
solutions	(originality)
G. Choosing best solution	E. Generating detailed ideas
H. Applying the solution	(elaboration)
I. Monitoring acceptance of	F. Synthesizing information
the solution	
J. Drawing conclusions	V. Evaluative Thinking Skills
	A. Distinguishing between facts
II. Decision Making	and opinions
A. Stating desired goal/	B. Judging credibility of a source
condition	C. Observing and judging
B. Stating obstacles to goal/	observation reports
condition	D. Identifying central issues and
C. Identifying alternatives	problems
D. Examining alternatives	E. Recognizing underlying
E. Ranking alternatives	assumptions
F. Choosing best alternative	F. Detecting bias, stereotypes,
G. Evaluating actions	clichés
	G. Recognizing loaded language
III. Inferences	H. Evaluating hypotheses
A. Inductive thinking skills	I. Classifying data
1. Determining cause and	J. Predicting consequences
effect	K. Demonstrating sequential
2. Analyzing open-ended	synthesis of information
problems	L. Planning alternative strategies
3. Reasoning by analogy	M. Recognizing inconsistencies
4. Making inferences	in information
5. Determining relevant	N. Identifying stated and unstated
information	reasons
6. Recognizing relationships	O. Comparing similarities and
7. Solving insight problems	differences
	P. Evaluating arguments
B. Deductive thinking skills	
1. Using logic	VI. Philosophy and Reasoning
2. Spotting contradictory	A. Using dialogical/dialectical
statements	approaches
3. Analyzing syllogisms	
4. Solving spatial problems	

This matrix is based on a compilation and distillation of ideas from Bloom, Bransford, Brunner, Carpenter, Dewey, Ennis, Feuerstein, Jones, Kurfman and Solomon, Lipman, Orlandi, Parnes, Paul, Perkins, Renzuili, Sternberg,
Suchman, Taba, Torrance, Upton, the Ross Test, the Whimbey Analytical Skills Test, The Cornell Critical Thinking Test, the Cognitive Abilities Test, the Watson-Glaser Critical Thinking Appraisal, the New Jersey Test of Reasoning Skills, and the SEA Test.

Table 5 One perspective on critical thinking skills & their constituent competencies Gubbins, E. J. "Matrix of Thinking Skills" (unpublished document). Hartford, CT: State Department of Education, 1985.

to point out that BIL-School links have important advantages for BIL as well. Among these are:

– Presentation of BIL's perspectives to a whole future generation of citizens and policy makers.
– The opportunity to fulfill the social responsibility of BIL in an efficient manner.
– Exposure to an alternative, non-inhouse mode of thinking that frequently raises questions about BIL's status quo.
– The opportunity to screen, develop and select potential talent without incurring he extensive commitments required by government labor policies
– The chance to tap into the pool of academic research and development personnel facilities, often at costs substantially below what would be required to maintain one's own R & D program

3 On the Joys of Speculation

Finally we are at the crux of our week again together, namely a detailed exploration of the intersection of:

1. Advanced educational technology
2. Technological literacy
3. Business/Industry/Labor links with the schools

Each of these focuses has been presented in the previous sections of this paper and key features outlined. But, now comes the exciting part of our time together-- namely the knowledge development part. As in Gibson & Sterling's speech to the National Academy of Science's Convocation on Technology and Education, "we need to make some conscious decisions to reinvent our information technology as if the future mattered". So, I invite you to share in some consensual hallucinations, the chief tools for which so far have been analysis and speculation. Five among the more challenging possibilities afforded us at the cyberspace intersection of AET, technological literacy and school-business links, are:

1. Embedded training, in private and public sectors, wherein the day-to-day production machines incorporate AI-based operation monitoring interfaced to an interactive video-supported CAI system that trains the operator as needed.
2. The use of AET via simulations, virtual reality and/or interactive modeling programs for purposes of enhancing the design and/or problem solving processes
3. The use of global computer networking, gopher space and heuristic student-driven front ends to encourage collaborative, goal-focused activity and exchange the ability to access and reduce information masses.
4. The uses of AET to support video and other forms of interactive conferencing, to bring school and BIL personnel closer
5. Establishing BIL-based certification systems to qualify students, and perhaps even teachers, via AET-based adaptive testing and portfolio data banking

Let me end in the spirit of Jacques-Yves Cousteau who, in addressing UNESCO's International Forum on Scientific and Technological Literacy for All, and speaking of technological challenges and understanding, said:

"let us not forget that what is at stake is who will win the race between schools and cradles...between an orderly human community, or chaos. We can only win this challenge if we have the courage to face such realities without flinching."

References

1. American Psychological Association: Taxonomy of educational outcomes (Bloom, Krathwohl et al.), circa 1956
2. Anderson, J. R., Kline, P. J., Beasley, C. M.: A general learning theory and its application to schema abstraction. Technical Report 78-2. Pittsburgh, PA, Carnegie-Mellon University 1978
3. Cousteau, J. Y.: A race between school and cradle. Keynote presentation to the International Forum on Scientific and Technological Literacy for All., Paris, France, UNESCO 1993, July 3
4. Dale, E.: Audio-visual education: The cone of experience. Columbus, OH, The Ohio State University, circa 1960
5. Dyrenfurth, M., Kozak, M. (eds.): Technological literacy. Council on Technology Teacher Education Yearbook. Peoria, IL, Glencoe 1991
6. Gattiker, U. E (ed.): Technological innovation and human resources. COMSERVE E-Mail message on INTERCOM 1993

7. Gibson, W., Sterling, B.: Technology and the future. Presentation to the Convocation on Technology and Education. Washington, DC, National Academy of Sciences 1993, May 10

8. Gubbins, E. J.: Matrix of thinking skills. Hartford, CT, State Department of Education 1985

9. Hamilton, J. B., Wonacott, M. E.: Updating teachers for tomorrow's technology: A strategy for action. Research & Development Series No. 242. Columbus, Ohio The National Center for Research in Vocational Education 1984

10. Hayes, C.: Four national training systems compared: Achievements & Issues. Occasional Paper No. 114. Columbus, Ohio, The National Center for Research in Vocational Education 1986

11. Henderson, J. V.: "Virtual Realities" as instructional technology. Journal of Interactive Instruction Development, pp. 24-30 (1991, Summer)

12. Hill, F.: Tomorrow's learning environment--Planning for technology: The basics. An ITTE Technology leadership Network Special Report. Alexandria, VA, Institute for the Transfer of Technology to Education, National School Boards Association 1988, December

13. Lipson, J. I.: Educational technology in vocational education. Information Series IN 268. Columbus, Ohio, The National Center for Research in Vocational Education 1984

14. National School Boards Association: New technologies: Key to more productive schools. NSBA Leadership Report, Volume 1. Alexandria, VA, NSBA 1985

15. National Science Foundation: Studies in science, technology and society: Program guidelines. Washington, DC, NSF 1991, October 28

16. Office of Technology Assessment.: Information technology and its impact on American education. OTA Report. Washington, DC, OTA 1982

17. Technology Transfer Institute: Computer and networking conferences and seminars. Santa Monica, CA, TTI 1993

"Working with Projects" Stimulates Basal Aptitudes

Fritz M. Kath
University of Hamburg
Sedanstr. 19
Hamburg, D-20145, Germany

Abstract. "Working with projects" as a teaching form is approached, discussed and judged mainly from an objective point of view even today. And indeed, one can affirm it a great deal. In discussing the so called "key-qualification", "working with projects" is connected with the reorganisation of the metal and electrical trades (1987) and by the same token with the reform of apprenticeship.

In future, "working with projects" will gain in significance, because when teachers and learners are working together in this form basal aptitudes will be stimulated which we call "key-dispositions".

In paper basal aptitudes are differentiated into (key-)qualifications and (key-)dispositions. The difference is cleared up between an "Industrial Training Act" (Britain) and a "Vocational Education Act" (Germany). Ways are considered to enable teachers to prepare themselves to stimulate (key-)dispositions in learners.

Keywords. Working with projects, basal aptitudes, key-qualification, key-dispositions

1 Introduction

"Working with projects" as a teaching form (1) is approached, discussed, and judged mainly from an objective point of view even today. And indeed, it is appreciated quite positively. In discussing the so-called "key-qualifications", "working with projects" is connected with the reorganization of the trades and by the same token with the reform of apprenticeship.

In future, "working with projects" will gain further in importance. When teachers and learners are working together in this teaching form those basal aptitudes will be stimulated which are called "key-dispositions".

2 Two Types of Basal Aptitudes

Basal aptitudes (3) are understood as preconditions of man's activities of such complexity that they may be expounded widely and differently. But they form nevertheless entities which one lives as unities of experience. Thus basal aptitudes are necessarily very abstract categories, for example "conclude consistently" or "to carry responsibility (to be responsible)". Each of these aptitudes may present itself in different contents: "to conclude consistently" for instance demands entirely different activities of thinking when somebody works empirically or hermeneutically, meaning interpreting texts or works of art; the phenomenological way of thinking differs certainly from the deductive way - to mention only a few ways of thinking; to each of them a specific scientific method is assigned; "to carry responsibility" is a basal aptitude of an entirely other type; an example: notwithstanding consistent reflecting I may say, "This person is very dear to me; he is really sick; the medical man doesn't know if he will ever recover; and nevertheless, I will take care of him (though it will not be easy for me)".

These two examples show that basal aptitudes may be essentially the base of two fundamentally differing activities; the first example points on cognitive aptitudes (which express themselves in kinds of skills), and the second one on affective aptitudes (which express themselves in kinds of attitudes). The group of cognitive aptitudes we call (in German) "key-qualifications". These include instances like:

- to think analytically,
- to think decidedly (the above formulated "to conclude consistently" may be included here),
- to think contextually (3, p. 205).

It is a matter of "qualification" "to think", that means a matter of definable skills which man can acquire (2, p. 101). Cognitive qualifications - and this is valid similarly for motoric ones - may be acquired as kind of skills in courses, and whithin a given time. It may be a short time if the skills are simple, as for instance the reading of a measuring instrument, but if the skills are complex, such as the planning of the cycle of operations for a CNC-lathe, supreme mental efforts are to be provided for.

The group of *affective* basal aptitudes we call "key-dispositions" (in German). They include examples like:

- to be flexible,
- to cooperate (to be cooperative),
- to act responsibly.

Here we speak about "dispositions", meaning physical or psychic potentialities of man to be active. Key-dispositions are mainly affective categories. Therefore it is so difficult to describe them objectively. Dispositions develop in each person individually. Thus they are most subjectively and may be assessed only indirectly.

But "dispositions" are learned, too. Yet, as distinguished to the learning of qualifications to promote dispositions is not possible, in a "course for flexibility" or in a "course for responsibility" for example. Dispositions need a long time to develop and the psychical mechanisms for it are still quite unknown. By initiating "social techniques" which may be observed by teachers they may be able to influence -indirectly - such potentialities of their learners.

Only for a few decades we know that (cognitive) qualifications and (affective) dispositions are initiated and controlled by different centers of the human brain. However, generally it is still believed that desirable dispositions seem to develop by themselves.

3 The Reorganization of the Trades and the Reform of Apprenticeship

In 1987 the industrial metal and electrical trades have been rearranged. It was intended, inter alia, to take into account the technological changes. The trades have been arranged anew, now, more according to what they have in common. To point to their differences and organize trades to come to even greater specialization was abandoned. And so 40 metal trades for were reduced to 17, and 20 electrical trades to 8. In 1989 the metal and electrical trades of the Crafts followed suit, and about a year later some of the commercial ones. So we can really speak of a "reorganization of trades".

For more than 10 years many issues have been discussed including those which lead in addition to the reorganization of trades to a reform of the apprenticeship. In this nexus it is important to mention that for the first time it is written in a Training Act (the "...Reorganisation ...Act"): " ... apprentices should plan, execute, check and evaluate the work done in their own responsibility ..." (3). Obviously, for a craftsman it is not enough any more to master the skills needed for one's trade. 'Self-confidence in working' and a 'sense of responsibility' should be demanded explicitly of today's craftsman.

The promotion of basal aptitudes in young people is today a political demand. For years pedagogues have emphasized these objectives to be introduced in training. This means for us, here and now, to direct our special attention to key-dispositions. For, there is no doubt about it that apprentices shall acquire kognitive and motor skills (qualifications): for instance they must learn to find the source of trouble when the production line comes to a halt. But, how should young people learn to become cooperative (this is another key-disposition)? They have been trained by society to live competitively for years!

4 How May Dispositions Be Promoted?

After these preliminary considerations the following way may be offered:

- 1.We have not only to know but to convince ourselves that "learning" is a completely personal process. Yet, it is *not* a process *from within* meaning it is not developed biologically - such processes are called ripen. Learning is interpreted as a personal answer which is initiated by impulses *from without,* by communication of any kind.
- 2. The teaching person has to organize situations that may cause communication which may lead to learning.
- 3. The teaching person has to prepare himself thoroughly to be able to plan differing situations which may suit different learners. For, it is the teacher who is responsible that the apprentices will learn what he intends.

ad 1: It is still common place to believe that the teacher teaches and instructs the learners thinking he is conveying contents to them. This is based on the erroneous assumption that information may be transmitted by means of communication; in other words: information may be conveyed from one person to the other. We have to learn that the meaning of a word or a gesture (that's the information) is not found in the word or in the gesture themselves (i.e. *in* the information) but in the way one reacts to them. In other words: communication does *not depend* on the information which are brought forth, but it rests upon *the reaction* of the person who receives the information. And this depends on the mental structure of his brain which is the result of his personal experiences.

ad 2: Another expression for "organizing learning situations" is "to choose forms (methods) of teaching or instruction". The first expression directs to a real pedagogical engagement the second one underlines a methodical point of view.

When the objective of teaching is, for instance, to promote self-confidence or to strengthen the sense of responsibility then "working with projects" (sometimes it is spoken about "project-oriented teaching" or "project-method") is a suitable means. It is a teaching form in which each learner has to tackle the subject-matter by himself. Alone or in groups the learners will decide about specific objectives concerning the subject-matter. They will plan, design, sketch out, discuss, reject, plan anew, redecide, execute the work, check and evaluate it. And all this they will do by themselves. In all the publications about this teaching from the authors agree that the most important aim of the joint effort may be expressed like this: pass responsibility to the learners, and they will carry it; if they succeed in carrying it their self-confidence will be strengthened; they will learn to communicate one with the other and to cooperate; this style of learning will be better and more proficient than regular class-room work. And the learners will come - now almost casually - to a much deeper understanding of the subject-matter, that is the material target of their work.

This means neither more nor less than the teaching person who decides to introduce "working with projects" as a teaching form must change his personal approach to his work with the learners entirely:

The principal objectives for choosing "working with projects" as a teaching form are to promote key-dispositions within the learners. If this is successful then the subject-matter - this is the target of the work - will be appreciated in special ease and depth - and in a way effortlessly.

It goes without saying that especially here the teacher needs his whole proficiency.

ad 3: How should the teacher prepare himself to promote key-dispositions? Some suggestions are proposed in my paper (3). In this context it must be sufficient to say that key-dispositions can be differentiated into "dispositional elements" for which "social techniques" can be formulated (3, p. 206). Using these techniques the teacher enables himself to evaluate the dispositions of a learner and may draw a structogram of his basal aptitudes (Fig. 1).

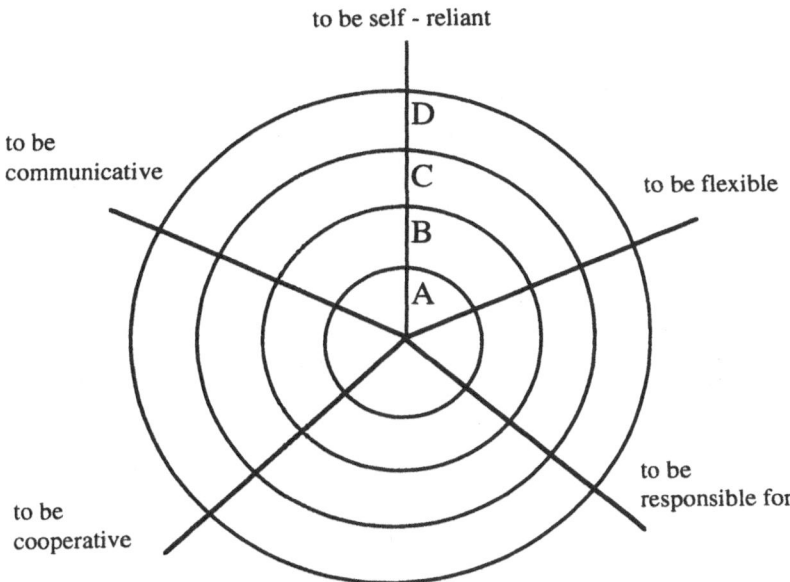

Fig. 1

If a teacher is willing to examine and to tackle the problem of dispositions in this way then he will come to a profound understanding of what dispositions mean. He will then be able to initiate and induce suitable social techniques while organizing learning situations. To what extent these techniques will be accomplished by the learners can not be tested by the teacher, but he may recognize and appreciate it very well.

References

1. Kath, Fritz M.: Die Realisierungsphasen beim "Arbeiten mit Projekten". In: technic didact, 10, 1985, 2, 81-93 (1985)

2. Kath, Fritz M.: Schlüsselqualifikationen - Vorwärts in die Vergangenheit? In: Reetz, L., Reitmann, Th. (eds): Schlüsselqualifikationen. Symposium in Hamburg. Hamburg, Feldhaus 1990

3. Kath, Fritz M.: Das Entfalten von Grundbedürfnissen im Rahmen der Neuordnung und die Arbeit des Unterrichtenden. In: Berufsbildung, 45, 1991, 5/6, 203-209 (1991)

Technological Literacy and Humanization

Ervin Szücs
Eötvös Loránd University
Faculty of Sciences
Rákóczi út.5, Budapest, H-1088, Hungary

Abstract. The difference between the animals and humans: the possibility of transforming the environment to their demands (the ancient Greeks coined for it the term techne). The human is a "tool developing animal". The process of developing creates a whole system: technology. This made it possibile to build a third (technical) environment; without this no human life can be imagined. General culture should include knowledge and values in connection with all of the three environment's types. There is no general culture without natural, social, and technical knowledge. In our age technical knowledge is an organic part of general culture, and without it no general culture (and no humanization, as well) is possible.

Keywords. Technology, culture, literacy, techne

There is a new "popular" word using by policy makers for the "democratization" of education. (Some people are using this word again for technology education!) For example, this year there was a conference in Bulgaria with the title: "Humanization of Schools". What is the meaning of this word "humanization"? The definition in the Longman Dictionary is: humanization = to cause to be human. In Webster's Dictionary: humanization = the fact or condition of being humanized, and humanize = to make human; to have or spread a civilizing influence. In my opinion, really it means not simply human, but "cultured human". Two questions are connected with this:

1. What is the difference between the animals and humans?
2. What do we mean by culture?

1 The Difference Between the Animals and Humans

All living beings are natural beings. Plants and animals are continuously in interaction with their natural environment. The equilibrium of nature is a necessary condition of life, at all. The human is, however, not only a simple natural being; no humanity can exist without society and/or outside of society.

"A being that could live outside society may be a wild beast or a god, but in no way could it be a man ." (Aristotle)

But there are a lot of species living in a so-called society (e.g., ants, bees live in "animal communities"). What is the basic difference between socialized animals and humans? We search for it in the process of activity.

Some animals use some objects found in nature. If the outcome satisfies demands, they use this object (or a similar one) again. From time to time the object may serve as a part of tools (e.g., some monkeys, birds).

The human, beyond the simple biological assimilation, has possession of possibilities of transforming the environment according to their demands.

Humans were created by productive work. They rose out of the animal kingdom because they used not only objects found in nature (as tools), but also developed them to suit their purpose. A human, therefore, is a "tool-developing animal". It must be emphasized that we speak of the development of tools and not simply of their use, as there are examples for the latter even in the animal kingdom. But, only humans are capable of recognizing the imperfection of a tool; they use, shape and modify it to the form best suited to their preconceived purpose. We need a historical approach, without which it is impossible to understand the development of culture and the role of technology. The historical approach needs a sense of direction in the processes of development of technology.

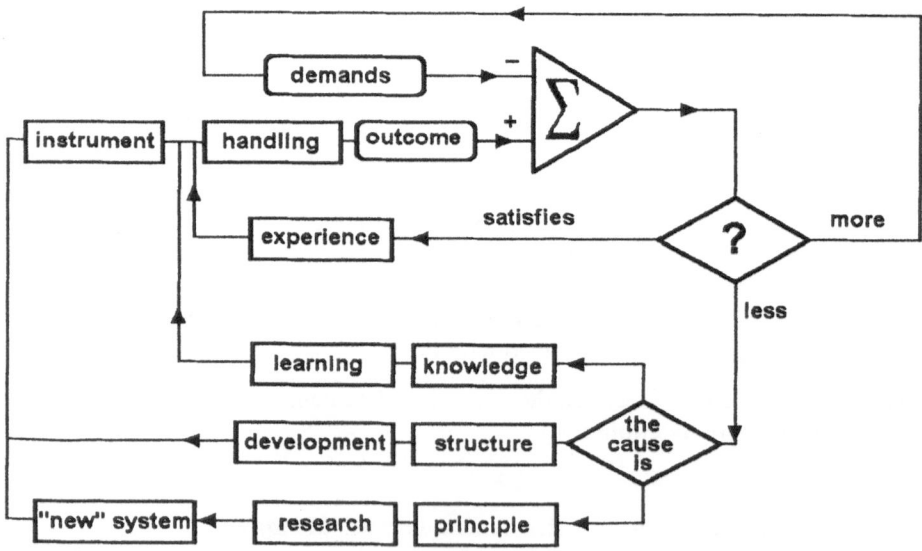

Fig. 1 Form of development of technology

For demonstration, only one example: what is a new device? Is it absolutely new indeed? In fact, technology development has an iterative character (Figure 1). In the beginning we have an instrument. We have to use it, because we had an "a priori" demand. After the handling there are three possibilities:

1. The outcome corresponds to the demand. In this case we have new experience, and we go on with the application.
2. The outcome is beyond expectation. In this case the demand develops further.
3. The outcome does not satisfy our a priori expectation.

In this case we have to analyse: what is the cause? We may be handling (acting) wrong. Then we must learn the correct usage, and after it the application follows. Maybe the system we are using is not "perfect". Now the task is to develop our system. But the most interesting problem is when the basic principle of our instruments is wrong (accordingly: the instrument is out-of-date). In this case we have to research the possibilities to create a new one. But nothing comes out of nothing; the *new* is never absolutely new; "only" a continuation of the past is possible.

This skill or ability belongs only to mankind, and the ancient Greeks coined for it the term techne. The process of developing tools is of paramount importance: on the one hand, it affects human biological development; on the other hand, the individual tools become a whole system, i.e., technology. This made the possibility of building a third (technical) environment; without this no human life can be imagined. This process is characteristic only for mankind. And by developing technology the human develops, too. Therefore, the most important part of humanization is technological literacy.

2 The Meaning of Culture

The basic components of culture can be understood in that case if we know the structure (the most important subsystems) of the environment. As may be seen, there are three parts of the environment. The first is nature, the second society, and the third one technology (as a whole system).

General culture should include knowledge and values in connection with all of the three environments types. There is no general culture without natural, social, and technical knowledge.

Nowadays a person cannot be called qualified and educated unless he or she has got some technical knowledge as well, i.e., the combination of knowledge and purposeful activity that make one able

- to orient herself or himself in the technical environment,
- to adapt herself or himself actively to the natural, the social, and the technical environment,
- to protect and develop the environment (by means of technology),
- to develop personal knowledge and activity.

From these conclusions logically follow: in our age technical knowledge is an organic part of general culture, and without it no general culture (and no humanization, as well) is possible.

This is not a technocratic view. On the contrary, it reflects the fact, that the human with technical illiteracy can destroy the natural environment of mankind and the social environment, as well. In that case the main conditions of human life and humanity will be destroyed.

There are numerous people who think that technological knowledge is a superfluous burden and hinders the development of their personality. The essence of this view is that technical knowledge belongs to the sphere of professional education, while general culture contains purely humanistic elements (or at best "some traces" of natural sciences).

Can such a view be maintained in an age where it is generally recognized that "knowledge has become a direct productive force"? This means among other things that the existence and development of society, and of the individual within it, cannot be imagined without science and its technological application.

In our age there are fashionable trends of thinking which bitterly condemn technology, identifying it with inhuman mechanization. They blame technology for everything, from changes in weather conditions to the spread of cancerous diseases and the pollution of water. Proclamations and literary works are written against "dehumanizing technology". Their authors try to revive the slogan "back to nature", they hold a lot of conferences on the dangers, the curse, and the dehumanizing role of technology and science. These antitechnical manifestations misunderstand the essence and role of technology, because of the following three arguments:

- First, humans were made by work, by the use and development of tools. There exist no art and no human way of life without technology.
- Second, the technical environment is an objective reality.
- Third, the threat to mankind does not consist in technology (and its instruments), but in its inhuman use.

Lamenting over certain harmful effects of technology is as senseless as grieving over the harmful effects (hail, storm, earthquake) of the natural environment while doing nothing against them. Of course, the crucial difference is that natural effects are independent of humans, whereas the effects of the technical environment are man-made. Therefore deliberate human behavior, also taking into account the secondary effects, has a much greater role in weakening - and in certain cases eliminating - the adverse effects of technology.

Humans cannot neglect the technical environment; it only shows her or his lack of knowledge if, instead of trying to live in it and with it, she or he begins to be afraid of it (asking mystical forces to help) or wants to get rid of the environment. There is only one kind of relationship that a cultured human may have with her or his environment (including the man-made environment): to study and classify the phenomena, to recognize their essence and laws, then, in possession of this knowledge, to strive to strengthen the advantageous effects and to reduce the harmful ones.

On the third point, more and more people recognize that technical development, if it is subordinated completely to profit-making, exerts a destructive effect on human relations, culture, and the living world, i.e., on both the social and the natural environment.

We must emphasize that not the technology itself, but its utilization may become dangerous and inhuman. There is no such thing as a humanitarian or an inhuman technology, only technology subordinated either to humanitarian or to inhuman interests, and there are views, goals of development, and uses of technology which are determined by political attitudes.

One of the basic principles (one might say the credo) of our ideology is inherent in the statement that our ideal is not "technicized man", but an anthropocentric technology. The level of technology is determined not only (and not primarily) by the technical perfection of the devices, but by the objectives and direction of their use and by their effect on the development and welfare of the whole society.

For that very reason I am convinced that no humanization is possible without technological literacy, and no humanization in the process of training is possible without general technology education.

4. Didactical Concepts for Advanced Technology

Advanced technology is closely related to the understanding of innovation and as such it will become a significant part of technology education in the future. However, a caution is important. The question is not, for example: Which advanced technology should be explained to learners? Much more important is the question: How can we use advanced technology to develop a better understanding of technology? This leads us directly to the concept of powerful intellectual tools which we will have to use much more in the future than we are doing at present. The identification of intellectual (logical) as well as mental (e.g., positive thinking) tools as a part of innovative thinking represent key initiatives which will become more and more important.

Here again the ARW participants called for both a higher standard and a greater quantity of fundamental work in this arena. They stressed the insight that we must learn to change the paradigms defining our didactic approach. For example, the participants often noticed that we try to develop students' capability with the newly evolved self-learning skills by using traditional instructional methods. This was clearly viewed as undesirable.

Among the innovative approaches a new arsenal of skills has emerged. This includes, but is not limited to, interpersonal didactic group discussions, alternative approaches to the development of problem solutions, and group process approaches to learning. All these activities have the common purpose of developing a transferable picture of the existing and future technological environment and of our capabilities through advanced didactic concepts.

These perspectives were enriched by de Fabio's injection of language and thought concepts into the group's consideration of didactics. Similarly, the notion of modeling has significant generalizable value when extended to didactics. Then too, the unique demands on didactics imposed by the factors associated with sparse populations, self-sufficiency, and great distances as highlighted by Haché and Sharpe stimulated the participants of the workshop to significantly different perceptions of learning.

The macro view of technology, i.e., explorations of how people actually address complicated problems and the didactics associated with the development of more effective capabilities in this arena was presented in a most stimulating fashion by Johnson. The participants noted that ultimately all learning occurred at an individual level, despite many settings where group interaction facilitate the process.

Thought, Language, and Technology in School-Industry Link Projects

Roseanne DeFabio
New York State Education Department
Albany, New York 12234, USA

Abstract. Underlying all school-industry link projects is the assumption that people learn from experience as well as from direct instruction. The Russian psychologist, Lev Vygotsky, emphasized throughout his work the relationship between concepts developed through experience (spontaneous concepts) and those acquired through the mediation of others (scientific concepts). School-industry link projects exemplify the process by which the two types of concepts are brought together in technology education. In this paper we consider how students can be provided with experiences that will develop the spontaneous concepts related to advanced technology and how, through reflecting on those experiences and discussing them with more experienced learners, the spontaneous concepts can be generalized, extended, and developed into scientific concepts. We explore the relevance of Vygotsky's "Zone of Proximal Development" to advanced technological studies. Attention is devoted to the development of the learner, to the roles of the mentor and the teacher, to the concept of "loan of consciousness", and to the relationship between instruction and development. We consider the value of guided practice, keeping in mind Vygotsky's contention that "consciousness and control appear only at the late stages of the development of a function, after it has been used and practiced unconsciously and spontaneously. In order to subject a function to intellectual control, we must first possess it." School-industry link projects can provide students with the spontaneous concepts, the language, and the technological skills for mature functioning in industry.

Keywords. School-industry link projects, Vygotsky's theory of learning, observation, experience, language, technology

"Without action, thought can never ripen into truth." Emerson

There is an ancient and persistent tension between practical, technical education and intellectual, academic development. Plato, in the Republic, presents training in handicraft, trade and the working professions as corrupting of the mind and spirit and detrimental to a man's striving for excellence. Few people today share Plato's view of work and technical education, yet a false dichotomy persists in our division of education into academic and technical programs, and, worse yet, our division of students into academic and technical students. Such division is a disservice to the students and to our society and a contradiction of the life experience of most educated people today. Growing recognition of the benefits of technology education for all students and increasing availability of school-industry link projects may help to heal this harmful division.

It is particularly ironic that a disdain for technical education should exist even in American society where there is a long tradition of respect for the contribution of industry to the development of nations and of individuals. In "The American Scholar," the nineteenth-century writer Ralph Waldo Emerson includes action, or work, among the influences on the scholar. Emerson mentions a number of benefits that the scholar attains from a life of action, and principal among them is language.

"If it were only for a vocabulary, the scholar would be covetous of action. Life is our dictionary. Years are well spent in country labors; in town - in the insight into trades and manufactures; in frank intercourse with many men and women; in science; in art; to the one end of mastering in all their facts a language by which to illustrate and embody our perceptions. . . . This is the way to learn grammar. Colleges and books only copy the language which the field and the work-yard made."

Emerson's recognition that labor is valuable not only for its own sake but for giving us a language by which to make sense of our world is an important one that I will return to, but his argument that work is essential to the full development of all people is especially pertinent today. He concludes his discussion of the benefits of action with an acclamation:

"I hear therefore with joy whatever is beginning to be said of the dignity and necessity of labor to every citizen. There is virtue yet in the hoe and the spade, for learned as well as for unlearned hands."

Emerson's recognition of the value of action and work for developing thought and language reflects a typically American respect for industry and points out the essential relationships among experience, thought, and language. It calls into question the division between academic study and practical work experience. Many recent proposals for restructuring education reflect that same concern in their recommendations that academic education be integrated with experiences from the world outside of school. Ernest Boyer in High School: A Report on Secondary Education decries the practice of "putting students into boxes" labeling some students "academic" and others "non-academic." "Students," he says," are divided between those who think and those who work, when, in fact, life for all of us is a blend of both." (p. 126) Boyer goes on to propose high schools in which academic and work-related education are integrated, and he concludes:

Clearly, if high schools are to offer advanced academic study and career exploration, they must recognize they cannot do it all. High schools must become `connected' institutions, creating networks and specialty schools, drawing upon resources beyond the campus. Part-time lecturers from business and industry and other professionals should be used. And students themselves must be given more responsibility for their education. New teachers, new locations, and new technology are important (p. 129).

Boyer's comments point out not only the importance of "connectedness" in learning but also the necessity of involving business and industry professionals in education if that connectedness is to be experienced by students. Similar sentiments are expressed by John Goodlad in A Place Called School. Arguing for the value of work-related experience for all students, he writes: General education is the best preparation for effective individual functioning and responsible citizenship. . . Vocational education including guided work experience, is an essential, not merely an elective, part of general education. . . This means that vocational education is for all students, not just an alternative to academic studies for the less academically oriented. I want the college bound students to include vocational studies too, just as I want to be sure that students not going to college secure a balanced program in academic subjects. . . . The issue is. . . what kind of education contributes most to economic competence and satisfaction in work and life (pp. 147-??8).

Goodlad and Boyer both make strong cases for the inclusion of work-related education in the programs of all students, but even they seem to see the two aspects of education as separate. It is important and valuable to investigate the "connectedness" of academic and experiential learning, and to examine how they contribute together to the development of the learner. The work of the Russian psychologist, Lev Vygotsky, focuses on the relationship between contextualized, experiential learning on the one hand and formal instruction on the other.

Vygotsky's theory of learning provides a useful framework for analyzing the elements of learning and development and particularly for understanding the relationships among experience, thought, and language. A number of aspects of Vygotsky's theory are particularly relevant to our discussion of advanced technology in school-industry link projects:

– spontaneous concepts - those concepts acquired through our experiences in and observations of the world around us. Such learning is often unconscious and is acquired "incidentally" as the learner tries to accomplish some real purpose.
– scientific concepts - those concepts that are formally taught and that are essential components of a discipline.

"These concepts are schematic and lack the rich content derived from personal experience." (Vygotsky, Thought and Language, p. 108)

The Zone of Proximal Development -

"the distance between the actual developmental level as determined by independent problem solving and the level of potential development as determined through problem solving under adult guidance or in collaboration with more capable peers." (Mind and Society, p. 86)

Vygotsky's research indicates that:

"what is in the zone of proximal development today will be the actual developmental level tomorrow -- that is, what a child can do with assistance today she will be able to do by herself tomorrow." (p. 87)

loan of consciousness - the process by which a competent adult lends his consciousness and control to the learner to help the learner move through the Zone of Proximal Development.

"It is an account of how the more competent assist the young and less competent to reach that higher ground from which to reflect more abstractly about the nature of things. . . .It involves the passing on of ideas from the more able or advanced to the less so. And the medium in which the transmission occurs is language and its products: literacy, science, technology, literature." (Bruner, pp. 73-74)

*the Second Signal System - the world as processed through language in contrast to the world of the senses. This concept, which Vygotsky took from Pavlov's later work, stood for nature transformed by history and culture.

1 Spontaneous and Scientific Concepts

In Vygotsky's view learning is the result of the interpenetration of spontaneous and scientific concepts.

"Two contrasting motions are necessary for the interpenetration of these two types of concepts. Spontaneous or experientially-learned concepts are helped `upward,' as it were, to self-conscious understanding by the path of the scientific or formally-learned concepts 'downward.' But scientific concepts are only helped downward or fully experienced -and thus fully able to be applied to unfamiliar instances - to the extent that spontaneous concepts have worked their way up to actualize them." (Elbow, 1986, pp. 18-19)

This interpenetration is a dynamic process but not an automatic one. For Vygotsky, "the mind grows neither naturally nor unassisted." (Bruner, p. 141) The references to concepts being "helped" in both directions is significant. The helping is provided by the more experienced members of the community who collaborate with the learner. Vygotsky begins Thought and Language with a quote from Francis Bacon, "Nec manus, nisi intellectus, sibi permissus, multam valent; instumentiis et auxilibus res perficitur." (Neither hand alone, nor mind alone can accomplish much without the aids and tools that perfect them.) Bruner explains that as meaning that "intelligence, for Vygotsky, is readiness to use culturally transmitted knowledge and procedures as prostheses of mind," (p.141) Students are helped to acquire the knowledge and procedures they need by their engagement in the purposeful activity of the people around them. Children who come from homes where gardening is a family pastime acquire considerable knowledge and skill in gardening through joining in that activity. Young people engaged in a school-industry link project in landscaping will acquire similar knowledge and skill through joining in the work alongside the professionals and through joining in conversation with them about that work. The resulting knowledge and skills constitute spontaneous concepts that the student acquires, often without even being aware of it.

When students in work-related projects are engaged in classroom study of advanced technology at the same time, they are able to acquire the scientific concepts necessary for consciousness and control of their learning. They acquire an understanding of the concepts observed or experienced in the work experience. They hear from the teacher of other instances of those concepts. They learn technical terms for activities and phenomena and use those terms in describing their own observations and experiences and in listening to the observations and experiences of their peers. The classroom discourse, like the work project, reflects the central Vygotskyan belief in the social nature of learning. "Human learning," he says, "presupposes a specific social nature and a process by which children grow into the intellectual life of those around them." (Mind in Society, p. 88)

When school and industry cooperate to provide students with projects that involve them in work-related experiences a number of benefits accrue to the students:

1. Through engagement in the work-related experience, students have an opportunity to develop those spontaneous concepts related to the technological experiences they encounter.
2. The guidance of an experienced practitioner from the field enables the students to accomplish tasks they are incapable of performing independently.
3. Through formal instruction, students acquire the scientific concepts directly related to the advanced technology learning they are engaged in.
4. In classroom discussion and writing, students use the scientific concepts to reflect on their experience, make connections between prior and new knowledge, and apply those concepts widely.

1.1 Loan of Consciousness

The roles of the adults in the school-industry link projects are crucial to the success of the students. The industry partners (whom we will call "mentors" for convenience) and the classroom teachers are essential to the development of both spontaneous and scientific concepts, though the balance may differ in each case with the mentor holding more responsibility for providing experiences that will lead to development of spontaneous concepts and the teacher for providing the formal instruction that supplies the scientific concepts.

1.2 Zone of Proximal Development

Ideally, both the industry mentors and the classroom teachers will be operating in the student's zone of proximal development. Their responsibility is to observe what the student is almost ready to do and to learn, that is, what he is capable of with collaboration, direction, or some kind of help. That zone is not limitless, and for every learner it will be somewhat different. Vygotsky points out the importance of determining the individual's potential for moving to a higher level of development through collaboration:

It is well established that the child can imitate only what lies within the zone of his own intellectual potential. If I am not able to play chess, I will not be able to play a match even if a chess master shows me how. If I know arithmetic, but run into difficulty with the solution of a complex problem, a demonstration will immediately lead to my own resolution of the problem. On the other hand, if I do not know higher mathematics, a demonstration of the resolution of a differential equation will not move my own thought in that direction by a single step. To imitate, there must be some possibility of moving from what I can do to what I cannot. (Thought and Language, p. 209)

The individualizing of instruction and experience suggested by the need to operate within the learner's zone of proximal development is a positive feature of many school industry link projects. The industry mentors in such projects introduce students to the activities of the industry gradually, moving them through a wide range of experiences as the students demonstrate readiness. Individual pacing allows more able and experienced students to attain a level of mature functioning in the advanced technology related to that industry and all students to acquire at least the relevant spontaneous concepts. The academic teachers, too, try to pace their instruction to the students' development, providing more complex and sophisticated reading material for advanced students and introducing concepts and material more gradually and with more explanation for the less well prepared.

2 Instruction and Training

A major pedagogical element in these projects is imitation. Working alongside an experienced mentor the student imitates the performance of the mentor, solving problems and accomplishing tasks that she could not perform independently. This imitation, however, is not a purely mechanical activity. The purposefulness of the demonstrations and the imitation are indicative of the difference between instruction and training, a distinction that Vygotsky found lacking in many theories of instruction. He describes the difference by referring to Kohler's experiments with animals.

The ape can meaningfully carry out through imitation only what he can carry out independently. Imitation does not move the chimpanzee further along in the domain of intellectual operations. Of course, through training, the ape can learn to carry out much more complex operations than would have been accessible to its own mind. Here, however, the operation is carried out automatically and mechanically as a meaningless habit. It does not constitute a rational and meaningful solution of a problem. Comparative psychology has established several indices that allow us to distinguish intellectual, meaningful imitation from automatic copying. In the first case, the resolution of a problem is learned suddenly - once and forever. It does not require repetition. The error curve falls steeply and suddenly from one hundred percent to zero. Every indication of an independent, intellectual solution is manifested. This solution is attained as a consequence of grasping the structure of the field, of grasping the relationships among objects. With training, however, learning proceeds by trial and error. The learning curve representing mistaken solutions falls slowly and steadily. Learning requires frequent repetition. The training process manifests no meaningfulness and no understanding of structural relations. It is realized blindly and without structure. (Thought and Language, p. 210)

That distinction between instruction and training is essential to insuring that the school-industry link projects result in real learning in advanced technology that contributes to the development of students' intellectual capacities, as opposed to the acquisition of a few specialized, technical skills. There may be a place for training within those projects -keyboarding, for example, is an essential technical skill that can be acquired through training - but the focus of the projects should be on the full development of the student as a thinker and learner. The most important element in meaningful instruction and learning is language.

3 Second Signal System

Vygotsky saw thought and speech as instruments for planning and carrying out actions. In an essay on "Tool and Symbol in Child Development," he writes: Children solve practical tasks with the help of their speech, as well as their eyes and hands. This unity of perception, speech, and action, which ultimately produces internalization of the visual field, constitutes the central subject matter for any analysis of the origin of uniquely human forms of behavior. (Mind and Society, p. 26) The use of speech as a tool distinguishes human learners from the animal subjects in Kohler's studies whose tool use was independent of sign or symbol use. Human learners, in contrast, use language as the principal tool for accomplishing tasks and planning future actions.
According to Vygotsky:

"... the most significant moment in the course of intellectual development, which gives birth to the purely human forms of practical and abstract intelligence, occurs when speech and practical activity. . . converge." (p. 24)

From that moment speech and action become "part of one and the same complex psychological function" directed toward the solution of practical problems, and the more complex the problem is the greater importance played by speech in the functioning.

Sound pedagogical practice provides for the necessary combination of speech and action and recognizes that programs that privilege action at the expense of language opportunities are as inadequate as those that privilege learning through language to the exclusion of practical experience. Exemplary programs are those in which the practical experiences and the language experiences are integrally related.

What kind of language activities might we expect to see in successful school-industry link projects? First we look for a great deal of conversation between the student and the mentor and teacher. Language scholars stress the importance to children's language development of frequent opportunities to try out their thinking in conversation with trusted others. Michael Halliday argues that:

"What matters most to a child is how much talking goes on around him, and how much he is allowed and encouraged to join in. There is strong evidence that the more adults talk to a child and listen to him and answer his questions, the more quickly and effectively he is able to learn." (p. 201)

Early in their experiences in a project, students may spend more time listening to the talk of the more experienced people around them than in speaking. Gradually they acquire the vocabulary not only to ask specific and pertinent questions but also to describe what they are doing or observing. Continued experience leads to an ability to pose problems, propose solutions, report observations, predict consequences, and so on. Those abilities will be essential for the student trying to communicate meaningfully with others in the project about the work they are engaged in. Trying out the language of advanced technology is a crucial step in solidifying and clarifying their own understanding of that technology and its uses.

Shirley Brice Heath, in Ways with Words, points out the importance of talk to students' intellectual development. In order to achieve academic success, she says, students must be immersed in talk with members of the academic community, and that talk should be talk about the work of that community of learners, talk that poses problems and investigates them, and, especially, "talk about talk" with the teacher pointing out the language conventions that are used within a particular discipline.

The mentor, as we saw earlier, necessarily involves the student in many of these forms of talk as they work together. The questions and comments that pass between mentor and students, the directions given, followed, and repeated, and the reports on results of their mutual endeavors - all immerse students in technological language.

The classroom teacher, however, may have the greater responsibility for calling the students' attention to that language - pointing out to them particular vocabulary they are acquiring and the fine distinctions that vocabulary allows them to make, analyzing with students the differences between common use of some terms and their technical meanings, and helping them extend their emerging technological understandings from the immediate context of the project to a wide range of contexts.

Heath's belief in the importance of talk is corroborated by Mike Rose in Lives on the Boundary with its descriptions of the instructional practices that he first came to appreciate as a student and later adopted as a teacher. Rose describes the value of talk in his own education:

"My teachers modeled critical inquiry and linguistic precision and grace, and they provided various cognitive maps for philosophy and history and literature. They encouraged me to make connections and to enter into conversations - present and past - to see what talking a particular kind of talk would enable me to do with a thorny philosophical problem or a difficult literary text." (p. 58)

Rose's experience confirms the importance not only of talk but of the particular type of talk that is most valuable to students who lack prior experience in the area of study (i.e. they lack the spontaneous concepts). Like Heath, he emphasizes the value of talk about talk --- talk that makes explicit the connections between newly encountered concepts or events and what was previously experienced, talk in which the teacher openly models the thinking and the language that students are trying to acquire.

Not only talk but also reading and writing are essential tools for students in advanced technology study. Spoken and written language have different functions within every discipline, and for full participation in the discourse of that discipline students need proficiency in the written language as well as the spoken. As with the acquisition of oral language, immersion in the language is the most important factor in the development of proficiency in writing within a discipline. That immersion requires extensive opportunity to read and to write within the discipline.

Like every other discipline, advanced technology has its own literature, with distinctive conventions. Students learn those conventions through reading extensively in the literature of the discipline. In their reading they encounter the conventions of language and form, but they may not consciously focus on them. They acquire, as we saw in the explanation of spontaneous concepts, an unconscious awareness of what constitutes good writing in that discipline at the same time that they are grappling with the ideas and content of the discipline.

In providing regular opportunities for students to write about their experiences and understanding of advanced technology, the teacher helps them to achieve conscious awareness of their learning. Bacon's assertion that "writing makes an exact man" is pertinent. To make her thinking clear to an [absent] audience, the student must not only formulate precisely her own understanding of the concepts she is writing about, but she must also elaborate her own thinking to a much greater extent than is required in face to face conversation.

Many kinds of writing are valuable for students in school-industry link projects. Informal writing-to-learn activities give students a chance to explore and develop their own emerging understandings, and has enormous heuristic value for the students. Writing that is more public and more formal gives the student a chance to be part of the professional discourse of that discipline.

The report of the Secretary's Commission on Achieving Necessary Skills (SCANS) of the U.S. Department of Labor, like other major reform reports, identifies reading, writing, listening, and speaking as "basic skills" that students need for the workplace. But in that report those basic skills are defined in a rather limited way to "reflect the workplace contexts in which they are applied." (p. 4) More helpful to understanding the complex demands of language use that is necessary for today's students is Naisbitt's Re-Inventing the Corporation in which he argues that an educated, skilled work force for the new information society needs three "new basics" - Thinking, Learning, and Creating. Naisbitt defines "thinking" as:

"... the ability to synthesize and make generalizations, to divide into categories, to draw inferences, to distinguish between fact and opinion, to put facts in order to analyze a problem" (p. 126)

Identifying areas of consonance and dissonance with the opinions of others in discussion groups, keeping a dialogue journal in which to record an ongoing conversation with the texts read in the class, and writing to discover and to convey one's own opinions, judgments, and analyses are all experiences in thinking and using language critically.

Naisbitt makes a strong case for the relationship of writing to thinking, learning, and creating. He quotes William Zinsser's statement that "clear thinking becomes clear writing: one can't exist without the other" and reasons from that to the conclusion that we must "strengthen the writing curriculum as an avenue to sharpen thinking." The experiences for strengthening the writing curriculum that he suggests include wider dissemination of the National Writing Project model of teachers and students writing together, increased participation of professional writers in teaching creative writing in the schools, and attention to writing across the curriculum where "the idea," as Naisbitt puts it, "is not to 'teach' writing as such but to use writing to teach all subjects." (p. 134) Evidence of the value of writing for students in occupational and technology programs is abundant.

The work of Naisbitt and the research of Rose, Heath, and Halliday suggest some common principles for instructional practices to develop students' proficiency in technological discourse:

1. Classroom experiences involve students in many different kinds of talk. Especially important are opportunities to describe experiences, summarize readings, label and classify features of objects or events, and compare and analyze experiences.

2. Much of classroom talk is "talk about talk" --- calling attention to features of the thinking and the language use that the class is engaged in.
3. Teachers model and explain the kinds of thinking and language use that they want students to learn --- pointing out the connections they are making, the questions they are posing, the criteria they are using to evaluate something, and the particular language forms they are using.
4. Writing-to-learn activities are a regular part of the daily classroom experience and provide opportunities for students to try out thoughts and language before going public with them.
5. Mini-lessons focus on direct instruction of particular skills or language conventions and are followed by immediate opportunity for applying the skill in a piece of real writing.
6. Reading, talking about reading, writing about reading, and reading each other's writing are essential to learning the conventions of written language.
7. Every discipline that students study in school has its own language conventions. Students learn both the concepts and the language of those disciplines by immersion and guided practice in the ongoing conversation of the discipline.

4 Model Programs

In one technical high school, students in an animal care program kept extensive written records of the operation of the program, including design and maintenance of the facility, plans for expansion and improvement, and the daily diet and activities of each of the animals. They used technical language that they had acquired from consulting manuals for the care of each species. Guiding visitors through the "zoo," the students showed remarkable poise and authority in explaining the distinguishing features of each animal or species, pointing out which ones were compatible with one another and which were not, describing the dispositions and natures of all the creatures, indicating which ones needed special care, and reminding us, ever so gently, of the realities of the food chain when we approached the cage of mice kept conveniently near the python. The engagement of those students in the activities of the animal care program looked much more like a professional business than a typical classroom, and their ability to read, write, listen, and speak to acquire, interpret, and transmit information and to analyze problems and make judgments and decisions was evident in everything they were doing.

The sad fact is that in that school the same engagement and the same rigorous thinking and language use were not evident in the other areas of the curriculum. No attempt was being made to connect the knowledge and understanding and language skills that the students acquired in the animal care program with their other courses. Even in the English class there was no evidence of students' writing of stories, poems, or even reports that drew on their specialized knowledge and no evidence of opportunities for reading literature and non-fiction related to their interests as a way of broadening their language competence. As a result, many students were not successful in the other areas of the school program and most of them had poor scores on the traditional measures of verbal ability. Good thinking and language use require constant and connected opportunities to talk about and write about important ideas and topics and to build on and expand areas of competence.

Some programs focus on connectedness. At another vocational high school where the major emphasis was on programs in building trades, students in the English class were competing in a local speech contest sponsored by a real estate agency. They had researched the building codes and zoning restrictions for their neighborhood and were using their technical knowledge of the material and labor costs to argue for the development of low cost single dwelling homes to replace decaying apartment complexes. In the same school another English class was working with a visiting poet to write poems of their own personal experiences.

Another school had a media program which involved students in writing, producing, and editing videos on current issues (e.g. gun control in the schools, AIDS prevention, teenage depression). To research the material and techniques for their own videos students viewed a number of professional documentaries on similar topics, visited the local cable station to consult with technicians there, did research in the library, and interviewed students and community members. They took notes, discussed script ideas, wrote and edited their scripts. They rehearsed their parts in the video, taped and re-taped section after section, directed and critiqued each other's performances, and edited and released the final product. All of this activity took place in an atmosphere that, like that of the animal care program, was more like a professional business than a typical classroom --- and this in a high school for students who could not function successfully in a regular high school. The focus of the program was media technology, but the range of language experiences and learning, as well as the understanding of significant concepts from across the curriculum, was impressive.

One final example --- in an alternative high school in a large city school system, students who had dropped out of regular programs or returned to school after release from drug rehab programs or prison terms were enrolled in a variety of vocational programs: health care, technology, and cosmetology. In that school the main text in the eleventh grade English class was an anthology of writing by former students of the school. The students read and analyzed poems and stories by young people like themselves. They talked about the writing techniques the authors had chosen; they evaluated pieces and compared them to each other and to the work of professional writers. They worked on pieces of their own to be included in future editions, meeting with their peers in writing groups to critique each other's work and offer suggestions for revision and to decide which pieces from the class should be recommended for the anthology. In the same school the journalism class produced a newspaper that contained news articles, feature stories, and editorials on topics of concern to the community. Issues like child care, public health programs, employment counseling, and unemployment regulations figured in the pages of the newspaper as they did in the lives of the students. The classroom teacher was assisted regularly by a professional newspaper reporter who helped the students not only with the technical concerns of layout and printing but, more importantly, with the techniques of information gathering and reporting.

All of these programs were in high schools especially for vocational education, but in every one of them excellent opportunities for thinking, learning, and creating were present. The students were not limited to filling out application forms, composing memos, writing business letters, or filling out order forms or insurance claims --- the kinds of writing often associated with the workplace and far too often the extent of the writing opportunities in programs for the non-college bound. The students were engaged in rigorous and diverse activities that allowed them to develop the knowledge and the language of mature thinkers. These programs illustrate the real value that school-industry links projects can have for students and suggest several points about the role of technology education:

1. Technology education, like vocational education, is, as Goodlad argued in
   A Place Called School, "an essential, not merely an elective part of general
   education. . . . This means that vocational education is for all students, not just
   an alternative to academic studies for the less academically oriented." (p. 147)
2. Advanced technology is an important area of academic investigation in its own
   right. Not only is a combination of experiences in the arts, sciences, and
   technology beneficial for all students in high school, but college degree
   programs are available in all of those areas. Students who choose to pursue a
   degree in technology will require a thorough understanding of the theory and
   practice of that discipline, just as they would in any discipline.
3. The integration of academic study and hands-on experience is an effective way
   of helping many at-risk students to achieve the desired learning outcomes set
   for all students. Academic study is made easier when its application to real
   world situations is apparent. The Grant Commission on The Forgotten Half:
   Non-College Youth in America endorses "a combination of conceptual study
   with concrete applications and practical problem-solving" as most effective for
   many students. (p. 129)
4. The goal of vocational programs and of school industry links projects,
   according to the interim report of the Grant Commission is not to prepare
   students for specific jobs but to motivate students "to acquire the skills and
   knowledge they need for both work and active citizenship." (p. 51)

School-industry link projects are not a substitute for academic study but a way of connecting academics to the world outside of school. They should not limit the future possibilities of students but should open up new possibilities for learning, thinking, and creating.

References

1. Boyer, E.: High school: A report on secondary education. New York, Harper Collins 1985

2. Bruner, J.: Actual minds, possible worlds. Cambridge and London, Harvard University Press 1986

3. Elbow, P.: Embracing contraries: Explorations in learning and teaching. New York, Oxford University Press 1986

4. Goodlad, J.: A place called school. New York, McGraw-Hill 1984

5. Halliday, M. A. K.: Language as social semiotic. Baltimore, MD: University Park Press 1978

6. Heath, S. B.: Ways with words: Language, life and work in communities and classrooms. New York, Cambridge University Press 1983

7. Naisbitt, J.: Reinventing the corporation.

8. Rose, M.: Lives on the boundary: A moving account of the struggles and achievements of America's educational underclass. New York, Penguin Books

9. The Secretary's Commission on Achieving Necessary Skills: What work requires of schools: A SCANS report for America 2000. Washington, DC U.S. Department of Labor 1991

10. Vygotsky, L.: Thought and language. Cambridge, MA: M. I. T. Press 1962

11. Mind in society: The development of higher psychological processes. In: M. Cole, S. Scribner, V. John-Steiner, E. Souderman (eds.). Cambridge, MA: Harvard University Press 1978

12. Youth and America's Future: The William T. Grant Commission on Work, Family and Citizenship. The Forgotten Half: Non-college youth in America. Washington, DC, The William T. Grant Commission on Work, Family and Citizenship 1988

Technology Education: The Rural Context Factor

George J. Haché and Dennis B. Sharpe
Memorial University of Newfoundland
Faculty of Education
Prince Phillip Drive, St. John's, A1B 3X8, Canada

Abstract. The delivery of an effective technology education program in rural communities, where less than ideal circumstances may exist, typically presents many challenges to educators compared to teaching in the often relative affluence of urban centres. The unique characteristics of rural communities, as well as their particular social and cultural milieu, must be considered along with a variety of program delivery options that utilize resources from both within and outside the community.

Keywords. Technology education, rural communities, curriculum delivery, constraints, options, choices

1 Introduction

A recent document entitled A Lot to Learn contains a discussion and recommendations for the future of education and training in Canada. In it, the Economic Council of Canada (1992) indicates a need for a coherent educational system that includes the need for greater linkages between learning and the labour market and the development of partnerships in education. This is supported by many other current government documents in Canada which additionally concur on the importance of tecnological development and technological literacy (see for example, Canada Prosperity Secretariat, 1992; Human Resource Development Committee, 1990). A perusal of educational and training developments of most other countries reveals similar perspectives. Kerre (1990), in his article Technology Education and World Development, summed it up by saying "it is becoming increasingly evident around the world that technology education is of national priority and that each learner in school should be exposed to it" (p. 40).

Responding to the need for a quality, relevant technology education program is not unique to Canada but an international challenge. An examination of recent curricula across several countries reveals a wide variety of approaches, each with a unique view of technology education (Ratt, 1992; Bensen, 1992). It is understandable, that in a world consisting of communities spread through diverse urban, rural and remote areas, there are wide ranging views and controversy on this subject. Definitions of technology education abound, and dialogue on what constitutes a good curriculum stimulates discussions at regional, national and international gatherings.

Identifying an appropriate program of technology education has provided educators with an opportunity to reflect on how standards for technology education can serve to enhance the opportunity for youth to have meaningful school experiences, regardless of the communities in which they reside. Those educators attempting to incorporate a worthwhile technological education program in rural, remote, and economically less affluent communities are hampered by conditions that are peculiar to these areas (Elliot, 1987).

The premise on which much of technology education is derived has been a dynamic interaction based with on an assumption that resources are available for curriculum development and implementation. This is plausible in the relative affluence of many urban and suburban school settings, however, the often resource poor, isolated, rural communities with their schools and students are often forgotten or neglected as educators ponder over curriculum issues. Sharratt, McClain & Zehm (1992) depict this problem by stating that:

"Educators in rural high schools are faced with a severe challenge: how can we prepare our students for life and work in a rapidly changing world when the schools are located in isolated settings, and lack the resources or incentives necessary for change? Rural schools, which have difficulty securing adequate resources for program innovation and which offer limited partnerships with diverse businesses and industries, find themselves caught in the difficult position of trying to prepare their students for a rapidly changing technological society." (p. 21)

It is the delivery of technology education under such difficult, challenging and less than ideal circumstances that this paper attempts to address.

2 Technology Education

The literature shows that fundamentally, all technology education programs are rooted in social and economic factors that determine the manner of existence of communities (Hendley & Lyle, 1992; Nováková, 1992), but there are considerable variations in the direction taken by different nations. These range on a continuum from utilitarian, with a focus on acquiring pre-employment knowledge and skill development, to the attainment of general technical knowledge and concepts and attitude formation for academic education (Prime, 1992; Ropohl, 1992; and Lauda, 1992)

In general, communities respond with unique programs of technology education, each designed to offer youth a broad range of opportunity (Haland, 1992). A close review of the various programs reveals that they have some common characteristics. They frequently attempt to simplify a growing technological knowledge base with a focused curriculum activity. They espouse liberal use of hardware, ranging from traditional craft tools to advanced computerized systems.

Technology education generally extends an empowering characteristic through the development of knowledge, skill, and attitude. Respectability of the subject is sought by providing an environment that allows individuals to acquire confidence to learn and use the method and content of technology and to eventually lead productive lives (Page, 1992). Prevalent, is the indigenous technology that exists in the area of the community. Characteristically, each application strives to foster positive attitudes towards technology, contribute to a perspective on future occupations, and offer a structure to encourage children toward a productive livelihood. Educators use technology education to provide a realistic contextual perspective of an increasingly complex world. Among the determinants that share the technology education agenda are a range of social factors. These are not as explicitly stated in curriculum descriptions but become evident in the context used to describe each program. Readiness for a livelihood in a technological world, employment, choosing a career, and decision making related to a host of technological problem scenarios ranging from environmental protection to learning how to become a contributor in a learning culture are but a few examples. (Richardson, 1992; DeVries, 1992; Dugger, 1992; Plant, 1992; Donghong, 1992).

With the diverse collection of social and contextual considerations that contribute to, and influence technology curriculum, and which tend to be unique for each nation, it is expected that a commonly agreed upon ground for what may be called technology education may be evasive. In particular, it will likely be less evident for rural communities.

3 What Are Rural Communities?

Like a definition of what constitutes a relevant technology program, a definition of a rural community may be nationally or locally defined. Population size may be a consideration. In parts of Canada, for example, towns with populations up to 10,000 people, villages up to 1,000, and hamlets with less than 100 persons may be considered rural (Hodge and Qadeer, 1983). Britain's Department of the Environment uses a size of 10,000, the United Nations uses 20,000, while Japan uses a ceiling of 30,000 people as defining a rural community (Lewis, 1979). What appears to be a pattern is that rural is defined in comparison with the larger population centres in each country.

Rural areas are characteristically different from urban areas in ways other than population size and density. In the context of education, geographic location and isolation, access to resources and communication links to and from other communities also distinguish what is rural (Szücs, 1992), and tend to compound the delivery of even basic educational services let alone a technology education program.

Access to and use of technology is also a distinguishing characteristic between rural and urban communities. Although residents in rural areas have an increasing access to much the same materials and information technology that residents of urbanized areas do, there are noticeable differences in how they perceive and deal with the technology (Jeffery, Lehr, Haché, 1992).

Culture, particularly evident through the expectations and behaviour of residents, also distinguishes rural from urban centres. Cohen (1982) points out that rural cultures are not inherently international in perspective; rather they are defined through their own characteristics and culture in terms of inherently unique experiences that are usually not as heavily steeped in technology in the same manner evident in urban centres. He also states that it is the locally defined experiences that have value in that they mediate the identity of a nation.

Research and literature provides evidence that the particular social and cultural characteristics evident in rural areas are factors in youth's equitable access to a formative view of the technological world. For example, the presence of jobs (that utilizes technology available in the local area) for youth to observe, contributes, in a limited way, to their knowledge base of existing career options. Access to persons and services that can supply or lead to information on technology may well enhance a youth's career options (Jeffery et al., 1992). However, the mere opportunity to seek information about what it is like to work in a technological world, or in some centre other than the one in which the individual resides is often unavailable. This general paucity of a technological presence, of "mentors" or persons that serve to create dreams, images, or visions that encourage and challenge youth to search the technological world is therefor a disadvantage for rural youth, and contributes to a relative absence of strategies that youth collect during school years, strategies used to focus on finding work, creating enterprise, and making career decision (Jeffery et al., 1992).

Also evident in rural areas are the close physical and psychological ties to adult members that serve as reference groups for youth. Rural adult members are more likely to have "similar" interest background, training, technological perspectives and status. Beyond internalizing opinion from community reference groups, rural youth typically gather career related information in schools and largely rely on parents for opinion to explain or compliment the information they have collected. Parents, on the other hand, are not entirely familiar with career counselling and struggle when attempting to provide assistance to youth, particularly on matters related to technological careers.

Overall, career and guidance opportunities are not uniformly available in rural communities. In their absence, youth are forced to proceed with a reliance on individual notions of common sense, casual advise from friends, and the influence of dominant cultural values when contextualizing the technology useful in their lives and future options. For youth this results in a modulated view of technological career expectations.

4 Affect on Rural Education

However, there are deviations in the above scenario, especially when we survey the growth of technology education in other nations. Not all communities experience equal growth with the "new technology" in the same manner. Although present communication facilities are serving as a new basis for the distribution of technological knowledge and advancements, not all communities have equal access to these resources and are compelled to rely on the technology that exists in their communities (Londono, 1992). The menace is that an ever expanding technological capability, evident in nations that can afford the advanced technology, will pattern a definition of what constitutes a meaningful experience in technology education for others. What challenges educators is the development of a perspective of technology education that harmonizes the relative differences and degree of technological sophistication acquired by various populations and experienced in various communities in regions of the world.

There are departures that encourage this challenge and which serve to provide strength to definitions of technology education. Educators from rural and less affluent areas report of technology education they believe to be relevant in the context of their particular country and culture (Ridgeway, Passey, 1992). Environmental influences in technology education, indigenous technology, advocating a technology that can improve the human condition of a community, seeking a technology education program which is "accountable for" (with a clear connection to its contribution to sustaining a livelihood in that nation) are among the examples (Kapiyo, 1992; Richardson, 1992; Plant, 1992). Generally, these variations of technology education collectively contribute to a larger view of what constitutes a meaningful technology programs.

5 Options and Constraints

In any given school situation there are typically options and constraints on the delivery of the technology curriculum. Basic elements are:

(a) the nature and composition of the curriculum;
(b) teacher attitude and expertise;
(c) locally accessible community resources;
(d) availability of external resources;
(e) in school resources; and
(f) the students of different ages, levels and abilities.

Each of these may vary in any school setting and are subject to change. All are influenced to some extent by the changing external context which is composed in part of the economy, government policies and funding, political forces, and technological advancement. The ruralness of the school, as discussed earlier, flavours each element and variable. Curriculum delivery options are therefore not static, but are dependent upon a composite, at any given point in time, of all components working together (the more harmoniously the better!).

The actual technology education curriculum is obviously a key part of this construct. Its organization and the level of specificity of the composite elements may or may not allow individual school or teacher choices in terms of modification, adaptation or delivery. Often though, student assignments, tasks, projects and activities (including design and problem solving) allow for local input and determination, and can thus be oriented to a particular (rural) community setting and deal with critical issues within that context. "Local" options may, with some foresight, be built into an effective technology education curriculum. This would allow for individual schools to develop locally needed curriculum content.

Teachers are among the most influential variables in the struggle to operationalize a culturally relevant technology education program. Successful teachers recognize the technology resources and conditions that are potentially useful in each community to build confidence and technological ability in the context of rural cultures. They need to have considerable initiative and be able to adapt to potentially difficult conditions; have an intuitive view of the local culture; and build a resource base with the variety of options that exist in the community. Additionally, a number of social characteristics of rural youth may need to be considered by the technology teacher. These include:

(a) the bonding strengths of the young person to parents, peers, other significant adults, home and community;
(b) acceptance of the notion that a rural home community may be the best or only place to be for individuals;
(c) recognition that fear of not being able to compete successfully elsewhere is real for youth who reside in remote communities;
(d) be able to identify role models in rural communities that have achieved success using the technologically productive implements found in local situations (in instances, the adaptation may be one of "surviving" with few or no career prospects); and
(e) recognition of the difficult path young people take when they leave a home community for career purposes by building manner of locating support networks that reside in unfamiliar communities.

Overall, teachers need to be able to function in environments that are not only culturally latticed, but need to see that in spite of a scarcity of advanced technological resources, there is still a technological education to be developed and delivered.

In addition to the above considerations, the teacher also needs some tangible resources to work with. Under the typical constraints of a rural teaching situation, the potentially available and accessible resources within the local community and the school, as well as those external to the community, need to be taken into account. Locally, there may be individual expertise, or on a larger scale, business/industry partnership opportunities (facilitating for example, cooperative type learning experiences); while external resources such as satellite access, distance education and computer networking might be utilized to provide an expanded use and perspective of technology education beyond the confines of the local community. Within the actual school site, facilities typically exhibit tremendous variety, ranging from the very rudimentary shared classroom space to well equipped laboratories for technology education. There may also be facilities outside the confines of the school building that can be accessed. Each situation presents a range of options for program delivery and will often test the ingenuity of individual teachers.

In a "broader" community, the sharing of resources may be possible where air, road or sea transportation is available. Riggs (1987), in his report on improving education in small schools, recommended that the use of mobile laboratory units be made available. He also strongly supported the notion of using distance education technology to help deliver programs.

6 Delivery Choices

The delivery of a program for technology education needs to be considered from the perspective of a strategy that focuses continuous development. Mosna (1992) indicated that it is best to start with a rudimentary group of activities and then strive to reach a maximum delivery model. Also, in the context of an ever expanding base of information, the delivery of a particular pattern of technology education may need to adjust to a view that the implementation needs constant vigilance and adjustment.

Strategies useful in responding to a need to develop an appropriate and culturally relevant technology education for rural schools might consider various combinations of the following approaches:

(a) Greater use of simulation and modelling of technological conditions and events that are identifiable to teachers and students in their own communities while continuing to be relevant within the educational requirements of local or national curriculum. (Note, many Canadian schools are authorized and encouraged to develop "local options" programs in technology education, and thus directly deal with local needs and activities.)

(b) Use of enterprise type education to focus technology education. This recognizes the unique relationship that school can have to enhance the economic awareness in rural communities as well as address entrepreneurial skills within a technology focus.

(c) The adopt-the-school process by business or industry can potentially offer the dramatic technological availability found more usually in urban centres (Ross, 1989). It is interesting that this approach can be used with industries or businesses from outside the local area as well as within.

(d) Recognition of the power of media such as video and tele-conference that promote distant delivery of technology programs. Satellite links to urban centres, and work emulations that promote exchange of services from remote areas with the use of computers and modems readily demonstrate technology as well as bring resources into the school. Bulletin boards that open channels of communications between rural schools and information sources have greatly expanded the technological awareness of youth in some locations. (For example: the Province of New Brunswick in Canada offers Bulletin Board Service (BBS); and Newfoundland is currently developing a similar service called STEMNET. Both offer teachers and students a means of capturing information and technology from other locations.)

(e) Communities use of distant career counselling for parents and adults in partnerships with technology education along with the establishment of "Career Hot-Lines" that can respond to both youth and parent career inquiries over telephone lines and facsimile where available.

(f) Pursuit of regional perspectives that are unique yet in harmony with that of other communities can be facilitated by the sharing of resources such as mobile facilities. This additionally provides flexibility to rural regions by diminishing the expense of a technology program for a single community.

(g) More deliberate integration of other subject matter into technological activity and vis-versa. An "across the curriculum approach" that utilizes mathematics, science, social studies, and other academic subjects creates relevance in technological activity (McKitrick & Nagel, 1986). Systematic modelling of multi-discipline technological activity using not only all the relevant subjects in a school but also the information and technological sources found in community business and individuals adds a greater dimension to the program.

(h) Greater use of tele-conference technology to build a profession of active technology teachers who can generate curriculum, in-service peer teachers, share expertise, gather the latest news on technology education developments, and exchange views with other technology teacher groups.

In conjunction with many of the above suggestions, design and problem solving processes might be considered very applicable. In fact, Williams (1992) suggests, in his discussion of technology education in less developed areas, that such approaches "apply to students regardless of the cultural context of the school or country" (p. 53). Certainly they would apply in many rural settings.

7 Conclusion

The need for a quality technology education program is well established in most countries, and numerous approaches have been developed in terms of curriculum development and delivery, but such approaches have not typically or specifically considered the unique problems and circumstances of rural, isolated areas (no matter how they are defined). Yet through a variety of delivery mechanisms, within a framework of options and constraints, opportunities for quality programs that enhance the development of rural youth within the context of their own community, social milieu and country, can be utilized in an effective way.

References

1. Bensen, J. M.: Technology & education: global perspectives, opportunities and challenges. In: D. Blandow, M. Dyrenfurth (eds.) Technological literacy, competence and innovation in human resource development. Proceedings, Weimar 1992

2. Brook, M.: Rural outreach: Connecting distance networks. Paper presented at the Annual Convention of the American Psychological Association. Los Angeles, CA. 1985 (ERIC document Reproduction Service No. ED 268 417)

3. Canada Prosperity Secretariat. Inventing our future: an active plan for Canada's prosperity. Ottawa: author, 1992

4. Cohen, A. P. (ed.): Belonging: identity and social organisation in British rural cultures. Manchester, U. K., Manchester University Press and St. John's, Institute of Social and Economic Research, Memorial University of Newfoundland 1982

5. Donghong, C. H.: A successful example of out-of-school education biological technology education. In: D. Blandow, M. Dyrenfurth (eds.) Technological literacy, competence and innovation in human resource development. Proceedings, Weimar 1992.

6. Dugger, W.: Mission 21: a new approach to teaching technology education in primary schools. In: D. Blandow, M. Dyrenfurth (eds.) Technological literacy, competence and innovation in human resource development. Proceedings, Weimar 1992.

7. Economic Council of Canada.: A lot to learn: education and training in Canada. Ottawa, Minister of Supply and Services 1992

8. Elliot, J.: Students at risk. (Report No. RC 016 362). Washington, DC, Office of Educational Research and Improvement (1987 (ERIC Document Reproduction Service No. ED 285 708)

9. Haland, B.: Technology as a subject in general education: trends from selected western countries. In: D. Blandow, M. Dyrenfurth (eds.) Technological literacy, competence and innovation in human resource development. Proceedings, Weimar 1992.

10. Hendley, D., Lyle, S.: Vocational education and the role of technology. In: D. Blandow, M. Dyrenfurth (eds.) Technological literacy, competence and innovation in human resource development. Proceedings, Weimar 1992.

11. Hodge, G. D., Qadeer, M. A.: Towns and villages in Canada: The importance of being unimportant. Toronto, ON: Butterworth 1983

12. House, J. D.: Going Away And Coming Back: Economic life and
migration in small Canadian communities. St. John's, NF: Institute of Social and
Economic Research, Memorial University 1989
13. Human Resource Development Committee:Learning to win, training and
national prosperity. Ottawa, National Advisory Board on Science and Technology
1990
14. Jeffery, G., Lehr, R., Haché, G.: Empowering parents to support youth career
development: An interim report. In: Canadian Journal of Counselling, 26, 4, 240-
255 (1992)
15. Kapiyo: Technology education in democratic Kenya. In: D. Blandow, M.
Dyrenfurth (eds.) Technological literacy, competence and innovation in human
resource development. Proceedings, Weimar 1992
16. Kerre, B. W.: Technology education and world development: challenges and
opportunities for education in Africa. In: Journal of Epsilon Pi Tau, XVI (1), 40-
46 (1990)
17. Lauda, D.: Internationalization the curriculum in technology education. In: D.
Blandow, M. Dyrenfurth (eds.) Technological literacy, competence and innovation
in human resource development. Proceedings, Weimar 1992
18. Lewis, G. J.: Communities. London, David & Charles 1979
19. Londono, E.: The role of technology education in the national development of
third world countries. In: D. Blandow, M. Dyrenfurth (eds.) Technological
literacy, competence and innovation in human resource development. Proceedings,
Weimar 1992.
20. McKitrick, S., Nagel, R.: Future tech super tech. Don Mills, Ontario
Secondary School Teachers Federation 1986
21. Mosna, F. (1992). Technology eduction in the national context: views from
the eastern perspective. In: D. Blandow, M. Dyrenfurth (eds.) Technological
literacy, competence and innovation in human resource development. Proceedings,
Weimar 1992
22. Novakova, H.: The role of technology education as an organic part of general
education. In: D. Blandow, M. Dyrenfurth (eds.) Technological literacy,
competence and innovation in human resource development. Proceedings, Weimar
1992
23. Page, R.: Creating effective environment for teaching technology. In: D.
Blandow, M. Dyrenfurth (eds.) Technological literacy, competence and innovation
in human resource development. Proceedings, Weimar 1992
24. Plant, M.: Ecological principles and technology education. In: D.
Blandow, M. Dyrenfurth (eds.) Technological literacy, competence and innovation
in human resource development. Proceedings, Weimar 1992
25. Prime, G.: The relationship between exposure to technical curriculum at
secondary school and attitude toward technology in Trinidad. In: D. Blandow, M.
Dyrenfurth (eds.) Technological literacy, competence and innovation in human
resource development. Proceedings, Weimar 1992

26. Ratt, J.: Some international developments in technology education for elementary schools. In: D. Blandow, M. Dyrenfurth (eds.) Technological literacy, competence and innovation in human resource development. Proceedings, Weimar 1992

27. Richardson, R.: Vocational education in Papua New Guinea secondary schools. In: D. Blandow, M. Dyrenfurth (eds.) Technological literacy, competence and innovation in human resource development. Proceedings, Weimar 1992

28. Ridgeway, J., Passey, D.: Developing skills technology: the theoretical bases for teaching. In: D. Blandow, M. Dyrenfurth (eds.) Technological literacy, competence and innovation in human resource development. Proceedings, Weimar 1992

29. Riggs, F.: Report of the small schools project. St. John's: Department of Education, Government of Newfoundland and Labrador 1987

30. Ropohl, I. E.: Philosophy of technology education. In: D. Blandow, M. Dyrenfurth (eds.) Technological literacy, competence and innovation in human resource development. Proceedings, Weimar 1992

31. Ross: Building partnerships together for today and tomorrow. Internal policy documents. Quelph, Ont.: The Wellington County Scool Board.

32. Sharratt, G., McClain, C. R., Zehm, S.: Vocational education in America: an agenda for the 1990's. Rural Educator, 14, 1, 21-26 (1992)

33. Szücs, E.: Technology, culture and education. In: D. Blandow, M. Dyrenfurth (eds.) Technological literacy, competence and innovation in human resource development. Proceedings, Weimar 1992

34. UNESCO (eds.): The integration of general and technical education and vocational education. Paris, United Nations Educational, Scientific and Educational, Scientific and Cultural Organization 1986

35. Williams, P. J.: Design: an appropriate technology education methodology in less developed countries. Journal of Epsilon Pi Tau, XVIII (1), 53-59 (1992)

Implications of Cognitive Science for Technological Problem Solving

Scott D. Johnson
University of Illinois
Department of Vocational and Technical Education
1310 South Sixth Street, Champaign, IL 61820, USA

Abstract. This paper discusses three predominate perspectives of human problem solving and justifies the role of cognitive science as the most relevant approach for the study of problem solving performance. Studies of cognition are examined which identify nine generalizations about the nature of expertise and provide a model describing the acquisition of high level cognitive skills. Building on the results of cognitive research, seven recommendations for instruction in technology education are provided.

Keywords. Problem solving, cognitive science, expertise, technology education

1 Introduction

Technological development and innovation impacts every aspect of life. We rely on the computer controlled engines in our automobiles; the microcomputers in our homes, classrooms, and offices; the programmable compact disc players in our home stereo systems; and the automatic teller machines which provide access to the money necessary to buy supplies for sustaining our existence. Technological innovation will continue to expand at an ever-increasing pace in the years to come. Technological breakthroughs will bring new devices, new methods for doing things, and new technology-related problems into the world. As a society, we must be prepared to face these challenges.

Advances in technological equipment, processes, and approaches are having a profound effect on the educational needs of the population. Professionals, managers, technicians, care and service providers, and general laborers will all be involved in making decisions and solving problems related to the application of technological innovations and information. This need was recognized firsthand by the Employment and Training Division of the U.S. Department of Labor in a study conducted to determine the types of skills and abilities the workforce needs to possess (Johnston, Packer, 1987):

To adapt quickly to new workplace demands, employees must know how to learn. They need problem-solving skills to overcome barriers that arise in new situations. And in addition to feeling comfortable with innovation, they must be able to think creatively as they cope with new challenges (p. 2).

Before designing effective instruction to enhance high level cognitive abilities, educators must understand how experts think and solve problems and how their approaches differ from those of weaker performers. By recognizing the differences between strong and weak performers, educators will have a better chance of developing appropriate and effective instruction. This chapter reviews the research literature that relates to technological problem solving and describes the implications of that research for education that strives to enhance technological problem solving ability.

2 Psychological Perspectives of Problem Solving

Over the years, three distinct psychological perspectives of problem solving have gained acceptance. These include the behaviorist's stimulus-response theory, the Gestaltist's "holistic" approach, and the cognitive scientist's information processing perspective.

In the behaviorist theory of thinking, prevalent between the 1920s and the 1950s, problem solving is described as a trial and error application of common tendencies or habits. With its roots in behavioral psychology, this view assumes that for every problem situation there are responses that are selected according to the strength of the association between the problem and the response. In a problem solving situation, the problem solver, through a trial and error process, tries different responses until an effective solution results.

The stimulus-response theory of problem solving does not describe the problem solving process in adequate detail. This theory ignores the complex nature of the human problem solver by being overly concerned with the associations between stimuli and responses and ignoring the cognitive processes that occur in the mind.

A second perspective, popular between the 1920s and the 1940s, is based on the Gestalt theory of thinking. According to the Gestalt psychologists, problem solving involves a search for relationships between various aspects of the problem situation to discover how all parts in a problem fit together to reach a solution. This search involves reorganizing various aspects of the problem until it can be solved.

Much of the Gestalt perspective on problem solving is based upon the principle of insight (Wallas, 1926). Insight is thought to occur during the problem solving stages of incubation and illumination. During the incubation stage, the problem solver does not consciously think about the problem. The illumination stage occurs when the problem solver realizes suddenly how to solve the problem. Although the concept of insight is supported with many fascinating historical accounts, it does not accurately describe the problem solving process for most of the problems people encounter (Green, 1966). Ericsson and Simon (1984) found that the ideas that arise from the illumination stage do not occur as a sudden insight. By tracing problem solvers' lines of reasoning through verbal protocol analysis, Ericsson and Simon have shown that what appears to be a unique and creative solution that arrives "out of the clear blue" is actually a mental continuation or reorganization of the search for the solution. In other words, the magical principle of insight can be explained as a cognitive process involving knowledge structure reorganization.

A third problem solving perspective developed in the 1960s when Newell and Simon (1972) studied the cognitive aspects of problem solving. Their research led to the development of a model that depicted human problem solving as an information processing system. The information processing model consists of three structures — sensory register, short-term memory, and long-term memory — which perform input, encoding, storage, and transformation functions within the mind.

Newell and Simon (1972) explored the operation of the human information processing system through the development of computer programs that simulated cognitive processes. Their model postulated that problem solving involves searching for solutions through a "problem space." A problem space consists of a mental representation of the initial problem conditions, the final goal, the intermediate states that could occur between the initial conditions and the solution, and the operators or strategies for moving from one state to the next (Mayer, 1983).

Problem solving in the Newell and Simon model begins by analyzing the initial problem information to produce an internal representation of the problem. The problem solver then selects and uses a problem solving method that has some relationship to the desired solution. If the problem solver is unable to find a solution using that method, another method may be selected, a different representation of the problem may be developed, or the problem may be abandoned.

Both the Behaviorist and Gestalt perspectives on problem solving suggest that human problem solving is a passive event. The behaviorists emphasize the importance of previously learned associations between stimuli and responses to solve problems while the Gestalts elaborate on the role of insight. In contrast, the cognitive view of problem solving recognizes that the problem solver is an active processor of information and consciously searches for and manipulates information to arrive at a solution. By viewing problem solving as an active process of information processing, educators can develop instruction that emphasizes the cognitive skills needed for problem solving.

3 Cognitive Science

Cognitive science is a domain of scientific inquiry that originated in 1956 (Simon, 1980). Cognitive psychologists, artificial intelligence researchers, linguists, and philosophers worked together to create this new "discipline" focused on understanding the human mind. The primary goal of cognitive science is to seek an understanding of human intelligence and use that understanding to develop intelligent technological systems. With its focus on the working of the mind, cognitive science represents a philosophical shift away from the behavioral psychology focus on observable behavior. Rather than analyze overt behavior as it results from external stimuli, cognitive scientists concentrate on the intellectual elements that form, organize, and guide behavior.

Much of the early research in cognitive science was devoted to investigations of problem solving ability in an attempt to identify general problem solving strategies. These early studies were based on the assumption that a class of problem solving strategies existed that could be used to solve a wide variety of problems. In an attempt to discover the general problem solving strategies that were assumed to exist, researchers studied how people solved various types of problems. The problems used in these studies were typically puzzles or logic games such as the water jug and river crossing problems, the Tower of Hanoi puzzle, and the game of chess. With the exception of the chess studies, most of these studies used problems that had little relevance to real world activity, were very well-structured, and required little domain knowledge to arrive at a solution. This line of inquiry did lead to an identification of several general problem solving methods and an enhanced understanding of the human information processing system.

While the early research in cognitive science advanced the field considerably, it soon became apparent that problem solving involved more than a set of general strategies. In an attempt to understand the content and structure of expert knowledge, cognitive scientists soon discovered that good problem solvers in one domain acted like novices in other domains. While general problem solving strategies can be useful for solving puzzles and game problems, they are less useful for solving the realistic, ill-structured problems faced in daily life. By studying problem solving performance in areas such as medical diagnosis, financial reasoning, electronic troubleshooting, and architectural design, cognitive researchers soon realized that expert performance relies heavily on domain-specific knowledge and skill. This realization led to more elaborate models of performance and a characterization of problem solving ability as a developed skill that cannot be easily generalized to a wide range of domains.

4 The Nature of Problem Solving Expertise

Expertise can be defined most simply as highly adaptive behavior. People who have expertise seem to have a "magical power" that allows them to solve problems fluently and efficiently. Experts are able to solve problems with little apparent mental effort and are able to get results in fewer steps and in less time than novices. Expertise also appears to be adaptable to novel situations. Experts are able to generate new knowledge in unfamiliar situations through their great depth of knowledge and experience, are introspective about the knowledge they possess, and have the ability to learn from past experience (Kolodner, 1983).

4.1 Generalizations About the Nature of Expertise

The following summary from the expertise literature provides a base for later discussions of instructional approaches for the enhancement of technological problem solving abilities.

1. Experience plays an important role in the development of expertise. However, more experience does not necessarily result in greater expertise. The type of experience is more important than the amount. For example, an apprentice who troubleshoots faulty equipment will be more likely to develop problem solving skills than another apprentice who spends time simply replacing parts that someone else has identified as faulty. The development of expertise also seems to be dependent upon the importance of the activities or problems. For example, if one begins using a new word processing program and has little need for page layout and graphics functions, the level of expertise gained with that program will only develop to a certain level. If page layout and graphics functions become important, one's level of expertise will increase as those commands are learned.

2. One of the key characteristics of expertise is an apparent ease of performance. Experts are able to perform quickly, fluently, and efficiently. Their speed is acquired as a result of many hours of practice. Through many repetitions solving similar problems, the problem solving processes and procedures of experts become virtually automatic. They seem to perform without thinking. There is general agreement that practice is essential for the development of quick and accurate performance. While practice may not lead to perfection, it does lead to an increase in the speed of task completion and a decrease in error rate (Phye, Andre, 1986).

3. Although experts generally arrive at solutions faster than novices, they spend more time than novices tying to understand the problem. Experts try to understand a problem before acting while novices jump right in and attempt a solution (Chi, Feltovich, Glaser, 1981; deKleer, 1985; Larkin, McDermott, Simon, D. P., Simon, H. A. 1980). Experts attempt to build a mental representation of a problem so they can infer relationships, define the situation, add constraints to the problem, and plan an approach to solve the problem. Once the problem is represented and understood, experts then solve the problem. In contrast, novices

typically consider the problem information that is initially available and then attempt to solve the problem. In practice, the novice approach brings about industry's concern for "preconceived notions" which lead maintenance workers to jump to conclusions and replace parts that are not faulty.

4. Experts represent problems at a deeper, more principled level than novices. A study by Chi, Feltovich, and Glaser (1981) found that experts and novices approached mechanics problems very differently. Subjects were asked to sort cards that contained mechanics problems into piles of similar groupings. It was noticed that the experts sorted their problems into piles based on the underlying physics principles and theories while the novices sorted the cards according to the surface-feature of the problems. The better performance of the experts was attributed to their deeper understanding of physics principles. Without this deep understanding of the domain, the novices' intellectual processes proved to be inadequate for solving similar problems.

5. Experts have the ability to perceive large, meaningful patterns. This pattern recognition ability takes on the character of "intuition" and was once thought to be the result of superior perceptual and mental abilities. Given that working memory can hold only a finite amount of information (Miller, 1956), people work around working memory limitations by organizing their memory into "packages" that contain related information (Chase, Ericsson, 1982). Due to their memory organization, experts possess a large knowledge base organized into elaborate, integrated structures while novices possess less knowledge that is not as coherently organized. The classic study by Chase and Simon (1973) found that the superior performance of chess masters was a result of their ability to recognize board layout patterns from past experience rather than from superior mental capability. In a similar study, Egan and Schwartz (1979) asked expert and novice subjects to briefly study electronic drawings and then reconstruct the drawings from memory. The results showed that when presented with realistic drawings, the experts, as expected, were able to recall significantly more of the drawing than the novices. However, when shown drawings with random placement of electronic devices in a circuit, the experts performed no better than the novices. This study suggests that the memory of expert technicians is based on "conceptual" chunks. The experts were able to recall portions of the drawings as chunks of information (i.e., amplifier circuit, tuner circuit, etc.) rather than as individual components.

6. In addition to having their knowledge better organized than novices, experts are able to use their knowledge to form mental and physical representations of the problems that confront them. Mental models based on physical systems and objects are one form of representation relevant to technological problem solving (Brewer, 1987; deKleer, 1983; White, Frederiksen, 1987). Mental models help to predict or explain our interactions with people and equipment and can also improve performance on cognitive tasks such as problem solving and decision making (Bouwman, 1983; Kieras, Bovair, 1984; White, Frederiksen, 1987). Causal mental models improve human performance in several ways (Williams, Hollan, Stevens, 1983). First, mental models can be used to predict the behavior

of physical systems by "running" or simulating the function and operation of a system in the mind. For example, it is relatively easy for an expert troubleshooter to mentally insert faults into a mental model and analyze the effects of those faults on the system. Second, causal mental models can help explain the behavior of a system. By comparing the observed symptoms of a faulty system to an existing mental model, a problem solver can reason why a system behaves as it does and learn from the analysis. Third, mental models can serve as mnemonic devices to facilitate remembering.

7. Experts work around their limited mental capacities by focusing their attention on relevant aspects of the problem. Research shows that experts are able to process a large amount of information when solving problems while novices often get "mentally bogged down" when confronted with lots of information. Experts accomplish this by directing their attention to appropriate aspects of a problem through the use of their large knowledge base while novices' attention seems to be guided by their senses (Johnson, 1989; Thomas, 1988). Experts are able to confine their attention to smaller portions of a problem space and retain only the information that is most likely to help solve the problem. In contrast, novices are less able to discriminate between relevant and irrelevant information, obtain less useful information for a given amount of effort, and do not efficiently reduce the size of the problem space they are considering.

8. Experts rely on stronger problem solving strategies than novices (Chi et al., 1981; deKleer, 1985; Larkin et al., 1980). Experts incorporate more powerful methods and are not dependent upon a single strategy to facilitate the problem solving process (Johnson, Flesher, Ferej, Jehng, 1992). In contrast, novices tend to rely on weak strategies and lean toward one favorite problem solving strategy. The ability to select an appropriate strategy is an essential element of the problem solving process. Weak strategies, such as visual inspection, can only find the most symptomatic faults, and a strict topographic search can easily miss a problem. Experts are generally able to use more powerful strategies and change their strategic approaches if necessary. Novices tend to use weak strategies and then make them even less powerful by overusing them. For example, novice troubleshooters have been observed checking the continuity of every conductor or component in the system (Johnson et al., 1992) and making multiple checks of switches using the same test that was previously unproductive (Johnson, 1987).

9. Strategic knowledge, or what is often called *metacognition*, refers to awareness of one's own thinking processes. Brown (1978) states that:

"the ability to monitor one's own understanding . . . is an essential pre-requisite for all problem solving ability." (Brown, 1978, p. 83)

Metacognition involves the planning that takes place before engaging in a thinking activity, regulation of one's thinking during the activity, and evaluation of the appropriateness of one's thinking performance upon the completion of the activity (Brown, 1978). Metacognition includes strategies such as self-monitoring, advance planning, self-checking, questioning, summarizing, predicting, generating and evaluating alternatives, and evaluating learning. Experts have stronger metacognitive skills than novices. They are more aware of their own mistakes, they know when they do not understand, and they know when they need to check their solutions.

4.2 Acquisition of Problem Solving Expertise

While it is often easy to recognize expertise, it is not as easy to determine how the expertise was attained. In spite of considerable cognitive research in the past two decades, it is unfortunate that the current theories do not adequately specify the "mystical ingredients" that are needed to advance to the level of expert. One model developed by Anderson (1982) clarifies the development of expertise by describing the acquisition of skill through three stages:

(a) the declarative stage,
(b) the knowledge compilation stage, and
(c) the procedural stage.

In the first stage an individual obtains information about the content being learned (i.e., facts, principles, theories, procedures). This is the most basic learning stage where the learner tries to determine what to do and how to do it. Considerable mental effort is required at this stage because of the limited mental capacity of the human memory system. Limited short term memory capacity forces the individual to focus on each specific piece of information because it has not yet been compiled into a cohesive knowledge structure. The individual acquires and uses the knowledge during the second stage of skill acquisition. In this stage an individual practices the task until it is done fluently and efficiently and begins to make the transition from controlled processes to automatic processes (Schneider, Shiffrin, 1977; Shiffrin, Dumais, 1981; Shiffrin, Schneider, 1977). Controlled processing requires conscious attention to information, which places a heavy load on working memory.

In contrast, automatic processing uses highly developed processing skills that place little strain on limited processing capabilities. Automatic processing develops through extensive amounts of practice which result in over-learning skills. The change in processes leads to the third stage of the skill acquisition model. At this stage the individual has adequate knowledge and has automated the skills needed to use that knowledge effectively. The individual is now able to generalize existing knowledge to new situations, make intelligent selections of strategies, and further refine and strengthen the acquired skill (Anderson, 1982).

It must be understood that this model of skill acquisition does not imply that all individuals who go through these three stages will become experts. There is some evidence that the development of expertise is also influenced by the individual's level of cognitive development. Days, Wheatley, and Kuhm (1979) found that problem solving processes or strategies become more systematic and logical as age increases. The biggest change occurs between the ages of 11 and 13. This finding stresses the importance of problem solving instruction at the early grade levels, particularly at the late elementary and middle school grades.

5 Strategies for Teaching Problem Solving

Building on what is known about the nature of expertise and human problem solving processes, numerous recommendations can be made about the teaching of problem solving in schools. The recommendations that follow depend heavily upon the ability of teachers to design instruction and manage classrooms and laboratories in ways that support the development of problem solving abilities. When teachers want to emphasize problem solving in their curriculum they must be facilitators of learning rather than transmitters of knowledge. Teachers must stand back and allow students to experiment with various techniques while solving problems (Swedlow, 1979). This does not mean that students are allowed to solve the problems in isolation so the teacher does not know how the student solved the problem. Teachers must be attentive to students' progress during problem solving and be ready to intervene before students become frustrated.

One of the best examples of the role of the teacher in developing problem solving abilities is provided by Schoenfeld (1983). In his approach, Schoenfeld teaches a set of strategies for solving mathematical problems to his students. His teaching involves showing students how he, as a mathematician, solves problems. However, unlike many teachers, he does not work the problems out in advance in order to show the students a smooth and successful solution. He even encourages his students to bring problems to class for him to solve. By being confronted with unfamiliar problems, Schoenfeld is forced to solve them as a mathematician would: by using a variety of strategies and by making errors. Through this technique, the students have the opportunity to see that there are many ways to solve mathematics problems and that even expert mathematicians make mistakes. Schoenfeld does not stop his problem solving activity when an answer has been found because mathematicians in the "real world" continue looking for alternative solutions and easier ways to solve the problem, and then attempt to generalize the solution to other problems.

Technology-oriented courses need to emphasize problem solving and Schoenfeld's instructional approach can be easily adapted to the technology education classroom. Technology teachers need to act like technologists in their classrooms. They need to solve unfamiliar technological problems for students and not be afraid to make errors or have difficulties finding solutions. By serving as a role model, technology teachers can show students how to collect and use information to solve technological problems and help them realize that not all problems have straightforward and simple solutions.

5.1 Focus on Processes, Not Just Information

Webb (1979) argues that instruction tends to place too much emphasis on information and too little on process. The predominate mode of instruction promotes the one-way transmission of facts, skills, and values from teachers to students. Metaphorically, this approach to education characterizes students' minds as "empty vessels" which teachers must fill by pouring information into their heads. Teaching is viewed as a process of transmitting information from teacher to student in much the same way as water flows through a conduit (Royer, 1986). Educators who adopt the "transmission" philosophy of education embrace the mechanistic view of human behavior based on behavioral psychology principles. Behaviorism advocates breaking human activity into specific responses and emphasizes the development of skills through specific instructional strategies. Curriculum developed under this philosophy stresses mastery of subject matter, traditional teaching methods, and places considerable emphasis on textbook learning. The current competency-based education movement is an operational example of the transmission approach to education.

If educators are genuinely interested in helping students develop problem solving skills, then directed effort must be made to address the process of problem solving within the curriculum. This will entail adopting a cognitive view of learning in which students construct meaning through their experiences. Instructors must develop learning environments that facilitate experiential learning and support problem solving activities. Through a cognitive approach to instruction, teachers become managers of instruction and facilitators in the learning process rather than purveyors of information.

5.2 Develop Experts Not Novices

In spite of their good intentions, many instructors actually teach their students to be novices rather than experts. This is especially common in subjects that rely heavily on algorithms. For example, electronics courses typically stress the importance of equations (e.g., Ohm's law) for solving various circuit design problems. Students are taught the theories that underlie the equations and are shown how to apply the equations to calculate various circuit conditions. While this instructional strategy is intuitively appropriate, it actually teaches the students to solve circuit problems like novices rather than experts.

As discussed earlier, experts spend a great deal of time analyzing a problem qualitatively before taking action while novices tend to jump right in and attempt a solution (Chi et al., 1981; deKleer, 1985; Larkin et al., 1980). When confronted with a problem, novices immediately look for a quantitative solution to it. When solving word problems in mathematics and electronic courses, students begin by looking for a formula that fits the information in the problem. In contrast, experts approach problems by analyzing problem information in order to better understand it. After the problem is understood the expert then begins looking for a solution.

Rather than emphasize the way novices approach problems, instructors need to concentrate on the methods and actions of experts. Students need to be taught how to think, plan, and act when confronted with problems.

5.3 Explicitly Teach Problem Solving

Courses typically place little emphasis on actual problem solving instruction. Rather, most problem solving strategies are latently designed into instruction. Class projects and assignments are assumed to improve problem solving skills without explicit instruction devoted to problem solving skills and strategies. Studies, however, have shown that students do not pick up strategies on their own (Schoenfeld, 1979b). When problem solving strategies are directly taught, student problem solving performance increases (Houtz, Denmark, 1983; Schoenfeld, 1979a) and the impact on students' problem solving performance is substantial (Schoenfeld, 1979b). Students need to be taught explicitly how to analyze initial problem information, how to represent the problem through diagrams and mental models, and how to perform various problem solving strategies.

5.4 Do Problem Solving Rather Than "Exercise" Solving

Many of the "problems" presented to students in school are more accurately labeled "exercises". Exercises are well-structured problems that are clearly presented, contain all of the information needed to develop a solution, and have an appropriate algorithm or solution available. Completing exercises in class are appropriate activities for students because they can practice using the algorithms that have been taught. In contrast, "real" problems tend to be ill-structured because they often lack important information, may contain inaccurate information, and do not have clear paths to the solution. Problem solving requires analysis and reasoning while exercise solving involves simple recognition or recall from memory (Smith, 1991).

The difference between problems and exercises is not a question of difficulty or complexity, but one of familiarity (Bodner, 1991). Although both require similar cognitive tools to arrive at a solution, exercises are familiar enough to the problem solver to be solved routinely while problems are typically unfamiliar and therefore, are non-routine (Smith, 1991). When confronted with routine problems, experts tend to use a forward reasoning strategy to arrive at a solution (Patel, Groen, 1988). However, when problems are non-routine and cause problem solvers to be uncertain or unsuccessful, they rely on more powerful strategies for solutions.

When instructors provide real problems to students, the problems are often so simplified that they can hardly be called problems. To ensure that classes run smoothly, instructors will work through the problems they want students to solve in advance. By "pre-solving" the problems, instructors remove much of the uncertainty that takes place in real problem solving and turn what might have been a non-routine problem solving opportunity into a routine, mindless exercise.

Instructors also develop procedure sheets so students can follow the directions on them, step-by-step, until a solution is reached. While procedure sheets help students arrive at a correct solution, they reduce the opportunity for students to engage in real problem solving. In effect, students replicate the problem solution of the instructor instead of solving the problem. Exercises and over-simplified problems provide students with an unrealistic view of how problems are solved. Exercises provide little indication to students that real-world problems involve making mistakes, facing dead ends, and require considerable mental and physical effort (Herron, 1990). While schools have become effective at preparing good exercise solvers, they are is still less successful in teaching students to be good problem solvers.

5.5 Structure Problem Solving Activities Around Rich, Real-World Contexts

One way to emphasize problems rather than exercises is to simulate real-world problem solving in class. The problems and social situations faced in real life bear little resemblance to the exercises, activities, and problems found in most elementary and secondary school curricula. However, the context that surrounds a problem is an important factor in problem solving. For example, students solve arithmetic problems very differently in situations outside school. One study found that students could correctly solve 98 % of the arithmetic problems presented to them in a supermarket but could only solve 59 % of the same problems on a test (Lave, 1988).

Cognitive science research has consistently indicated that the context in which something is learned influences later use of that knowledge. New knowledge is "indexed" when it is learned so it can be retrieved when needed at a later time (Glass, Holyoak, Santa, 1979; Phye, Andre, 1986; Reiser, 1986). This concept is analogous to using a card catalog to "index" books in a library so specific books can be easily identified and located. While context plays an important role in learning, problem-oriented instruction too often takes place in contexts that are dissimilar from those the student will encounter later.

Situated cognition is a term that describes learning in contexts that reflect the way the knowledge and skills will be used in real life. Instruction must occur in contexts that support encoding and representation of new information so it can be indexed in ways that make it accessible at a later time. Experiences that occur within rich contexts reduce the chances of students developing "inert" or "fragile" knowledge: that is, knowledge that one possesses but does not use in problem solving situations (Perkins, Schwartz, Simmons, 1991; Whitehead, 1929).

5.6 Emphasize Problem Solving Competencies Rather Than Stage Models

The most popular method of teaching problem solving involves the use of stage models of problem solving. Stage models are simplified lists of the stages or steps involved in general problem solving. One of the first and most popular stage models of problem solving was developed by Polya (1945). Polya's model suggests that problem solvers complete the following four steps when engaged in a problem solving activity:

1. Understand the problem
2. Devise a plan
3. Carry out the plan
4. Look back

Other popular models of problem solving are shown in Figure 1. Many of these models have been adapted for technology education and are shown in curriculum documents and posters attached to classroom walls in elementary and secondary schools.

Stage models are simplified representations of the problem solving process. While they provide a general framework for problem solving, they are not particularly useful in instruction. Stage models were developed from studies of puzzle solving and describe how experts solve *exercises* (Bodner, 1991). Unfortunately, they are too general, too simple, too linear, and too inflexible to describe accurately the steps used to solve real, ill-structured problems. To illustrate the weaknesses of stage models for describing problem solving processes, think back to the last time you solved a real technical problem. Did you follow Polya's four step model? Did you begin by trying to understanding the problem and then devise a plan? Did you then carry out the plan and look back over your result? Instead of following such a linear approach, you probably solved the problem in a more flexible fashion.
Troubleshooters, for example, begin by collecting enough information to understand the problem and determine several reasons why the equipment is not functioning properly. Then, instead of developing a complete plan, they choose a fault that is likely to be the main cause of the problem and run some tests or make adjustments to see if it is the real fault. If it is not the fault, they choose another potential fault and test that hypothesis out. This process continues until the fault has been identified. As shown in this brief example, stage models are limiting because they fail to clarify the processes that are actually used during problem solving. In examining Polya's model, Bodner (1991) suggests that all of

Wallas (1926) studied the phenomenon of insight as related to creativity and developed a problem solving model that contained four distinguishable and overlapping stages:

1. Preparation — the problem is investigated as completely as possible.
2. Incubation — the individual does not consciously think about the problem.
3. Illumination — the appearance of the solution.
4. Verification — the individual evaluates the worth of the solution.

Hayes (1981) describes the problem solving process in a six step model developed from an information processing viewpoint:

1. Finding the problem — recognizing that there is a problem to be solved.
2. Representing the problem — understanding the problem through the development of both internal and external representations.
3. Planning the solution — choosing a method that may solve the problem.
4. Carrying out the plan — attempting the proposed solution.
5. Evaluating the solution — asking "How good is the result?" once the plan has been carried out.
6. Consolidating gains — learning from the experience of the solving.

Bransford and Stein (1984) synthesized numerous research studies before developing their "IDEAL" model of problem solving.

1. Identify potential problems — often the most difficult part of problem solving.
2. Define the problem — similar to Hayes' "representing the problem" stage.
3. Explore alternative approaches — emphasis is on selecting problem solving strategies.
4. Act on a plan — carry out the strategy.
5. Look at the effects — see what impact the strategies had on the problem.

Fig. 1 Three popular problem solving stage models

the activities that could be considered as problem solving actually occur within Stage One of the model. Once you fully understand the problem you have actually solved it. Carrying out the remaining stages are merely a process of verifying that your solution is correct.

Many educators have noticed that even though students possess knowledge and skills, they often fail to use them when confronted with situations where they would be appropriate. This holds true for instruction that emphasizes stage models of problem solving. Bransford and Stein (1984) taught a five step problem solving strategy to college students. Even though the students found the strategy easy to learn and could use the strategy when prompted, they often failed to apply the model when faced with problems that were conducive to the use of the model. The reasons for their inability to apply the five step model of problem solving are unclear but do raise serious questions about the usefulness of such models for enhancing problem solving ability.

Studies have shown that technical problem solvers solve problems in very different ways. Simon (1979) noticed diversity in approaches to problem solving by subjects from the domains of physics and chemistry. In a study of troubleshooting expertise, Johnson (1987) noticed that individual experts and novices had their own unique approaches to problem solving. It appears that technical problem solvers have preferred styles of problem solving that conform to the type of problem and their personal and professional backgrounds (Johnson, Flesher, in press). Since technical problem solving differs across individuals and domains, how can a simple stage model be adequate for teaching problem solving processes?

Rather than emphasizing stage models of problem solving that do not accurately describe the process people use to solve real problems, it may be best to help students acquire the competencies they need to be successful problem solvers. Figure 2 contains an incomplete list of the problem solving competencies that people need to become successful technical problem solvers. These competencies should receive explicit attention in technology courses while the stage models of problem solving should be given secondary emphasis.

5.7 Provide Opportunities to Practice Problem Solving

Acquiring expertise requires extensive opportunities to practice developing the competencies shown in Figure 2. In many technology courses however, students actually have few opportunities to practice developing the necessary competencies. Instruction often takes the form of teacher-directed lectures and skill development activities in a laboratory (Johnson, 1990). Students tend to be passive receptors of information during lectures and often spend their laboratory time replicating activities that have already been performed by the instructor. In addition, students typically solve only a limited number of technological problems in a semester. This is due to a combination of factors. First, technological problem solving is time consuming because of the time it takes for design, collecting relevant information, locating tools, accessing components, running tests, disassembling and assembling systems, and verifying results. Second, few school laboratories have sufficient work stations to allow an entire class to engage in technological problem solving at one time. Without sufficient numbers of work stations, instructors must be creative in their selection of activities so students remain busy during lab time. Third, it has become a tradition in many technology-oriented classes to emphasize individualized problem solving rather than group efforts. The individual emphasis places more constraints on instructors and facilities and

To become competent problem solvers, students should gain the ability to:
- Identify both given and needed information.
- Obtain problem information via the senses.
- Obtain relevant information from technical manuals and other resources.
- Use technical devices to collect problem information.
- Create a simplified, abstract problem space.
- Create models to simplify the problem by using diagrams, tables, charts, graphs.
- Develop a mental image of the problem.
- Use analogies/metaphors to look at the problem from different angles.
- Plan before taking action.
- Recognize patterns.
- Reason hypothetically.
- Estimate.
- Apply domain specific algorithms.
- Utilize general search methods (trial & error, blind, systematic, exhaustive)
- Utilize proximity search methods (hill climbing, means-ends analysis, topographic)
- Utilize fractionation search methods (split/half or bracketed)
- Utilize knowledge-based search methods
- Solve a simpler problem.
- Work backwards.
- Utilize metacognitive skills such as planning, predicting, evaluating, reflecting.

Fig. 2 Competencies needed for successful technical problem solving

hampers the instructors' ability to provide adequate problem solving experiences for students.

While creative instructors will be able to structure and manage their courses to increase the amount of time students spend on problem solving activities, using instructional technologies may be a way to significantly increase the amount of problem solving experience students gain through instruction. Building on the current capabilities of computer technology, high fidelity problem solving scenarios have been designed for technological problem solving (Bransford, Sherwood, Hasselbring, 1986; Johnson et al., 1992; Lesgold, Lajoie, Bunzo, Eggan, 1989; Wenger, 1987; White, 1988). These simulations allow students to solve technological problems faster than they could on real equipment because they do not have to spend time doing things like physically removing panels and loosening bolts. By simply adding a computer to a laboratory environment, additional work stations are provided. Through the use of computer-based problem solving environments, extensive practice opportunities can be provided for students which help them quickly develop the same mental patterns that are developed by expert problem solvers through many years of experience (Nichols, Pokorny, Jones, Gott, Alley, 1989).

6 Summary

Technological problem solving is a very complex task. Not only is it a difficult task to perform, it is also difficult to teach. These difficulties lead to a dilemma for the education and training community. Can problem solving abilities be improved through instruction? If so, what instructional design and implementation strategies must be utilized? It is fortunate that so many teachers are interested in problem solving. Many teachers attempt to teach problem solving to their students and provide experiential opportunities through various activities and assignments in spite of the fact that they have received little guidance from the research community on effective ways to teach problem solving.

As discussed in this paper, problem solving is primarily a cognitive activity. Through studies of the cognitive processes of low and highly skilled individuals on a variety of problem solving activities, cognitive scientists have clarified the knowledge structures, processes, and dispositions utilized while solving problems. Cognitive research has also described the process involved in the acquisition of high level skills. Through basic research studies into human performance, cognitive scientists have clarified the instructional requirements for problem-oriented instruction and have led to the seven instructional recommendations offered in this paper. These recommendations need to be implemented in technology classrooms and studied critically by applied researchers. Through collaborative efforts by classroom technology instructors and applied researchers, an even greater understanding of the acquisition of expertise and instruction's impact on problem solving ability can be gained.

References

1. Anderson, J. R.: Acquisition of cognitive skill. Psychological Review, 89, 369-406 (1982)
2. Bodner, G. M.: A view from Chemistry. In: M. U. Smith (ed.), Toward a unified theory of problem solving (pp. 21-33). Hillsdale, NJ: Erlbaum 1991
3. Bouwman, M. J.: Human diagnostic reasoning by computer: An illustration from financial analysis. In: Management Science, 29, 6, 653-672 (1983)
4. Bransford, J. D., Sherwood, R. D., Hasselbring, T. S.: Computers, videodiscs and the teaching of thinking. Paper presented at the meeting of the American Educational Research Association, San Francisco April 1986
5. Bransford, J. D., Stein, B. S.: The ideal problem solver: A guide for improving thinking, learning, and creativity. New York, Freeman, 1984

6. Brewer, W. F.: Schemas versus mental models in human memory. In: P. E. Morris (ed.), Modelling cognition (pp. 187-197). New York, Wiley, 1987

7. Brown, A. L.: Knowing when, where, and how to remember: A problem of metacognition. In: R. Glaser (ed.), Advances in instructional psychology (pp. 77-165). Hillsdale, NJ: Erlbaum 1978

8. Chase, W. G., Ericsson, K. A.: Skill and working memory. In: G. Bower (ed.), The psychology of learning and motivation (pp. 1-58). New York, Academic 1982

9. Chase, W. G., Simon, H. A.: The mind's eye in chess. In: W. G. Chase (ed.), Visual information processing (pp. 215-281). New York: Academic 1973

10. Chi, M. T. H., Feltovich, P. J., Glaser, R.: Categorization and representation of physics problems by experts and novices. In: Cognitive Science, 5, 121-152 (1981)

11. Days, H. C., Wheatley, G. H., Kuhm, G.: Problem structure, cognitive level, and problem solving performance. In: Journal for Research in Mathematics, 10, 2, 135-146 (1979)

12. deKleer, J.: AI approaches to troubleshooting, (Report No. AD-P003 918). Denver, Denver Research Institute 1983

13. deKleer, J.: How circuits work. In: D. G. Bobrow (ed.), Qualitative reasoning about physical systems (pp. 205-280). Cambridge, MA: MIT Press 1985

14. Egan, D. E., Schwartz, B. J.: Chunking in recall of symbolic drawings. In: Memory and Cognition, 7, 2, 149-158 (1979)

15. Ericsson, K. A., Simon, H. A.: Protocol analysis. Cambridge, MIT Press 1984

16. Glass, A. L., Holyoak, K. J., Santa, J.: Cognition. Reading, MA, Addison-Wesley 1979

17. Green, B. F.: Introduction: Current trends in problem solving. In: B. Kleinmuntz (ed.), Problem solving: Research, methods, and theory. New York, Wiley 1966

18. Hayes, J. R.: The complete problem solver. Philadelphia, Franklin Institute 1981

19. Herron, J. D.: Research in chemical education: Results and directions. In: M. Gardner, J. G. Greeno, F. Reif, A. H. Schoenfeld, A. A. diSessa, E. Stage (eds.), Toward a scientific practice of science education (pp. 31-54). Hillsdale, Erlbaum 1990

20. Houtz, J. C., Denmark, R. M.: Student perceptions of cognitive classroom structure and development of creative thinking and problem solving skills. In: Educational Research Quarterly, 8, 20-26 (1983)

21. Johnson, S. D.: Knowledge and skill differences between expert and novice service technicians on technical troubleshooting tasks (Report No. 20). St. Paul, University of Minnesota, Training and Development Research Center 1987 (ERIC Document Reproduction Service No. ED 284 054)

22. Johnson, S. D.: A description of expert and novice performance differences on technical troubleshooting tasks. In: Journal of Industrial Teacher Education, 26, 3, 19-37 (1989)

23. Johnson, S. D.: Current practice in preparing the future workforce: An analysis of advanced technology programs in Illinois community colleges. Springfield, Department of Adult, Vocational and Technical Education, Illinois State Board of Education 1990

24. Johnson, S. D., Flesher, J.: Troubleshooting styles. Technical and Skills Training (in press)

25. Johnson, S. D., Flesher, J. W., Ferej, A., Jehng, J. C.: Application of cognitive theory to the design, development, and implementation of a computer-based troubleshooting tutor (Report No. 265). Berkeley, National Center for Research in Vocational Education 1992

26. Johnston, W. B., Packer, A. H.: Workforce 2000: Work and workers for the 21st century (Report No. HI-3796-RR). Indianapolis, The Hudson Institute, Employment and Training Administration, U. S. Department of Labor 1987

27. Kieras, D. E., Bovair, S.: The role of a mental model in learning to operate a device. In: Cognitive Science, 8, 3, 255-273 (1984)

28. Kolodner, J. L.: Towards an understanding of the role of experience in the evolution from novice to expert. In: International Journal of Man-Machine Systems, 19, 497-518 (1983)

29. Larkin, J., McDermott, J., Simon, D. P., Simon, H. A.: Expert and novice performance in solving physics problems. In: Science, 208, 1335-1342 (1980)

30. Lave, J.: Cognition in practice. New York, Cambridge University Press 1988

31. Lesgold, A., Lajoie, S. P., Bunzo, M., Eggan, G.: SHERLOCK: A coached practice environment for an electronics troubleshooting job. Paper presented at the meeting of the American Educational Research Association, San Francisco March 1989

32. Mayer, R. E.: Thinking, problem solving, cognition. New York, W. H. Freeman & Company 1983

33. Miller, G. A.: The magical number seven, plus or minus two. In: Psychological Review, 63, 81-97 (1956)

34. Newell, A., Simon, H. A.: Human problem solving. Englewood Cliffs, Prentice-Hall 1972

35. Nichols, P. D., Pokorny, R., Jones, G., Gott, S. P., Alley, W. E.: A cognitive theory-based evaluation of an intelligent tutoring system. Paper presented at the meeting of the American Educational Research Association, San Francisco March 1989

36. Patel, V. L., Groen, G. J.: Toward a unified theory of problem solving: A view from medicine. Paper presented at the meeting of the American Educational Research Association, New Orleans April 1988

37. Perkins, D. N., Schwartz, S., Simmons, R.: A view from programming. In: M. U. Smith (ed.), Toward a unified theory of problem solving (pp. 45-67). Hillsdale, Erlbaum 1991

38. Phye, G. D., Andre, T.: Cognitive classroom learning: Understanding, thinking, and problem solving. New York, Academic Press 1986

39. Reiser, B. J.: The encoding and retrieval of memories of real-world experiences. In: Galambos, J. A., Abelson, R. P., Black, J. B. (eds.), Knowledge structures (pp. 71-99). Hillsdale, Erlbaum 1986

40. Royer, J. M.: Designing instruction to produce understanding: An approach based on cognitive theory. In: Phye, G. D., Andre, T. (eds.), Cognitive classroom learning: Understanding, thinking, and problem solving (pp. 83-117). New York, Academic Press 1986

41. Schneider, W., Shiffrin, R. M.: Controlled and automatic human information processing: I. Detection, search, and attention. In: Psychological Review, 84, 1, 1-66 (1977)

42. Schoenfeld, A. H.: Can heuristics be taught? In: Lochhead, J.,Clement, J. (eds.), Cognitive process instruction: Research on teaching thinking skills (pp. 315-338). Philadelphia, Franklin Institute 1979a

43. Schoenfeld, A. H.: Explicit heuristic training as a variable in problem-solving performance. In: Journal for Research in Mathematics Education, 10, 173-187 (1979b)

44. Schoenfeld, A. H.: Problem solving in the mathematics curriculum (Report). The Mathematical Association of America 1983

45. Shiffrin, R. M., Dumais, S. T.: The development of automatism. In: J. R. Anderson (ed.), Cognitive skills and their acquisition (pp. 111-140). Hillsdale, Erlbaum 1981

46. Shiffrin, R. M., Schneider, W.: Controlled and automatic human information processing: II. Perceptual learning, automatic attending, and a general theory. In: Psychological Review, 84, 2, 127-190 (1977)

47. Simon, D. P., Simon, H. A.: A tale of two protocols. In: Lochhead, J., Clement, J. (eds.), Cognitive process instruction (pp. 119-132). Philadelphia, Franklin Institute (1979)

48. Simon, H. A.: Cognitive science: The newest science of the artificial. In: Cognitive Science, 4, 33-46 (1980)

49 Smith, M. U.: A view from Biology. In: M. U. Smith (ed.), Toward a unified theory of problem solving (pp. 1-19). Hillsdale, Erlbaum 1991

50. Swedlow, R.: Problem solving on the playground. In: Science and Children, 16, 7, 20-21 (1979)

51. Thomas, R. G. (ed.): Thinking underlying expertise in specific knowledge domains: Implications for vocational education. St. Paul, University of Minnesota, Minnesota Research and Development Center for Vocational Education 1988

52. Wallas, G.: The art of thought. New York, Harcourt, Brace, & World 1926

53. Webb, N. L.: Processes, conceptual knowledge, and mathematical problem solving ability. In: Journal for Research in Mathematics Education, 10, 2, 83-9? (1979)

54. Wenger, E.: SOPHIE: From quantitative to qualitative simulation. In: E. Wenger (ed.), Artificial intelligence and tutoring systems: Computational and cognitive approaches to the communication of knowledge (pp. 51-78). Los Altos, Morgan Kaufman Publishers 1987

55. White, B. Y.: Thinkertools: Causal models, conceptual change, and science education (Report No. 6873). Cambridge, BBN Laboratories 1988

56. White, B. Y., Frederiksen, J. R.: Causal model progressions as a foundation for intelligent learning environments (Report No. 6686). BBN Laboratories 1987

57. Whitehead, A. N.: The aims of education. New York, Macmillan 1929

58. Williams, M. D., Hollan, J. D., Stevens, A. L.: Human reasoning about a simple physical system. In: D. Gentner & A. Stevens (eds.), Mental models (pp. 131-153). Hillsdale, Erlbaum 1983

5. Principles of Engineering Courses and Apprenticeship Entry Requirements

Industry, i.e., one half of the school-industry link partnership, uses the term engineering to collectively refer to the high-level use of technological procedures to achieve its ends. Consequently, the planners of the ARW invited Liao to provide an overview of a National Science Foundation (USA)-funded model program to introduce the principles of engineering into the schools of America.

However, because of the workshop's structure and goals, it was imperative to include industry's perspectives on the same topic. To this end, Buresch highlighted the goals and core beliefs of an industry-leading corporation with respect to the high-level systems view of both technology and the learning of technology. The workshop was even further enriched by Stern's insightful contribution of Asian industry and education perspectives on the same theme.

One of the outcomes of these presentations was the new research area identified by the combined interaction of the engineering areas, the structure of the learning situations employed, and the strategy of thinking. The issue is, how does one bring people from multiple disciplines and backgrounds together and organize their interaction for maximum effect? The crux is, how do we advance innovative thinking by exploiting the creative tension between integrating and individualizing and between logic and intuition?

Participants raised questions related to the translation of needs between the universities and the factory/companies.

Learning in Technical Work Systems - Industrial Training Models

Jürgen Buresch
BMW AG
Department of Development of Human Resources
Petuelring 130, D-80807 München, Germany

Abstract. The general conditions in modern industrial companies determined by the development of society and technology and the new demands for qualification of the employees arising from changing production organisation are used as starting points to describe principles and methods of vocational and further education. The main goal is to strive for producing extensive acting competence; the way is to reinforce project work and team work.

Personal related aspects will be characterised as essential disruptive elements of high automated production. These aspects reveal themselves especially by one-sided sensitivity and one-sided structured knowledge of the employees. As didactical-methodological consequence for efficient vocational and further education the author points out a problem-genetic optimisation of the transfer effect in technical instruction systems inside for a curriculum of acting oriented learning.

Keywords. Vocational and further education, technical instruction systems, acting oriented learning

As an educator, Socrates gave nothing, but caused others to bring it forth. He made seemingly wise persons aware of what they did not know and in this way allowed them to find genuine knowledge for themselves. In other words:

"Everyone must discover knowledge for himself, it cannot be transferred like a product, it can only be aroused." (cf. Jaspers, 1992, p. 4)

I believe that we all experience the same problems - at least far as education is concerned; be it at universities, at schools providing general education, at vocational training schools or in industry - where they in turn apply to both and advanced vocational training. Although we see them from a different point of view, we can none the less learn from one another.

On this note, my thanks are due to WOCATE, the World Council of Associations for Technology Education, for making this exchange possible. Let us seize this opportunity, for according to Jaspers:

"Education is evident in the ability to ask questions which, in specific cases and with the aid of previously acquired knowledge, are capable of penetrating to the heart of the matter." (cf. Jaspers, 1992, p. 114).

With regard to my chosen subject: "Learning in technical work systems" I would first like to describe the fundamental changes in modern industrial companies and deal with the models and methods currently practised in the field of internal basic and advanced training.

Starting with the conditions prevalent in everyday technical work systems, I will then refer to a specific example to demonstrate how we are trying to increase the flexibility of our employees in highly automated production areas by communicating to them the basic principles of information, control and regulating technology.

The model which I intend to present is the one we are currently testing; it concerns optimisation of the problem-genetic transfer effect for technical instruction systems.

Finally, I will sum up our picture of the consequences for education and training on the basis of what has been said.

1 On the Fundamental Changes in Modern Industrial Companies

1.1 Changes to Qualification Requirements

In the past few years, the level of automation has increased significantly in BMW production areas. These changes have led to demanding physical activities such as loading, operating and removing being replaced increasingly by functions such as controlling, monitoring and maintenance of the system. Physical demands have been overtaken by psychological ones, combined with the need to observe parameters such as quality, full utilisation of machine capacity and preventive maintenance.

Linked to this are the higher training standards which operating and maintenance personnel are expected to satisfy. These changing qualifications open up possibilities for new forms of work structures, work organisation and employee co-operation, with corresponding repercussions on management structures. In practice, this leads to the gradual breakdown of hierarchies and to the transfer of responsibility and tasks to operating personnel. One example of the increased flexibility already demanded of production and maintenance personnel is the use of industrial robots in flexible production systems.

As a consequence of endeavours to remain internationally competitive, the technological development outlined here will continue to accelerate, in the field of production it is determined by the following factors:

– a trend towards flexible, computer integrated production,
– greater use of sensor controlled robots and flexible production cells,
– a reduction in downtime and non productive time,
– automation of in-house transport and quality control,
– work time models for more efficient utilisation of capital intensive systems.

Such drastic changes are bound to have repercussions on the people actively employed in these areas, on the qualifications they need and on communication and co-operation patterns; this will apply to both operating and maintenance personnel working in highly automated production areas. Organisational structures, communication paths and the qualifications possessed by both employees and managers must be chosen appropriately if these technological changes are also to be controllable in terms of personnel policy.

1.2 New Requirements for Trainers to Satisfy

Extending and reorganising the scope for decision - making and action - taking requires employees to be prepared for these new tasks. Trainers too can only perform their task successfully if they have an active part to play in company developments and can make use to them in their own task area. The company assists trainers with advanced training measures.

At BMW, the objective of advanced training for trainers is to promote comprehensive, interactive skills. These are based on:

Subject competence	Special-subject knowledge and abilities
Methodological competence	Precise, methodical, planned ways of thinking and the development of problem solving strategies for specific tasks
Social competence	The appropriate communicative and co-operative behaviour

This calls for long-term planning of professional qualification and for trainers to be taught new techniques at an early stage. It includes transferring problems from a practical to a classroom setting, incorporating company-specific, character-forming factors relevant to training and integrating working and learning.

In addition to differing peripheral conditions such as the European Community, the growing together of European states (East and West) and international economic, technical, political and socio-political structural changes, we are also faced with better qualifications on paper and a different attitude to their vocational choice. The learning environment is therefore changing.

Different target groups, an increasing need for education, the call for lifelong learning and the compulsion to reduce costs all necessitate new training strategies and new training concepts. The steady reduction in working hours and the rising costs of education have led to a demand for part of advanced training to be transferred to leisure time. Examples of new learning techniques and methods of conveying knowledge include the use of new media and interactive teaching/learning systems, a stronger link between theory and practice as a consequence of on-the-job learning and new forms of self education in well equipped centres.

1.3 Models/Methods of Internal Basic and Advanced Training

As a rule, training structures are planned so that training increasingly takes the form of project and team work. The development of key qualifications is anticipated in all training sections from the start. According to the new concept of acquiring vocational qualifications, that is to say independent planning, implementation, monitoring and assessment, training is moving away from its intensive support role and taking on a more advisory character as training times increase in length (fig. 1).

The monitoring of learning success relates to the attainment of learning and training goals and to progress in vocational qualification, in other words to the acquisition of abilities, skills and behavioural patterns. It is linked with analysis, assessment and measurement of achievement.

One thing which must remain open is whether people will behave in the appropriate way in a future situation. There are no criteria suitable for measuring this. We must not only be able to do something, we must also do it.

– On-the job training
– Training on the job furthers the desired link between theory and practice.

Quality circle/ "learning shop". The BMW - "learning shop" promotes organisational development within the company. The "learning shop" is important because it embodies action, experience and actual practice; it has developed from internal company requirements. The "learning shop" is where working groups come to terms actively with topics both related and unrelated to work. Group work achieves a balanced relationship between individual and group activity and topic orientation. The main objectives are to develop human potential and to improve quality and productivity.

Personal study centres. The company provides the foundation on which the employee can build outside working hours. The on-site study adviser can be consulted if required.

Correspondence courses. BMW has made rooms at its Munich plant available to the correspondence university. The correspondence university is a popular choice among participants in the Munich region and BMW employees.

Independent learning using guide text. Guide texts include information and instruction on how to solve set tasks independently.

The systematic procedure in 6 steps concern:

1. Information on the task,
2. The work plan,
3. Technology, work aids,
4. Implementation,
5. Monitoring,
6. Assessment by the trainer.

1.4 Project Oriented and Transfer Oriented Training

A predefined task can be tackled in three organisational learning forms:

1. Self-controlled individual work
2. Group planned individual work
3. Group work

The aim is to satisfy the requirements of the new concept of professional development by reorganising the vocations for which training is required. Emphasis should be placed on personal control of the learning process in order to promote independence and the ability to work in teams.

Interactive teaching/learning systems. In addition to interactive teaching/learning systems, which are already applied in a wide area, it is no longer possible to conceive of teaching without the simulation of technical procedures and the examination of computer programs (e.g. for the control of machine tools). Video tapes, video discs and compact discs are used as data carriers.

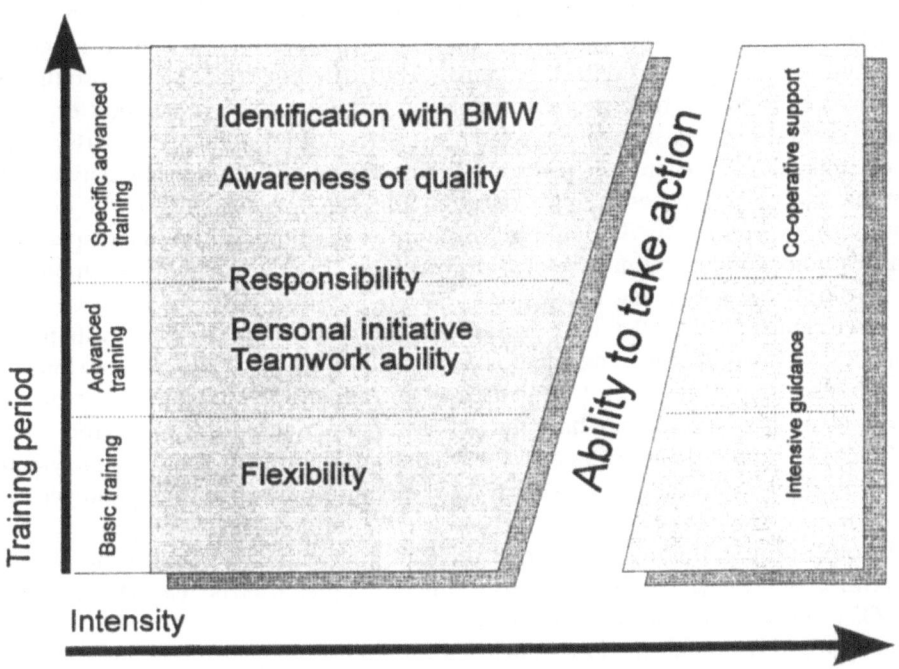

Fig. 1 From intensive supervising to co-operative advising

2 PROTEUS - An Example of Learning in Technical Systems

PROTEUS - Programm zur Optimierung des Transfereffektes in technischen
    Unterweisungssystemen (program for optimising the transfer
    effect in technical instruction systems)

PROTEUS: In Greek mythology, a sea god who was able to make prophecies but,
because he could change his shape at any time, was difficult to catch.

The "capricious nature of the object" in technical systems would seem to be very protean; but by optimising the transfer effect, we hope to be able to get the root of this troublesome problem with the aid of the PROTEUS´ special skill, name his ability to change his shape.

2.1 Problems Inherent in Technical Systems

To be able to ensure internationally competitive quality standards in the production area calls for independent, problem solving, co-operative and skilled workers. Production quality depends on employees abilities; it can no longer be guaranteed by quality control systems. The efficient use of new production techniques is therefore largely dependent on employees` learning abilities, since these are used in raid succession in the most varied of production areas. But if this more intensive use of technology is not accompanied by adequate interactive skills on the part of employees, training requirements are increased and, in the event of faults or equipment modification during start-up, production is interrupted and causes non-productive time and costs to escalate. The responsibility of employees accordingly takes on a new dimension.

An example: With the introduction of interlinked production systems for manufacturing brake discs, demands similar to those described above were made of employees as a result of technical and organisational changes. Production employees, however, did not have the necessary experience on which to rely.

Training requirements and costs for preparing employees to use such systems were high; nevertheless, the result of work using the new machines and systems were not satisfactory.

In our opinion, this was not due to the fact that employees were insufficiently flexible, but to lack of suitable training concepts; this is the area at which PROTEUS project is specifically aimed. The situation outlined here does not just concern BMW, but all modern industrial companies. It is the consequence of the fact that optimisation of the transfer effect in instruction systems for highly automated production areas has been neglected up to now (and was previously unnecessary).

What kind of problems are facing us, and what are the interference factors ?

Our observations were based on representative fault analyses during the period in which employees were familiarised with interlinked production systems. Among other things, fault analyses differ according to location, cause and type of fault.

For example, the types of fault varied according to technology, mechanics, electric's/electronics, pneumatics and hydraulics. In particular, however, it was possible to identify abnormalities during the work process with the resulting consequential faults. Aspects of disruptive situations for which people were responsible included:

- Differences in anticipatory behaviour during the work process,
- Varying fault diagnosis procedures,
- The differing degrees to which associated measures - necessary for problem solving were taken.

To be more precise: the problem solving process was often disturbed by imbalances of emphasis and knowledge structure. The information available in interlinked systems was not utilised sufficiently (collecting data, analysing data, forming and examining hypotheses, taking decisions capable of solving specific problems and acting appropriately during work).

Based on these findings, we tried to determine the constitutive factors in the peculiarities noticeable in the interaction of individuals working in disruptive situations. This led us to the question:

What causes the problems and the differences which occur when individuals interact in a working environment ?

Our results revealed:

1. Varying attitudes to and concepts of theory and practice,
2. Varying levels of perceptive transformation.

In a practical working environment, this is expressed in the internal mental conversion of a two-dimensional representation (for example, reading a technical drawing) into a conception of a three-dimensional object and in the conversion of a three-dimensional object back into a two-dimensional representation. These tasks must be performed when writing the machine tool control program and when simulating the process.

The trainer is faced here with the problem of didactic reduction, in order to make the necessary transformation work comprehensible. If didactic reduction does not go far enough, the trainer will not be understood; if it goes too far, then the problems of reality between three- and two-dimensionality are not seen. The trainer is often unaware that his knowledge and his experience make him perceive things differently.

Some examples to demonstrate this. To start with, a few comments concerning the frequently encountered misunderstanding of theory and practice. Even Kant commented on the common saying: What may be right in theory may not apply in practice.

"The veritable epitome of practical rules is called theory if these rules or principles are of a certain general nature and derived from a number of conditions which have a mandatory influence on their implementation. On the other hand, practice does not refer to all work, but only to the accomplishment of a purpose which is conceived as adherence to certain general principles of the process." (cf. Kant, 1981, p. 127).

For Kant, theory and practice were two sides of one coin. He continues:

"In other words, nobody can claim to be practically proficient in a science and then ignore the theory without simply admitting that he is ignorant about his subject; by believing that he can get further than theory is able to bring him by fumbling around with trails and experiments without assembling certain principles (which actually make up what is known theory) and without having thought in holistic terms about his activities (which, if done methodically, is referred to as a system)." (cf. Kant, 1981, p. 128).

Now for two examples from the dimensional ontology for transformation tasks performed as part of the perception process, according to Frankl (fig. 2).

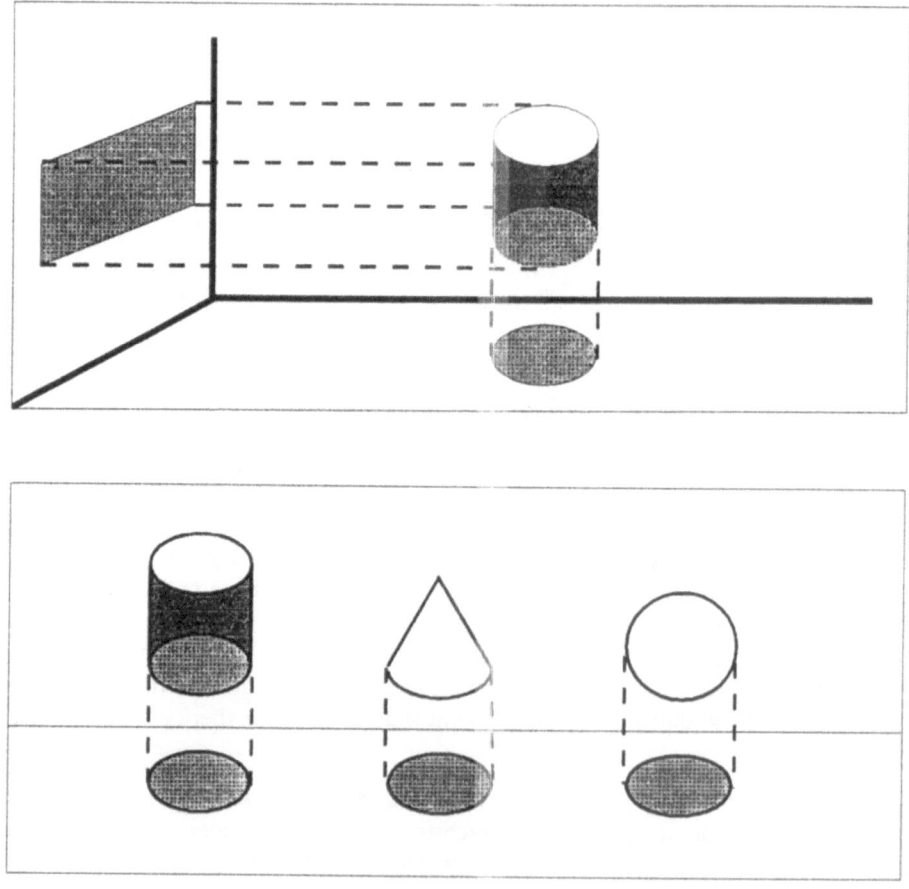

Fig. 2 Illustration showing two laws of dimensional ontology (V. E. Frankl)

"One and the same thing projected from its own dimension into different dimensions which are lower than its own is reflected in such a way that the images contradict one another. If, for example, I project a drinking glass (Cylinder), or, in geometrical terms, a cylinder, from a three-dimensional space into the two-dimensional planes of horizontal projection and side elevation, then in one case a circle is produced, in the other case a rectangle. Moreover, the projection is also contradictory, because in both cases the figure produced is closed although the drinking glass is an open vessel." (cf. Frankl, 1985, p. 24).

These are the demands made of perception in the simulation of technical processes, for example CNC simulation.

The second law of dimensional ontology (fig. 2) is:

"(Not one and the same but) different things are projected out of their own dimension (not in different dimensions but) into one and the same dimension which is lower than their own, and are reflected in such a way that the projections (do not contradict one another but) are ambiguous. If, for example, I project a cylinder, a cone and a sphere from a three-dimensional space into the two-dimensional plane of horizontal projection, then a circle is produced in each case. If we regard the cylinder, the cone and the sphere as casting shadows, these are ambiguous in the sense that, because they are identical, I cannot tell from them if they are cast by a cylinder, a cone or a sphere." (cf. Frankl, 1985, p. 25).

Another example is Piaget's "mountain exercise" (fig.3), which is comparable with the demands made when reading technical drawings and the transformation work involved in imagining the different views of a drawing such as in plan, in elevation or in any possible section.

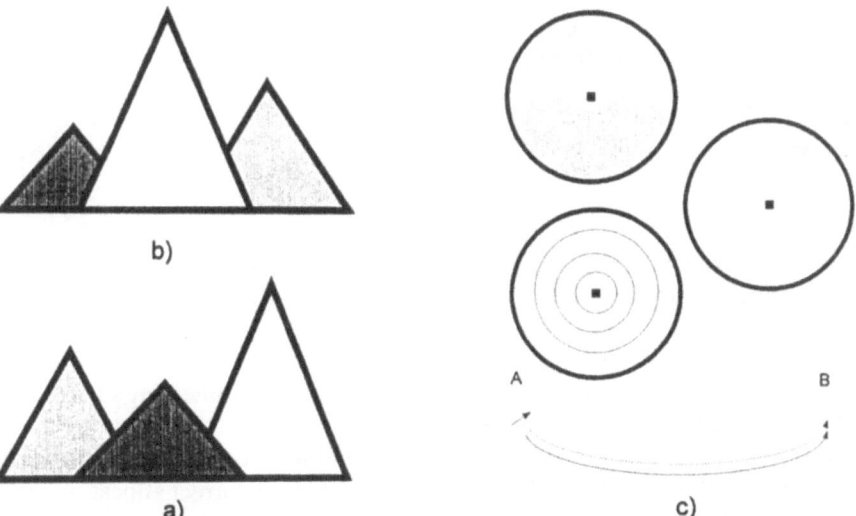

Fig. 3 Piaget's mountain exercise (according to Klix 1971)

Figure 3 a shows the initial view and figure 3 b a different view from which the task is to reconstruct the observers position. Figure 3 b thus shows the final state of a transformation of characteristics to which an observers position (fig.3 c) is to be assigned in Piaget´s mountain exercise. According to Klix, the demand presupposes a forward and an inverse transformation (determining the change of location between a and b, transposition from b to a). To clarify the required transformations, figure 3 c shows the positions and distance relationships seen from above. From here, it is possible to view the observers change of location simultaneously (cf. Klix 1971, p. 539).

Figure 4 is an example indicating the limits of recognition of topological equivalent configurations. The figures marked A and A` and B and B` in figure 4 are topological equivalent, but are not perceived as "similar" configurations. They are perceptively different figures. However, with the aid of abstract rules of recognition, it is possible to learn that they are equivalent (according to Minsky).

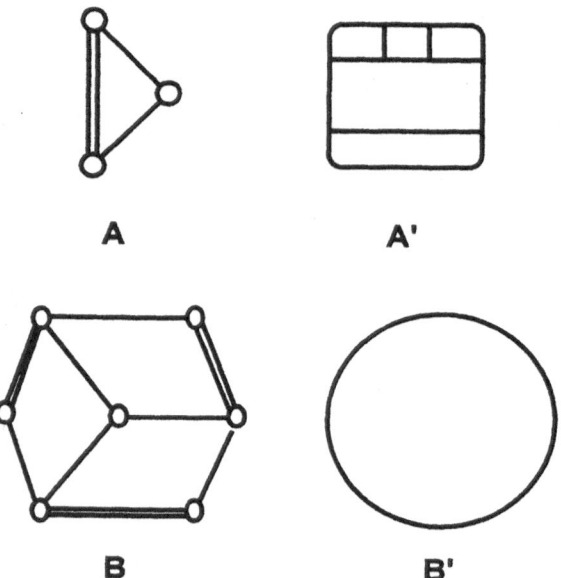

Fig. 4 Examples showing the perceptive limits of recognition of topological
equivalent configurations (Klix)

Also according to Klix, these and similar models teach us something else: that all processes of recognition includes decisions.

According to this, it is the "decision made combining object recognition with behaviour which leads to the consequences of correct or incorrect allocation". This shows "that even the most elementary signal reception tasks can involve decision processes by way of memory structures which have to be learned".

"This network of phylogenetically pre-formed stimulus processing and learning-related differentiation processes in perception represents a significant basic requirement for the potential development and training of higher cognitive processes." (cf. Klix 1971, p. 283).

Accordingly, cognition is a procedure that generates comprehension systems by learning. The cognitive requirement priorities in disturbance situations concerning technical working systems are to be found in particularly in the absorption of information, its processing and the decisions to be taken in connection with the necessary action. Accordingly, the action to be taken in disturbance situations is mainly determined by the ability to master these cognitive demands, and is therefore bound to exhibit considerable inter individual differences.

However, if cognition is a process which "generates comprehension systems by learning", awareness of the relationship between the demand situation and the action necessary to satisfy that demand must surely offer interesting methodical scope for determining the necessary approaches to learning. The relationship between the orientation stimulus (that is to say the adoption of an approach designed to filter out the evaluate relationships between features), behaviour program and transformation sequence can be seen in figure 5 (cf. Klix 1971, p.546).

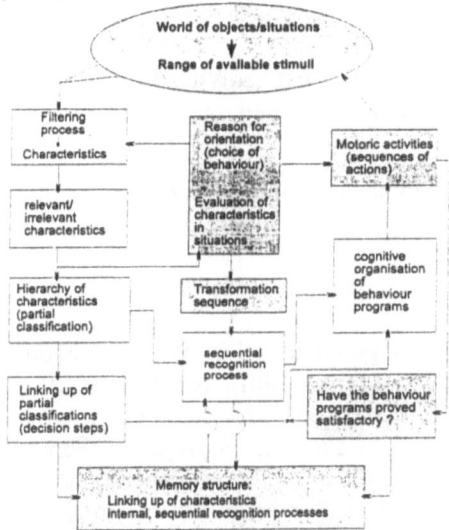

Fig. 5 Relationship between orientation stimulus, behaviour program and transformation sequence

According to Klix, the sequence of transformation stages and their effect on perception give rise to a memory structure, which calls for recognition processes which have been built up step by step. After this has taken place, the memory structures can set off and also control sequential recognition processes. In this way, transformation of characteristics triggered off by actions have the effect of changing ambient conditions. According to Klix, this process leads to the "discovery" of the depth structure information sources.

It permits cognitive structural formations to be implanted into individual memories although containing ambient characteristics which cannot be perceived.

2.2 Regarding the Problem-Genetic Method

In simplified terms, in case of the evolutionary recognition theory approach, the recognition path leads from the phenomenon to the essential, from the collecting, comparing and sorting of facts to the relevation of their internal, general and essential inter-relationships and to the determination of the laws with which they conform (cf. Bührdel 1988).

The genetic teaching/instruction method supports and promotes the development and the ability to analyse and solve problems. The continuous posing and solving of partial tasks (Fuchs 1980) takes place on the basis of heuristic principles.

As early as 1837, Mager produced a three-point summary of the principle of the genetic method:

1. The exploration (induction) or analysis of the initial source material,
2. The conclusion drawn from known points with regard to the new one being sought,
3. The build-up of new structures from elements obtained analytically, either by a freely creative combination process or a genetic one based on known laws (cf. Mager 1837).

A method of training and instruction which employs and communicates heuristic rules and takes account of recognitive genesis is referred to as a problem-genetic method.

Knowledge of problem solving strategies is a precondition for the transferability of those receiving training.

Practical ability, however, is acquired by independent action. Successful action presupposes the presence of the appropriate cognitive skills (cf. Hacker 1979), something which leads any conventionally described separation between theory and practice ad absurdum. The overall objective of the PROTEUS project is therefore to develop and test a curriculum from the production and plant engineering area for the improvement of skill-flexibility and co-operative problem solving among skilled personnel. As a means of communication and furthering the main key qualifications (the ability to solve problems, independent planning and monitoring), teaching and instructional methods based on problem-genesis and education by personal control are to be used.

The "education of personal control" method to be adopted for the model process is based on the findings on the ORIGIN concept (De Charms 1973) and the results from the work in learning shops and quality circles (Grau/Klaus 1988).

By means of an action oriented learning curriculum in training, it is intended to communicate all-embracing principles by examples in all cases. This is with the intention of building up a common knowledge structure for all vocations in industrial production and plant engineering, as a precondition for the competent, skilled and co-operative solution of problems in the work area. This knowledge structure at the same time forms a basis for communication on various hierarchical levels within the working environment. The structure of industrial vocations (basic vocational training, expert training in specific fields) is equivalent to the manner in which various working activities are networked within the production process. As far as these activities are concerned, increasing importance is now attached not only to the qualifications referred to above, and derived from the new demands made on skilled personnel, but also the inter-subject qualifications referred to as key qualifications.

Selected aspects of the content of experimental model planning:

PRELIMINARY WORK ON CURRICULUM DEVELOPMENT
– Describing representative inter-subject tasks to be solved,
– Establishing inter-subject problems and methods of solving them,
– Drawing up evaluation criteria,
– Describing tasks aimed at monitoring transfer work,
– Stating principles for the communication of meta-knowledge or knowledge in depth,
– determining the joint minimum requirements in the information, control and regulation technology areas,
– Compiling a qualification profile.

DEVELOPING THE CURRICULUM
– Deciding on the structure of the curriculum's learning objectives,
– Learning objectives in specific subject areas and covering several subjects,
– Reducing presence and catalogue knowledge,
– Structuring the content of study material according to the problem genetic method,
– Integrating the PROTEUS curriculum into the training vocations` subject and timetable structures.

CREATING THE PRECONDITIONS NECESSARY FOR THE CURRICULUM TO BE INTO EFFECT
– Producing training material,
– Installing and operating the technical equipment,
– Obtaining qualified instructors,
– Having training documentation drawn up (by trainers),
– Holding a trainers seminar to co-ordinate and optimise the training material drawn up by the trainers.

IMPLEMENTING AND OPTIMISING THE PROTEUS CURRICULUM
– First implementing cycle and its evaluation,

– Assessment of results and revisions to curriculum,
– Second implementation cycles and its evaluation at additional BMW training
  points,
– Project reports,
– Interim reports and exchange of conclusions,
– Presentation, final report and exchange of conclusions.

2.3 Consequences for Education and Training

In conclusion I would like to attempt to supply answers in the form of these to a
number of questions related to the educational and training consequences. These
questions are:

1. Is there a connection between the technical area and society ?
2. Do we need ethical standards when shaping the future ?
3. Do we need to educate people on technical matters ?
4. What course of actions should we adopt ?

2.3.1 Is There a Connection Between the Technical Area and Society?

– Technical development provides a basis for economic and social progress.
– Advanced technology not only creates jobs but also helps to safeguard
  our future.
– Technology is an element in our culture.

Conclusion. Technology is part of our society; we live with and it forms a
basis for our survival.

2.3.2 Do We Need Ethical Standards When Shaping the Future?

– We have no need either to idolise or decry technology.
– We must confront its risks, but fear is a poor counsellor in such cases; we need
  an open minded approach to technology with all its advantages and
  disadvantages.
– The character of a civilisation and therefore the way in which people concern
  themselves with technology is governed by the ethical and cultural values to
  which they adhere.
– The increasingly technical character of our industrial society has always been
  accompanied by fears, criticisms and appeals of various kinds; the rejection of
  technology is as old as its history.
– Responsibility is preparedness to stand up for ones own actions or one's failure

to act, and accept the resulting direct consequences. Responsibility includes knowledge of the limits of one's own awareness and ability to act.
– Responsibility can only be perceived as an element in an overall view; this calls for interdisciplinary discussion and co-operation.
– According to Weber, every individual is responsible for the future, not merely those with technical skills.

Conclusion. We need ethical standards when shaping the future.

2.3.3 Do We Need to Educate People on Technical Matters?

– People have to confront the environment into which they are born (Karl Marx).
– When we encounter the modern working world, we not only need to think systematically and in networked relationships, but also to make the connection between theory and practice, a desirable step which makes a worthwhile contribution towards the vocational orientation of young people.
– We need technical education from an early age, beginning when the child is being brought up by its parents.
– Genuine progress presupposes that we handle technical matters with responsibility and attach a higher value to knowledge than to technology and its ambivalent effects.
– "We are not only responsible for what we do but also for what we do not do." (LAO-TSE)

this also applies to the dialogue between school and industry.

– We must learn to master technology so that it does not master us.
– Changes in technology and in the industrial society compel us to rethink the positions of education and the school in a changing society and to arrive at the correct conclusions in good time regarding the educational system.

Conclusion. We need technological education.

2.3.4 What Course of Action Should We Adopt?

We must ensure that there is awareness inside the school of changes taking place outside it. This means creating a basis for the comprehension of social and economic relationships and providing information on technical processes and their effects. This can be achieved as follows:
technical education at an early age, starting in the hole and in nursery schools or equivalent units.

– practical orientation (a link with the world of business and labour) as a fundamental educational task from primary through high school.
– a greater degree of co-operation between schools/high schools and industry.

This will entail:

– utilising modern knowledge of a teaching and behavioural psychology,
– contemporary pedagogic and adult educational methods,
– introduction of modern media,
– giving consideration to the type of pupil,
– suitable learning conditions,
– motivation of teachers and pupils, enthusiasm for the task,
– promoting life-long learning as a pleasurable task,
– encouraging commitment and personal initiative,
– an inter-disciplinary teaching principle (the world as a unit),
– the communication of knowledge structures.

If our young people can be prepared for life in this way, we can face technical and social changes without anxiety and be confident in humanity's ability to shape its future in a responsible manner.

References

1. Bührdel, Ch.: Unterrichtsmethodik Maschinenwesen. Berlin, Verlag Technik 1988
2. de Charms, D.: Ein schulisches Trainingsprogramm zum Erleben eigener Verursachung. In: Edelstein (ed.) Bedingungen des Bildungsprozesses. (p. 60-78), Stuttgart, Klett 1973
3. Frankl, V.: Der Mensch vor der Frage nach dem Sinn. Zürich: Piper 1985
4. Fuchs, R.: Einführung in die Lernpsychologie. Darmstadt: Wissenschaftliche Buchgesellschaft 1980
5. Grau und Klaus: Untersuchungen zur Kausalanalyse des Transfereffektes von Vorübungsprogrammen. In: Erziehungswissenschaftliche Forschung 1975
6. Hacker, W.: Allgemeine Arbeits- und Ingenieurpsychologie. Stuttgart, Huber 1979
7. Jaspers, K.: Was ist Erziehung? München, Zürich, Piper 1992
8. Kant, I.: Schriften zur Anthropologie, Geschichtsphilosophie, Politik und Pädagogik. In: Weischedel, W. (ed.) Band 9, Erster Teil. (pp. 127-128) Darmstadt, Wissenschaftliche Buchgesellschaft 1981
9. Klix, F.: Information und Verhalten. Kybernetische Aspekte der organismischen Informationsverarbeitung. Einführung in naturwissenschaftliche Grundlagen der Allgemeinen Psychologie. Berlin, Deutscher Verlag der Wissenschaften 1971
10. Mager, K.: Wissenschaft der Mathematik nach heuristisch genetischer Methode. Berlin, Förster 1837

Principles of Engineering Course: School and Industrial Collaboration

Thomas T. Liao
State University of New York at Stony Brook
Department of Technology and Society
Engineering Building, Room 210, Stony Brook, NY 11794-2250, USA

Abstract. Engaging students in design and problem solving activities that are related to actual industrial systems and problems is an optimum way of providing contextual or situated learning. In the high school course, Principles of Engineering (POE), many schools have developed innovative school and industrial partnerships that are symbiotic. All parties in the collaboration benefit and each organization's missions are enhanced. Some of the case studies or curriculum units have been developed in a collaborative manner.

In this paper, after discussing the design features of the POE course, several examples of school-industrial symbiosis are described. New curriculum materials that have been developed with the help of company personnnel and private sector support are highlighted. The unique features of school/industry alliances will be presented. The paper concludes with a description of how the POE course has been designed to mirror the engineering team approach to design and problem solving that is used in industry as well as the recommendations to the US Department of Labor's SCANS report.

Keywords. Engineering education, contextual learning, school-business collaboration, technology case studies

1 Design Criteria for Development of Instructional Systems and Curriculum

Learning only becomes meaningful and interesting if students perceive connections between what they know and what they are trying to learn. Thus, contextual or situated learning should be the paradigm for instructional design. Students need to learn concepts, strategies, and habits of the mind that help them see how the various aspects of an increasing technological world are connected. [2]

We need new interdisciplinary courses that engage students in relevant problems and the study of technological systems. These courses besides providing contextual learning and study of unifying concepts that connect seemingly unrelated events, must also provide many opportunities for cooperative learning. We should design learing environments (curriculum and instruction) that develop skills for carrying out the adult roles that high school students will soon have to assume. Being able to be an effective team member is one such skill.

We should also design learning environments that model some of the highly successful techniques that are used by today's business and industry. For example, the just-in-time manufacturing approach can be applied to education in what can be called just-in-time learning. In this approach to learning, concepts and skills are learned as needed to solve problems or design systems. A second example is the use of the notion of concurrent engineering in programs that are designed to achieve outcome-based education. In other words, the various aspects of a contextual learning systems must be integrated so that we can design more optimum learning environments. For example, in studying the evolution of conventional TV systems to a HDTV (High Definition Television) system, students need to integrate the study of human factors, governmental regulatory agencies, the science of pulse code modulation and the mathematics of digital systems as well as the ideas of consumer acceptance and international competitiveness.

Business and industry besides providing metaphors for curriculum design and development can also be collaborators in the design and development of instructional systems and curriculum that are based on the design criteria that are discussed above, namely :

- Contextual Learning
- Connections via Unifying Concepts
- Cooperative Learning
- Concurrent and just-in-time learning

A fifth "C" that can be added to already discussed 4 "C's" of educational reform is constructivism. The constructive approach suggests design criterion that specifies design features which result in learning activities that provide opportunities for engagement, exploration, explanation, elaboration and evaluation. A modern learner-center instructional system can be designed using the five "C's" of educational reform and the five "E's" of the constructivist approach to learning. The most compeling reason for using these design criteria is that the resulting learning environments will promote life-long learning.

In the past six years, the author of this paper has been collaborating with a group of colleagues in New York State, USA, in the design of a high school course, Principles of Engineering, which used these design criteria (5 C's and 5 E's).

The purpose of this paper is to describe how these design criteria guided the development of the learner-centered Principles of Engineering course that is centered around six major conceptual areas and uses. Real - world case studies are used to help students learn how the concepts are applied to the study of real problems and systems.

After providing an overview of the Principles of Engineering course, the paper will discuss two types of school-industry collaboration. Some of the case studies and curriculum units have been developed with mini-grants from industry-based foundations, which supported the work of educators and professionals from industry, working as a team. The second type of collaboration is in the form of school-business alliances that resulted in projects that are symbiotic. This type of win-win cooperation produces synergistic outcomes.

The paper concludes with a discussion of how the Principles of Engineering course is an exemplary response to the US Department of Labor's recently published SCANS report which described what high school graduates ought to be able to do as future employees in US companies.

2 Overview of Principles of Engineering Course

Currently, about sixty high schools in New York State are teaching a newly developed course called Principles of Engineering. This course, designed for college-bound 11th and 12th grade students, uses the case study approach to help students learn and apply six major conceptual areas of engineering. During the 1992-93 school year, the following five case studies were field-tested:

1. Auto Safety
2. Ergonomics of Communication Technology
3. Machine Automation
4. Structures: Emergency Shelters
5. Energy Case Studies

This author is part of the curriculum development team and is writer for the second case study. These case studies or mini-courses are vehicles for helping students learn and use the six major concepts. In order to convey the scope of this course and the six conceptual areas, the following performance objectives are reproduced from the curriculum guide. [3]

Upon completion of the set of case studies in the course, students will be competent in:

1. Modeling
   a. Use of words, pictures, and mathematics to describe a system.
   b. Manipulation of models of systems through the use of apparatus, computer simulations, and mock-ups.

2. Systems
   a. Describing a system in terms of input and output.
   b. Explaining and demonstrating how a specific system is made up of subsystems.

c. Demonstrating how a system is controlled through feedback.
d. Contrasting open- and closed-loop systems.

3. Optimization
   a. Explaining the consequences involved in trade-off situations.
   b. Setting criteria in real-world decision-making situations.
   c. Explaining how constraints often conflict with the ability to meet the desired outcome in decision-making situations.
   d. Developing the ability to use techniques such as applying algorithms and appropriate trial and error in making decisions.
   e. Using cost-benefit analysis and cost-effective analysis in making decisions. Cost is considered as human, societal, political, environmental, as well as economic.

4. Technology-Society Interaction
   a. Applying the system of technology assessment regarding the future impact on society of the application of specific technologies.
   b. Describing the process of considering alternative approaches to the solution of technology-society problems. These alternatives fit into the categories of:
      1) Education (behavior modification)
      2) Legislation (rules and laws)
      3) Technological fixes (applying technology to the solution of a problem)
   c. Actually getting involved in voluntary action such as lobbying, recycling, and/or developing a technological fix in a real-world situation.

5. Design
   a. Participating in the design process.
   b. Considering human and environmental factors in the design of a system or device.
   c. Applying design principles such as form and function, color, balance, unity, etc. in the design process.
   d. Selecting appropriate materials when designing.
   e. Considering the effect of production capabilities, marketing, time and cost in designing a product.

6. Engineering Ethics
   a. Considering the legal and professional responsibilities of contractual agreements and activities.
   b. Exhibiting social responsibility by considering:
      1) Benefit or risk to society.
      2) Benefit or risk to individuals.
      3) Environmental risk.
      4) Long-term vs. short-term risk and gains in making decisions.
   c. Being aware of the moral dilemmas involved in employment.
      1) Do you blow the whistle on your employer even at the risk of losing your job?
      2) How do you weigh the benefit vs. risk in making a decision?

3 Industry-Based Curriculum Units

A number of curriculum units contain case studies that were developed with support from private foundations. The energy case studies were developed with a grant from the New York State Power authority. The passive solar home case study engages students in the design and construction of a model of a commercially available passive solar home. The other two solar energy case studies deal with the design of a model solar powered vehicle and the study of efficient homes and electrical appliances.

A new set of case studies that relate to the theme of Designing Technology for People with Disabilities is being developed and field-tested. This project, supported with a grant from NEC of America Foundation, involves students in human factors engineering (ergonomics).

All three case studies are driven by scenarios that describe the needs of a person with some type of disability. One of the case studies challenge the students to design and construct systems to aid a new student with limited vision to become familiar with a new school. The other two case studies deal with the design of adaptive devices to overcome various types of physical disabilities.

A set of technology learning activities has been developed for high school students using a professional engineering software called Mannequin. Five POE teachers working with the education director of Bio-Mechanics Corporation developed a curriculum unit that provides an introductin to ergonomics using the Mannequin software and a pocket ergometer. This is an excellent example of how business people and educators can collaborate on a new educational product.

4 School-Industry Partnerships

In order for high school students to begin to learn the skills to become an effective employee, they need to have meaningful contacts with professionals in various occupations. In the POE course, a number of schools have started or are participating in programs that make it possible for professional engineers to interact with high school students.

Some schools have formed school/business alliances to promote collaborative programs. For example, Sachem H. S. on Long Island, New York is now involved in alliances with two companies: CYBEX Corporation and Symbol Technologies Inc. The goals of the Sachem School/Business Alliance and its mission is to provide an enhanced relationship between Sachem and the business community so that their students will be the best prepared for tomorrow. They believe that by providing educational opportunities such as:

- improving communications and the exchange of information between the business community and the schools
- formally advising the schools
- providing professional assistance to schools

- assisting the business community
- helping in the transition for the students from school to work

the community of Sachem and the economy of Long Island will be improved. The following meeting agenda provides a glimpse of the activities of the alliance:

Sachem School-Business Alliance Meeting
Wednesday, June 9, 1993
Sachem High School, North Campus

Agenda:

I.   Student Outcomes Subcommittee
        A. Employer survey
        B. Mission statement

II. Sachem/CYBEX Partnership
        A. Project presentation by Advertising, Marketing and
        Engineering students.

III. Sachem/Symbol Technologies Partnership
        A. Engineering Students Mentoring Report

IV. Sachem Corporate Adventure - Harry Einbinder

V.   Carpentry/Construction CTP Update - Dominick Messina

VI. Renaissance Update - John Heslin

In the fall of 1993, the Department of Technology and Society of SUNY at Stony Brook's College of Engineering and Applied Sciences will be hosting the second National Engineering Design Competition (NEDC). This regional competition is coordinated by JETS (Junior Engineering Technical Society) and winners go on to the National Competition in Washington D. C., USA.

NEDC is an exciting program in which teams of students design, fabricate, and demonstrate solutions to a defined problem. At all levels of competition, students present, demonstrate, and defend both their design and development process and their solutions to a panel of experts who serve as judges.

Engineers from local companies can serve as advisors as well as judges. In last year's competition, we had volunteers from Bio-Mechanics and CYBEX Corporations serve as judges. Other engineers seved as advisors during the preparation prior to the competition. In both cases, the engineers seved as positive role models for the high school students.

(VI) POE: An exemplary response to the SCANS recommendations

"Nothing is more important to the future of this country than the effective education of our young people. An informed and literate nation is essential to our nation's productivity and standard of living. We can't afford anything less than a well educated and well prepared workforce"[4] William E. Brock, Chair Secretary's Commission on Achieving Necessary Skills U. S. Department of Labor

On April 5, 1990, US Secretary of Labor Elizabeth Dole announced that William E. Brock, a former secretary of labor, will chair a new Secretary's Commission on Achieving Necessary Skills (SCANS). The above quote was a part of a statement made by Brock on the occasion of his appointment as chair of SCANS. To highlight the need for SCANS , Dole said:

"Skills levels for today's jobs are increasing, yet 700,000 young people drop out of high school each year, and another 700,000 graduate without the skills necessary to survive in the workplace. Further, some estimate that as many as one-fourth of our current work force faces substantial literacy problems."

The focus of SCANS is to develop guidelines that define the skills needed to get and keep entry-level jobs for high school graduates who are not planning to enter college--"the forgotten half" is the apt terminology of the William T. Grant Foundation Commission on Work, Family, and Citizenship [1]. Many American secondary school students consider school a waste of time. The complaints are familiar to parents and teachers: "It's boring." "Why do I need to learn this?"

Even students who plan to go to college have difficulty seeing the relevance of what they are studying in the classroom. For example, in studying science and mathematics they are not provided with interesting examples of how concepts from these disciplines are used in various fields of engineering. Thus, there is a need to provide secondary school students with concrete and meaningful examples of how what they are studying to relates to future employment and to college programs that prepare them for professional careers.

5 Conceptual Approach to SCANS Project

On August 9 and 10, 1990, this author was invited to join 16 other professionals representing various industries, educational institutions, and government agencies to review a draft document that describes the conceptual approach to the SCANS Project. We met with a member of the Commission and staff from the US Labor Department who were working on this project.

At the "meeting of experts," a working document developed by the SCANS staff was reviewed. This paper, Conceptual Approach to the Definition of Necessary Skills in Work, contained the following opening paragraph:

- The two basic objectives of SCANS are to
  a) recommend the skills that students leaving high school should have in order to perform effectively at work (and be capable of continuing to learn on the job and progress in their career), and
  b) provide a reliable means of assessing those skills at different levels of perfomance.
- The skills needed for work comprise only a part of what students should learn in high school for fully participating in society as citizens, parents, and individuals --however, a very important part. All indications are that the capabilities of the students coming out of high schools fall considerably short of the increasing demands of the workplace [5].

In order to operationalize the identification of necessary skills and the means of assessing attainment of these skills, the SCANS Project is focusing on three major aspects:

- identification and description of functional skills,
- identification and description of enabling skills, and
- learning in context.

6 Functional Skills and Enabling Skills

Existing research shows that the functional skills of people at work involve the exercise of different and more complex capabilitites of thinking and behavior than what most students are normally taught in schools. In order to perform functional skills, a set of enabling skills is needed. These are the more familiar verbal and quantitative competencies learned in schools.

One of the problems in today's classrooms is that enabling skills besides the main part of the curriculum are often learned in a vacuum. What is needed is more emphasis on the study of generic functional skills that involve the performance of multiple enabling skills. For example, the ability to manage resources (time, finances, materials, and people) effectively can certainly involve, to varying degrees, many different acts of reading, writing, quantitative analysis, etc. The group of experts that met in August was charged with the task of identifying a list of 20 to 40 functional skills that satisfied the following criteria. The functional skills must:

- be important to the effective performance of a broad range of jobs
- adequately represent the complexities of work
- encompass a wide range of enabling skills
- have a hierarchy of performance levels
- be testable, so that a person's performance can be evaluated
- be teachable, so that instructional programs can be developed

After much brainstorming and discussion, a tentative list of 27 functional skills was identified. The 27 skills were grouped in five major skills categories as follows:

A. Resource Management: Identifying, organizing, planning and allocating resources
  1) Time: can understand, follow, and prepare a schedule
  2) FInancial: can prepare and follow a budget
  3) Material: can select and use materials and tools
  4) Human: can choose and develop cooperative working groups

B. Information Management: Acquiring and using necessary information
  1) Identifying, finding, and selecting necessary information
  2) Assimilating and integrating information from multiple sources
  3) Representing, conveying, communicating information to others effectively
  4) Converting information from one form to another
  5) Preparing, interpreting, and maintaining quantitative and nonquantitative records and information including visual

C. Social Interaction
  1) Participates as an effective member of a team
  2) Facilitates group learning
  3) Teaches others new skills
  4) Serves clients/customers
  5) Influences (informs, explains, persuades, convinces) an individual or group
  6) Negotiates to arrive at a decision
  7) Works with human diversity
  8) Understands how the social/organizational system works

D. Understanding Systems Behavior and Performance
  1) Understanding how system comments interact to achieve goals
  2) Identifying, anticipating, and managing consequences
  3) Monitoring and correcting performance--identifying trends and anomalies
  4) Linking symbolic representations to real-world phenomena
  5) Integrating multiple displays

E. Human and Technology Interaction
  1) Selecting and using appropriate technologies
  2) Visualizing operations and program machines to perform work
  3) Employing computers for input, presentation and analysis
  4) Troubleshoot and maintain technologies
  5) Design systems to perform complex tasks efficiently

7 Learning in Context

The third aspect of the conceptual approach to SCANS is that people learn skills best when they are learned in context. Establishing the connection between skills and real-world situations is equally important to the learning of both functional and enabling skills. Ideally, students are places in a real work situation. Problems are posed and functional skills and related enabling skills are learned to facilitate the search for solutions.

Given the list of funcitonal skills and the recognition that contextual learning is important, the next step for the SCANS Project is to generate descriptions of how the functional skills relate to various work environments. Equally important is the development of a set of evaluation instruments for determining if students have learned the functional and enabling skills. In 1992, the US Department of Labor published the SCANS report which was based on the work that was described above [6].

8 Principles of Engineering and SCANS

Although the SCANS Project findings mainly deal with skills for students who do not plan to go to college, they can be used to assess courses for college-bound students. Many of the functional skills that are needed in the workplace are also needed for success in college. Contextual learning is the primary design criterion of the Principles of Engineering course. Using the case study approach makes the learning of engineering concepts relevant. Using computer technology to support instruction provides students with examples of how technology is used in the workplace.

All five fuctional skills categories are well represented in the Principles of Engineering course. Students will learn functional and related enabling skills that will serve them well in college. Cooperative Learning addressed explicitly the development of social interaction skills.

The POE curriculum and the various types school/industry collaborations are all designed to achieve the learning outcomes that are described in the SCANS. Thus, the POE course can be used as a model for designing other programs that are more learner-centered and prepare students to be participating adults of the 21st century.

References

1. Hamilton, S. F.: Is There Life After High School? In: The Harvard Education Letter, July/August 1990
2. Liao, T. T.: Liberal Education in Mathematics, Science and Technology. In: The TIES magazine, March/April 1993
3. New York State Education Department: Principles of Engineering, Curriculum Guide and Engineering Case Studies. Albany, 1989
4. U. S. Department of Labor: Labor Secretary Dole Announces Workplace Skills Commission. News Release, April 5, 1990

5. U. S. Department of Labor: Conceptual Approach to the Definition of Necessary Skills in Work. Working Paper, Washington D.C., 1990
6. U. S. Department of Labor: The SCANS Report. Washington D.C., 1992

Creativity at Work: Implications for Education About Work

Sam Stern
Oregon State University
School of Education
Corvallis, OR 97331, USA

Hisaaki Komazaki
Tokyo Institute of Technology
Department of Systems Science
4259 Nagatsuta-Cho, Midori-Ku, Yokohama 227, Japan

Abstract. This paper describes the results of a two-year study of the development and expression of creativity in Japanese companies, and describes the implications for work-related education. The distinction between individual and corporate creativity is discussed, and a definition of corporate creativity is proposed. The results of this study indicate that education and training can influence the expression of creativity at work through the promotion of problem finding and self-managed activity. Implications for educational programs are described.

Keywords. Creativity, education, Japan, work

1 Introduction

While the development and expression of creativity is widely recognized as important to individual, social, and economic development, there is little agreement on what creativity is or how it can best be developed. Most research on creativity has focused on the expression of individual creativity in non-company settings. Advances in technology and the reorganization of work have increased the need for creativity in the workplace (Carnevale, 1991; Secretary's Commission on Achieving Necessary Skills, 1991; and Wirth, 1993). The well documented performance of Japanese companies has attracted the attention of companies throughout the world who want to know how to balance creative growth with effective performance (Drucker, 1985; Murakami and Nishiwaki, 1991; Quinn and Rivoli, 1991; Tatsuno, 1990; Torrance, 1980).

Based on the results of a two-year study of the expression of creativity in Japanese companies, the authors believe that problem finding ability and a willingness to engage in unofficial or unassigned work are important to creativity. In educational programs, these two types of activity may be best described as self-initiated and self-managed activity. This paper will provide an overview of related research; presentation of case study and survey data from our study of the development and expression of creativity in Japanese companies; and a discussion of the implications for educational programs.

1.1 What is Creativity?

The definition and use of the term creativity has been described as elusive by philosophers, psychologists, economists, and educators alike (Barzun, 1989; Drucker, 1985; Hausman, 1984; Perkins, 1988; and Torrance, 1988). Barzun (1989), believes that there is no other word in our contemporary culture that is put to more frequent and varied use. Torrance (1988) who has been involved in the measurement and study of creativity for more than 40 years, believes that the term defies precise definition.

The difficulty in arriving at a commonly accepted definition of creativity may be caused by the existence of multiple perspectives or views of creativity. Several researchers have suggested that there are four major ways of viewing creativity: from the perspective of a person, process, product, or place (MacKinnon, 1978; Rhodes, 1961). Although each of these perspectives are highly interrelated, they each present a distinctive research perspective.

Early research on creativity can be characterized as person centered. It was closely associated with the study of genius and intelligence. Using standard measures of intelligence or indicators of exceptional talent, researchers attempted to identify characteristics or behaviors that are associated with intelligence (Galton, 1869; Terman, 1925). Since creativity was thought to be closely related to intelligence, it was assumed that characteristics or behaviors that were associated with high intelligence were also associated with high creativity. In his presidential address to the American Psychological Association, Guilford (1950) argued that creative ability is distinct and separate from intellectual ability, as commonly measured. Guilford's hypothesis was supported by the research of Getzels and Jackson (1962), MacKinnon (1971), and Torrance (1960) who found no correlation between measures of intelligence, such as IQ scores or grades and measures of creativity. It is important to note that all of the above researchers took care to distinguish between a prerequisite level of intelligence for creativity, and correlation between intelligence and creativity. By way of example, MacKinnon, who conducted in-depth studies of the characteristics and backgrounds of creative architects, estimates that an IQ score of approximately 120 is necessary to be an architect. Therefore, MacKinnon believes that it is necessary to have an IQ of approximately 120 or greater to perform the work of an architect, but IQ scores above 120 will not necessarily result in higher levels of creativity by architects.

Another view of creativity is the view provided by looking at the creative process. From the perspective of the creative process, research questions include: What are the stages of the creative process? Is the creative process similar in different domains? Are the processes for problem solving similar to the processes for creativity? Can the creative process be taught?

Wallas (1926) provided one of the earliest descriptions of the creative process. He described four stages of the creative process: preparation, incubation, illumination and verification. Osborn (1953), the originator of "brainstorming," identified five stages of the creative process: orientation (picking out the problem), preparation (gathering relevant material), analysis and ideation (seeking possible solutions), incubation (a time lag for the mind to synthesize the problem and solutions), and evaluation (putting the pieces together and verifying the solutions through further testing or evaluation). The study of the creative process continues to interest researchers who are investigating the related areas of metacognition, teaching for thinking, and problem solving.

Recognizing the difficulty in separating a person from the product of their activity and environment in which they work, other researchers (Amabile, 1983; Csikszentmihalyi, 1988; Simonton, 1984) use a systems approach. They believe that the expression of creativity is dependent on the interaction between problems, skills, individuals, and the overall environment.

Regardless of whether an investigation of creativity focuses on an individual, the processes used, and/or their environment, the initial point of research entry is typically made through the identification of a product that has been recognized as creative. A creative work of art, piece of music, technological invention, or scientific discovery leads to the identification of a person or persons who produced a creative product in a particular environment. Although some may argue that it is possible to be creative without ever producing a creative result, most researchers believe that the identification of creativity depends on the recognition of a creative product.

1.2 Creativity and Problem Finding

Problem finding is a particularly important part of creativity because it occurs first, and because it is important in determining the quality of the solutions. Csikszentmihalyi and Getzels (1971) were among the first to investigate creative problem finding. They presented art students with a set of objects, and asked the students to arrange the objects and make a drawing. The students were observed while they worked, and their "discovery-oriented" behaviors were recorded. Discovery-oriented behavior was defined as the number of objects used before drawing, the uniqueness of the stimulus used, and changes in media or perspective. The drawings were rated for their originality, aesthetic value, and craftsmanship.

The results of correlational analysis indicated that the ratings of discovery-oriented behavior was significantly related to the originality, aesthetic value, and craftsmanship of the completed drawings.

Runco and Okuda (1988) investigated the role of problem discovery in the divergent thinking and creative performance of adolescents. Three divergent thinking tests were administered to a group of adolescents. Each test contained three given problems and one discovered problem. The discovered problem allowed the subjects to think of a problem and then to provide solutions. Comparisons indicated that the subjects generated significantly more responses to the discovered problems than the given problems.

The research of Csikszentmihalyi and Getzels (1971) and Runco and Okuda (1988) suggest that students who work on problems that they discovered or found themselves are more likely to be highly involved in their solution and more likely to arrive at creative solutions.

1.3 Creativity and Self-Managed Activity

Independence has also been closely associated with creativity. In particular, the ability to make independent judgements, independently organize highly complex or chaotic situations, and to work apart from others are characteristics of creative persons that have been identified by researchers (Tardif, Sternberg, 1988). Although there is little empirical research to show that self-managed activity is directly related to creativity, it is an emerging area of inquiry in the field of cognitive science. Cognitive scientists (Glaser, 1985) report that the use of self-regulating skills are an indicator of higher order achievement, and important to their development.

There is also evidence that self-managed unofficial activity by R&D personnel, sometimes described as "under the table," "bootleg," or "skunkworks" activity, is closely related to creative R & D (Amabile, 1987; Lehr, 1988) Although several companies, including Toshiba, 3M, and Corning Glass Works have established corporate policy that encourages researchers to dedicate 10 to 15 % of their time to unofficial research activity, Lehr (1988), the former Chairman and Chief Executive Officer of 3M, notes that only a small percentage of researchers are actively involved in unofficial activity at any given time. In other words, even though unofficial activity has been closely associated with creative R & D, and several companies actively encourage such activity, the majority of researchers are either unable or reluctant to engage in substantive unofficial activity.

2 Research Methodology

In recognition of the importance of the study of creativity and the need for international collaboration, the Japan Management Association (JMA) endowed the JMA Creativity Development Chair at Tokyo Institute of Technology in January 1990, with an open ended charge to study factors that contribute to the expression of corporate creativity. To better understand the development and expression of creativity in companies, the JMA Study (Stern, Iguchi, Komazaki, 1992) conducted interviews and surveys with three groups of personnel associated with R & D projects. Group 1 was composed of winners of the Kagaku Gijutsu Korosho Award from Kagaku Gijutsu Cho (Ministry of Science and Technology) and national awards from Hatsumei Kyokai (Institute of Invention and Innovation) between 1986 and 1990. Group 2 and Group 3 were randomly selected companies that did not receive either awards between 1986 and 1990. In Group 2, R & D projects were selected by R & D managers as being representative of a creative project. In Group 3, R & D projects were selected by R & D managers as being representative of a typical project. Table 1 shows the sampling method and number of projects for each group. It should be noted that Group 3, identified as typical projects, were R & D projects that resulted in successful business activity, but were not judged as being creative.

Table 1 Group Composition

Group	Sampling Method	Number of Projects and Respondents
1	Kagaku Gijyutsu Cho & Hatsumei Kyokai award winning projects.	120
2	Identified by R & D top management as creative projects.	76
3	Identified by R & D top management as typical projects.	97

Note: Total number of projects and respondents = 293. The response rate for Group 1 was 62.5%; Group 2, 15.2%; Group 3, 19.4%.

Group 1, the recipients of awards from Kagaku Gijutsu Cho and Hatsumei Kyokai between 1986 and 1990 were used as a sample of highly creative corporate activity. Each year these two organizations present awards to individuals who have made significant and creative contributions to science and technology. The recipients of these awards are primarily R & D personnel of Japanese companies. Awards received by individuals who work in a non company setting were not included in the sample.

In the case of both Kagaku Gijutsu Cho and Hatsumei Kyokai, the awards were granted to one or more individuals in recognition of their work on a specific project. After eliminating those awards that were received by individuals working in a non-company setting, such as universities or public research institutes, a total of 192 projects that received awards from Kagaku Gijutsu Cho and Hatsumei Kyokai from 1986 to 1990 were identified. These projects represent 148 companies and more than 400 researchers. In many cases more than one researcher received an award for the same project; in some cases one company received more than one award between 1986 and 1990; and in one case a single project received an award from both organizations. In this paper, the project that they worked on is referred to as the "specified project." For Group 1, the specified project was a project that received an award from either Kagaku Gijutsu Cho or Hatsumei Kyokai. For Group 2, the specified project was selected by an R & D manager as being representative of a creative project. For Group 3, the specified project was selected by an R & D manager as being representative of a typical project.

2.1 Interview Sample

In the first stage of the JMA Study, interviews were conducted with personnel associated with 22 (11.5%) of the 192 Group 1 projects. A major R & D effort, such as those in the interview sample, is complex. In an attempt to investigate the effect of the researcher(s), the management environment, and the HRD environment, three separate interviews were conducted in each company. Interviews of about two hours each were conducted with members of the R & D team that received the award, a top-level manager of R & D, and a manager of human resource development. The interview sample was selected to reflect the diversity of the total group. About half of the interview sample received awards from Kagaku Gijutsu Cho and about half from Hatsumei Kyokai. Some were the R & D efforts of very large companies such as Matsushita and Mazda. Others were the R & D efforts of smaller companies such as Seiki Corporation, a 300 person company in Yonezawa that manufactures machines for runnerless injection molding. Some of the award winning R & D projects in the interview sample are well known, such as the development of the world's first completely autofocus camera by Minolta or the method for computer entry of kanji characters developed by Fujitsu. Others are less well known, but equally as important, such as the process developed by Mitsubishi Electric for data compression in facsimile machines that permits the rapid transmission of data by facsimile transmission.

2.2 Survey Sample

Based on interview results it was hypothesized that creative projects were more likely to have been initially proposed by individual researchers and more likely to have long periods of unofficial activity. To investigate these hypotheses and others, surveys were sent to researchers who worked on Group 1, 2, and 3 projects. As noted in Table 1, the response rates varied by group. Aided by the support of both Kagaku Gijutsu Cho and Hatsumei Kyokai, the response rate for Group 1 was 62.5%. Although the response rates for Group 2 (15.2%) and Group 3 (19.4%) are lower, it should be noted that both groups were randomly selected from the Jojo Kigyo list, a listing of Japanese companies whose stock is openly traded.

In comparing the results by group, it is important to note that Group 1 contained significantly more large companies than either Group 2 or 3. As shown in Figure 1, approximately 60% of Group 1 researchers work for large companies with 5,000 or more employees, as compared with 18% of Group 2 researchers, and 10% of Group 3 researchers. Although Group 2 contains somewhat more large companies than Group 3, the difference is not significant. Survey results revealed no significant differences between Group 2 and Group 3 companies in company sales; total number of employees; number of R & D employees; annual R & D budget; or ratio of basic, applied, and developmental research. Similarly, there were no significant differences in the ages, educational background, or position of Group 2 and Group 3 researchers.

As noted in Table 1, the response rates varied by group. Aided by the support of both Kagaku Gijutsu Cho and Hatsumei Ky_kai, the response rate for Group 1 was 62.5%. Although the response rates for Group 2 (15.2%) and Group 3 (19.4%) are lower, it should be noted that both groups were randomly selected from the Jojo Kigyo list, a listing of Japanese companies whose stock is openly traded.

3 Results

3.1 Initial Proposal Source

The beginning of any R & D activity is the identification of a potential research problem. As such, the selection of an R & D problem, sometimes described as R & D target setting, profoundly influences the expression of corporate creativity. If potentially creative R & D activities are not first identified for consideration, they can be neither approved nor realized. More than half (54.6%) of the 22 interviewed projects (all of which were award-winning) were first proposed by individual researchers. The remainder were first proposed by management (top-down) or others. Based on the analysis of the projects and interviews with personnel associated with bottom-up and top-down projects, it was hypothesized that differences between personnel and projects may be associated with the initial within-company proposal source.

Since the initial selection of the R & D target is important in determining the potential for the expression of corporate creativity and the results of interviews suggested a relationship between the initial proposal source and creativity, the surveys asked the researchers to identify the original source of the proposal for the specified project. Table 2 shows a comparison of the percentage of projects that were first proposed by management (top-down); first proposed by an individual researcher (bottom-up); and those proposed by others, such as a different section, committee, or user.

As shown in Table 2, the results of chi-square tests for significance revealed that significantly more Group 1 projects ($p < .05$) were first proposed by individual researchers (43.5%) than Group 3 (24.0%). Correspondingly, significantly ($p < .05$) more Group 3 projects were first proposed by top management (60.4%) than Group 1 (40.9%). Although the difference is not statistically significant at the conventional .05 level, more Group 2 projects (30.3%) were first proposed by individual researchers than in Group 3 (24.0%).

Table 2 Project Proposal Source (%)

Proposal Source[b]	Group[a]			Contrasts	(chi-square)	
	1	2	3	1 vs 2	1 vs 3	2 vs 3
Top-Down	40.9	53.9	60.4	2.841	7.997[c]	0.863
Bottom-Up	43.5	30.3	24.0	3.149	8.811[c]	0.964
Other	15.6	15.8	15.6	0.004	0.000	0.004

[a]Group 1 = award winning projects, n = 120; Group 2 = projects identified as creative, n = 76; Group 3 = projects identified as typical, n = 97;
[b]Top = proposals initially proposed by management, Bottom = proposals initially proposed by individual researchers, Other = proposals initially proposed by other sections of the company, users, or others;
[c]$p < .01$.

3.2 Unofficial Activity

Based on interviews with researchers who worked with award winning projects, it was hypothesized that long unofficial periods are a characteristic of creative R & D. To test this hypothesis researchers were asked to report the total length of the specified project and the length of the unofficial, basic, developmental, and preparation for business stages. Table 3 summarizes the average length of the project stages in years for each group. The unofficial stage describes the time when one of more researchers worked on the project in an unofficial capacity. The basic stage describes the time when the project members were exploring a wide variety of possible approaches to the research problem. The developmental stage describes the time when the project members developed a preferred approach to the research problem. The preparation for business stage describes the time when preparations were being made for the commercial introduction of the research results.

Table 3 Length of Project Stages (average number of years)

Project Stages	Group[a]			Contrast (t-values)			
	1	2	3	F	1 vs 2	1 vs 3	2 vs 3
Unofficial	1.1	1.0	0.7	3.98[b]	0.765	2.734[c]	1.343
Basic	0.9	0.9	0.8	0.18	0.194	0.566	0.449
Developmental	1.6	1.3	1.3	1.05	1.306	1.451	-0.086
Preparation	1.3	1.2	1.0	1.25	0.369	1.761	0.748
Total Length	4.9	4.3	3.6	3.48[b]	0.926	2.776[c]	1.343

[a]Group 1 = award winning projects, n = 120; Group 2 = projects identified as creative; n = 76, Group 3 = projects identified as typical, n = 97;
[b]$p < .05$;
[c]$p < .01$.

One-way ANOVAs revealed significant differences in the total project length
($P < .05$) and the length of the unofficial period ($P < .05$). Comparison of means
with t-tests revealed that the total project length, from the unofficial start until the
results of the research were commercially available, of Group 1 projects
(4.9 years) was significantly greater ($p < .01$) than Group 3 projects (3.6 years).
Although each stage of Group 1 projects is somewhat longer than in Group 3
projects, only the unofficial stage of Group 1 projects (1.1 years) is significantly
longer ($p < .01$) than the unofficial stage of Group 3 projects (0.7 years). The
length of the unofficial stage of Group 2 projects (1.0 years) is very close to being
significantly longer ($p = 0.063$) than the length of Group 3 projects. The longer
unofficial periods of Group 1 and Group 2 projects support the hypothesis that
more creative projects have longer unofficial periods than less creative projects.

4 Two Case Studies

The following are descriptions of two case studies that illustrate the nature of
creative R & D and its relation with the proposal source and unofficial activity.

In 1990, Tomoshige Hori of Snow Brand Milk Company, a leading Japanese
producer of dairy products, received a national award from Hatsumei Kyokai for
developing a process that is changing the way that cheese is made throughout the
world. The story of this award winning R & D activity began in 1980 when Hori
heard a lecture given by a Keio University professor about the problems of
measuring temperature convection in a fluid. During the lecture, the professor did
not refer to the possibility of using milk or any other dairy product as the liquid,
and the lecture itself was not particularly related to Hori's research area. After
hearing the lecture, Hori decided to experiment with the measurement of heat
transfer in milk. Working after regular hours, he conducted experiments for about
three months without the official support of his company. While conducting the
experiments, he noticed that a large change in temperature occurred when the milk
began to clot. The change was so dramatic and observable, that he doubted the
operation of his experimental apparatus. After carefully repeating the experiments,
he determined that there was a significant and reliably detectable change in
temperature during the time that milk clots.

At the time that Hori conducted his initial experiments, he had no application in
mind. His previous research was unrelated to cheese making and he had no
knowledge of cheese making. During his initial experimentation, he began to read
about the cheese making process. He learned that one of the major problems of
making cheese is determining exactly when milk clots. At that time, the accepted
method required the subjective judgement of a skilled technician. Cutting the curd
too early results in a poor yield, while cutting it too late results in poor taste
quality. Hori quickly realized that his discovery offered the possibility of replacing
the skilled technician, who used subjective judgement in deciding when to cut the
curd, with an automated reliable process. Hori told his manager about his

discovery and his belief that Snow Brand Milk should pursue the development of this process. Although he was disappointed when his manager did not support his idea, he continued his work on an unofficial basis. During that time he published his experimental findings in the leading international journal in his field, The Journal of Food Science. Encouraged by the positive response, he again approached management. This time, he received the enthusiastic support of several R & D managers. Today, approximately ten years after Hori first started working on the project in an unofficial capacity, he heads a ten person research, development, and marketing team that continues to conduct research and development on the use of a hot wire method for fluid measurement. Based on Hori's research, Snow Brand Milk Company now uses and sells systems for in-line fluid measurement in Japan, the U. S., and Europe. In 1990, approximately 20,000 tons of cheese were made using the process developed by Hori (Hori, 1991).

In 1989, Kenzo Hatada, a researcher at Matsushita Electric Industrial Company, one of the world's largest consumer electronics companies, received national awards from both Kagaku Gijutsu Cho and Hatsumei Kyokai for developing a new technology for semiconductor mounting. From 1976 to 1979, Hatada participated in the development and application of a process for the mounting of LSI's (large scale integrated circuits) for thermal printers. In spite of substantial difficulties, the two-year project was successfully implemented at the end of 1978. During the project, Hatada became aware of the limitations of the existing technology and realized that the increasing use of LSI and VLSI technology would require the development of a new approach to semiconductor assembly.

He began an unofficial study of current and evolving technology, including the careful study of patent applications and references. His review of current and evolving technology did not identify anyone else who was pursuing a new type of technology for semiconductor mounting. Independent experiments and discussions with colleagues led to the development of an entirely new method now known as "bump transfer mounting technology." After approximately two years of unofficial research he described his ideas for a new semiconductor mounting technology to his manager. His manager asked him if any other maker was studying it and what was the probability of success. Hatada answered that no other maker was studying it and the estimated probability of success was only a few percent. In spite of the challenges, he told his manager that he was deeply committed to continuing his research. Although the project was not officially approved, a limited level of continuing unofficial research was tolerated. Approximately a year later, with the support of a manager who was familiar with Hatada's previous work, the project was finally given official approval. The development and application of the new technology was very successful and is now used in LSI and VLSI semiconductor mounting technology throughout the world (Matsushita Electric Co. Ltd., 1987).

Both of the above examples were award winning projects that had high levels of newness and success, as viewed from the perspective of their companies. They were both initially proposed by individual researchers who encountered substantial resistance to their ideas. Both examples had relatively long unofficial periods of three years during which the researchers continued research activity without official approval.

5 Discussion

5.1 Problem Finding and Self-Initiated Activity.

As described earlier in this paper, previous research has shown that problem finding to be an important part of creativity. The results of our study support the idea that problem finding is important to creativity in the R & D setting, and establish a link between problems that are first proposed by individual researchers and the expression creative R & D. One of the major findings of the JMA Study was that the creative sample included significantly more projects that were first proposed by individual researchers than by management. In other words, problems that were self-selected by individual researchers were more likely to result in creative activity than problems that were assigned to researchers by managers.

One of the implications for the development of creativity in the workplace is that companies that want to increase their creative activity should encourage research proposals from researchers. However, simply encouraging a larger number of research proposals that are first suggested by individual researchers by itself, will not necessarily result in greater creativity. To successfully initiate ideas that lead to creative activity requires both problem finding ability and a willingness to pose such problems.

Consider the case of Hatada, the Matsushita researcher who received awards from both Kagaku Gijutsu Cho and Hatsumei Kyokai for the development of a new semiconductor mounting technology. After successfully completing the initial project, he initiated an unofficial effort to develop a new type of mounting technology, and, in spite of resistance, persistently proposed that his company officially engage in the proposed research. During our interview with Hatada, we asked him to identify the factors that contributed to the creativity of his activity. He told us that he believes that the ability to think of future research problems while working on current research projects contributes to creativity. In his case, the drive to continue searching for problems, even after arriving at an accepted solution, made his creative activity possible.

5.2 Unofficial Research and Self-Managed Activity

The results of our study support the idea that a willingness to engage in unofficial research is also important to creativity, and establish a link between the length of the unofficial period of research activity and the expression of creative R & D. One of the major findings of the JMA Study was that creative R & D projects had significantly longer periods of unofficial research than typical projects.

One of the implications for the development of creativity in the workplace is that tolerance of unofficial activity is important to creativity. However, as noted earlier in this paper, even in companies where unofficial activity is encouraged, many researchers find it difficult to engage in substantive unofficial activity. The expression of creativity, in or out of the workplace, requires successful activity in new areas. However, movement into new areas will inevitably encounter resistance. The results of our interviews with personnel associated with creative projects support the idea that the expression of creativity involves overcoming substantial barriers.

The case of Hori, the Snow Brand Milk researcher who developed a new process for making cheese, is a good example of how the willingness to engage in unofficial research contributed to the expression of creativity. Although Hori's research was initially rejected, he continued unofficially for three years. During that time, his work was entirely self-managed. His ability to successfully manage the research during the unofficial stage without the official support of his company enabled the successful expression of creativity. As with Hatada, we asked Hori to identify factors that contributed to the expression of creativity in his award-winning project. He told us that in his case, the ability to pursue independent work while doing assigned work is especially important to the expression of creativity.

5.3 Implications for Educational Programs

While it is evident that the development and expression of creativity in a work setting is complex, involving many individual, procedural, and environmental variables, the results of our study support the idea that problem finding and engagement in unofficial activity are closely related to creativity. Both of these activities can, and should be, encouraged in creative educational environments.

Students in an educational setting, as are researchers in the R & D setting, are regularly challenged to respond to and solve problems. Irrespective of the subject domain, problems can be categorized, on the basis of their source, as being given problems or found problems. Typical school activity is characterized by students solving problems that are given to them directly by teachers or indirectly through a variety of educational materials. In schools, students are required to provide answers to given problems much more often than they are required to analyze complex information and, based on that information, pose challenging questions. As experienced educators know well, asking good questions can be far more difficult than finding correct answers.

We believe that it is important for schools to help students develop their ability to find and propose problems. Previous researchers (Arlin, 1975; Runco & Okuda,

1988) report that problem finding is a developed skill that becomes distinct from problem solving during adolescence. As such, educational environments should support the development of problem finding skill in a wide variety of subjects at the appropriate developmental stage. Equally important is the need for educational environments to facilitate the willingness of students to propose problems in a variety of settings.

In addition to the importance of problem finding, our research also indicated that engagement in unofficial research is associated with creativity. We believe that unofficial research activity in an R & D setting is related to self-managed activity in an educational setting. Even if students are able to find and propose problems that lead to creative solutions, to successfully realize those solutions they must also be able to self-manage. Just as it is difficult for researchers to conduct research independent of their organization, so is it difficult for students to engage in self-managed activity without the highly structured support that is typical of educational activity.

References

1. Amabile, T. M.: The social psychology of creativity. New York, Springer-Verlag 1983

2. Amabile, T. M.: The motivation to be creative. In: S. G. Isaksen (ed.), Frontiers of creativity research (pp. 223-254). Buffalo, Bearly 1987

3. Arlin, P. K.: Cognitive development in adulthood: A fifth stage? In: Developmental Psychology, 11, 602-606 (1975)

4. Barron, F.: An eye more fantastical. In: G. A. Davis, J. A. Scott (eds.), Training creative thinking (pp. 181-193). Huntington, Robert E. Krieger Publishing 1978

5. Barzun, J.: The paradoxes of creativity. In: The American Scholar, 58, 337-351 (1989, Summer)

6. Carnevale, A. P.: America and the new economy. Alexandria, American Society for Training and Development 1991

7. Csikszentmihalyi, M.: Society, culture, and person: A systems view of creativity. In: R. L. Sternberg (ed.), The nature of creativity (pp. 325-339). Cambridge, Cambridge University Press 1988

8. Csiksentmihalyi, M., Getzels, J. W.: Discovery-oriented behavior and the originality of creative products: A study with artists. In: Journal of Personality and Social Psychology, 19, 47-52 (1971)

9. Drucker, P. F.: Innovation and entrepreneurship: Practices and principles. New York, Harper & Row 1985

10. Galton, F.: Hereditary genius. London, Macmillan 1869

11. Getzels, J. W.: Creativity, intelligence, and problem finding: Retrospect and Prospect. In: S. G. Isaksen (ed.), Frontiers of creativity research (pp. 88-102). Buffalo, Bearly Limited 1987

12. Getzels, J. W., Jackson, P. W.: Creativity and intelligence: Explorations with gifted students. New York, Wiley 1962

13. Guilford, J. P.: Creativity. In: American Psychologist, 5, 444-454, (1950)

14. Hausman, C. R.: A discourse on novelty and creation. Albany, State University of New York Press 1984

15. Hori, T.: Objective measurements of the process of curd formation during rennet treatment of milks by the hot wire method. In: Journal of Food Science, 50(4), 911-917 (1985)

16. Lehr, L. W.: Encouraging innovation and entrepreneurship in diversified corporations. In: R. L. Kuhn (ed.), Handbook for creative and innovative managers (pp. 211-219). New York, McGraw-Hill 1988

17. Matsushita Electric Industrial Co., Ltd. . Bump transfer mounting: A development story. Unpublished manuscript, 1987, May 25

18. MacKinnon, D. W.: Educating for creativity: A modern myth? In: G. A. Davis, J. A. Scott (eds.), Training creative thinking (pp. 194-207). Huntington, Robert E. Krieger Publishing 1971

19. MacKinnon, D. W.: In search of human effectiveness. Buffalo, Creative Education Foundation 1978

20. Murakami, T., Nishiwaki T.: Strategy for creation. Cambridge, England, Woodhead 1991

21. Osborn, A. F.: Applied imagination. New York, Scribners 1953

22. Perkins, D. N.: The possibility of invention. In: R. L. Sternberg (ed.), The nature of creativity (pp. 362-385). Cambridge, Cambridge University Press 1988

23. Quinn, D. P., Rivoli, P.: The effects of American and Japanese style employment and compensation practices on innovation. In: Organization Science, 2, 4, 323-340 (1991)

24. Rhodes, M.: An analysis of creativity. Phi Delta Kappan, 42, 305-310 (1961)

25. Runco, M. A., Okuda, S. M.: Problem discovery, divergent thinking, and the creative process. Journal of youth and adolescence, 17, 3, 211-220 (1988)

26. Secretary's Commission on Achieving Necessary Skills (SCANS). What work requires of schools: A SCANS report for America 2000. Washington, DC, U.S. Department of Labor 1991

27. Simonton, D. K.: Genius, creativity, & leadership. Cambridge, Harvard University Press 1984

28. Stern, S., Iguchi, T., Komazaki, H.: The development and expression of corporate creativity (Educational Science and Technology Research Report 92-1). Tokyo, Tokyo Institute of Technology, Educational Science and Technology Research Group 1992, January

29. Sternberg, R. J.: A three-facet model of creativity. In: R. L. Sternberg (ed.), The nature of creativity (pp. 125-147). Cambridge, Cambridge University Press 1988

30. Tardif, T. Z., Sternberg, R. J.: What do we know about creativity? In: R. L. Sternberg (ed.), The nature of creativity (pp. 429-440). Cambridge, Cambridge University Press 1988

31. Tatsuno, S. M.: Created in Japan: From imitators to world-class innovators. New York, Harper & Row 1990

32. Terman, L. M.: Genetic studies of genius: Mental and physical traits of a thousand gifted children. Palo Alto, Stanford University Press 1925

33. Torrance, E. P.: Educational achievement of the highly intelligent and the highly creative: Eight partial replications of the Getzels-Jackson study. Research Memorandum BER-60-18, Bureau of Education Research, University of Minnesota 1960

34. Torrance, E. P.: Lessons about giftedness and creativity from a nation of 115 million overachievers. In: Gifted Child Quarterly, 24, 1, 10-14 (1980)

35. Torrance, E. P.: The nature of creativity as manifest in its testing. In: R. J Sternberg (ed.) The nature of creativity (pp. 43-75). Cambridge, Cambridge University Press 1988

36. Wallas, G.: The art of thought. New York, Franklin Watts 1926

37. Wirth, A. G.: Education and work: The choices we face. In: Phi Delta Kappan, 74, 5, 361-366 (1993, January)

6. Design Methodology and Theory-Practice Links

The design of the ARW drew on the critical mass of work in the realm of design education and its implications for the development of new, higher level and generalizable technological capabilities. To this end, Bayazit presented a careful exploration of the interrelationships between design knowledge, research, practice and education. Added to these perceptions were de Vries' methodological analyses of design as a tool for learning about technological developments in industrial settings. Similarly useful, Blandow shared a structure that could be used to guide overall methodology choices.

The participants observed an ever increasing recognition of knowledge and basic/fundamental understanding (elements and laws/principles) that correlates positively with the increasing influence of technology in our world. As more and more insights and knowledge are put into practice, each succeeding generation finds it increasingly difficult to work with the accumulated experiences because of their geometrically increasing number and complexity. Based on these insights the workshop's participants reached the conclusion that it should be possible to exchange ideas and strategies for introducing technological subjects using elements, principles, and laws of technology that would be the same all over the world.

Technology was viewed as an essential vehicle to develop interdisciplinary thinking. The interdisciplinary nature of technology is the background for interpersonal teaching activities and this in fact also guides us towards new didactic structures that were explored throughout the workshop.

Interrelations Between Design Education, Design Practice, Design Research, Design Knowledge

Nigan Bayazit
Istanbul Technical University
Department of Industrial Product Design
Faculty of Architecture
Teknik Universite, Istanbul Taksim, 80191, Turkey

Abstract. The aim of this study is to try to investigate the relationships between design research, education, and practice. Design education is considered as the learning of complexity, in relation to the learning styles of designers. Working with computers in design professional practice as well as in design studio education and trying to decode the knowledge of the professional practice into computers to be used by the professional practitioners in turn is accepted as one of the interaction points. Creating tools of advanced educational technology for design students, depending on the knowledge acquired and elicited from the professional practice is the other subject of discussion. Design research is accepted as the key course of action in this respect. Understanding design knowledge, a part of design research, requires the investigation of design activity in professional practice. In all the disciplines, designing demands collaborative and interdisciplinary team work to investigate the nature of design knowledge, design education, and practice. Design research forces researchers to apply miscellaneous techniques and the methods of different disciplines including information sciences.

Keywords. Design education, design research, design knowledge, knowledge acquisition, philosophy of design

1 Interrelation Between Education, Research and Practice

A theoretical model of the Computer Aided Design (CAD) Education and Research is published in an article by Bayazit (1987) related to the CAD laboratory established in Istanbul Technical University Faculty of Architecture in 1987 for the purpose of combination of research and education. Since then, the applications in the laboratory and research works are based on the principles established in that paper. This model has three exhibited (education, research and evaluation) and one hidden (practice) components. The first and the second (education and research) will be developed interactively. There are various internal and external characteristics of the components in such a model of design education and design research. External characteristics relate to social technology, organization, resource allocation, roles, funds, experts, etc. 'Internal characteristics relate to the mental, cognitive development of learners like, i.e., psychology of learner, tutor, researcher, experts, etc.' (Bayazit, 1987). In the same article learning system in the CAD laboratory is explained as 'A learner and the process of learning are basic elements of learning system to meet the goal, for which we generally design some packages and deliver knowledge neglecting the requirements of the learner.... In our case, the instructor provides a kind of guide to assist the learners in their approach to design. 'This guide should be called "language of design" or, as by some cyberneticians, "metaphors" ' (Bayazit, 1987) (Fig. 1). In the same text it is explained that the interaction between the learner and instructor is provided by analogy and metaphor through conversations of any kind. The major objective of the CAD curriculum is explained as the improvement of learners' ability in making a transition from visual perceptual to representational thinking. 'The CAD curriculum should include both perceptual and content oriented materials as well as representational and process-oriented materials. .... Form, color, texture, proportion, pattern rhythm, order are main concepts to be learned, and students should be able to transfer, code and analyze comparative differences and dichotomies in form and other perceptual elements. Expression and representation of them in a visual language are the main issues, to be improved in the learners and represented on the computer screen' (Bayazit, 1987). CAD studies help students in the development of their personalities. They learn how to investigate by themselves. Instead of abstract studio applications students work with the design languages of the CAD programs and meet the real world conditions in front of the computer screen.

2 The Requirements of the Professional Practice

The demand of the industry from educational institutions needs to be better and more regularly defined. This leads us to do research into the production modelling and methodology of the design practice and design education in the industry.

2.1 Design Education-Industry Relations

In relation to industry, design education policy for the development of a curriculum must be faithful to the professional practice, giving enough consideration to the problems. Design education policy must consider the nature of design phenomena, the nature of developing designerly knowledge, understanding, competence, learning through designing. The other considerations are the developmental stages of design education, constraining factors on

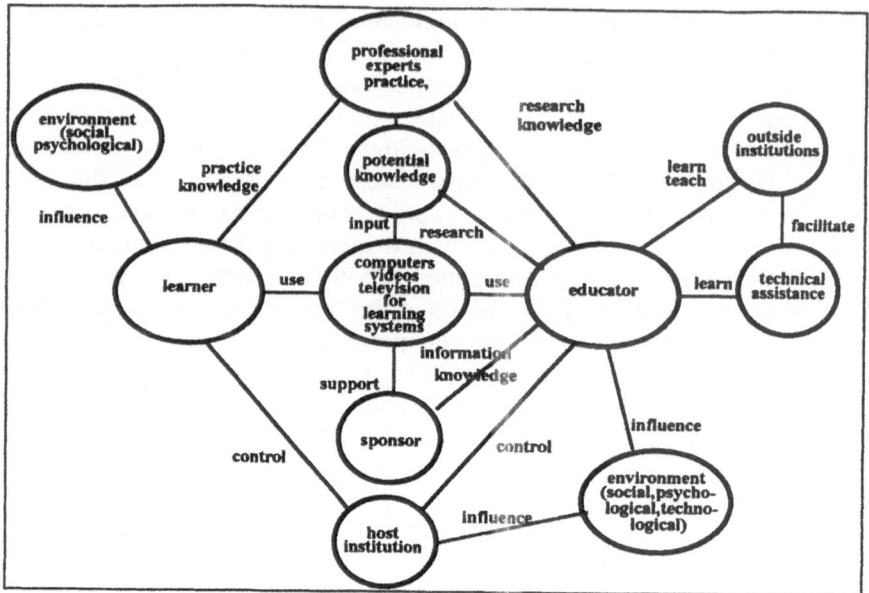

Fig. 1 Relations model of the design, education, research.

educational institutions, cultural context of design phenomena. To meet the requirements of industry, designers need continuing education either at school or in the practical life. In the professional practice they must refresh their education and learn new high technology and its facilities for the organization as well as design purposes.

The success of a designer depends on the commercial success of the product. Therefore, design education should be related to the problems of the business. The designer must be strong on concepts, must avoid using clichés, must search for the new, unproved but attractive solutions rather than the straight but proven ones. A designer must have a foundation of engineering principles, a wide range of support subjects, aesthetic and ergonomic principles. A designer must know how to get the help of the other specialists and where his/her own weakness lies and must know how to work in a team on common projects with colleagues and must learn to learn from others.

3 Design Education

3.1 The Philosophical Background of Design Education
Design is the essential part of industrial production. Designers at the beginning of their education, in any one of the design professions, generally have a limited perspective of the profession and industry, the world of artificial and causes behind

the artificial. The education in this respect brings the design students into contact with the domain of product design that does not exist without the perceptual as well as knowledge amplitude of the learner. We can say that the real world only "exists" for the designer or with the approval of the designer who dictates his or her principles to the real world.

Relations between the real world and the designer as explained above are the subject of "subjective ontology". 'Ontology is a philosophy that considers the role of the subject in an important place. Depending on this view it is possible to postulate the existence of reality and generation of reality from the acceptance by the subject. Ontological principles are valid for the knowing and thinking. There are no principles of things in subjective ontology, but there are principles that are the organizing principles of experience according to Kant and these principles are only tools for the collection of knowledge for empiricists.'(Bayazit, et al., 1993 a) Principles are tools to understand something as a whole. No fact exists or is alive by itself. Nothing exists without a reason in the mind of a subject. No explanation can be considered correct without enough reason. These principles are accepted for the initial stages of design, influencing the way of looking to the research actions into the world of education and practice.

3.2 Learning the Complexity of Design

The artificial around us concerning to design is very complex for the beginners and lay people. Apprehension of the complexity of the artificial needs guidance by the tutors. 'No one has succeeded in giving a definition of "complexity" which is meaningful enough to enable one to measure exactly how complex a given system is. Obviously, it is something to do with the number of elements that can be separately identified in the system, and with the number of ways in which they are related; but it is a matter of choice how many elements one wish to distinguish, and how far one wants to follow up the ramifications of their relationships and interconnections' (Waddington, 1977). These sentences of the Waddington lead us to think about the definition of the degrees of the complexity we wish to make students to discover. The increase in the number of things and concepts increases the complexity of relations and frames generated in the minds of the students. We can only help them to generate their own cognitive frames of the rules and principles of the real world. We can teach them some principles or rules of our own cognition and let them to make combinations of rules and/or principles of their own.

3.3 Learning Styles

To achieve our goals, we have to investigate the learning styles of the students and their proficiency situation in the traditional and CAD studio teaching.

Learning styles of tutors are also important areas to be investigated in relation to students'. Many cognitive scientists from design education viewpoint tried to find different explanations to demonstrate diversified aspects of designers' cognitive behavior while they are designing. Differences in cognitive styles are also important in many experiments in design research that require a number of subjects to tackle. The differences constitute a variable that is not being controlled. Cross and Nathenson (1981) distinguish four different categories of learning styles such as:

1. Convergent and Divergent
2. Impulsive and Reflective
3. Field-independent and Field-dependent
4. Serialistic and Holistic

In "convergent" thinking an individual takes the information and converts it towards the single right answer. In contradiction to this the person who thinks "divergent"ly deals not with one correct answer, but a wide range of answers. The "reflective" thinking is the style attached to the persons who tend to consider the relative accuracy of the alternative answers before responding a solution to a given problem. On the contrary "impulsive" learner tends to put forth the first answer that presents itself to him/her. Witkin (1969) put forward the other learning styles as "field-dependent" and "field-independent". He found that people differed from one another in the way they perceive the domain of the problem and themselves. Witkin uses the concept of field-dependent to characterize the person who is influenced by the domain and field-independent characterizes the person who is free from the domain. The last learning style is put forward by G. Pask and Scott as serialist and holist. "Serialist" people learn gradually step by step in logical small phases, tries to make every point clear before moving on to the next point and take a straight route through teaching material with no digression or unnecessary information. "Holist" people pick up small bits of information that is not logically necessary, but which help him/her to remember certain facts, and like learning things in different ways....and then learn, remember and recapitulate as a whole in terms of "high-order" relations' (Cross, Natheson, 1981).

Newland, Powell and Creed (1987) found this classification of learning styles inadequate and proposed another model mainly depending on the Kolb-Leary predicted relationships. Their classification is oriented towards the personality characteristics of designers. In this study, architect designers are grouped into four categories, as a consequence of discussion on learning styles and communication between the people. These categories are as follows:

1. Common Sense Learners
2. Dynamic Learners
3. Contemplative Learners
4. Zealous Learners

According to the above authors, "Common Sense" learners are abstract thinkers who have learned to exist as effective designers by combining this ability with active experimentation. These designers are self disciplined, dominant but not domineering and are good listeners. They attempt to construct a reasonable understanding of the world by seeking out underlying patterns.' "Dynamic" learners are defined as in a continual process of being shaped by their surroundings and gregarious for variety in an attempt to widen their perspectives, trying anything new as long as they are actively and personally involved' (Newland, Powell, Creed, 1987). In the same article "Contemplative" learners are defined as struggling to find the existence of a unique wholeness in life. They do this by desensitizing over plenty of data picked up from carefully studying the many facets of that whole. 'These designers are those who like to consider a montage of information; if well structured and complete, such a montage can result in attitude change and the shaping of new behavior. "Zealous" learners' reality is also a montage of information ....Such groups learn through practical action and doing. Useful information which helps them to do best what they want to do is readily accepted by them' (Newland, Powell, Creed, 1987). These two groups of learning styles and designing personalities can be found in combinations.

3.4 Systemic View of the World in Design Education

From the point of view of complexity and fundamental transformation of our perception, the real world can be taken as a holistic whole. Holism is a reductive principle. Then we can ask how do we compose a generic system and conceive the systemic thinking. The answer lies in the representation of the object world. 'In classical ontology, and in systems science terms, objects are mere appearances, that is, simplified unidimensional constructions. They are objects mutilated and removed from the complexity of physical and psycho-cultural organization. The initial notion of systems may have brought changes to our vision of things, in that objects were represented in terms of an assembly of macro-, meso-, microsystems, but the fundamental ontological conception system-things was not changed. The accumulation of the learned knowledge of designer constructs his/her schematic frames of the world.

3.5 Teaching Design

Teaching method of a design course at the beginning should be such as to make a gradually increased demand on individual frames of the real world. This includes the development of the professional concepts. 'Traditional craft programs derived their educational justifications from their contribution to the emotional and physical development of children, design courses are increasingly recognized for their contribution to intellectual development. The abilities to reason and make judgment in the light of available and relevant data is rightly regarded as one of the foremost intellectual skills, but the traditional academic route to such excellence too often failed to recognize that a child's conceptual development, whilst resulting in the ability to deal with abstractions, must start with experience of concrete. Design courses offer a rare opportunity to develop the minds of children through the disciplined application of design experience to solving of material problems' (Kimbell, 1982).

'Teaching in architectural design lacks the sufficient scientific foundation, the scientific principles, and is guided by specialized empiricism, intuition and experience. The deficiency of architectural design education is the critical and comparative feedback based on generally accepted principles. There are some questions to be answered. Can a scientific theory of design be developed? There are fundamental differences among the various fields of architectural design education and there are various tutor, student and organization related variables to make any sort of common theory possible' (Bayazit, 1992).

Design in architecture and in industrial product is abstracted essence of the field; it is what the whole process is about, but there is also a great deal to the process of architecture and industrial product that is not identifiable as design. The students in a school get the deformed view of what the field is like, because in schools most of the time design is accepted as a personal process. On the contrary in practice, design is a collaborate, co-operative or corporate activity. Schools generally ignore what happens in professional practice.

3.6 Design Education in Studio Domain

Teaching design is still conducted within the studio environment in the fashion of master-apprentice relations. For the investigation of the present situation in architectural design studios, we can ask some questions to generate new theories and to identify the variables.

What a curriculum for design education can teach to the students is the main question to be answered. Are we able to help students to identify and define real world problem situations based on their own experience? Is it possible for the students to elicit and determine relevant sources of information? Are we able to help students to analyze problem structures and situations? Are we developing judgment to discriminate and distinguish essential and technical problems? Are we teaching students how to investigate the real organization of the buildings so that they can apply them to their designs? Are we establishing concepts and skills in the minds of the students for problem solving strategy applicable to architectural design? What kinds of specific skills and techniques must students know if they engage in design as professionals?

Teaching design in architecture is different from the teaching any kind of skill that contains the components of craft characteristics of a profession. Most of the teachers in design try to give the patterns and frames in their mind to the students to copy them as their own designs while learning to design.This becomes a failure when students are left alone to make their own designs. Some of them withdraw from designing because of that reason. The main objective is to seek to learn how to learn for a dynamic (re)construction of knowledge.

In the transition from traditional design studio teaching to CAD studio teaching, the requirements for a CAD expert system as studio tutor and the behavior of the student in this new environment can be studied to raise awareness and generate discussion about the present and projected future of the design studios in the schools of architecture, industrial design, etc.

3.7 Requirements of Students in a Traditional Studio

Design studio requirements of the students in traditional studio environment while doing design works can be explained in relation to the problems of the studio work such as cognitive, environmental, and crowding. The requirements of the students are clarified depending on the results of an empirical study by Uluoglu (1990) who explained the communication between the tutor and the student working in an architectural design studio, in her thesis. She put into a rank order the different types of difficulties the students faced in the studio teaching. In this study the studio environment is accepted as a one-to-one interaction between the tutor and the student.

1. having no information about references such as books, brochures, journals to be used for the specific design task
2. the difficulties of the realization of ideas and thoughts he/she has in mind
3. the low qualities of studio conditions
4. not knowing the starting point of design
5. having difficulties in the application of presentation techniques
6. the lack of data in the specific design problem area
7. having difficulties in the visualization of the dimensions in the real world
8. having difficulties in the visualization of the proposed end of the studio project
9. having difficulties in the visualization and understanding of the 3-dimensional drawings of design
10. having difficulties in the communication with the studio tutor

In this study other aspects of studio learning are examined asking questions about what students learn at their first studio experience or the schematic expression of the students in their approach to design. The responses of the students to questions about what they pick up during their first experience in the studio learning are ranked as follows: 50% space organization, 33.3% architectural language, 33.3% user and equipment dimensions, 30% functional relations of the spaces, 16.7% user requirements, needs and expectations, and so on. The students' expression of the design process of their own is analyzed in relation to gathering data, initiation of the design process which comprises analysis, direct entry and starting from an abstraction of design. This information is altered to delineate common schemas of the design process. The following categories are selected as the most commonly applied starting stages in the design process by the students.

1. gathering data, and/or making functional analysis or a single design solution, the development of the design, and/or functional analysis and relational graphs, making single design solution, the development of the design.
2. making direct entry, and/or making a single design solution and reaching the end design, and/or making a single design solution, space and block organization of building.
3. making an abstraction (mental) of the process and/or defining goals of design, and/or developing an idea or thinking of a life style, and making a single design solution.

3.8 The Knowledge Presentation of Studio Tutors

In the design studio education in the form of master-apprentice relation, tutor's presentation of his/her knowledge is the most crucial aspect of design education. In Uluoglu's thesis (1990) architectural studio tutors are also studied in relation to their professional (as architect) and educator characteristics applying another survey and protocol analysis in the domain of studio environment. The universal and individual aspects of design knowledge possessed by the studio tutors are investigated, in relation to the extrinsic characteristics of design knowledge, applying extensive analysis techniques. Knowledge interpretation channels of studio tutor to students are externalized as written below.

- Interpreting and making critique
- Orientation
- Questioning
- Exhibiting solution
- Explanation
- Talking about the past examples
- Reminding something
- Talking about the design problems
- Talking about the design downfalls
- Talking about the positive aspects of design
- Making analogy
- Displaying examples
- Talking about the scenario of the design
- Talking about the conflicts in design

3.9 Requirements of Students in a CAD Studio

Students who select the CAD studio try to make at least one of their studio projects using a CAD program like AutoCAD. These students are patient learners of the CAD program. Each student has a different approach to CAD design: 1) The first group learns CAD skillfully while doing subordinate drawings such as facades of the existing buildings or site plans, etc., and continues sketching their designs on the computer. 2) The other group of students uses computer only for the drawing purposes. After carrying out their design phases with pen and pencil and completing all the necessary decisions, they begin drawing on the computer, equivalent to drawing with a pen on a sheet of paper.

One of the difficulties of these students in a CAD studio generates from the inadequate knowledge of how to do design efficiently as well as inadequate knowledge of how to use efficiently a CAD software simultaneously. CAD softwares are not mature enough to meet the requirements of the students who are at the beginning can be considered as layman of the profession, even those of an architect. It is not easy for an unskilled person to manipulate fuzzy knowledge in front of a computer program. Computers can not help at present to design thinking. They can only be used to generate patterns, prepare symbols, even symbol libraries, and can call existing designs whenever necessary. There are quite a lot of restrictions in the use of CAD softwares, not only for the students, but also for the professional designers. Most popular softwares as AutoCAD are originally designed to meet the requirements of mechanical engineers. Therefore the requirements of architects and industrial designers are not well covered.

3.10 Differences Between the Traditional and Computerized Studio Teaching

The differences between the traditional and computerized studio teaching generate not only from the equipment used during the design, but also from the behavior of the students. The CAD studio is composed of students, tutor, design discourse, the studio itself, similar ingredients of the traditional studio, plus machines and softwares. Students require extra time and learning effort and performance to achieve a solution graphically. Students' achievement in learning depends on their learning styles in relation to the present qualities of CAD softwares existing in the studio. Convergent, serialist and field-dependent students can adapt themselves to the CAD studio more easily than the others. On the other hand their personality in terms of Newland, Powell and Creed approach, can be well suited to dynamic, contemplative and zealous learning styles. A student with a contemplative and zealous learning style easily assembles montage of elements to construct a whole design. Holist, divergent, field-independent, reflective and impulsive students prefer to work without computer at the beginning and sometimes all through the studio works. This is easily understandable from their viewpoint. This is also true for common sense learners who are more abstract thinkers. When students have an experience with a term project and learn how to complete a design work with a computer, they achieve designing better than the fuzzy approaches of traditional studio teaching. On the other hand originally good creative designers may leave working with computers or increase their ability with additional softwares to help them in their creative works.

4 Learning About Design Knowledge

Design knowledge can not be segregated from the theory of knowledge in philosophy. At present we are working with computers and trying to interpret the methods of the professional practice into computers to be used by the professionals in the practice. These approaches lead us to the investigation of the designer's design knowledge while they are working in the domain of professional practice.

We can define knowledge as truths, concepts, approaches, judgments, norms and methodologies that are available to administer particular situations. There are two considerations of design knowledge: the computer scientists' interpretation of the knowledge is programming experts for the purpose of representation into the computer, and cognitive scientists' approach to the knowledge of the expert is to understand the designers in the real world. These two considerations are intermingled in many publications and are not clearly distinguished from each other. Most of the computer science publications try to name the programmable aspects of design knowledge as the knowledge that causes a kind of conceptual chaos. It is necessary to examine at some length the relation between the known knowledge by designers and its consequence as the design that has semantical content.

We can distinguish the different patterns of knowledge that have their own dynamics. First of all design knowledge can be axiomatic in character or it can be causal. Design knowledge may also relate to conventions and experience with little basis in certainty or apparent logic as indicated by Coyne and others (1990). Also a distinction can be made as certain and uncertain knowledge. Design domain knowledge has many facets such as procedural knowledge, normative knowledge, concrete knowledge, positive knowledge, craft knowledge, knowledge of design discourse patterns. Some academicians define knowledge only on account of procedural and declarative. This common classification does not comprise the whole space of design knowledge that needs much deeper explorations to be done. The knowledge of the expertise area of a specific design system is called domain knowledge. Domain is the professional environment that comprises co-operation of the expert team members who participate in a design activity. Therefore we can not dispute the single domain of a designer as an expert and his/her knowledge of the domain. We have to consider the participants of the design team as expert designers having different roles.

4.1 Knowledge of Design Process

Our main concerns are the investigation of the design process related procedural knowledge that relates to the cognitive processes and interpretation and/or representation of this knowledge into the computers. Procedural knowledge is concerned with descriptions and explanations of the process which is the result of a set of functions for an unexisting artifact. The evolution of the artifact eventuates in the design process that occurs in the mind of the designer or is exhibited by the designer during the design activity as stages. Procedural knowledge can be subdivided into different patterns, such as operational knowledge, situational knowledge, strategic knowledge, interpretive knowledge, generative knowledge, control knowledge, craft knowledge.

Operational knowledge relates to the use of declarative knowledge in certain processes and situations, that contains actions and manipulations. Situational knowledge is the conditional knowledge that comprises the understanding about when and where to access certain facts or employ particular procedures. Situational knowledge depends on intuition and experience that comes from the practice of the perception of the circumstances related to the design problem. Strategic knowledge is another pattern of procedural knowledge that provokes consciously acquisition and utilization of knowledge with effort and plan. Strategic knowledge can be defined as the possible action sequences, i.e., the selection and ordering of design tasks. Strategic knowledge is a part of control knowledge that is described as the mapping between the items of knowledge by Coyne and others (1990). Control knowledge makes design tractable through the reasoning process, is therefore that which defines spaces of possible action sequences such as forward or backward chaining. Generative knowledge (Syntactic knowledge) describes the relational rules of the components of a design and how these components fit together. Design descriptions can be regarded as sentences in natural language. They are explicit strings of symbols. In an interpretive system the idea of grammar seems to be a useful device in design. Grammar in design provides formal way of representing knowledge (the rules about how things are put together) about the composition. In design, system words are replaced with components as vocabulary elements. If the sentence is equal to the syntax of the system, then the process of substitution produces the start state. Interpretive knowledge relates to the meaning in design, like in linguistics, that is not explicit in a sentence. The meaning of a sentence can be considered as all those objects and ideas to which the sentence refers, and must be derived by means of interpretation. We can name it semantic space. The knowledge learned by doing is simply called craft knowledge. Industrial design and architecture possess craft skills of many kinds. Skill is the efficient and effective application of knowledge to produce solutions in some problem domain. Craft knowledge is a kind of procedural, i.e., operative knowledge. This inexplicit knowledge is hard to differentiate from the other kinds of explicit knowledge. Reasoning can be accepted as Procedural Knowledge. Reasoning is defined in Webster Dictionary as 'The drawing of inferences; thinking with a view to a conclusion believed to be valid.' It relates to the justification of an act or procedure, and to the considerations, motives, judgments leading to an action. Reasoning is the logical form of a plan of actions in the design process. Procedural knowledge can be composed of reasoning to derive information about a design problem under analysis, reasoning to derive knowledge about the existing or available knowledge, reasoning to generate hypotheses based on design domain knowledge and information which can be assumptions, statements and facts. Procedural knowledge can be about the direction of the reasoning process that can be chained forward or backward or can be bi-directional in nature. In computer applications, reasoning can be defined as the control and establishment of order for the rules of the knowledge.

4.2 Declarative or Expressive Knowledge

Declarative or expressive knowledge refers to the "knowing what" or "knowing that" type of factual information about design and design process. Expressive knowledge means indicated, demonstrated, articulated knowledge. Publicly or officially known knowledge according to rules, customs, etc., falls into this category. Declarative knowledge can be subdivided to design discourse, positive knowledge, symbolic knowledge, concrete knowledge. Most of the scientific or non-scientific publications, documents, standards, specifications, written or unwritten information about design fall into this category.

Positive knowledge theory in design is an attempt to explain the accumulation of facts about the world. 'Positive knowledge theory is intrinsically tentative and subject to revision in the face of the first deviant case that does not conform to its explanation and prediction' (Roberts, 1969). Positive knowledge in the literature for designers is related to the human beings, named as user requirements, user studies, user attitudes, men-environment relations, user behaviors, etc. searched under the scientific fields of ecological psychology, environmental psychology, ergonomics, marketing, etc. User requirement studies go back to the beginning of this century applying the social surveys, and work or job studies copied from the approaches of the Gilbert and Taylor. In the area of industrial product design first attempts for the positive knowledge have been made in the era of Bauhaus.

Concrete (substantive) scientific knowledge in architecture and industrial product design is concerned with the description and explanation of the physical nature of the products and the built environment-its material, space and structure. It comprises the segments of the environmental design knowledge. The emergence of building science in this century influenced the use of scientific information in architecture. For most of the architects, science is a useful source for facts and generalizations. There are organizations, standard institutes, laboratories and schools of engineering who work on the scientific and technological aspects of design to produce concrete scientific knowledge. This information must be put into a form easy enough to be learned and used by the design community who does not know scientific contents.

A discourse can be defined as a formation constituted by all that is said, written or thought in a field around some objects. A discourse actually refers to a referent, to an object outside it, or to things. The concept of knowledge of design discourse is an important term that comprises design practices, design studies, design theories- what exactly they are dealing with, discursive rules and formations. The subject of the design discourse is the objects, structure of the objects and the mechanisms of the discourse itself, the formations of the discourse as a network of relations as indicated by Teymur (1982). Most of the books, periodicals, standards, specifications fall into this category.

4.3 Difficulties in the Understanding of Design Normative Knowledge

According to the dictionaries norm is defined as 'a standard of proper behavior or principle of right or wrong 'and 'a usual or expected number, amount, pattern of action or behavior'. Normative knowledge relates to preferences, values, tastes, attitudes of designers. To some it means, "what has been as a consensus agreed upon, the norms for a given time"; to others it consists of statements on "what ought to be-what a good world is". Normative knowledge theory of design consists of value-laden statements of philosophers, politicians, and architects, among others, on what ought to be. This definition is too broad to explain the normative knowledge of an individual. When individuals with common motives or problems interact over a sufficient time span, social norms develop as a by-product. Universal aspects of culture can be described as normative as indicated by Malinowski (1961).

The acquisition and the structuring of the normative knowledge are challenging as much as the knowledge itself. There are two main design research areas in the study of normative design knowledge: 1) to make interpretive analysis of the design itself 2) to make introspective analysis of individual designers. The interpretive analysis of design is the most widespread approach among designers and art historians. The most challenging point is the interpretation itself that contains the normative values of the interpreter who belongs to a culture (Bayazit, 1993). Introspective analysis on designers is the most complex operation to achieve normative design knowledge. A set of normative knowledge is indispensable for every designer but some of it is relative to individuals. These normative values have a relational structure in a hierarchical order. Behavior scientists try to investigate the underlying values, motivations, ethical, religious, or aesthetic background of the values as a part of mental life of people. Therefore, it is possible for the design researcher to act like a psychologist to examine the mental life of a designer for a certain end. If there is an aesthetic requirement involved in an engineering design then we have to consider relative values of each designer. Normative knowledge of the present designers can be the subject of study by the design researchers and the behavior scientists in the future.

4.4 The Necessity of Collaborative Design Knowledge for Industry

Collaborative and individual design works are two different methodological approaches to design. At present collaborative design work is recognized as being more powerful than the individual design work for its various qualities. For some psychologists individuals can be more creative when they are apart from the others. On the other hand groups play a crucial role in the organization theory.

In primitive groups, man achieves his mastery over the environment and his competitors through co-operation. Co-operation means life in common. Both co-operation and life in common imply sacrifices and joint effort, subordination of private interests to mutual gain, the existence of rules, of authority, of constraint. There are several significant characteristics that make collaborative work powerful, such as co-ordination between the people, a co-operated goal shared by the participants, goal-directed behavior of the participants, distributed responsibilities of the work and work flow, a reward system for the participants, a shared responsibility between the participants, an organic learning process between the participants in the group, belonging to a social group, mutual interaction between the group and the individual.

The new computer technologies and international communication standards facilitate the co-operative work space activities. At present, multi-skilled participants are required in design teams at any stage of design. Scientific design management approaches are aiming at optimum use of human resources in design team activities. Expert systems and computer supported co-operative work studies are concerned with the development of systems that support individuals in this respect. Understanding collaborate knowledge will help to develop simultaneous distance design, education and decision making procedures and systems.

5 Design Science - Design Research

Design is planning and representation of any kind of activity consciously, toward a purposeful, intended end to impose a meaningful order. We are dealing with the meanings of design related to the human actions such as intention, contrivance, purpose, delineation, reasoning, proposition. The other meanings related to design as an artifact are not directly examined in this study. As a human activity design(ing) is a phenomenon that is studied by design science and considered essential for shaping and describing the design process and outcome. Doing research into the design process concerned many theoreticians who worked in close relations with industry. The source of scientific knowledge of design goes back to the emergence of technology. 'The experience-based know-how 'can be accepted as indicated by Sarlemijn (1993) as the beginning of scientific knowledge about design. Formal research for design was emphasized explicitly and taught first time in the school of Bauhaus in 1920's.

Design science and design research are the two concepts used interchangeably. Those two concepts deal with the study of design and designing. Gregory in 1965 used the concept of "design science" for the first time. "Design Science" is the investigation of designing activity and design methods put to use by the experts who develop their own methods through the experiences gained in the practice in their life-span. We are talking about the research into the process of designing scientifically. "We can say that we are at present at the very beginning of the design science"(Bayazit, 1993 b). Archer (1981) made the other definition for design research as follows: 'Design research is systematic inquiry whose goal is knowledge of, or in, the embodiment of configuration, composition, structure, purpose, value and meaning in man-made things and systems.' Design research obligates us to apply different approaches and the methods of different disciplines. In the investigation of the design knowledge we have to consider the information known by the designers, how that information is gained, how that information is processed, how it is used, and how it is decided to be necessary while solving a problem. Design research can be conducted in various directions utilizing approaches of various scientific disciplines developed for basic physical, human, etc. sciences.

5.1 Knowledge Acquisition for Design Research

Knowledge acquisition is an empirical approach developed utilizing the methods of cognitive science. 'It can be accepted as an empirical investigation tool for design research, in the exploration of design methods of expert living designers' (Bayazit, 1993 b). Knowledge acquisition deals with the known knowledge that can be procedural, normative, declarative or collaborate, and the relational rules and orders of the knowledge of experts. Knowledge acquisition employs a technique to elicit data (usually verbal) from the expert and helps to interpret these verbal data in order to infer what might be the expert's underlying knowledge and reasoning process. Knowledge acquisition uses this interpretation to guide construction of some model or language that describes (more or less accurately) the expert's knowledge and performance. In this process knowledge engineer has the main role to organize the whole activities associated with eliciting (or acquiring), codifying and encoding knowledge, conceptualizing and implementing knowledge-based systems, and engaging in activities to formalize knowledge and its use. Design researcher in this case acts like a knowledge engineer who organizes whole research activity during the knowledge acquisition and engages in activities to formalize knowledge and its use in the design process.

During the knowledge acquisition procedure there are problems of the research on the experts. Acquisition of verbal data can be incomplete and unstructured as well as unreliable and conflicting. The second problem originates from the required retrieval procedure of expert knowledge bases, because knowledge structure of the experts is not well structured and has no similar characteristics. Therefore, it is difficult to make updates. The other problem is in the performance of the expertise that may be hard to define, and this knowledge may not well fit to the requirements of its user. Experts do not only solve problems but they are competent in the communication with the environment (user, client, etc.), in order to elicit well specified problem statements and to carry out solutions. The recording of this communication is difficult to obtain. The complexity of the selected domain to capture knowledge of the experts is another problem. Research into the selected domain may not be feasible, socially wise and economic.

5.2 The Literature About Knowledge Acquisition

Knowledge acquisition applies the methods of cognitive science. The review of the knowledge acquisition methods is carried out to understand the ways a knowledge engineer works. In each new knowledge acquisition procedure, design domain is observed, data are collected, refined, rejected until reached to a satisfactory position. Then the knowledge is interpreted and concepts are structured. In this procedure review and analysis of design discourse is made, concepts are identified, depending on the initial approaches the expert knowledge is studied applying different techniques. Information gathering and development technologies are using already accepted quite common and basic techniques in many disciplines. Bayazit gives in her article a long list of these techniques (Bayazit, et.al., 1981) concerning to the related sciences. Design researchers widely use these techniques in the knowledge elicitation for miscellaneous purposes (Fig. 2). In the following lines a group of knowledge acquisition approaches are listed.

Searching for Documentary Evidence: Declarative or expressive knowledge as we mentioned before can be found in books, publications, reports, standards, codes of practice, specifications, videos, slides, or any kind of documentary evidence. We accept the objects as having patterns of relations that can be a set of theoretical relations or procedures as meant by C. Alexander in his studies. These relations can be in the form of a concrete knowledge such as a formula or a range of criteria. We can apply various models of cognitive semantics for listing and establishing relations between the objects that have an internal reality.

Congruence of Representation approach is used a rule-elicitation method. Lundell developed this method (1988). He controls the independent variables such as elicitation method, expert's level of expertise, and knowledge representation in the knowledge base, in his experiments.

Models of Verbalization deals with the direct vocalization of the information or the vocalization of initially encoded information as indicated by Ericsson and Simon (1984):

"The obvious implications of this for analyzing recorded verbalization is that the originally heeded information should be recovered by decoding the "encoded" verbalizations (i.e. those not originally in oral forms). The first step in such an analysis is to identify the verbalization units.... The second implication of the model is that each segment is verbalized independently of those that precede and follow it...A third implication of our model is that verbalizations should be encoded in terms of the heeded information they express."

This approach is for analyzing verbal reports of subjects. In this model, report can be obtained with a number of techniques. The earliest first verbal reports, "thinking-aloud", "talk-aloud" recording while a subject is solving a problem is developed by Ericson and Simon (1984). Stevenson et al (1988) developed another protocol analysis technique to make evaluation on the small groups depending on the theory of adaptive control of thought.

Computer Assisted Knowledge Acquisition is developed as a part of computer design assistance by several authors such as Ullman (1992), Deffner and Ahrens (1989) and many others. Ullman developed a tool for designers to obtain graphical knowledge of designers. Deffner and Ahrens developed a method that involves having a domain expert entering rules in a formal language. Then they used a refinement procedure to modify any ill-defined rules. They created experts in an artificial domain. In the other approach role of the personality differences of experts and the predictive accuracy of knowledge engineers and the knowledge acquisition method is tested in some experiments (Adelman (1989). The main concerns are the quality of domain expert's expertise, skill levels and the personality of the knowledge engineers. Another widely used approach is structured interview. In that approach, the control group of experts have their knowledge acquired through interviews. In this group of knowledge acquisition procedure pre prepared interviews are used after the production of a decision tree depending on the documented rules inductively. The purpose of this approach is to reach final decisions, making comparisons of the induction with the interview results. All interviews are tape recorded and transcripts are ordered. Kavakly and Bayazit (1993), and many others applied a structured interview technique on design offices of window producer firms.

Research Methods of Knowledge	Procedural Knowledge	Declarative Knowledge	Collaborate Knowledge	Normative Knowledge
Work Observations	o		o	
Questionnaires for Experts	o		o	o
Free Talks	o		o	o
Structured Interview	o		o	o
Think-Aloud Protocols	o		o	o
Computer Assisted KA	o	o		
Questionnaires for Users			o	o
Conversation	o		o	o
Congruence of Representation	o			o
Predictive Accuracy				
Searching for Doc. Evidence	o	o		o
Team Discussions	o		o	o

Fig. 2 Research methods for the patterns of knowledge

5.3 Knowledge Interpretation and Structuring

Methodology of the knowledge acquisition is the crucial problem in the investigation of designers' knowledge. In knowledge acquisition we can formulate three main functions: a) knowledge elicitation b) interpretation of knowledge c) structuring knowledge. Knowledge elicitation is the extraction of knowledge from the acquired knowledge such as coding, (Burton, et al., 1990), (Coyne 1990). structuring and modelling. Interpretation (Breuker, et al., 1987) and structuring are the most complicated stages in the knowledge acquisition procedure. We need a model in order to interpret verbal, written, and design data. Data interpretation model should be simple enough and robust (i.e., compatible with a wide range of alternative assumptions about human information processing) as Ericsson and Simon (1984) indicated in their book. During the verbalization procedure loss of information is recognized by Chafe (1984) and the written texts are preferred because of the slowness of writing which leads to quality which is called "integration". 'Integration as he indicated, shows up packing of more information into written idea units, through typical written devices such as normalization, the increased use of attributive adjectives (properties of entities) and particles, and so on' (Bayazit, 1990). Written reports are easy to analyze compared to oral reports. A method based on "Kinaesthetic Image-Schema" was developed by Bayazit (1990), principles taken from "Cognitive Semantics" (Lakoff, 1986)

Knowledge interpretations can not be completed without giving enough consideration to the knowledge structure of the referent expert. 'The basic assumption in expert system studies is to form a mental model that accurately represents the design as well as the process that can be performed by it and on it' (Sowa, 1984). The structure of the design knowledge is analyzed depending on the concepts, their understanding and meaning. Structure of concepts generates from the structure of the experience that takes place at two levels. Lakoff (1986) named these levels as "the basic level" and "the image-schematic level". Akyn (1986) makes distinction of general and specific purpose knowledge. He calls the general form of knowledge schemata and the specific form instances. According to him schemata represent knowledge that is equally applicable to many different circumstances or individual instances. Bayazit (1990) proposed four major schemas after Lakoff (1986), such as container, part-whole, source-path-goal, link.

5.4 Expert Systems for Design Studios as Teaching Tools

Development of expert systems for design education, as part of advance educational technology, bridges the gap between education and practice with the help of design research. Acting as a knowledge engineer to do design research on the teachers of design and experts in the professional practice should help to create new tools for design education environment. Utilization of a CAD expert system can eliminate most of the complications in the studio environment. The knowledge of tutors as well as expert designers can be fed into such a system for design education. In the light of the studies on the traditional studio teaching and the requirements of CAD studio learning we can determine the requirements of a CAD expert system for design. On the other hand it is possible to develop different expert systems for the studio environments for the students to better understand the problems of the industry, looking through the glasses of industrial experts. A general instructional system can be constructed to meet the basic conceptual requirements of different design problems. If we accept an expert CAD program as a studio tutor we can make a list of the required responses from a tutor in front of the student when making critique.

- better information
- guidance to the direction of the project
- explanation(s) to the project
- better access to user population
- asking right questions
- displaying past examples of solution(s)
- showing analogies
- reminding necessary information
- showing the problems of design
- showing the downfalls of design
- better understanding of the built environment
- better understanding of the nature of people
- better understanding of the nature of design process of designers
- better understanding of the interactions of the above three (environment, user, designer)
- better understanding of the nature of design practice
- better understanding of the modes of operating the process and of the different modes of professional-client relations

This system can have several subsystems and modules for the starters. Procedural requirements of the analysis stage that are explicitly written and told may be easily put into the expert system. For the purpose of giving information related to special design problems some instructional modules can be prepared to help students to find out where to start to a design problem. Declarative knowledge of human behavior, environmental qualities, legal documents, etc., may be located in the libraries of this system. Procedural knowledge may be simulated with lists of questions, flow diagrams, check lists, etc. Starting from the general system small different instructional expert systems can be developed to help the students with their library of symbols, well known buildings as well as problem pattern examples, thesaurus like shape libraries, etc. The difficulty of an expert CAD program is to turn this knowledge into a way of structuring the environmental knowledge, knowledge of users, knowledge of procedure, in other words the science of praxis.

6 Conclusions

The demands of the industry from educational institutions need to be better and more regularly defined. The role of the tutor changed in this context. The new technological advancements are forcing us to develop new design methodologies from a different perspective. If we are going to use computers as a part of our daily life, we have to develop new approaches to the investigation of design process. The major objective of the design education should be to enhance learners' ability in building own cognitive frames of the world and transferring this knowledge to representational thinking. Tutor is not a person dictating the viewpoints to students but helping them in this direction. Instead of teaching to the students the existing world by description, narration, explanation and interpretation pulled out from our own experiences as distorted views of the world, we must teach them how to perceive, how to investigate, how to structure, how to judge, how to explain and how to interpret the real world by themselves. Therefore teaching and educational technology must be oriented to the minds of the students. Knowledge about the learning styles of the students helps us to understand the evolution of the cognitive frames in the mind and their approach to the high technology.

There are big gaps between the research and practice of design. Many theories have been developed and new sciences are brought into existence in association with the design research since the beginning of the studies on explicit design methodologies. Design research bases are gained as a result of empirical studies in which objective research methods are applied with critical evaluation procedures of design knowledge. Design research can be considered to be wholly scientific in this respect.

Expert systems may help to the students at the beginning of their design studios in giving design information. We believe there are countless number of investigations to be completed and innumerable number of discussions to be made in the domain of CAD studio teaching. For further developments guidance from theory to practical systems is necessary. We consider this will improve the interactions between the theory and practice, theory and education. A CAD expert system for design studios can not replace the human experts, but may be of some help to them to introduce the expert knowledge from professional practice when educating the students if it is used appropriately.

References

1. Akin, Ö.: Psychology of Architectural Design. Pion (1986)
2. Adelman, L.: Measurement Issues. In: Knowledge Engineering, IEEE Trans. Systems, Man, & Cybernetics 19, 3, 483-488 (1989)

3. Archer, L. B.: A view of the Nature of Design Research. In: R. Jacques, J. A. Powell (eds.), Design, Science, Method. IPC Business Press 1981

4. Bayazit, N., Esin, N., Özsoy, A.: An Integrative Approach to Design Techniques. Design Studies, 2, 4, 215-223 (1981)

5. Bayazit, N.: Theoretical Basis of a Computer-Aided Design Education and Research Laboratory. Design Studies, 8, 3, pp. 138-149 (1987)

6. Bayazit, N.: Development of a Knowledge Acquisition Model for Computer Aided Design. In: V. Hubka, A. Kostelic (eds.), Proceedings of the 1990 International Conference on Engineering Design, ICED 90, Heurista and Yudeko, Dubrovnik-Zagrep 1990

7. Bayazit, N.: Requirements of an Expert System for Design Studios, EDCAADE Barcelona Conference, 12-14 December 1992

8. Bayazit, N., Demir, Y.: Ontological and Cognitive Perspective of Design Education for Beginners. In: Architectural Education Programs, EAAE/ACSA Schools of Architecture Conference, Prague, 11-15 May 1993 a

9. Bayazit, N.: Designing: Design Knowledge: Design Research: Related Sciences. In: M. J. de Vries, N. Cross, D. P. Grant (eds.), Design Methodology and relationship with Science. Kluwer Academic Publishers 1993 b

10. Breuker, J., Wielinga, B.: Use of models. In: A. L. Kidd (ed.), The Interpretation of Verbal Data, in Knowledge Acquisitions for Expert Systems: A Practical Handbook, Plenum Press, New York 1987

11. Burton, M. Shadbolt, N.: Knowledge Elicitation. In: J. R. Wilson, E. N. Corlett Evaluation of Human Work, London, Taylor and Francis 1990

12. Chafe, W.: Cognitive Constraints on Information Flow, Institute of Cognitive Studies, University of California at Berkeley 1984, July

13. Coyne, R. D., Roseman, M. A., Radford, A. D., Balachandran, M., Gero, J. S.: Knowledge-Based Design Systems. Addison-Wesley, Reading, MA 1990

14. Cross, N., Nathenson, M.: Design Methods and Learning Methods. In: R. Jacques, J. A. Powell (eds.), Design: Science: Method, IPC Business Press 1981

15. Deffner, G., Ahrens, R.: On the Use of Formal Language, and Ill Defined Quantifiers in Knowledge Acquisition. Proceedings of HFS 33rd Annual Meeting, Perspectives, 1, pp. 356-360 (1989)

16. Dressler, G.: Organization Theory: Integrating Structure and Behavior., Prentice- Hall, Englewoods Cliffs, NJ 1986

17. Ericsson, K. A., Simon, H. A.: Protocol Analysis: Verbal Reports as Data, MIT Press, Cambridge MA 1984

18. Gregory, S. A.: The Design Method, Butterworth, London 1966

19. Kavakly, M., Bayazit, N.: Knowledge Elicitation and Structuring for the Synthesis of a System Component in Design. Knowledge Elicitation and Structuring Workshop, I. T. U. Istanbul 5th February 1993

20. Johnson, L.: The need for competence models in the design of expert systems. International Journal in Systems Research, and Informational Science, 1 (1985)

21. Kimbell, R.: Design Education. The Foundation Years. London, Routledge & Kegan Paul 1982

22. Lakoff, G.: Cognitive Semantics, Institute of Cognitive Studies. University of California at Berkeley, March 1986

23. Lundell, J. W.: Knowledge Extraction and the Modelling of Expertise in a Diagnostic Task. University of Washington Seattle (Ph. D. dissertation), 1988

24. Malinowski, B.: The Dynamics of Culture Change. New Haven. Yale University Press 1961

25. Newland, P., Powell, J. A., Creed, C.: Understanding Architectural Designer' Selective Information Handling. Design Studies, 8, 1, pp 2-16 (1987)

26. Roberts, E.: Theory Building. New York, Free Press 1969

27. Sarlemijn, A.: Design are Cultural Alloys, 'Stempje' in Design Methodology. In: M. J. de Vries, N. Cross, D. P. Grant (eds.), Design Methodology and Relationship with Science, Kluwer Academic Publishers 1993

28. Sherif, M., Sherif, C.: An Outline of Social Psychology. Harper and Brothers, New York 1956

29. Sowa, J. F.: Conceptual Structures, Information Processing in Mind and Machine, Addison-Wesley, Reading, MA 1984

30. Stevenson, J. R., Manktelow, K. I., Howard, M. J.: Knowledge Elicitation Dissociating Conscious Reflections from Automatic Process. In: D. M. Jones and R. Winder (eds.), People and Computers IV, University Press, Cambridge, UK 1988

31. Teymur, N.: Environmental Discourse. London, ?uestion Press 1982

32. Uluoglu, B.: Mimari Tasarim Egitimi. Tasarim Bilgisi Baglaminda Stüdyo Elestirileri (Architectural Design Education: Design Knowledge Communicated in Studio Critiques), I. T. U. Fen Bilimleri Enstitüsü, Istanbul (Ph. D. Thesis in Turkish) 1990

33. Waddington, C. H.: Tools for Thought. Granada Publishing, St Albans, UK 1977

34. Whitkin, H. A.: Some Implications of Research on Cognitive Style for Problems of Education. In: M. B. Gottesgen, G. B. Gottesgen (eds.). Professional School Psychology, 3, Grime and Stratton, New York 1969

The Elements of Technology for Education

Dietrich Blandow
Eindhoven University of Technology
Department W and M
Den Dolch 2, 5600 Einhoven, The Netherlands

Abstract. Technology is the knowhow and creative process for using tools, resources, environmental conditions, and personal capabilities in order to realize objectives and change conditions as well as help individuals to overcome contradictions in typical situations.

The paper shows the resources of technology for developing human capabilities.

Keywords. Technology, innovation, vocational education, production process, tools, resources, environmental conditions, personal capabilities

Introduction

What I would like to explain with the following examples is that the accepted situation between humans and their technological environment is one of development relationships. We see this not only in the field of production, but also in our leisuretime, in our safety aspects, in the areas of sports, of communications and hospitality. But the relationships between humans and their environment are irreversible. You cannot omit some stages, nor can you ignore the existing levels. Yet the main point is that advanced technology itself is the result of human activities with their social, natural, and physical interfaces. At the same time, the man-used and man-made world is a result of both theoretical and practical efforts, and it is reflected in all aspects of our lives (see Fig. 1).

On the other hand, the relationships between humans and technology relations are already curious. More and more ideas are put into practice and each generation finds it increasingly difficult to work with accumulated experiences increasing exponentially in number and complexity. The consequences of this, the well-known knowledge-time problem, are accepted; however, the later consequences, the knowledge of technology, from which other things came, meals, safety, traffic, communications, medical health, our future ecological environment, is not yet accepted as a part of general education everywhere.

Fig. 1 Technology and human resource development

And hereby we include not only the young, but the older people, the unemployed as well as the daily workers should be kept in mind. In reality, most scientific results in the field of high technology never reach the people in practice.This raises questions about the different views of society and the purpose of maunfacture. And it involves the ethics of technology and the social responsibility of companies. During the UNESCO Bangkok conference on Technology Education in 1989 this phenomena was explained with the opposite term to technological literacy, namely technological illiteracy.

When we are looking for a starting point in order to explain the pedagogical dimension of the human technological interface and to understand the changes, risks, laws and principles of technology, we need to consult Fig. 2.
One outcome of this chart is the need to know what general culture is and which role technology plays in life. In my opinion, general culture (which is the basis of professional culture and economical success too) must be a symbiotic complex of related knowledge and purposeful behavior that enables people:

- to orient themselves to their environment (in space and time);
- to adapt themselves actively to that environment;
- to protect her or his environment and, finally,
- to develop themselves.

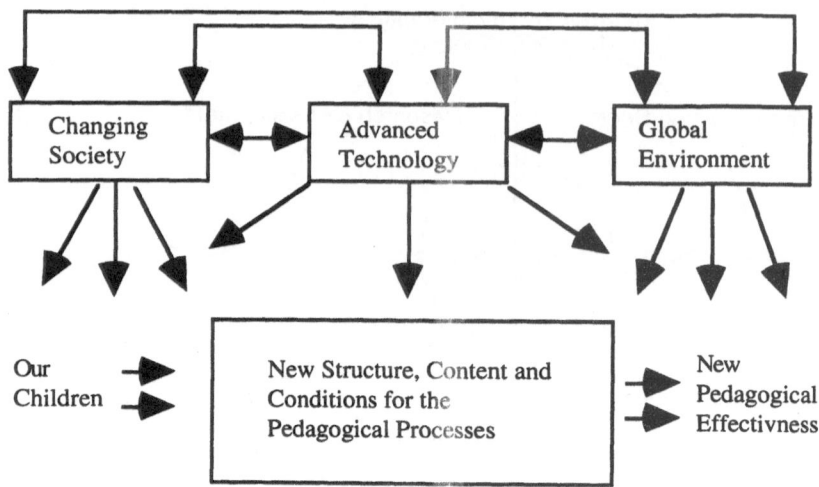

Fig. 2 Finding the starting point

Nowadays, technological education (which is synonymous with Technological Capabilities and Technological Literacy) is part of the general culture without which it would not exist. This is not a technocratic view. On the contrary, it reflects the fact, that illiterate people can destroy our natural environment and society too. Therefore the conditions of human life and humanity itself would be destroyed. Technological literacy and the success of society as a whole are irreversibly connected. Let me explain this with a simple example. One part of technological literacy concerns thinking in a hierarchical and time-oriented manner. Shortsighted thinking has consequences which become apparent later, sometimes years later, as shown in Fig. 3.

Before I explain the ideas behind the concept of technological education as a part of general education, let me highlight the paradigm changes in vocational training and engineering subjects. It is sometimes easier to solve your own problems if you know something about your colleagues.

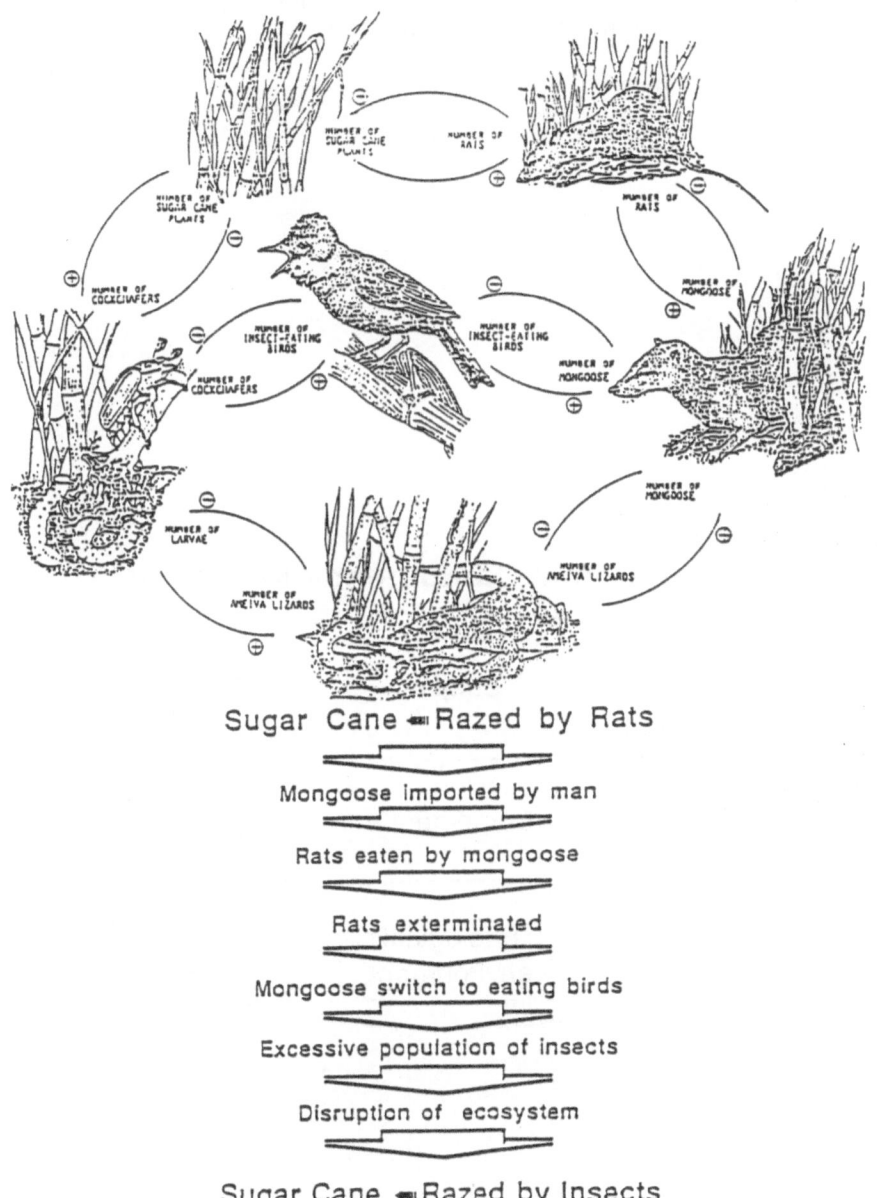

Sugar Cane ⟵ Razed by Rats

Mongoose imported by man

Rats eaten by mongoose

Rats exterminated

Mongoose switch to eating birds

Excessive population of insects

Disruption of ecosystem

Sugar Cane ⟵ Razed by Insects

Fig. 3 Consequences of short-sighted thinking

In vocational eduction, companies are using the so-called Synergetic Competence Model more and more as a starting point, refers Fig. 4.

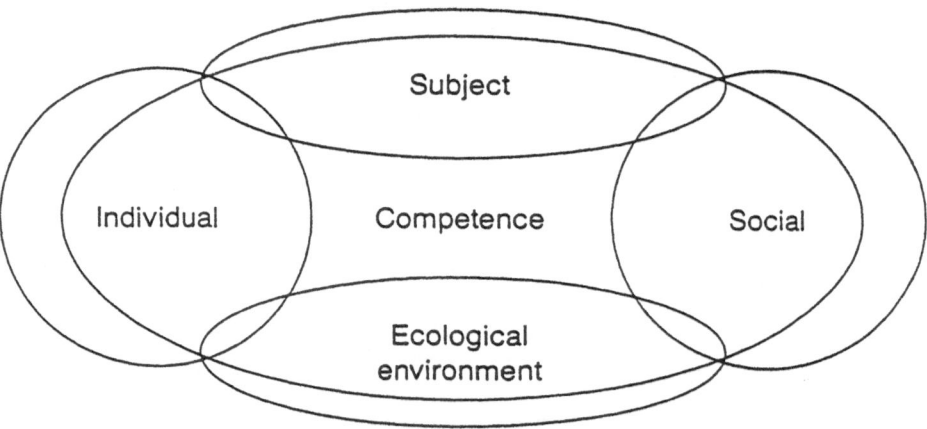

Fig. 4 Synergetic Competence Model

Theuerkauf works with VW for developing educational strategies. His starting point is nearly the same like Dyrenfurth, who works with Ford in the US. From such models, the demands on vocational training have been listed in Fig. 5.

TRAINING FOR		
	PRODUCTIVITY:	FLEXIBILITY:
special qualifications	requires abilities that fulfil the demands of the working place (highly qualified and specialized)	requires basic training for different work places (wide and applicable)
general qualifications	need to be ready for action, efficiency, high-quality work, resistant to stress and tireless	need to be adaptable, able to learn on the job, creative, ready to work elsewhere, ready to work in a team, analytic, capable of independent planning, discerning, communicative and ready to make a decision
PRODUCTIVE (PROFESSIONAL QUALIFICATION)	+ FLEXIBLE (VARIETY OF DEPLOYMENT)	= SKILLED WORKERS

Fig. 5 Demands on vocational eduction

These examples lead us directly to the key- strategy, to integrate technology in the field of general education as a useful instrument for developing personal competancies or personal capabilities.

Thinking of the technological knowledge-time-problem in engineering terms leads us directly to the structure of key-qualification. The example from BMW for instance compares not only the differences between the nominal profile of BMW and its trainees, but also between it and the graduates from colleges and universities too.

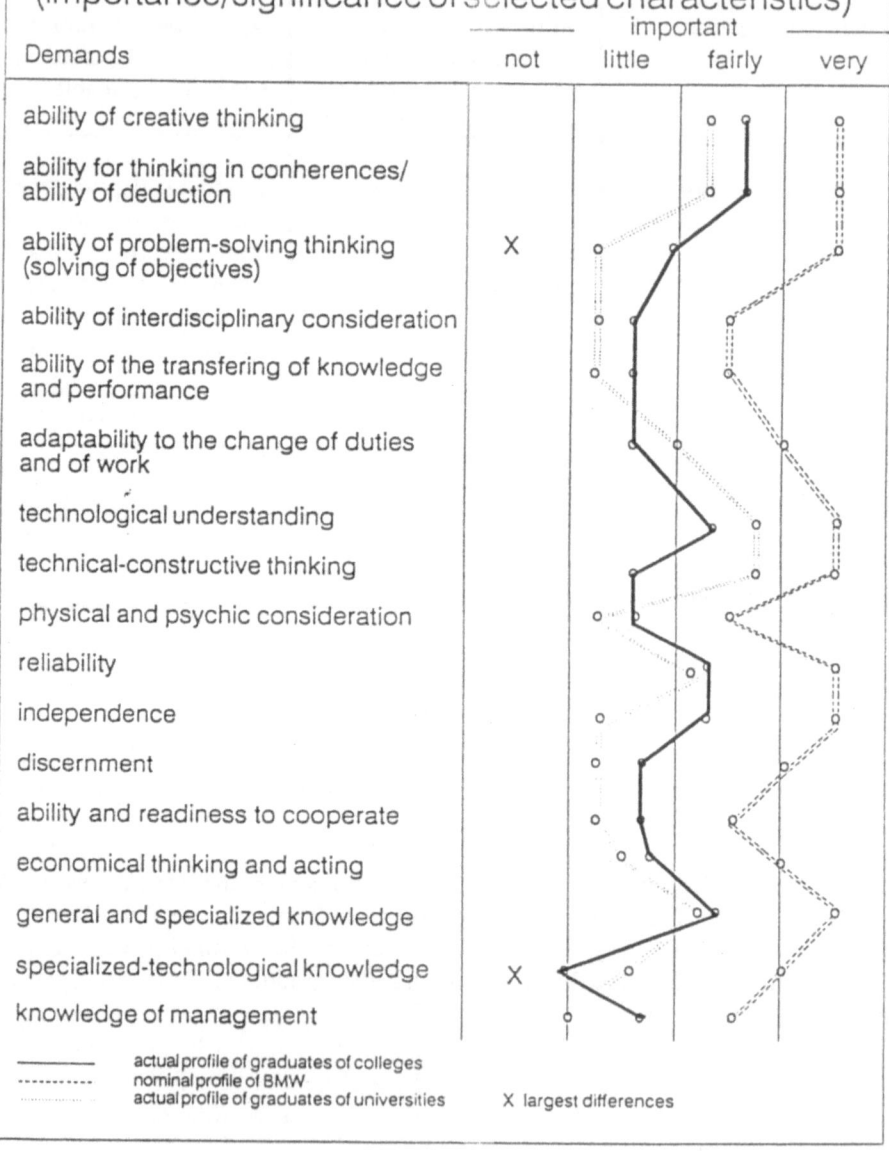

Fig. 6 Nominal-actual-profile comparison

Now, I must come back to technological literacy as a part of general education. I think that the general standard of technological education in our culture will be a precondition for success in the future and it will influence investors. This is especially important for Eastern Europe and developing-countries. In addition to natural resources and the social structure of a region the educational standard, the suitability of technical skills will influence the decisions of investors. Especially when we look at Eisenach, the new General Motors enterprise, or Jenoptic (the former Carl Zeiss Jena) or Chemnitz, Dresden and other places in Eastern Europe, the educational standard was and will still be an important decision criteria. Thinking in terms of systems, hierarchies and analogies, thinking in terms of variables, contradictions and compromises and being able to formulate technological problems are common denominators for a development-oriented educational system. Let me explain in more detail what are the starting points for the conception of technological education in the field.

Framework Model

The concept of technological capabilities is based on the pillars of general technology, technical systems (the theory of artifacts) and innovation and designing. This means that we have to accept a complex and interdisciplinary situation in association with a Metatheory, its language and structure. Therefore, we must be clear about two things:

1. There are natural overlaps between disciplines
2. The development of a framework depends on interrelationships
   between disciplines and differences between their perspectives and
   approaches.

Metalanguage includes:

Function: The ability of technical skills and technological conditions
           to design processes.
System: A complex set of connected components within a hierarchy.

Systemborder, systemheart, systemenvironment, structure and functional principles are terms that indicate the kind of thinking needed. The key to developing the ability to arrive at the correct answer is to find the right starting points; especially, for technological subjects, the key to all technological solutions are known from the terms Z and D Z (see Fig. 7).

258   Dietrich Blandow

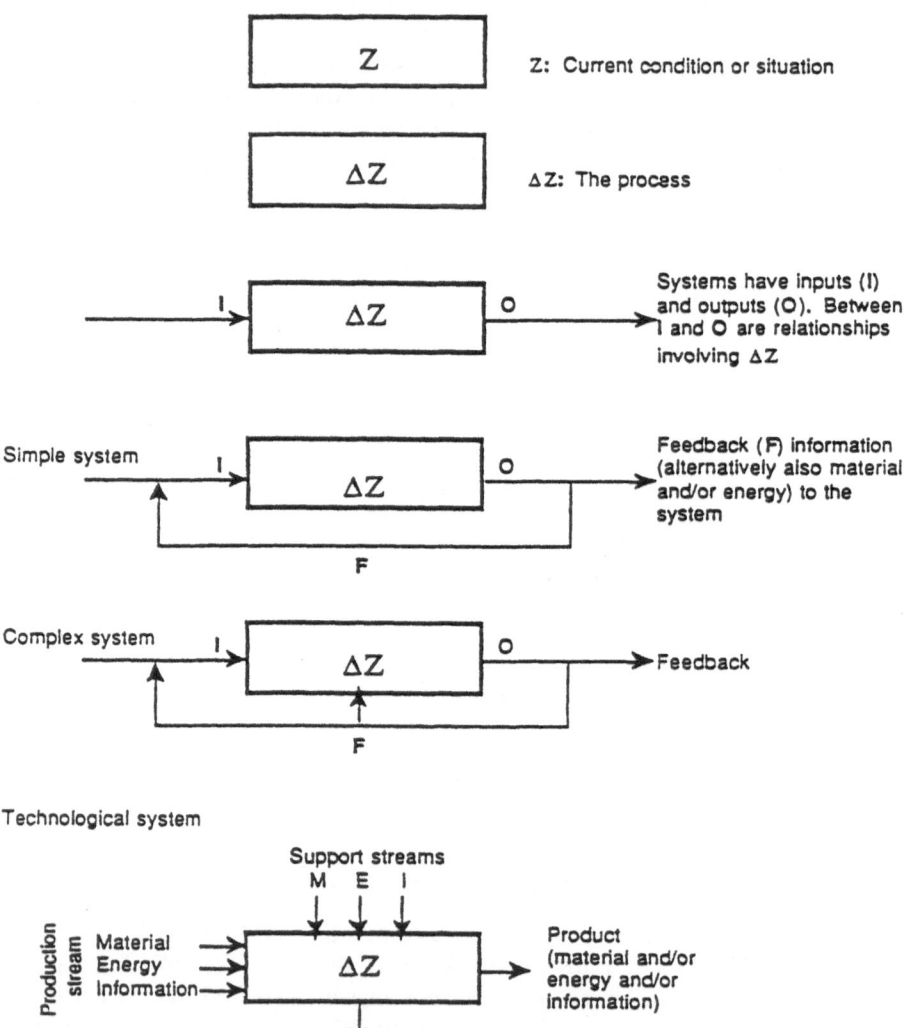

Fig. 7 Key elements of technological processes

Keypoints for understanding technical products and processes are the condition or situation, the changing of conditions or situations, the relations between input, output and feedback.

The pertinent question here is in fact the key question. It is not so important to know what is being produced. Instead, the salient issue is what changes and processes are being used, this means on which level we are processing. In other words, the profiles and interaction between the levels should be part of the technological education. In reality, those keys interact on various planes and levels (see Fig. 8).

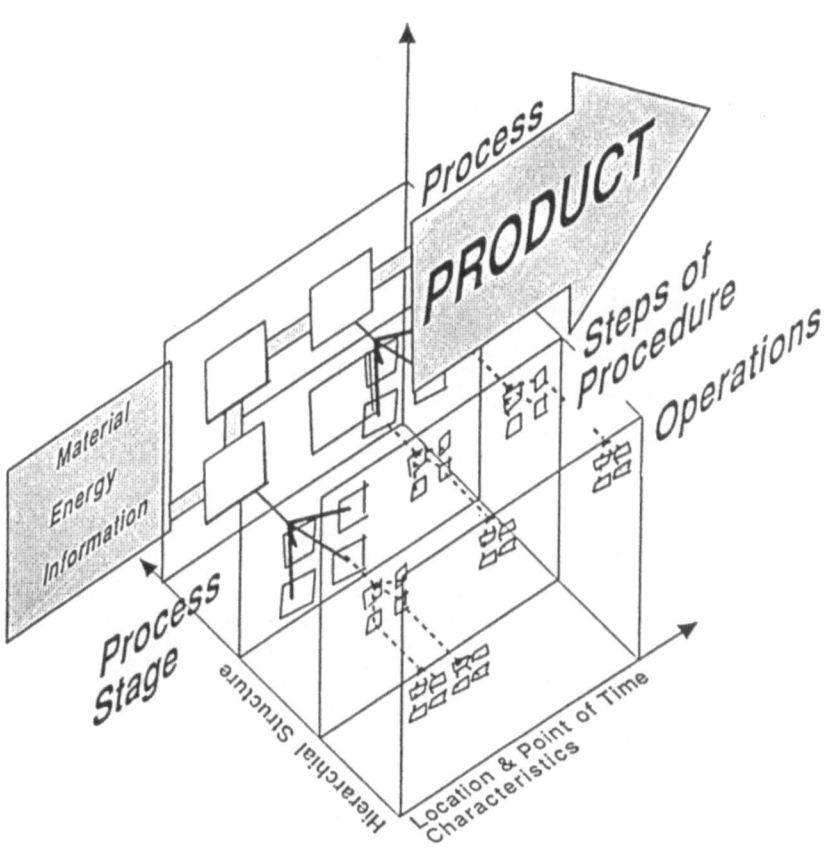

Fig. 8 Hierarchical structure of production process

The structure shown in Fig. 8 may be used to describe, explain or analyze production in any of the areas typically used by the learners. The model is equally applicable to traditional paper, metal, wood or plastics-industries, as well as, to food processing including cheese, sugar, meat and milk, or process industries such as petrochemicals, derated water or bio-technology. Furthermore, although less obvious the model clearly also fits agriculture. The same situation is shown in the hierarchy of technical systems, shown in Fig. 9.

FUNCTIONAL SYSTEM	W.O.	S.O.	T.O.	D.O.	G.O.	P.O.	C.O.	O.O.	EXAMPLE
TOOLS	+	+							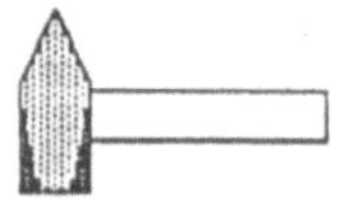
DEVICES	+	+	+						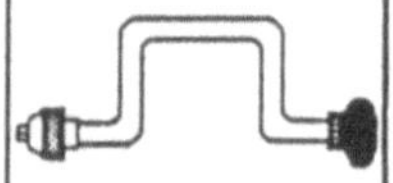
SIMPLE MACHINES	+	+	+		+	+			
TRADITIONAL MACHINES	+	+	+	+	+	+			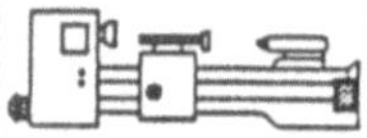
NC - MACHINES	+	+	+	+	+	+	+		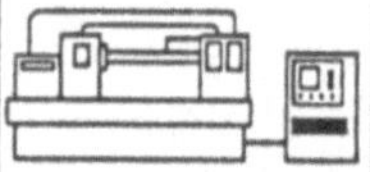
INTEGRATED MACHINES	+	+	+	+	+	+	+	+	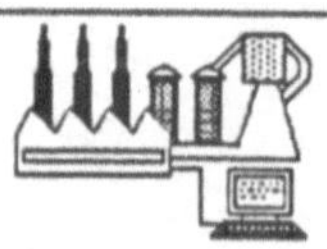

W.O.	WORKING ORGAN		D.O.	DRIVING ORGAN
S.O.	SUPPORTING ORGAN		P.O.	POSITION ORGAN
T.O.	TRANSMITTING ORGAN		C.O.	CONTROL ORGAN
G.O.	GUIDANCE ORGAN		O.O.	OPTIMIZING ORGAN

Fig. 9 Hierarchy of technical systems.

Other models of connecting are available for the different levels and stages in a so-called Life Cycle of Technical Systems.

As a result of this attempt to make sense of technology, it will be useful to make a model to represent the range of production, in the form of a matrix with three pillars (materials, energy, information) against the nature of change (shape, structure, location, time). It is shown in Fig. 10.

Object of work	Nature of Change			
	Form/ Shape	Structure	Location	Time
Material	Material shaping	Reconsti- tuting	Materials handling	Aging, Wine, Patina
Energy	Energy processing	Energy conversion	Energy transfer	Half-life
Information	Information handling	Information processing	Communi cation	Obsoles cence

Fig. 10 Matrix of objects of work against nature of change. (Blandow/Dyrenfurth, 1991)

If the principles of technological organization are included together with the proceeding matrix, one arrives at the principles of development for production. This combination is depicted in Fig. 11 and it will become a most useful tool to help us understand the strategies needed for solving specific technology/ innovation problems.

	Implications of the Goals on:			
Sample goals of process operation	Changing conditions or situations, Z_1, Z_2, Z_n	The process, DZ	Location and point of time characteristics	The technical artifacts/ means
Minimization of resources	Capitalization on material characteristics [Material structure]	Process integration WRT time [Work hardening]	Production timing (continuous/inter-mittent) [continuous casting, Just-in-time organizing]	Energy supply at point of use [Solar telephone, Integral wheel-motors]
Increase of variability	Substitution, Alternative sequences [Recycled material aggregate]	Adaptation [Photo-chromatic glass]	Flexible reactions [Combine threshing drum pressure]	Standardized components [Microchip logic elements]
Increase of stability	Feedback systems [Sensor technology, Dash warning indicators]	Networking, optimization [Feedback driven control systems, assembly line buffers]	Quality assurance [Zero defect programs]	Parallel/ redundant structure [Pilot/copilot]
Reduction of production cycle time	Activation characteristics [Catalysts, hardeners]	Increase of energy/work density at the work station [halogen lights, microcomputers]	Parallel processing, assembly lines [automobile manufacturing, Matrix computers]	Increase of frequency [Newspaper production]
Reduction of product planning and setup time	Standardized stock, modular construction components [Rolled steel, 4x8 panels, DIN paper]	Utilization of standardized (modular) process elements [Canned cycles in NC machines]	Modular machines, handling systems [Flexible manufacturing systems]	Automatic tool/jig fixture changers, robots [Computerized plant change over]
Increase in ecological responsibility	...	...	...	...
...	...	...	...	...

Fig. 11 Implications and goals of process operations.

First Consequences

The preceding analyses of technological systems and technical products led me to consider a modular concept for Technology Education. Fig. 13 presents an

overview of such a concept, it shows the constants of the problem-solving process at the Human-Technology-Interface along the X axis; the key objective of technology along the Y axis; and the key technological processes along the Z axis. And now, since I use it nearly every day, the model has led me to consider both education about technology and education through technology.

As we continue to provide technology education, it is possible to systematize this approach, and to improve its reliability and validity as well as basic consistency. It will include the following areas:

– the laws and principles of technology,
– the structure of technological processes,
– the design of technical products and
– the process and principles of innovative thinking.

Also, with such a modular concept of technology, innovation and work, we have a framework for building a database of examples which can be used to support an integrated technological education system that incorporates schools, industry and work. Then we will have an area for future reseach in order to help teachers set up technological projects. Let us go into some details.

1. When one combines the constants of objectives with the constants of technological processes, the planes of an overall model are given. One starting point is the invariants of the human-technology-interface like using, testing, serving, assessing, recycling.

2. The second plane is formed by combining the constants of processes, and objectives. Then, by adding the constants of technological interaction sites, a three dimensional model is produced that represents a matrix of technological activity. Selected contraversial examples might include (see Fig. 12) :

– Energy transport in space
– Energy storage in water
– Material transport in hospitals
– Material forming in space
– Information storage in water
– Information processing factories.

Those are not merely academic musings or wishful thinking. Immediately behind them are answers to questions regarding the emerging possibilities of technological capacity. For example, and rather practical than the previous examples, are:

– Lasers as surgical tools

– Lasers as dynamic measuring devices
– Electrophoresis gene identification
– Biotechnology for use in coal mines, etc.

Furthermore, the emergence of such technological possibilities brings with it an opportunity to incorporate forward-looking aspects of education of curricula for technology and, to learn at the same time, how to use heuristic knowledge for mobilizing our thinking.

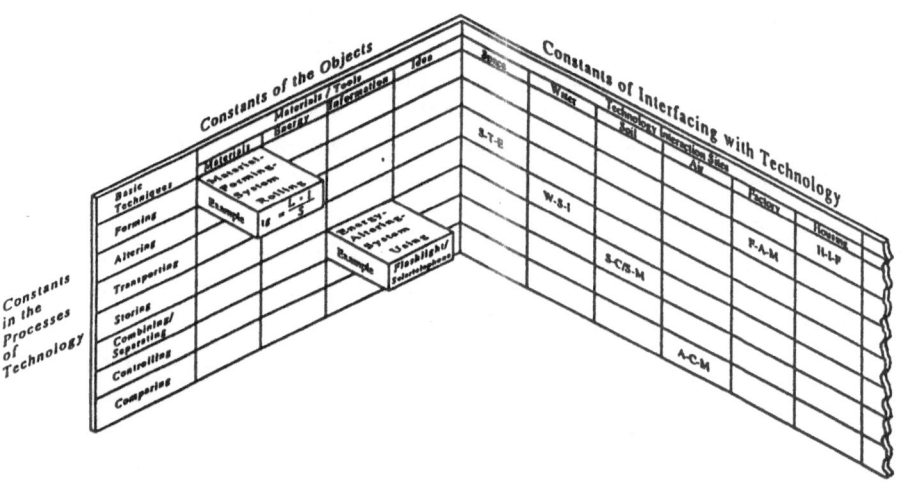

Fig. 12 Model planes : Constants of technological processes vs objects vs
     interaction sites.

3. The constants in the human-environment relationship, such as using, evaluating, etc. can be checked against other planes of the model in order to study new interaction fields. With this concept of modular planes, one has a useful methodology for organizing the variety of technological applications/examples; while on the other hand, it enables teachers and teacher trainers to generate

thousands of ideas and examples for teaching activities and the furthering of innovative thinking.

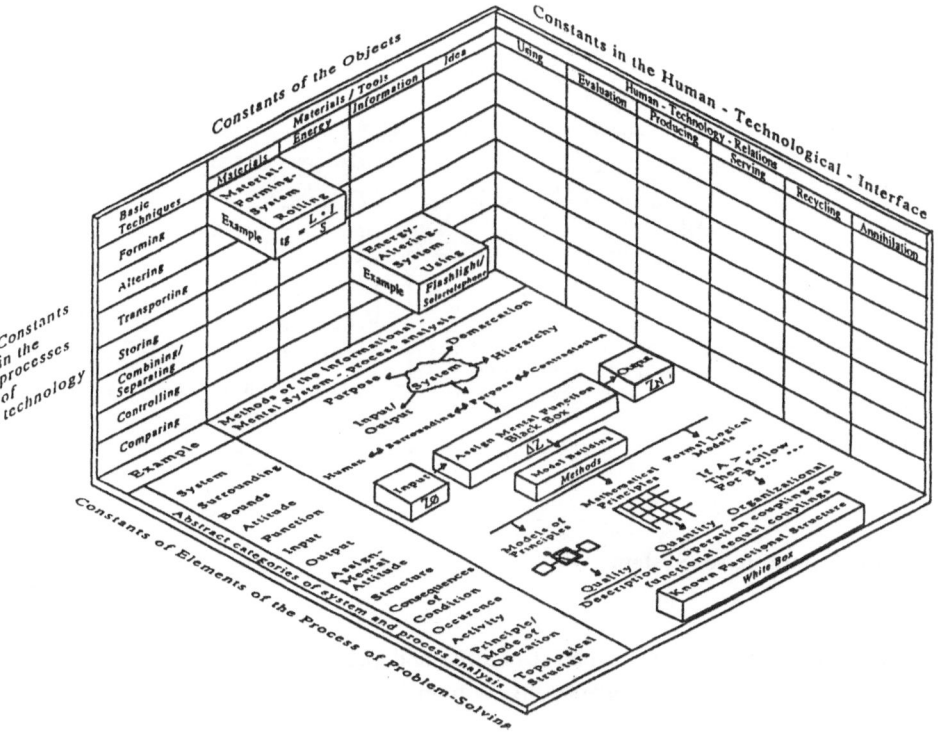

Fig. 13 The modular concept of technology and work

Second consequences

From the modular concept we can think of other alternatives:

– The same function can be realised through different structures.
– Correlations exist between function, shape, manufacture and
  materials for determining a compromise system (see Fig. 14).

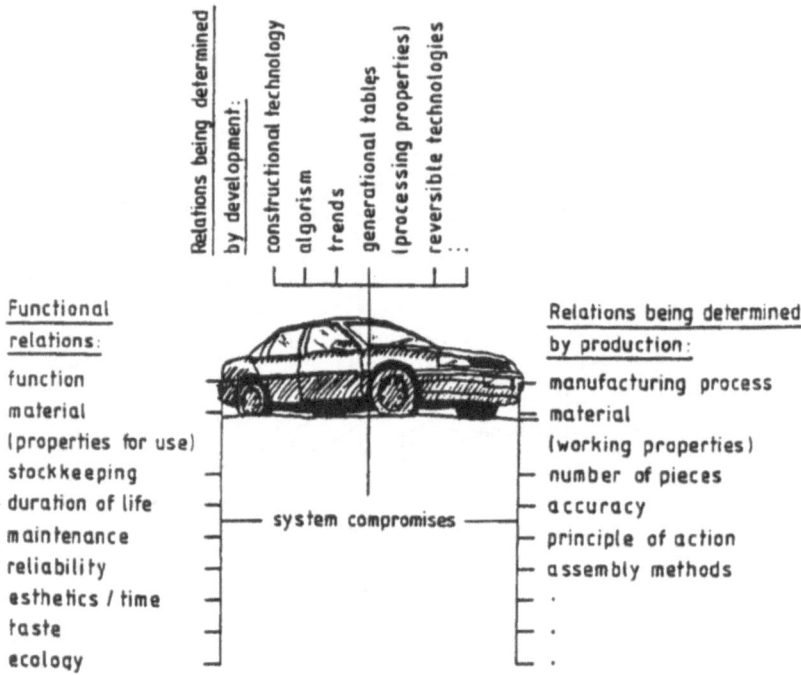

Fig. 14 Compromise System.

- The numbers of processes can be structured and classified according to their
  characteristics (forming, transporting, converting, warehousing, storing energy
  and processing information).

- All processes can be based on a model of active principles in order to change the
  operant conditions from Z_i to Z_{i+1}, see Fig. 15.

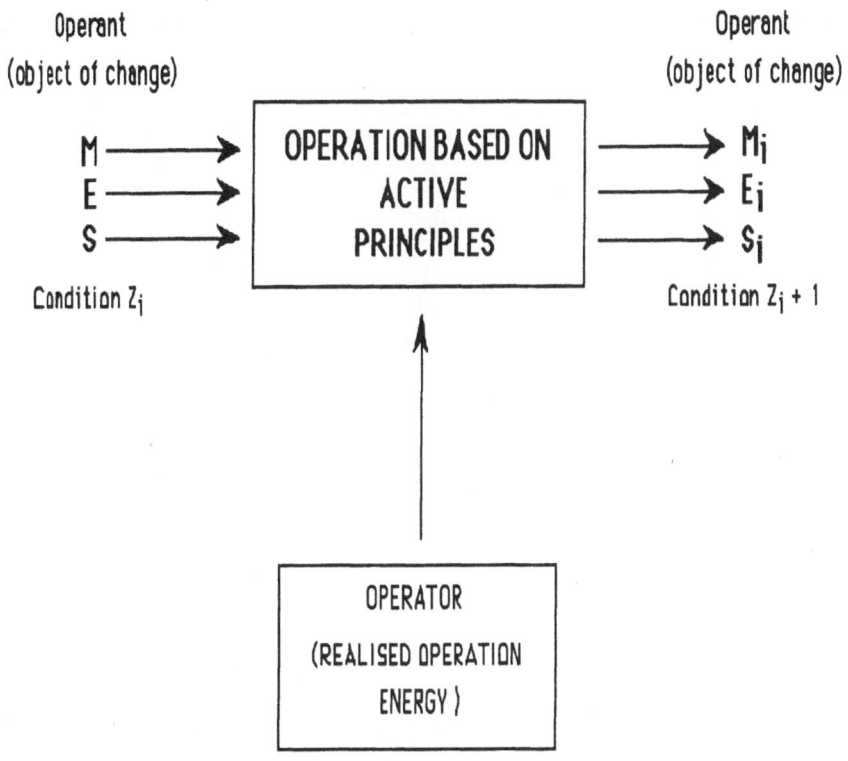

Fig. 15 The basic model to show an active principle.

- The active principles can use an analog or homolog as the starting point of morphological frameworks for product developments.

- The typical levels like needs, target, functioning principle, technical action principle, technical principle, dimensioning, can be used in processes of composition and decomposition.

- The hierarchical structure for evaluating user characteristics and technological assessment starts with the assumptions:

    - Ecological cleanness   = maximum
    - Sureness   = maximum
    - Life quality   = maximum
    - Environmental reflection   = minimum
    - Ideal-reality-difference   = minimum

The didactical simplification of these objectives leads us directly to the functional
and process understanding oriented strategy line of implementation, see Fig. 16.

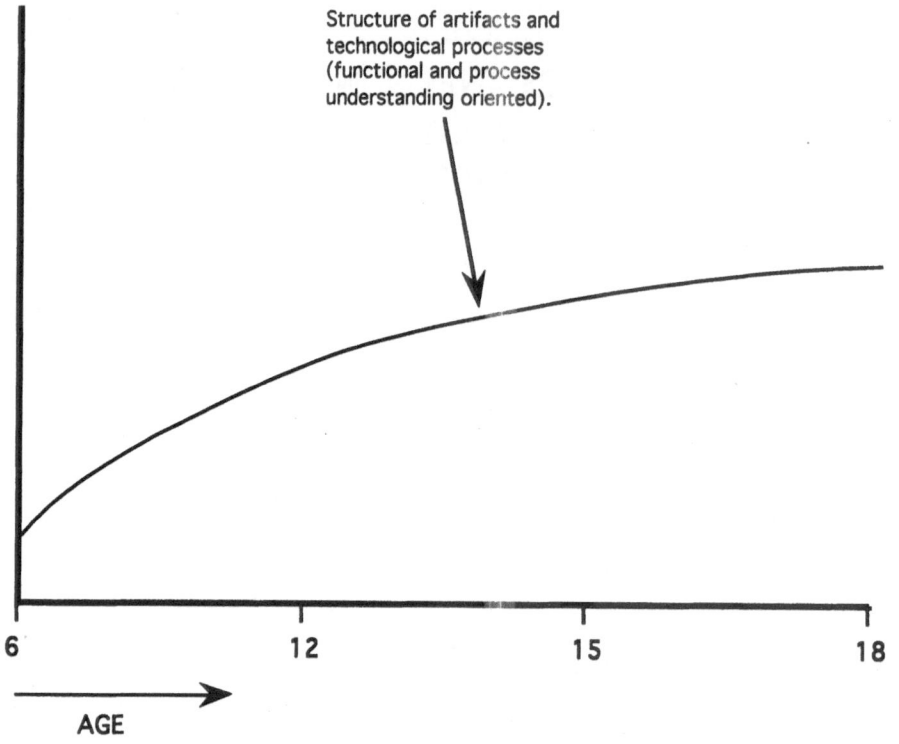

Selected Topics from the Framework Model (based on the modular concept)		
Working with construction kits	Function and structure of machines	Structure of technological processes in traffic, communication, services,...
Making models of known things	Electronic circuts	
	Technological processes and active principles	Principles of technology
		Material, energy and information flow

Fig. 16 Framework Model

To use these insights as resources for pedagogical processes, we need more insight into the pedagogical situation itself. Therefore, not only we have to structure the objective and principles of the processes, but also to determine the capabilities of the humans themselves.

Technology   Capabilities

All learning involves overcoming barriers and the role of education is to identify situations that help people develop the abilities to overcome barriers. It should be acknowledged, that human-technology interactions are a focus for development thinking. This has been agreed around the world, but it was known at the time of the fable about Daedalus and Icarus.

Daidalos und Ikaros nach einem deutschen Holzschnitt von 1497

Fig. 17 The fable of Daedalus and Icarus

The example of Icarus illustrates an important fact - that we should not consider the school as an exile or prison, because he was forced to learn to survive -- and to translate his wish for freedom into activity. His vision of a wider future, and

seeing the freedom of birds flying over him, triggered Daedalus to model their wings. The conclusion is well known (Icarus went higher and higher...).
This example has a lesson for today; it is shown in Fig. 18.

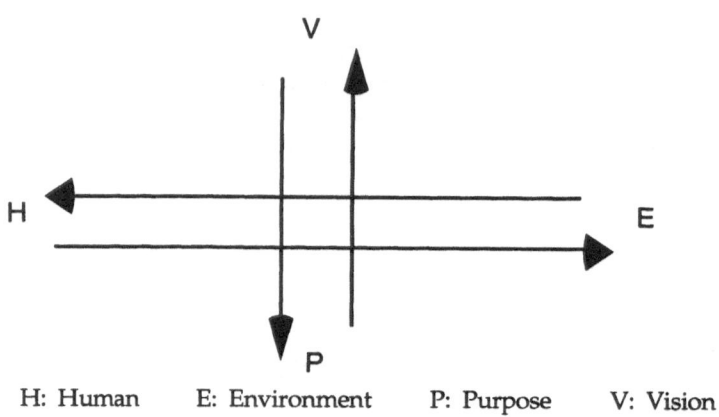

H: Human   E: Environment   P: Purpose   V: Vision

Fig. 18 Basic relations for starting points

When we ask for an answer, we must be prepared to evaluate it too. Daidalos made wings and attempted to escape. But before doing so, it was very important for him to have an objective, to have a vision.

Problematic situation (thought initiator) => Overcoming thought barriers => imagining a vision of a possible solution => model development (resolution of contradictions) => development of approach strategies => development of time and activity plan => execution of the plan => evaluation of the results => new situation/problematic situation

The cycle is important today. The example of the fable shows us today, as it did in the past, the relationship between the tangible world and our mental concepts of it, in order to translate our ideas into practice via a systematic strategy. In the following figures, we depict these concepts albeit with the addition of time and economics as factors, see Fig. 19.

But this example also shows us barriers to our thought processes and how difficult it is to overcome them. The problematic situation was the starting point/initiator for all the activities. Icarus had no concept relating to the warmth of the sun affecting his ability to fly high. In order to properly judge a situation, technological or otherwise, we must be aware of all its aspects.

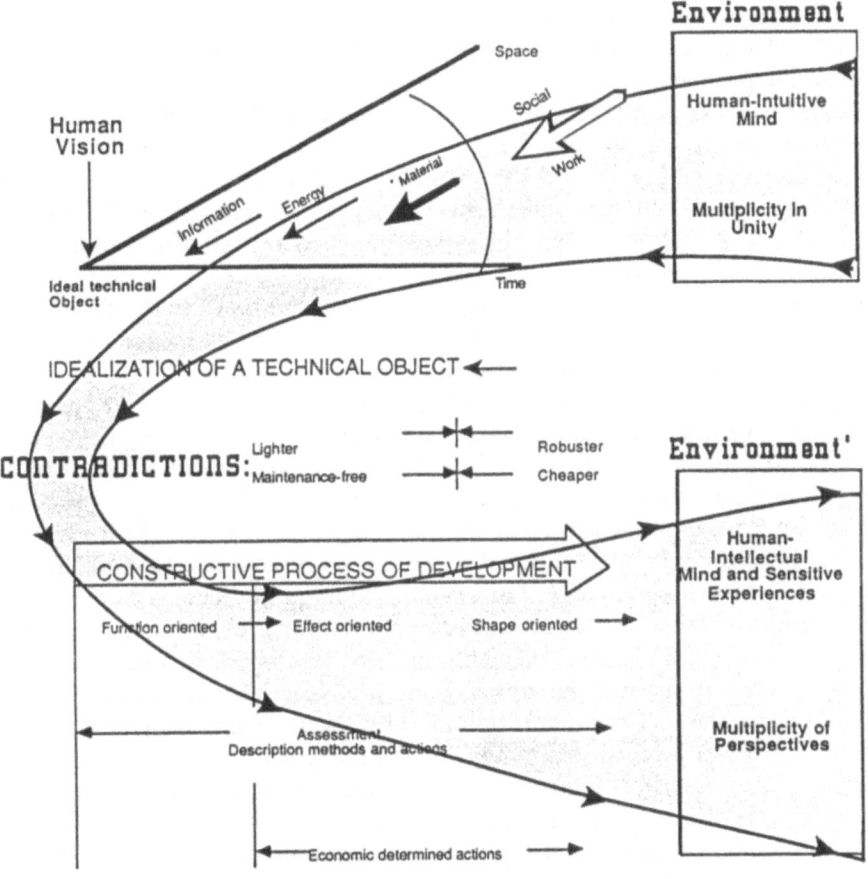

Fig. 19 Concrete - abstract - concrete' dynamic of technological competencies
(Blandow/Dyrenfurth/Schmidt, V., 1991)

However, we do not need to think of Icarus to recognize the lesson of his example. Consider the many calamities and problems that we have experienced recently: The Tacoma Narrows Bridge collapsed in 1940; various, dam disasters, the garbage avalanche, chemical catastrophes (Bophal), rocket explosions, Tjernobyl, hormone scandals and airplane crashes with a frequency that has almost made us become accustomed to them. The world experiences a new Icarus daily! However, today, the consequences of such failures affect many more people. Due to the power of technology, its consequences are felt by all humanity. This new dimension, namely that we are all involved, has consequences, that solving problems requires overcoming thought barriers first. Such an approach needs a wide awareness that cannot be obtained solely at school -- it necessarily requires an active involvement with the problem and its whole environment.

Given the problems, it becomes clear that current education does not develop awareness or make people sensitive to potential effects of technology or associated systems.

How can we help people to develop the skills for overcoming barriers? Obviously by beginning with basic concepts, considering the simplest proposition that combines the objectives between the starting point and the process for achieving them.

Some typical barriers between the stages are shown in Fig. 20. Furthermore, the entire process is set in a context that also colors/ affects the process itself. This is depicted in the following illustration, Fig. 21.

Together with the product levels (functional principle, active principle, designing, ...) and the typical methods or intellectual tools for changing over from one level to another (Trend Analysis, Generation Tables, Need-Aim-Integration, Determining Contradiction, Setting up Compromises,...) we have got the concept of Fig. 21. The basic structure of the two step model (Fig. 21) involves the analysis steps for everyone to use, abstraction, evaluation, etc. Here we also find the key for a teaching strategy. For example looking at students at the age 15+ years trying to find an alternative energy source for a cycle lamp we need an abstraction to the law of induction and from there we can ask for every alternative. But if we were to ask for other energy alternatives, we can change the active principles. Would we change the system, the bicycle as an element of a traffic-system, we again have other alternatives. On the grades 12 to 15, you can also work with the strategy of explaining the black box and its functional principles. (For windmills, the same function can be realised with different structures, etc.).

For the strategy model for implementation technology education as a part of general education we have an additional Figure for orientation.

Thought initiators,
stimuli, needs

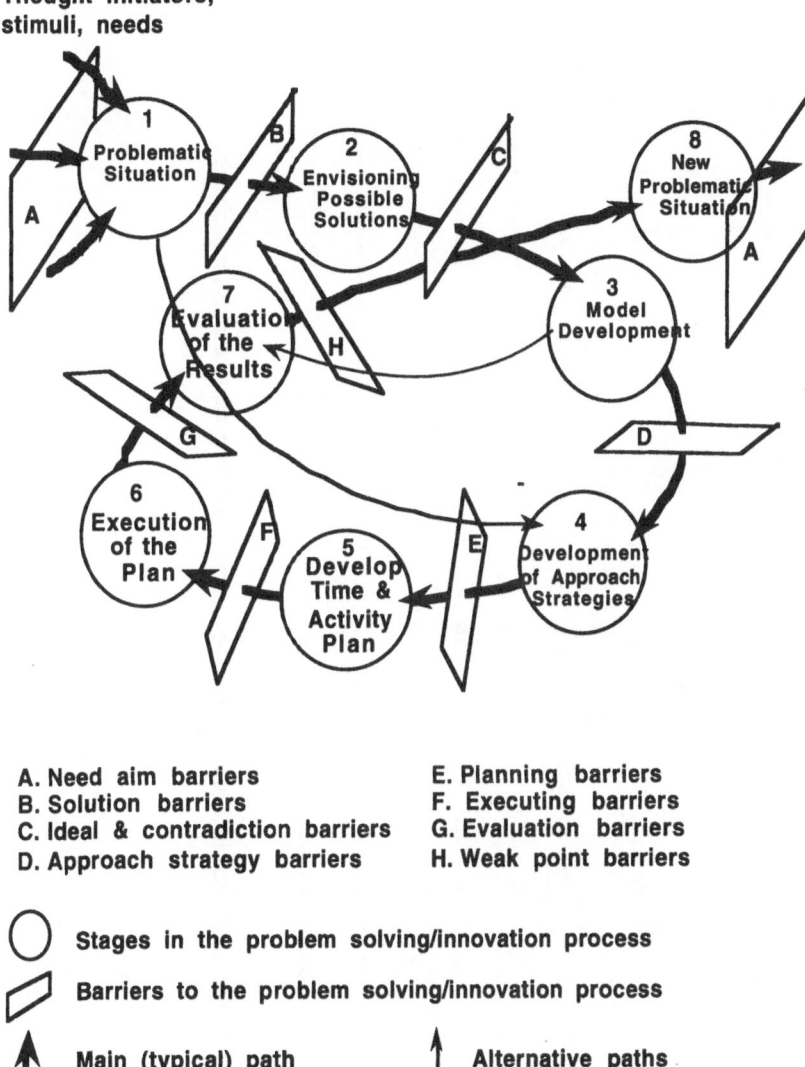

A. Need aim barriers
B. Solution barriers
C. Ideal & contradiction barriers
D. Approach strategy barriers

E. Planning barriers
F. Executing barriers
G. Evaluation barriers
H. Weak point barriers

◯ Stages in the problem solving/innovation process

▱ Barriers to the problem solving/innovation process

↑ Main (typical) path   ↑ Alternative paths

Fig. 20 Stages of the innovation process and typical barriers.

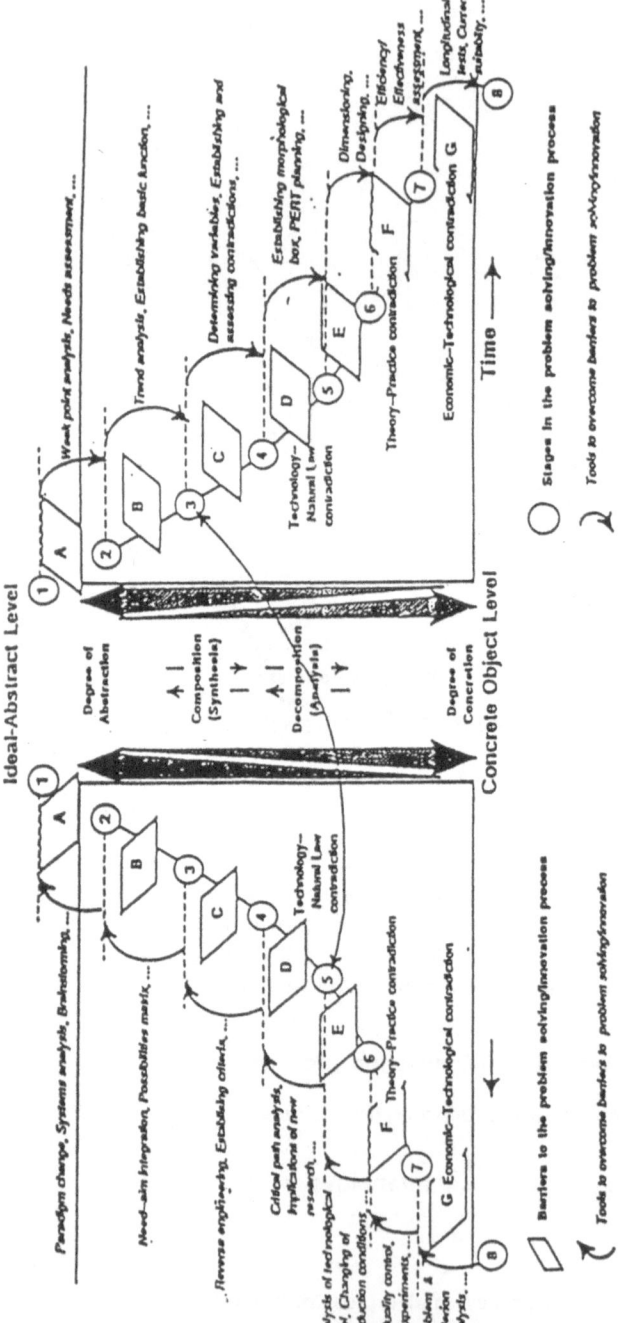

Fig. 21 Overview of problem solving, innovation stages, barriers and characteristic tools for implementing solution strategies.

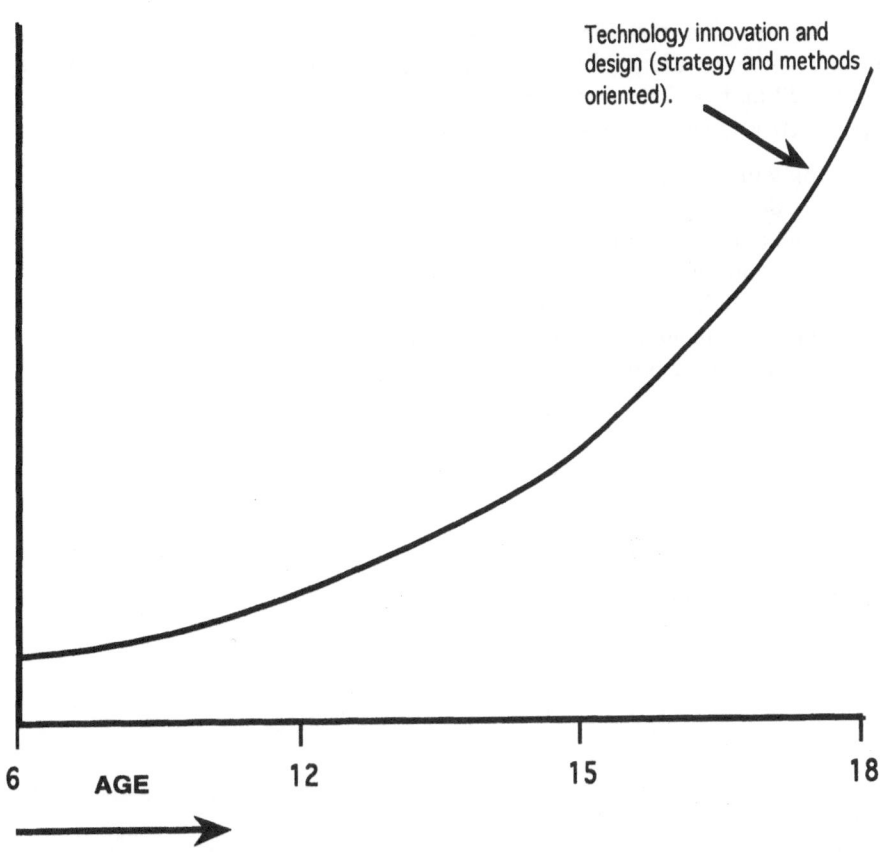

Selected Topics from the Framework Model (based on the modular concept)		
Modeling of a bridge Using natural materials for our living area	User characteristics and evaluation Technology in our life (environment, traffic, repairing, serving,..)	Life- stages of a product Trend analysis and success parameter System analysis, ideal product Contradictions and compromises Technological assessment

Fig. 22 Framework Model

With the structure of the levels and the intellectual tools to go from one level to another we have the preconditions for defining technological capabilities, see Figures 23 and 24. The competencies (or capabilities) are oriented to learning the appropriate knowledge and technological behaviour. They are based on:

- learning a metalanguage
- learning deconceptualising
- learning conceptualising
- learning contradiction and active principles
- learning variables und compromises
- learning assessment and evaluation
- learning workplace order.

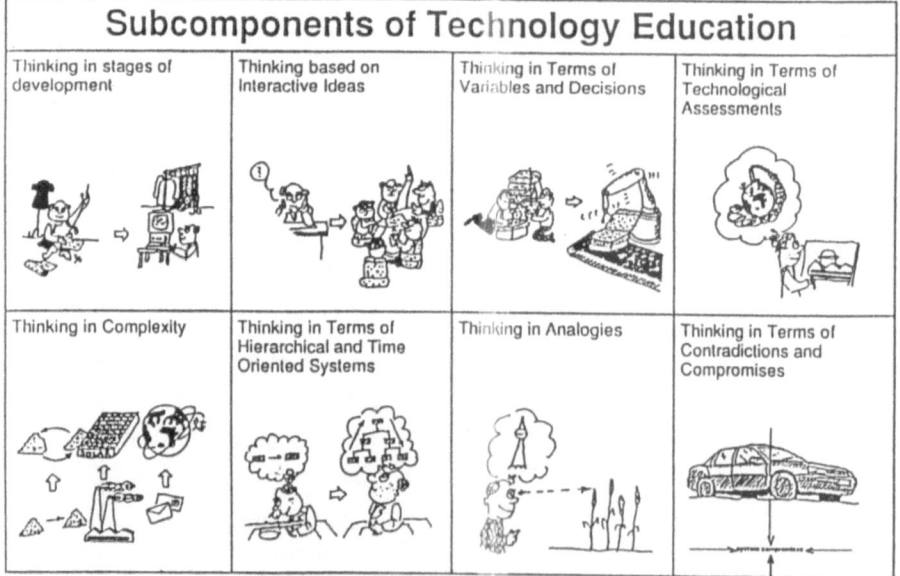

Fig. 23 Technological competences I

Fig. 24 Technological competences II

The sub-components of technological education can be expanded according to the age and interests of the students.

Implementation model

We may approach the basic principles in various ways. Some specialists will consider the activity as significant, others will consider the systems characteristics, while a third group could emphasize the aspect of social relationships. We may (moreover, have to) discuss it. We should, however, go beyond the debate and tolerantly look for those viewpoints which are common. I think those of my colleagues who think within the framework of the basic categories matter-energy-information and intellectual tool-system-model would not deny the importance of activity, construction and application, and vice versa. Similarly those colleagues who think within the framework of the economical and social relationships of technology would not deny the importance of aspects of household economy, preparation for life, or professional orientation, and vice versa. I think, only the stress is different, and they do not touch the very essence of our common endeavour.

As a useful tool for the implementation of technology as a school subject, we have - as a result of the ERASMUS-project Erfurt, Eindhoven and Leeuwarden - developed the Morphological Box, shown in Fig. 25. This model combines the possibility of composition and decomposition of projects. Combining of the stages of cognitive development with the stages of interests and activities allows the subject area to offer a strategy for thinking and acting. The box helps reduce the world of complexity to models of acceptance. The box helps to adapt a general scientific model to the actual problems. But also, it helps to adapt it to the person involved. Here, the term didactical simplification for setting up meaningful activities can be used.

From this model (Fig. 25), we can visualize the framework and the subjects needed for the curricula as described in Fig. 26. For setting up special projects, you should see from Fig. 27 that we should start with user characteristics. They are typical levels situated at the human technological interface. Then, we should go over to the structure of the processes and the products themselves.

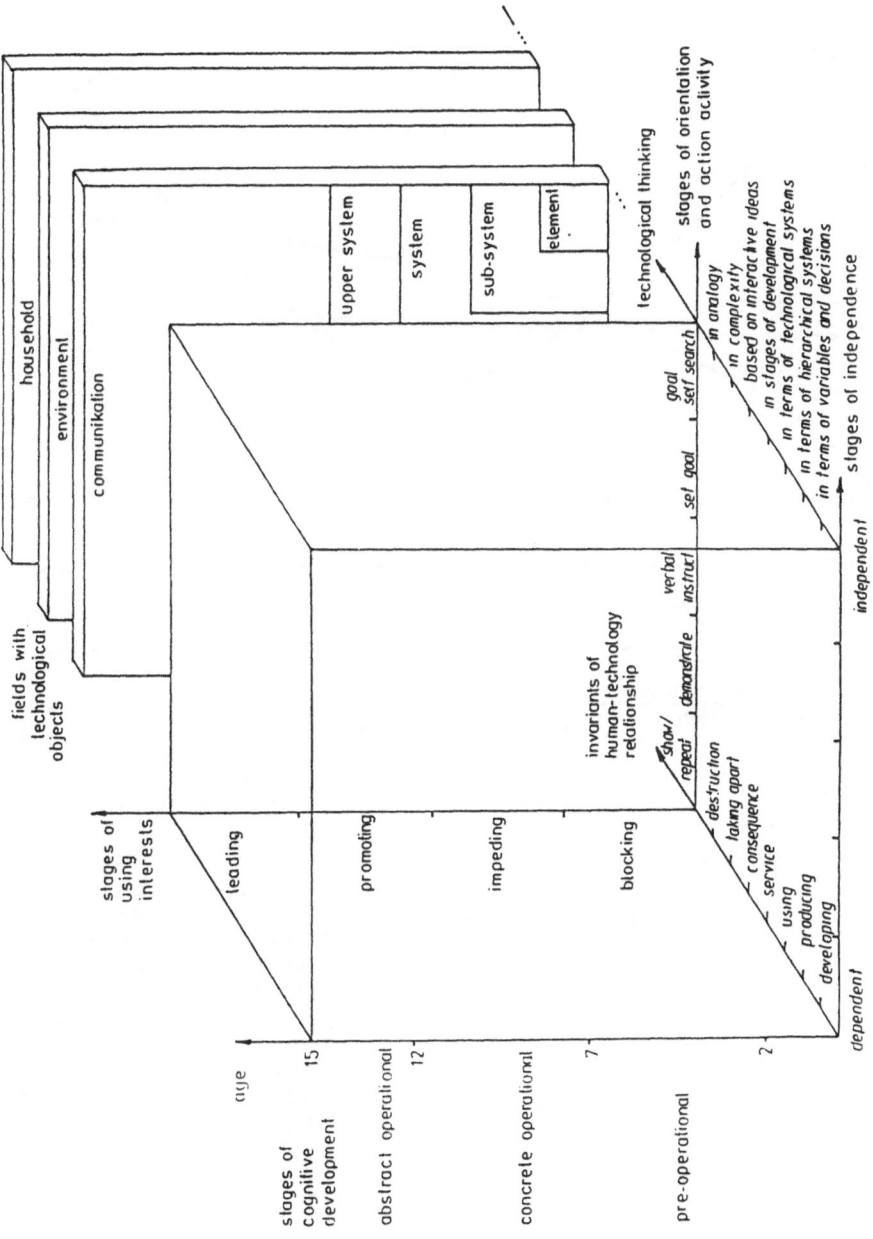

Fig. 25 Morphological Box

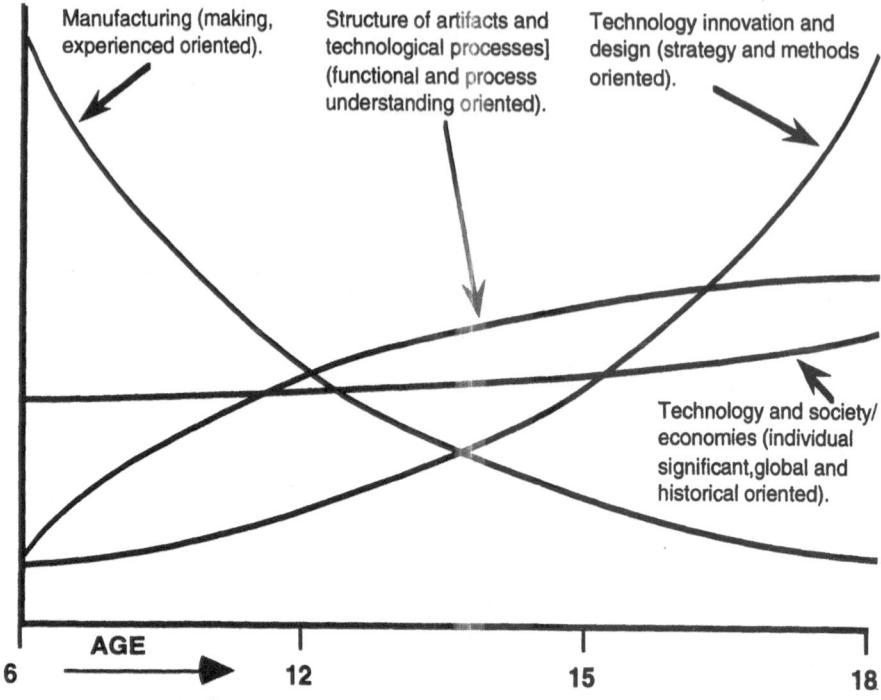

Fig. 26 Framework Model

Selected Topics from the Framework Model (based on the modular concept)		
Using natural materials for our living area Modeling of a bridge Working with construction kits Making models of known things	User characteristics and evaluation Technology in our life (environment, traffic, repairing, serving,..) Function and structure of machines Electronic circuts Technological processes and active principles Risks and resources of technology	Life- stages of a product Trend analysis and success parameter System analysis, ideal product Contradictions and compromises Technological assessment Structure of technological processes in traffic, communication, services,... Principles of technology Material, energy and information flow Production and recycling Social impacts of technology Technological standards anl lows in Europe Economy and technology Traffic and housing energy concepts

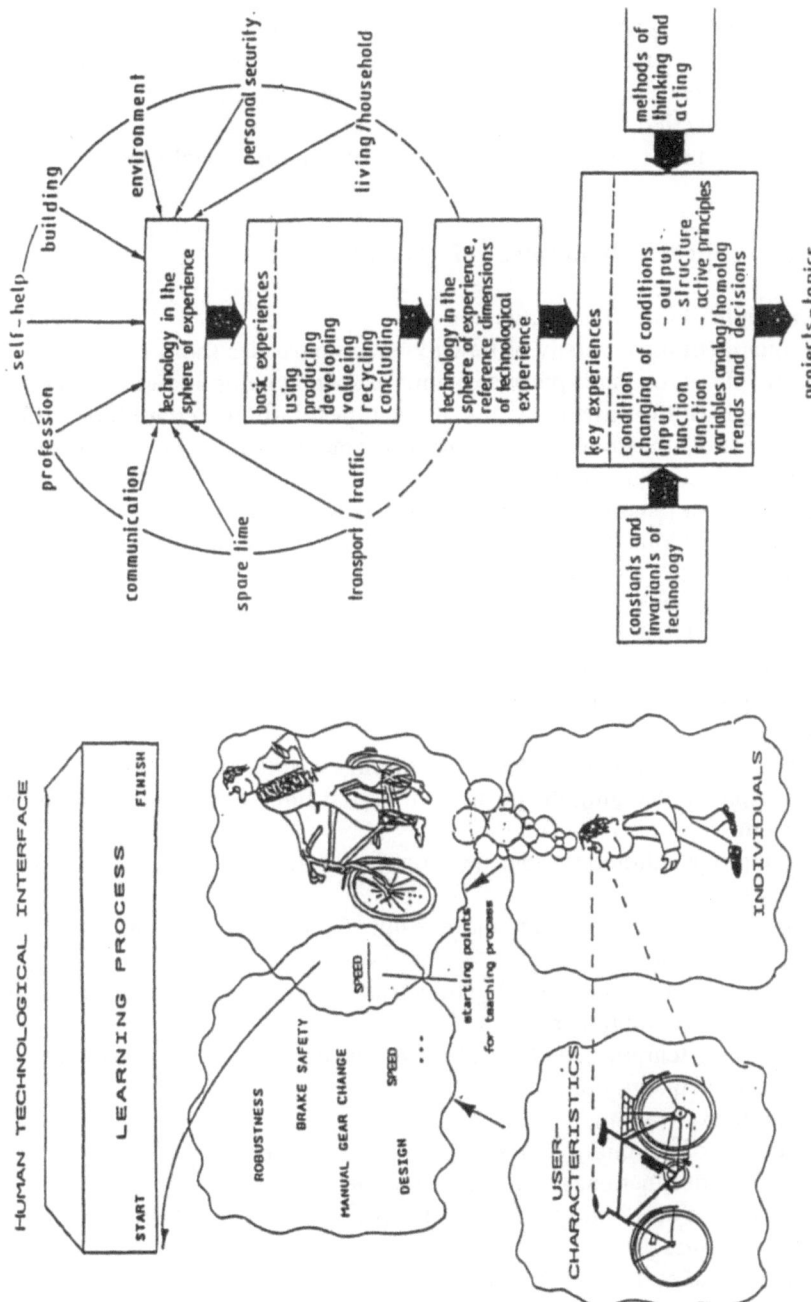

Fig. 27 Basic structure of technology projects.

To work with and in the field of technology, like all other subjects; it needs the knowledge and the principles of the subject area as preconditions for pedagogical activities. To understand the system compromises, the knowledge about the elements, the basic contradictions, or the principles that frame the solutions, will be the tools needed. From the catalogue of knowledge elements and basic principles, the most suitable principles are shown in the conclusion.

Catalogue Sheet: Principles of Technology:

1. Principle of the effects of natural laws.
2. Principle of the diversity of how to realize purposes (homology).
3. Principle of the multi-purpose nature of special natural laws (analogy).
4. Principle of the basic elements of machines: Driving, control, optimizing, supporting, transmitting and working elements of machines for material-, energy- and information processes.
5. Principle of the conditional constraint (using, local, time, economical).
6. Principle of transformation and integration of the function between man and machine.
7. Principle of reversible technological processes (recycling).
8. Principle of realizing the processes through connected materials-, energy- and information flows.
9. Principle of combining partial functions into a variety of functional systems.
10. Principle of contradictions and compromises (relative optimum).
11. Principle of changing the position of partial functions within a hierarchic system.
12. Principle of anhomogeneous development, principle of the existence of weak points.
13. Principle of using more and more results from the microcosmos for effects in macrocosmos
14. Principle of using functional-, structural- and organizational analogies from nature (also evolutionary).
15. Principle integrating the flow of materials, energy and information, (functional integration).
16. Principle of rhythm.
17. Principle of the multiple use of partial function elements.
18. Principle of functional realization through variation.
19. Principle of time and space hierarchy systems of oriented assessment (user characteristics).
20. Principle of realizing the main function through combining functional elements according to their sub-functions.
21. Principle of multiplication and minimization
22. Principle of higher density at the working points.

23. Principle of using all the characteristics of materials, energy and information.
24. Principle of interdisciplinary development of technological systems.
25. Principle of process development and flexible products.
26. Principle of benefitting from disadvantages.
27. Principle of ideal products and processes.

For further research, I would like to find out the correlation between types of activities in a subject area and the interests of students age 12 to 15. For the group 15+ it would be very interesting to start a course for young inventors. The question is how to develop their interests for technological subjects via innovation-oriented optional subjects I hope that we will have a chance to influence the situation, that more and more students will look for other subjects than mathematics and/or engineering subjects. But at the same time we should invite our Eastern European Colleagues via Tempus Projects which will help them to reach a better orientation and to restructure their production- oriented framework.

References

1. Blandow, D.: Probleme des Erkennens and Förderns wissenschaftlich - technischer Begabungen im Unterricht; Wissenschaftliche Schriftenreihe der Technischen Universität Karl - Marx - Stadt (Chemnitz), Heft 6, S. 19 ff (1989)
2. Blandow, D., Wolffgramm, H.: Zur Spezifik der fachwissenschaftlichen Grundlagen der Ausbildung von Diplomfachlehrern für Polytechnik. Wissenschaftliche Zeitschrift der Pädagogischen Hochschule "Dr. Theodor Neubauer" Erfurt,. 11(1), pp. 5-14, (1975)
3. Buresch, J.: Specialists with all-round competence -- A reflection on advanced technology in vocational training. International conference on technology education, Weimar, Germany, 1992
4. Dyrenfurth, M. J.: Rethinking Technology Education in the Secondary School: Missouri's Approach to Technological Literacy; Prepared for Landesfachkonferenz Polytechnik - Arbeitslehre. Thüringen, German Democratic Republic, 1990
5. Eder, W. E.: Science in engeneering, one component of the science of engeneering design. NATO ARW, Eindhoven, NL, 1992
6. Erasmus Projects Group: Pädagogische Hochschule Erfurt, Fachbereich Technik-Technology and the Christelijke Hogeschool Noord-Nederland, Leeuwarden, department for basic education. 1992
7. Herrmann Holliger - Uebersax: Morphologisches Institut Zürich. Integrale Systeme oder Denkkatastrophen. Technische Rundschau, Heft 34, (1987)

8. Hill, B.: Aufbau von biologischen Funktionsspeichern, ein Beitrag zur Überwindung von Barrieren im Analogiebereich. Pädagogische Hochschule Erfurt, Forschungsgruppe Polytechnik, 1990

9. Klix, F.: Erwachendes Denken. Deutscher Verlag der Wissenschaften. Berlin, 1987

10. Lutherdt, M.: Zu den konstituierenden Elementen ausgewählter technischer Wissenschaften; Wissenschaftliche Zeitschrift, Pädagogische Hochschule Erfurt, 1990

11. Nacken, W.: Lernen im Dialog: Jugend - Wirtschaft - Politik; in Sozialwissenschaften und Berufspraxis; Jahrgang 9 / Heft 4 (1986)

12. Raat, J. H.: Onderwijs in Techniek, afscheidscollege, gegeven op 18 november aan de T.U. Eindhoven 1988

13. Rubinstein, S. L.: Das Denken und die Wege seiner Erforschung; Deutscher Verlag der Wissenschaften, Berlin 1968

14. Schaefer, G.: Systems thinking in biology education; UNESCO, Paris 1989, Division of Science, Technical and Environmental Education; No. 33, Document Series 1989

15. Schmidt, V.: Bewerten technischer Objekte - ein methodologischer Ansatz zur Erschließung der Komplexität der Technik; Thesen zur Dissertation B, Pädagogische Hochschule Erfurt, 1989

16. Szücs, E.: Technology Education in General Culture. International conference on technology education, Weimar, Germany, 1992

17. Theuerkauf, W. E., Weiner, A.: Schlüsselqualifikation als eine Orientierungsmöglichkeit für eine technische Bildung. Hildesheim 1992

Design Methodological Analyses as a Tool for Learning About Technological Developments in Industrial Settings

Marc J. de Vries,
University of Technology Eindhoven
Department of Philosophy & Social Sciences
Den Dolch 2, P. O. Box 513, Eindhoven, NL-5600 MB, The Netherlands

Abstract. Design processes in industry are influenced by scientific, technological, market, political/juridical and aesthetical factors. In design methodological analyses these factors and their impact on the way a chain of designs is developed are studied. In a piecemeal rationality insight into the combination of these factors in a certain situation leads to decisions about the next step in the design process. This concept is illustrated by three case studies: the Brabantia corkscrew, the Philips Stirling (hot air) engine and the Philips Plumbicon (a television camera pickup tube). Differences between these three designs show the need to differentiate between the following kinds of technologies: experience-based technologies, macrotechnologies and microtechnologies.

This distinction gives us insight into the level of abstraction of the knowledge that is used in the various technologies and thus can be useful for determining the order in which the various technologies should be dealt with in education.

If we accept that one of the aims of Technology Education is to give a realistic idea of how technological developments take place in the industrial practice, these design methodological analysis can serve as a tool for teaching this school subject. This requires a didactical transformation of the academic way in which design methodological analyses are made into a more practical approach that fits with the abilities of pupils.

Keywords. Design methodological analyses, experience-based technologies, macrotechnologies, microtechnologies

1 The Nature of Design Methodological Analyses

1.1 Different Types of Analyses in Design Methodology

Design methodology is the scientific study of design and design processes. These processes can be studied in several ways. This is reflected in the different traditions in design methodology[1]. One group of studies deals with the structure of design processes and tools that individual designers or groups of designers can use to enhance their creativity. In most cases these studies do not differentiate between different types of technologies, but claims to develop theories and tools, that are independent of the type of technology. A second group of studies focuses on the various types of technological and social factors, that influences the design process. In such analyses it becomes evident that a differentiation between different types of technologies is necessary to understand the relationship between scientific knowledge and methods and the design process as a technological activity. This paper deals with the second group of analyses.

1.2 Types of Factors in Design Methodological Analyses

Design processes in industrial settings are very complex to manage. A number of relevant factors has to be taken into account when making decisions on the directions for future developments. Here we distinguish the following factors[2]:
Scientific factors. These factors are the natural phenomena that can be described in scientific theories. Examples: thermodynamic phenomena that are used in steam engines, electromagnetic phenomena that are used in radio transmitters;
Technological factors. These factors, together with the scientific factors give a complete description of a technological system. Examples: the hierarchy of a complex system like an airplane, the various types of processes for separating materials;

---

[1] In my introduction to the October 1992 NATO ARW on 'Design Methodology and Relationships with Science' I called these traditions 'the two cultures in design methodology' (after C. P. Snow's famous two culture lecture in which he described the cultural differences between natural and social sciences).

[2] The initials of the factors form the acronym STeMPJE, that can be use for ease of remembrance (that is why the spelling 'esthetical is used in stead of the more usual spelling 'aesthetical'). The name was used first in Sarlemijn 1993.

Market factors. These factors are the characteristics of the design with respect to the way the market sees it. Examples: the price of the design, its usability;

Political factors. These factors comprise the political decisions that are relevant to the design. Examples: the political choice of a television line system (PAL, NTSC, SECAM), the environmental regulations for refrigerators with respect to CFC's;

Juridical factors. Here one can think of existing patents, established norms (like DIN in Germany or NEN in the Netherlands),

Esthetical factors. These factors are related to outward characteristics of the design.

In a number of studies it was found that changes in the combination of these factors lead to changes in decisions with respect to further development and design. The rationale behind the chain of designs thus is not described by serendipity only, nor by a once-and-for-all set of requirements, but by a piecemeal approach: in each situation the specific state-of-affairs with respect to the factors has to be examined and combined into one comprehensive and multifactorial analysis, that forms the basis for design management decisions[3]. Such a piecemeal rationality can explain the success of an innovation.

1.3 Different Types of Technologies

To understand the relationship between scientific knowledge of the natural phenomena that are used and their application in technological systems, we have to distinguish three types of technologies:

Experience based technologies: here the scientific knowledge is no more than a collection of practical experiences that have been tabulated. Some simple relationships have been derived from these data without searching for more fundamental theories. An example: bridge for many ages have been designed by adapting other successful designs;

Macrotechnologies: these technologies are characterised by an interaction with more fundamental, abstract and idealised theories about natural phenomena. A technological system is optimised by applying knowledge that has been gained with the purpose of knowing more about the how and why of this system. An example: thermodynamics was developed in the context of steam and hot air engines and later on was used to improve these engines;

---

[3] Gardiner (1990) more or less discusses the same concept when he emphasizes that design methodology should not result in rigid methods and strategies, but should leave room for serendipity and that all aspects of implementation (cost, customer satisfaction, etc) should be taken into account in a very early stage of the design process.

Microtechnologies: here the level of abstraction is higher, because the theory deals with phenomena that are not visible, because they are on microscopic level. This means that the gap between the theory and the design reality is broader and the problem of bridging this gap is more difficult to solve. In microtechnologies the development of these theories precedes the technological applications. An example: solid state physics preceded the development of microelectronic devices.

2 Case Studies

To give a more practical meaning to the concepts that have been explained above three case studies will be presented, that illustrate the relevance of these design methodological considerations. They have been chosen in such a way that they represent the three types of technologies:

- the Brabantia corkscrew as an example of an experience based technology,
- the Philips Stirling (hot air) engine as an example of a macrotechnology,
- the Plumbicon (a television camera pickup tube) as an example of a microtechnology.

2.1 The Brabantia Corkscrew

In 1985 the Dutch firm Brabantia brought out a new type of corkscrew that was an immediate success on the Dutch market. When Brabantia wanted to bring out the same corkscrew on the UK market they were accused of infringement of a patent, owned by the Hallen company. In the juridical process that followed Brabantia had to reveal the design process and this yielded the data that were used to study the way Brabantia in their corkscrew design process based their management decisions on the factors that were mentioned in 1.2. The way they responded to the challenge of overcoming the juridical barrier they faced with the Hallen patent shows how a change in the combination of factors resulted in a new design that fits this new combination. This illustrates the concept of the piecemeal rationality: the new design only made sense in the new combination of factors and was not searched for in previous situations[4].

Brabantia is a metal processing firm that produces household gadgets, like bread bins, biscuit bins, and pedal bins. In 1976 the management decided to start developing a new set of kitchen gadgets, that would include a corkscrew. In accordance to Brabantia's general development policy to improve existing

---

[4] A more indepth description of this case is given in De Vries (1994).

products rather than designing completely new devices, Martin Verhoeven, one of their designers, did a survey into different types of corkscrew that were on the market already. A list of requirements was made, in which the results of a market research were used. This research had shown that a minimum of force needed to extract the cork and the possibility of ejecting the cork without touching it were important issues for customers.

At first Verhoeven had a preference for the rack-and-pinion type of corkscrew and made some preliminary designs. In 1972 his colleague Wiericks was made responsible for the corkscrew design and he developed a completely new type with two parallel helices to get a better grip on the cork. As usual with Brabantia there was a frequent interaction between the designers and the management and this resulted in the Wiericks type to be abandoned when Wiericks resigned in 1982. Verhoeven took over again and meanwhile had become interested in the selfpuller type. In particular he had come across an existing corkscrew of that type, named 'Screwpull', that was produced and sold by the Hallen company. A selfpuller type of corkscrew is operated as follows: the corkscrew is put on the bottle neck; then the handle is turned so that the helix is inserted into the cork. At a certain moment the helix cannot move downwards further and by continuing the rotation of the handle the cork is forced to move upwards along the helix. Then the cork can be removed easily by pulling up the corkscrew from the bottle neck. The friction of the helix was reduced drastically by coating the helix with Teflon. Verhoeven had found out that this corkscrew was rather successful on the British market. He realised that this Selfpuller had the potential of fitting the requirements that follow from the various factors, mentioned in 1.2 very well:

S-factors: it made use of the scientifically established properties of Teflon as a friction reducing material,

T-factors: it made use of the technological advantages of the selfpuller principle,

M-factors: by adapting the lay-out it could be improved with respect to the customer needs (the sharp point of the Screwpull helix was unprotected and the cork needed to be taken of by hand),

(P/)J-factors: no existing patent was found that protected the use of the combination of the selfpuller principle and the Teflon coating (and when it was found shortly before introduction of the Brabantia corkscrew on the UK market, it was estimated that a patent on this combination could be rejected because of obviousness of the idea),

E-factors: the outlook of the corkscrew could be redesigned to make it fit into the new Brabantia kitchen gadget series.

With these considerations in mind, Verhoeven designed the Brabantia corkscrew (see Fig. 1).

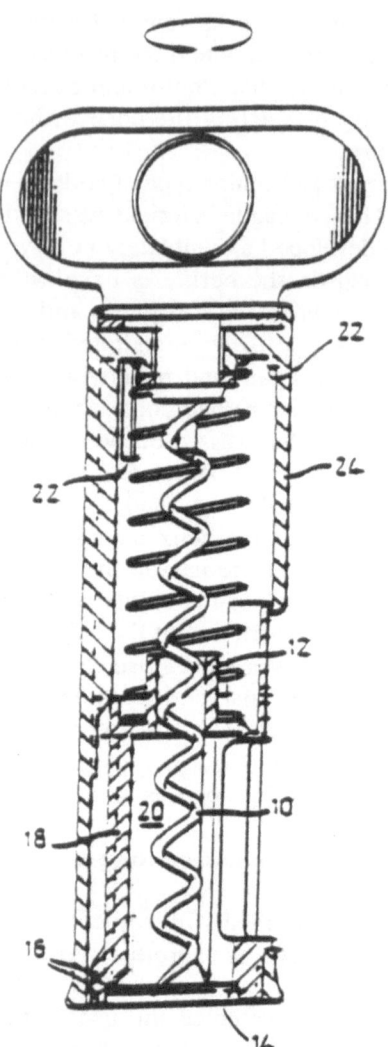

Fig. 1 The Brabantia corkscrew design by Verhoeven

The Hallen company, that saw its main income threatened by the introduction of the Brabantia corkscrew on the UK market, started a juridical process to force Brabantia to withdraw. They succeeded in proving that the patent was infringed indeed, because the main properties of the Brabantia corkscrew fitted the patent claim description very well. On the other hand Brabantia claimed that the patent was obvious. Their main arguments were: the selfpuller principle is widely known because of its ease of use; Teflon is known as a friction reducing material in a great variety of applications, so applying the coating to a corkscrew is not very new.

The final opinion of judge Aldous was that the patent was obvious, but he allowed the patent to be amended, so that more properties of the Screwpull were combined into one claim, that was not obvious any more. In particular the length of the guide passageway of the helix being as long as the pitch of the helix was merged with the combination of the selfpuller principle and the Teflon coating of the helix.

Now Brabantia was faced with a new combination of factors: the juridical factor no longer could be estimated to be favourable, as their design infringed the new Hallen patent (it had all the characteristics mentioned in the new claim, including the guide passageway as long as the pitch of the helix). How could the design be adapted to fit this new situation?

The way the solution was found shows the experience based character of the corkscrew design: by trying out it was found that the guide passageway could be reduced to half its length without hurting its guiding function[5]. Thus the design was adapted and the new corkscrew fitted the new requirements. Its commercial success proved that indeed that rationality that had led to it had taken well account of the technological and social factors that were mentioned earlier.

2.2 The Philips Stirling (Hot Air) Engine

In terms of the outcomes of the design process the Stirling engine case differs largely from the Brabantia corkscrew case. Here we see how problematic an innovation can be when it is not well possible to come to terms with the technological and social factors that are relevant for the development. Also the kind of scientific knowledge that is involved in the design is different: in the Brabantia corkscrew case, no fundamental, abstract theories were involved. In the case of the Philips Stirling engine, there was a gap between the abstract and idealised thermodynamical theories and the practical design situation. That makes the scientific factor more complicated to deal with.

The original idea of Robert Stirling was very promising: he invented an engine that is based on the following cycle: air is compressed in a cold room by a piston, transferred to a hot room by a second piston, called displacer, then the air expands in the hot room and finally is transferred back into the cold room (see Fig. 2).

---

[5] No fundamental, abstract theories were used to find this solution. That is why the corkscrew can be seen as an example of an experience based technology.

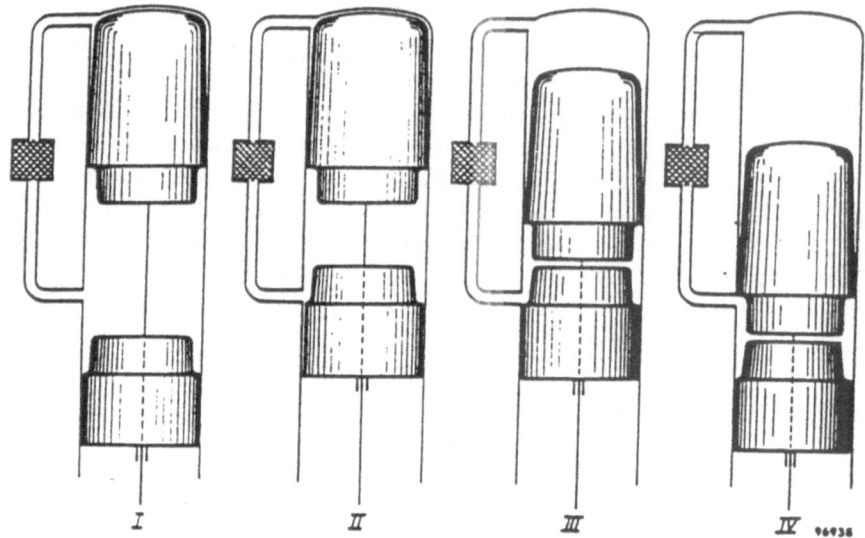

Fig. 2 The Stirling cycle

This process yield work and costs energy. Even though the thermodynamic description of the process did not exist yet, Stirling had found out, that a combination of a high pressure and a high temperature difference was needed to get a reasonable power output and efficiency. Alas this caused a serious problem, as there were no materials yet, that could resist this combination (the Bessemer process for making steel was yet unknown). The result was, that only engines with low power and a low efficiency were produced for relatively small markets (water pump drivers for example). The technological factor of lacking appropriate materials hampered the innovation.

A new start was made in the Philips Research Laboratories in 1938, when Gilles Holst (who at that time was in charge of the Labs) and Herre Rinia (the engineer with the 'golden fingers', who would be one of his successors) decided to take up the development of Stirling engines with the following considerations in mind:

S-factors: since Stirling's time a lot of knowledge had been gained about the thermodynamical process[6] in the engine, as well as knowledge of gas flows

---

[6] A rather idealized analysis had been given by G. Schmidt, a German engineer. He gave theoretical evidence for what Stirling already knew: the need for a combination of high pressure and high temperature. In fact the analysis did not mean much for the design. Only when some of the idealizations were abandoned more practical results came out, that improved the design. This shows the macrotechnological nature of the Stirling engine design: an idealized theory is developed from the need to improve an already existing design. Without the theory the design probably would have been improved also, but at a lower pace.

and heat transportation. This newly gained knowledge could improve the engine design substantially;

T-factors: steel was available now, so that the combination of high pressure and high temperature could be realised;

M-factor: the engine could be used as energy source for transportable radio transmitters and receivers (it was small and quiet!) that were to be used in developing countries and in other special situations where mobile electrical energy was needed. There is no evidence that P/J-factors were considered.

The situations soon changed when the battery took over the perceived market and although the engine was improved for moderate power demands, there was a need to look for another possible was of getting a favourable combination of the factors, mentioned above. This combination was found when R. Meijer invented a new type of crank mechanism (the so-called rhombic drive) that made it possible to make a much lighter construction with higher power output. Now a new market became interested in the engine: the car engine market. The next step in the development of the Stirling engine was guided by the following combination of factors:

S-factors: gradually better predictions for the behaviour of the engine became possible;

T-factor: thanks to the rhombic drive higher power output was possible;

M-factor: that opened a new market: the car engine application.

Again, no evidence has been found that P/J-factors played a role in the considerations. These factors became important when in the USA new laws were made to restrict air pollution by cars. On the one hand this factor caused General Motors, with whom Philips had a contract, to abandon all Stirling engine research and concentrate on improvement of the internal combustion engine and on the other hand it enabled Ford to raise government funds for a research programme to develop Stirling car engines in cooperation with Philips.

After six years of research the funds were exhausted and still the design was not ready to be produced in large numbers for a competitive price. Ford abandoned the research in 1978 and in the next year Philips decided to do the same. It had become clear that it had not been possible to make the combination of factors favourable enough to get a successful innovation:

S-factors: although more and more accurate and computerised theoretical computational models of the engine had become available,

T-factors: the materials and the production process were still too expensive to produce an engine for a price, competitive with the internal combustion engine, so that

M-factors: the engine was not suitable for the car engine market.

P/J-factors: the environmental policy of the governments were neither in the USA, nor in the Netherlands, severe enough to drive up the price of other engines high enough to make the Stirling engine competitive.

Although for Philips this meant the end of the Stirling engine research programme, in other countries, like Japan and the USA still a lot of research is going on in this field, but still without a real breakthrough.

2.3 The Plumbicon Television Pickup Tube

The Plumbicon is a television camera pickup tube that for several decades has been the most popular tube for professional studio use. A design methodological analysis helps us to understand the reasons why it was such a successful innovation. It was developed in the famous Philips Research Laboratories in the fifties by a team of researchers that had been given the assignment to work on the improvement of an existing type of tube by Gilles Holst, who then was in charge of the Research Labs and by Herre Rinia, whose name we have already met in the Stirling engine case. They based their decision on an analysis of the scientific, technological, market and political/juridical factors as they were present at that time.

The design of television pickup devices in fact started as an experience based technology: the Nipkov disc was a mechanical way of scanning pictures for television transmission. But soon it became evident that television would never become a real innovation without input from microtechnological approaches. Nipkov only allowed for transmitting static images with a high level of illumination. The discovery of the electron and later on the ability to handle electron beams, that enabled electronical scanning i.s.o. mechanical scanning, would make it possible to transmit moving pictures also and deal with lower levels of illuminations (e.g., in outside situations). The first pickup tube that had full electronic scanning was the iconoscope, that was invented in 1933 by Vladimir Zworykin, who worked at RCA in the USA. It functioned as follows (see Fig. 3):

– when light hits the target mosaic that consists of cesium grains, electrons are emitted from the mosaic: the higher the local light intensity, the more electrons are emitted, the higher the positive charge of the grains locally;
– the scanning beam, that is produced by the electron tube (lower left part of the tube), replaces the ejected electrons: the higher the positive charge locally,
the more electrons are replaced, the higher the resulting video signal. Thus differences in light intensity are transformed into differences in electric current
(the video signal). The scanning beam is steered by the plates V and H, so that the whole picture is scanned linewise.

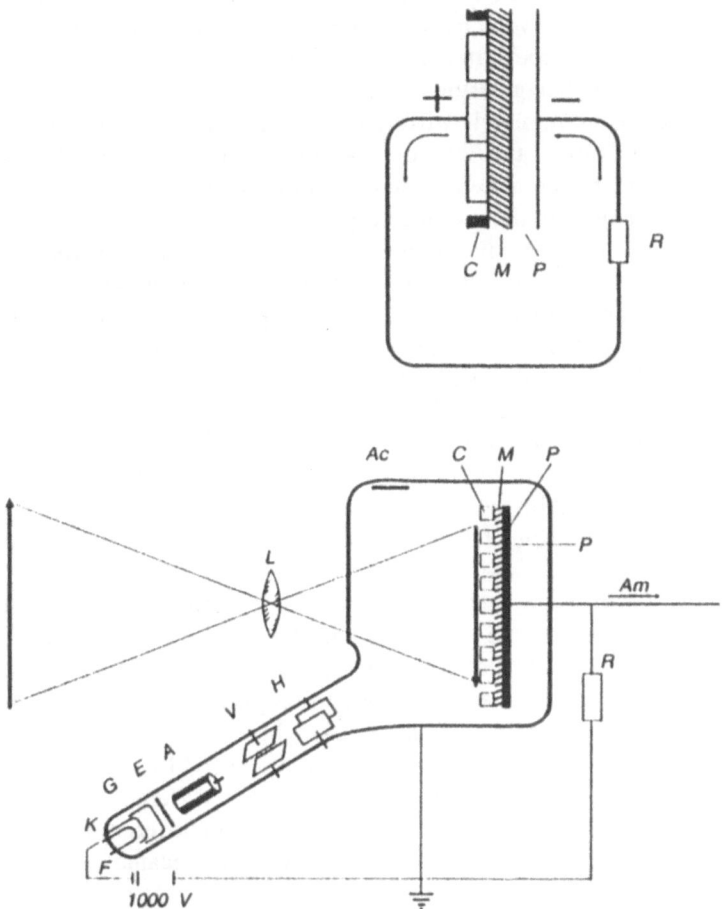

Fig. 3 Zworykin's iconoscope

The main advantages of this electronic pickup tube i.s.o. mechanical scanning, are:

- the speed of scanning is much higher, so that more lines per second can be scanned, which allows a sharper image,
- the light intensity can be much lower, because the light is used more efficiently (in the time between two local hits of the scanning beam, a positive charge is built up by the light).

The main problem with the iconoscope was that the scanning beam hit the target so hard, that new electrons were emitted and fell back on the target in a very uncontrollable way. This so-called 'secondary emission' hurt the quality of the image. Although all kinds of improvements were found (a continuous target i.s.o. the mosaic[7], a low velocity scanning beam i.s.o. the high velocity scanning beam of the iconoscope[8]), in the end it became clear that either a very complex tube (the so-called 'image orthicon') was needed for a sufficiently high quality of the image, or a completely different type of pickup tube had to be found. This new type of tube - the 'vidicon' - was developed at the RCA labs in the USA and used the phenomenon of photoconductivity of the target i.s.o. photoemission that was used in the previous types.

   All this time Philips in the Netherlands had been keen to keep informed about developments and sometimes did some minor development themselves, but did not yet see an opportunity for a real breakthrough until the vidicon was invented. But then they decided to start an intensive research to improve the vidicon, because of the following considerations:

S-factors: the main problem with the vidicon was, that it responded too slowly to quickly changing images (this causes a blurred image) and it had a 'dark current' (a video signal that runs even though no light hits the target. A different target material could be the solution to both problems[9]. To find this a research into properties of various target photoconductive materials would be necessary;

T-factors: the vidicon was the best starting point for further technological development work because it solved the problem of the secondary emission;

M-factors: the vidicon would be the only option for colour television, because there the light had to be split up into three parts, so that the light intensity per tube was much less then for black-and-white television;

P/J-factors: the vidicon was the solution to problem, caused by the political decision to have different numbers of lines in the image in different countries (we still have NTCS, PAL and SECAM today). This caused different tubes to fit the requirements of different countries (the iconoscope became a typical USA tube, the image orthicon became a typical continental tube). The vidicon could be used for all the line systems.

Here again we see a piecemeal rationality: the analysis of the factors mentioned above made it possible to take a logical next step in the chain of designs. In a

---

[7] This was done in the image iconoscope that Zworykin invented in 1934. Here the process of transforming light into currnt was split into two parts: first in a photocathode, then the resulting stream of electrons is directed to a target that emits several electrons when one photoelectron hits this target.

[8] This was done in the orthicon and image orthicon tubes. A second improvement in this type of tubes was the dubble sided target that allowed light to fall in from one side and pass through a transparent side, and the scanning beam to come from the other side. This allowed a much more compact lay-out of the tube.

[9] RCA saw this as an intrinsic property of photoconductivity and therefore did not look for other target materials.

few years the material research yielded lead oxide as a solution to the problems of the vidicon and a new type of vidicon - the 'Plumbicon' - was developed in the Philips Research Labs and would become the standard pickup tube for professional use from 1962 on for many years.

2.4 Comparison of the Case Studies

The case studies illustrate the need to distinguish between different types of technologies: the input from scientific knowledge is quite different in the three cases. General remarks about the science-technology relationships that can be found in literature (like 'technology is applied science' or 'in technology common sense is more important than scientific knowledge') only apply to limited groups of examples.

All cases also show that insight into the combination of scientific, technological, market and political/juridical factors help us to understand the innovation. When it is possible to make use of a favourable combination of these factors, a successful innovation can occur; when the combination of factors remains problematic, so does the innovation. This knowledge can be useful for decision making in design processes.

3 Implications for Technology Education

Design methodological analyses in the first place serve a scientific purpose: to help us to understand the science-technology-society relationships. In the second place they can be used to give a basis for design management decisions in industrial situations. These are the reasons that design methodology is part of the STS programme as it is taught at the Eindhoven University of Technology[10]. But these analyses also yield useful information for our thinking about technology education, and in particular for school-industry link projects, that form the focus of this conference. In the first place the differences between the three types of technologies have consequences with respect to the order in which we want to deal with these technologies in technology education. In the second place the types of factors that are studied in design methodological analyses are also relevant for design activities in the technology education curriculum.

---

[10] A brochure by Kroes that gives more information on this programma is available with the author of this paper.

3.1 The Order in Which Technologies Are to Be Taught in Technology Education Curricular

We have explained the nature of experience based technologies, macrotechnologies and microtechnologies in the same order as in which they emerged historically. It is also an order of an increasing level of abstraction of the scientific theories that are involved in these technologies. In education we deal with pupils that have a limited ability in abstraction. Therefore we need to be careful not to assume too much of this ability when we want them to understand the various types of technologies.

It seems to be advisable, therefore, to start with the technologies that have been developed in an experience based approach. An example of such a technology is the design of bridges. Although nowadays bridge designs are based on a theoretical analysis of partially idealised models, for many ages bridges have been designed without such models, and only based on rules of thumb, that had been derived from previous successful bridges[11]. Another field of experience based technologies are technologies in which knowledge of macroscopic material properties plays an important role. Here data from Material manuals and handbooks are the main scientific input for design activities.

When pupils have reached a certain level of abstraction the macrotechnological approach can be taught and used in classroom design activities. The main macrotechnological theories are the classical theories: classical mechanics, classical thermodynamics and classical electrodynamics. All three of these have many examples that can be used (and in many cases already are used) for technology education.

The highly abstract microtechnological approach must be reserved for pupils of a higher level of abstraction ability. Probably this type of technology is not appropriate until the higher part of secondary education (senior high school level). Of course it is possible to use the outcomes of microtechnologies, like transistors and microchips, as black boxes in an experience based approach. This happens in control technology education, where pupils design complex electronical circuits by using previous experiences and a certain 'Fingerspitzengefühl' and do not need an understanding of the natural phenomena on which the functioning of the elements of such circuits is based.

---

[11] Layton (1992) in a monograph for a liberal arts programme elaborated the case of James B. Francis, in whose work the transition from working with rules of thumb only to a more 'scientific engineering' approach can be seen quite clearly. Fairbairn and Rankine are two other 19th century engineers, who are well known for their work in making the transition from a experience based approach to a macroscopic approach in mechanical engineering (see Russel and Goodman 1972 for fragments of their writings).

3.2 Design Methodological Analyses at the Pupils' Level

In education we cannot learn pupils to work with the full complexity of industrial design practice. Even making excursions to industrial sites only gives them a vague and incomplete idea of this complexity. We will not expect from pupils that they will be able to make design methodological analyses at the level that we discussed in our case studies. And yet, the awareness that both scientific-technological and social factors have to be taken into account can be objectives for our technology education curriculum. If we could find ways to make didactical simplifications in the design methodological approach, we would have a valuable instrument that can be used by pupils in their classroom design activities.

Design activities increasingly are seen as a major element in technology education in many countries worldwide[12]. It is striking, though, that in most discussions about the way design should be implemented in the curriculum the focus is on the structure of design processes: what steps (and in what order) need to be taken by pupils to end up with a design? Much less attention is paid to the content of the knowledge that is necessary to get through a design process successfully. In technology education an integration of domain specific and procedural knowledge should be looked for[13]. There is some evidence that the learning of concepts enhances problem solving capabilities[14]. For technology education this means that both laws and principles of technology

and design and innovative thinking skills should be taught[15]. A problem here is that we hardly have any basis of didactical research on children's understanding of technological objects to build on[16].

---

[12] DeVore (1991) mentions the design focus in particular when he discussed technological literacy as an emerging paradigm for technology education. I identified the 'design approach' as one of the possible approaches in technology education (see de Vries 1993iii). It can be found in the UK in its purest form. In other situations, where design is an emerging issue in technology education, the result is a mixture of a different approach (e.g. the 'applied science' approach) and design activities. In some countries (like the Netherlands; see de Vries 1992) the introduction of design activities in technology education is still a problematic issue.

[13] McCormick 1993.

[14] Glaser 1992.

[15] Blandow 1992. Liao at a previous NATO ARW on Advanced Educational Technologies in Technology Education presented a 'Principles of Engineering' course, in which design is one of the fields of competence (Liao 1991).

[16] Cheek 1992.

Looking at the factors we have seen in design methodological analyses this would mean the following in terms of concepts that pupils have to use in their design activities:

S-factors: in their design activities pupils should realise what natural phenomena they use and what scientific knowledge about those phenomena is available. This will be limited to some macroscopic phenomena that they have become acquainted with in previous science or technology lessons. In particular the somewhat elder pupils can do experiments to make them aware of the gap between predictions that follow from idealised theories and the design reality;

T-factors: pupils will have to study the various technological aspects of their design: the availability of materials with certain characteristics and the various treatments that are available to put the materials into the desired shape. They will also become aware that shape, material and treatment are interdependent. A systems analysis is another way of describing the technological object to be designed and already now there are several examples of technology education curricula in which this plays a role;

M-factors: pupils should ask themselves questions that have to do with the market for which the design is made: who are the customers and what do they expect with respect to the properties of the design? What are they prepared to pay for the product and how many customers will possibly want to buy the product. The pupils should be encouraged to do practical research to find answers to these questions;

P/J-factors: here in particular the environmental requirements are a good example of such factors that pupils can take into account. In practice this will be the most difficult factor to deal with as political decisions usually are rather far from the daily experiences of the pupils. Here the teacher would have to assist by preparing sets of documents that can help the pupils to find the necessary information about these factors;

E-factors: this again is a type of factor that does appeal to the pupils and certainly should be taken into account when designing. In many practical examples this was the main focus of the pupils' designs.

The real meaning of the design methodological analyses, however, is not to treat the factors in an isolated way, but to combine them into one integral view on the situation in which the design activity takes place. Only this way of looking at the factors can yield the piecemeal rationality that we have seen in successful designs. In educational situations too, this is the real strength of the study of the factors. Therefore the pupils should combine the factors in the list of requirements they make at an early stage of the design process[17] and

---

[17] Except for the scientific and the political/juridical factors, these points of attention for a list of requirements are mentioned in the new proposal for Design and Technology in the National Curriculum for England and Wales (DFE and the Welsh Office 1992).

during the whole design process they should monitor to what extent they succeed in making the design match these requirements. They should also look for already existing designs, that are promising in terms of the combination of factors and can be adapted to make them fit the new set of requirements, just like we saw in the case of the Plumbicon (where the promising precessor was the vidicon) and the Brabantia corkscrew (where the precessor was the Hallen Screwpull)[18].

References

1. Blandow, D.: The elements of technology education. Eindhoven, University of Technology 1992
2. Cheek, D. W.: Thinking constructively about science, technology and society education. Albany, State University of New York Press 1992
3. Department for Education and the Welsh Office: Technology for ages 5 to 16. London, HMSO 1992
4. DeVore, P.: Technological literacy: the evolving paradigm. In: M. J. Dyrenfurth, M. R. Kozak (eds.). Technological literacy. Peoria, Glencoe Div., MacMillan/McGraw-Hill 1991
5. Gardiner, K.: Design: organisation and measurement. In: M. Oakley (ed.), Design management. Cambridge, Basil Blackwell Inc. 1990
6. Glaser, R.: Education and thinking: the role of knowledge. In: R. McCormick, P. Murphey, M. Harrison (eds.). Teaching and learning technology. Wokingham, Addison-Wesley 1992
7. Layton, E.: From rule of thumb to scientific engineering. James B. Francis and the invention of the Francis turbine. Stony Brook, Research Foundation of the State University of New York 1992
8. Liao, Th. T.: Pre-college technology education and instructional technology: preparing students for the workplace. In: M. Hacker, A. T. Gordon, M. J. de Vries (eds.), Integrating advanced technology into technology education. Berlin, Springer Verlag 1991
9. McCormick: Design education and science: practical implications. In: M. J. de Vries, N. Cross, D. P. Grant (eds.). Design methodology and relationships with science. Dordrecht, Kluwer Academic Publishers 1993
10. Russel, C. A., Goodman, D. C.: Science and the rise of technology since 1800. Bristol, John Wright & Sons 1972

---

[18] This suggestion differs from much contemporary educational practice in technology education, where pupils are supposed to start from scratch and think up a completely new design themselves. In fact this almost never happens in the reality of industrial design practice.

11. Sarlemijn, A.: Designs as cultural alloys. The STeMPJE approach in design methodology. In: M. J. de Vries, N. Cross, D. P. Grant (eds.) Design methodology and relationships with science. Dordrecht, Kluwer Academic Publishers 1993

12. Sarlemijn, A., de Vries, M. J.: The piecemeal rationality of application oriented research. An analysis of the R & D history of the Plumbicon in the Philips Research Laboratories. In: P. Kroes, M. Bakker (eds.). Technological development and science in the industrial age. New perspectives on the science-technology relationship. Dordrecht, Reidel 1992

13. de Vries , M. J.: Technology education in the Netherlands. In: R. McCormick, P. Murphey, M. Harrison (eds.). Teaching and learning technology. Wokingham Addison-Wesley 1992

14. de Vries, M. J.: The Philips Stirling engine development. A historical-methodological case study into design dynamics. Methodology and Science (in print) 1993i

15. de Vries, M. J.: Design methodology and science: an introduction. In: M. J. de Vries, N. Cross, D. P. Grant (eds.). Design methodology and relationships with science. Dordrecht, Kluwer Academic Publishers 1993ii

16. de Vries, M. J.: Approaches in technology education. In: A. T. Gordon, M. Hacker, Th. Liao, M. J. de Vries (eds.). Advanced Educational Technologies in Technology Education. Berlin, Springer Verlag 1993iii

17. de Vries, M. J.: Design process dynamics in an experience based context. A design methodological analysis of the Brabantia corkscrew development. Technovision (in print) 1994

7. Advanced Technology and Integrative Situations

The participants reported an almost universal trend where advanced technology was addressed in schools by adding ever more separate specialized subjects. They opined that this cannot be sustained by any training or educational system. Furthermore, such by-passing of an overview technology experience required of all students is counterproductive for several reasons. First, it substitutes short term, fad-like courses for more substantial, robust, and carefully developed scope and sequences of technologically-relevant learner outcome targets. Second, the fragmented addition of a multitude of individual courses has the tendency to remove many of the exciting, motivational, dynamic, and contemporary components from existing delivery systems, thereby soon relegating them to the scrap heap in any rapidly changing society.

Furthermore, because technology is integrative in nature there was the opinion, that this trend (of additional separate subjects) cannot be the right path to the future because it contradicts the nature of technology. Technology itself integrates materials, energy, and information. It necessarily assimilates ethical as well as environmental and sociological considerations and then involves their integration and interaction in daily life. As such, the fragmented nature of a plethora of individual courses works against the development of the very capabilities and understandings they were implemented to develop.

To enable the learner to structure information and to work with questions of increasing complexity and escalating volumes of information, it is increasingly important to engender thinking in terms of hierarchical information networks. Similarly, participants reached the conclusion that integrative situations would lead us to the recognition of constants such as: converting, structuring, storing, transforming, connecting, separating, etc. The participants indicated that enabling learners to work with volumes of information was a necessary precondition to interdisciplinary work .

Interdisciplinarity means at the same time composition and decomposition, modeling and simulation. Key processes also include technological assessment and evaluation. The participants worked out a clear statement favoring treatment of technology and its disciplines both as a separate subject and for the core of an integrative experience involving situation-based concepts (e.g., project engineering). The ARW participants called for pilot projects for both. They recommended use of a technology principle-based subject of technology as a freestanding course as well as for its use as a new integrative symbiotic. With respect to the school arena, i.e., technology education's classes 10 to 12/13, at the pre-university level, the participants called for an Integrative Symbiotic Science and Technology Curriculum.

The values of an integrated approach were depicted by Hacker, who also pointed out the urgent staff development needs engendered by such approaches. But these are not the only needs that emerged. Concomitant with a focus on the emerging higher level technological capabilities, is the need for improved assessment methodologies that yield better formative and summative information.

Bukovsky's example of Math Olympiad activities and the outcomes engendered by it worked well to reinforce the concept of integrated M/S/T situations. Kimbell persuasively presented the workshop participants with valuable techniques and a model for achieving this. Conclusively documenting the integrative nature of technology education was Hrivnak, who demonstrated the role of university-level technology education programs as important for the transition of the formerly Eastern-Bloc nations to a market economy, thereby spurring regional development.

The Goals of Mathematical Olympiad and Changing Society in Transition to the Market Economy

Lev Bukovsky
Univerzita P. J. Safarika
Jesenna 5, 04154 Kosice, Slovakia

Abstract. This note gives some information about the Mathematical Olympiad in Czechoslovakia and its goals, and discusses some related problems connected with the transition of Czech and Slovak society to a market economy.

Keywords. Mathematics, mathematicians, mathematical competition, the Mathematical Olympiad, goals

In this note I want to give some information about the Mathematical Olympiad in Czechoslovakia and its goals, and to discuss some related problems connected with the transiton of our society to a market economy.

It is very probable that things I will speak about like mathematics and mathematicians are true for any other scientific discipline and can be generalized. Anyway I have information and arguments only in the case of mathematics.

There are many definitions of a person being a mathematician. All those have a common attribute: interest in development of mathematics. The development is made by people. A part of the development of mathematics is the preparation of the mathematicians, i.e. mathematics education. It is well known that many outstanding mathematicians were and are deeply interested in teaching mathematics mainly at primary and secondary schools.

As a science, mathematics is rather a method of thinking and therefore the education of a mathematician is a long process, usually beginning very early. Many other scientific discplines need good knowledge of mathematics: physics, chemistry, technical disciplines, etc. On the other side it is common to consider mathematics as a very difficult science. So it turned out that a motivation for the study of mathematics is needed. Between the many methods of motivations the competition is probably one of the most efficient.

According to this, in many countries a mathematical competition has been created. This creation is very often connected with a name of a strong scientist. In Hungary a mathematical competition was initiated by Lorand Eotves in 1894, in Poland the creation of the Mathematical Olympiad in 1949 is connected with the name of the prominent mathematician Kazimir Kuratowski. In the Netherlands that was the excellent mathematician H. Freudenthal who was closely related to similar activities. We could give examples of other countries as well.

In June 1993 Czech and Slovak mathematicians together with many foreign specialists celebrated the hundredth anniversary of the birth of the outstanding Czech mathematician Eduard Cech. E. Cech was the founder (with the Italian mathematician G. Fubini) of the differential projective geometry, he contributed essentially to several parts of topology: dimension theory, homology and the theory of compactification. E. Cech contributed substantially to the development of mathematics in Czechoslovakia. He was deeply interested in the problems of teaching mathematics, mainly at the secondary schools. He was one of those mathematicians who understood that there should exist a close cooperation between university professors and secondary school teachers. Led by this conviction, he wrote several textbooks for secondary schools.

In 1951 Eduard Cech together with other prominent Czech and Slovak mathematicians proposed to create a mathematical competition for secondary school students in Czechoslovakia - the Mathematical Olympiad, in Czech and Slovak languages Matematicka olympiada. They prepared this competition in such a way that the Mathematical Olympiad started in the school year 1951/52. Main purpose of the Mathematical Olympiad was to motivate interest in deeper and more intensive study of mathematics by secondary school students in maximal possible extent and to look for mathematical talents - mathematically gifted students.

The structure of the Mathematical Olympiad was as follows. The competition has been divided in three (later in four) categories according to the classes of the students. In the first round during one or two months the students solved 4 - 8 problems. The authors of satisfactory solutions went to the second regional round where during 4 - 5 hours they solved usually 3 - 4 problems. In the highest category there was the third round for the best in the regional rounds from the whole Czechoslovakia. In this round the students solved 4 problems, later 6 problems during two days.

Preparation of problems for the Mathematical Olympiad was a nontrivial and very interesting process. It was necessary to choice problems available to secondary school students of different kind: easy, difficult. Neither the esthetic point of view was negligible.

However, such a competition needs some financial basis: preparation of texts, their distribution, covering the travel and stay expenses of staff and students during the competition etc. The rather uniform centralized administrative hierarchy of socialistic Czechoslovakia has been used for solving those problems. The financial support came from governement, the organization has been done by direction from the Ministery of Education and so on.

The competition had to motivate students for the interest in mathematics, systematic and deeper study of it. Of course, the students needed some help from their teachers. They organized working groups, usually called "Kruzok MO" - a circle for the Mathematical Olympiad. At regular sessions they solved series of problems related to the topics of the Mathematical Olympiad. The teachers of secondary schools also needed some help. The mathematicians from universities and research institutions (mainly from Academy of Sciences) prepared for them seminaries devoted to the topics connected with the Mathematical Olympiad. The organizing committee of the Mathematical Olympiad understood very soon that these activities must be promoted. Thus, for every year there were determined areas from which the problems of competition have been prepared. The areas were announced to the secondary schools and the teachers could help their students in study of corresponding material. However, the work became more and more complicated and very expensive. Mainly in centres of higher educations the working groups - circles, have been organized not for specific schools, but for the whole city and/or for the region and usually with the help of specialist from the higher education institutions. E.g., in Kosice, we had a circle in which worked students from Kosice, Bardejov, Presov, Poprad, sometimes from Michalovce, i.e. up to 100 km from Kosice.

The Czechoslovak mathematicians, mainly the university professors and research workers from Academy of Sciences, helped the Mathematical Olympiad with writing a series of booklet on different topics from mathematics at the level corresponding to the secondary school students. They wrote more than 70 very good booklets. Also, every year the annual report on the Mathematical Olympiad containing all problems and their solutions has been published. In this way the students obtained very good material for study.

It is well known that according to the planned economy, many deformation in thinking and behaviour of the people appeared. E.g., great number of students (fortunately not all) came to the universities not to study, but just to obtain diploma. Very often the good employment depended from the political connections. The diploma was needed of course. The knowledge and skills were not important. As a rule, the good results in the Mathematical Olympiad enabled to the student to be accepted for study at certain higher education institutions without entry examination. As a consequence the motivation for a deeper study of mathematics has often changed to the interest for good result in the Mathematical Olympiad.

Usually we follow two abilities of students: the ability of thinking (creativity, problem solving) and ability of hard working (concentration, fullfilling larger project). Those two abilities are very often in contradiction. The student able to solve problems is often lazy. Do not forget that the Mathematical Olympiad was a voluntary competition. The work in circles for the Mathematical Olympiad developed mainly the ability of thinking. The students became more able to solve, better to say - to find the idea of solution, but they had usually problems with written presentation of the solution (often just being lazy). So some other motivations were necessary. At several places the mathematicians started with the so-called Correspondence seminary for the Mathematical Olympiad - a distance seminary. The system was well developed at P. J. Safarik University in Kosice.

The students obtained a series of not very difficult problems for solving. The quality of written solutions was a basis for the ordered list of authors. Approximately every half year the first twenty - thirty students from the list have been invited for a very attractive week seminary, usually in some nice places (mountains, lakes).

This system was very successful: participants of the Correspondence seminary gained high positions in the competition and many of them became later good mathematicians.

In 1959 Rumanian mathematicians initiated an international competition - the International Mathematical Olympiad. This essentially changed the position of the Mathematical Olympiad. It had to be a tool for preparing and chosing the national team - participants of the International Mathematical Olympiad. Problems similar to the "amateur - professional problem" in sport arised.

A gifted student of a "Lyceum" in France or a "Gymnasium" in Czechoslovakia could not win the competition with the student (of the same age) prepared for this competition during 3 - 4 years at the Moscow University. In many countries, including Czechoslovakia, special mathematical classes supported by universities and the Academy of Sciences have been organized. Let me summarize the main goals of the Mathematical Olympiad:

1. motivation for the deeper study of mathematics;
2. good mathematical library for secondary school students;
3. development of additional and attractive education at
   mathematics;
4. close cooperation of university professors and secondary
   school teachers.

With transition of our society to a market economy several problems connected with the Mathematical Olympiad have appeared.

The first and very difficult problem is the problem of the organization and financial support. The Mathematical Olympiad depended on the administrative system of direction and was not prepared for changes. Now, dividing the money from the state budget between universities, nothing is left for the Mathematical Olympiad. Neither the minister can organize the competition by a direction.

It seems that it is not an accident that the system of mathematical olympiads has been developed best in former socialist countries (Soviet Union, East Germany, Rumania, North Vietnam). There are three possible answers to the question why it happened so:

1. the system of planned economy really needs a strong motivation for the
   study of mathematics (generally not very attractive);
2. according to the official ideology the governements really wanted to help in
   developing sciences and especially mathematics;
3. the mathematicians understood that the administrative system is very
   convenient for creating such an institution and, in a very clever way, they used

their opportunity for developing sciences and mathematics.

I am afraid that the mixture of 1. and 3. is the correct answer. The publishing of mathematical literature has been supported by state budget. Actually, every secondary school library obtained charge free copies of booklets prepared for the Mathematical Olympiad. I do not suppose that in near future somebody can find a financial support for publication of similar booklets (in spite of the fact that new technology enables to publish such booklets cheaper) and for some time, the prepared manuscripts will wait for publication.

As concerns the third and fourth goals, I suppose that mathematicians both in Czech and Slovak Republics will keep their important attribute - interest in developing the mathematics - with all necessary consequences and therefore, both seminaries and interaction with secondary school teachers of mathematics will go on.

Finishing my short note, I hope that both Czech and Slovak mathematicians will find ways out and will continue all positive activities developed for Czechoslovak Mathematical Olympiad.

A Model for Integrated Mathematics, Science, and Technology Education Staff Development

Michael Hacker
New York State Education Department
One Commerce Plaza Room 1619, Albany, NY 12234, USA

Abstract. In New York, as well as in other States, interest is expanding in coordinating and integrating instruction in mathematics, science, and technology education. In New York, nine broad learning outcomes for mathematics, science, and technology have been developed by a statewide commission. These will give direction to K-12 math, science, and technology education programs in the years ahead. To implement these major changes, substantial staff development is essential. A model has been developed which provides for large scale integrated staff development, and which will promote connections among mathematics, science, and technology educators. The United States National Science Foundation has indicated its support for this model, and will most likely fund a $US 1.6 million project which will prepare a staff development network of 120 New York State Technology Education mentors with enhanced technological, pedagogical, and leadership skills.

Keywords. Curriculum integration, inservice education, mathematics, science, staff development, technology education

1 Introduction

At a prior NATO Conference, in Eindhoven, The Netherlands, 1990, Dr. Marc J. de Vries made a strong case for Technology Education to assume the role of an integrating discipline [1]. In the United States, as well as other countries, Technology Education is a vehicle through which students are helped to synthesize their knowledge by applying mathematics and science to the solution of practical problems which exist in a societal context, and by presenting their results through the use of graphics, written and spoken language.

In 1992, New York State embarked on an effort to interrelate the teaching of Mathematics, Science, and Technology Education, as articulated in "A New Compact for Learning", the plan adopted by the State Board of Regents to initiate systemic reform. This new emphasis on multidisciplinary connections will generate new staff development needs. To this end, a three-year long project has been conceived to improve the quality of Technology Education in New York State through the establishment of the New York State Technology Education

Network (NYSTEN). The Network will provide contemporary technological and pedagogical enhancement to Technology teachers. In addition, awareness workshops will be conducted for other members of the school and local community to develop support for quality Technology Education programs, share current professional thought and practice, and thereby improve the chances for sustainable reform. The project will most likely be funded at $US 1.6 million through the National Science Foundation.

2 Technology Education

Technology Education is an emerging discipline nationwide and worldwide. In the United States, 40 states have developed or are developing Technology Education programs [1]. Internationally, the movement has taken root as well. The United Kingdom has identified Technology as one of the Foundation Subjects in the new National Curriculum and has mandated its study by all children from ages 5-16 [2]. The Netherlands mandated middle school Technology Education for all Dutch students in 1993 [3]. A NATO advisory committee of experts recommended that all NATO countries establish Technology Education programs for all students as part of their compulsory schooling [4]. In New York State, Technology Education is a required subject for each of the 170,000 full-time equivalent (FTE) middle school students per year. A full array of high school elective programs serves another 100,000 FTE students annually [5]. Since there are very few Technology Education programs at the elementary school level, the Project focuses on middle and high school teacher enhancement.

The National Science Foundation, in its Materials Development, Research, and Informal Science Education Program Announcement, indicates that:
A third area of special attention is that of technology education. In this sense, technology is not an instrument, but a field of study. It involves the application of learned principles to specific, tangible situations. Problems in technology typically consist of three components: a given set of resources, given conditions, or "constraints," and stated goals. Because these "design under constraint" problems have multiple solutions, students and teachers become focused on the *process* of problem solving; therefore, rather than constantly being faced with situations which can only result in success or failure, students experience situations in which each outcome offers some opportunity for learning. In using this approach, students not only learn techniques of design and engineering, but receive practical problem solving experience in the principles of mathematics and science [6].

In New York State, the Technology Education program complements well-established Mathematics and Science programs. A major Technology Education program objective is to help students synthesize learning in Mathematics and Science through technological activities [7]. Conceived as a hands-on, "design-and-construct," laboratory-based program, Technology Education provides engaging experiences through which students may be stimulated to discover their technical interests and talents and to pursue further studies in areas of mathematics, science, and technology.

3 Need for Staff Development

Technology Education has emerged from the Industrial Arts tradition in the United States and from Craft teaching in other countries, most notably the Netherlands and the United Kingdom. As an emerging discipline, Technology Education promises to contribute significantly to students' overall scientific and technological literacy. Fundamental to the attainment of this goal is the preparation of Technology teachers. In the United States, most Technology teachers were educated as Industrial Arts teachers. Preparation focused on skills and knowledges related to the processing of materials (woods, metals, plastics). Technology Education is very different from Industrial Arts in terms of its mission, content base, relationship to other disciplines (particularly mathematics, science, and the social sciences), and emphasis on higher-level thinking skills [8]. Technology teachers must be helped to assimilate new goals, methodologies, and content.

In New York State, Technology Education was given impetus by a statewide Futuring Project in the early 1980s, which brought together educators, industrialists, scientists, engineers, and sociologists for the purpose of reforming curriculum to meet the demands of the 1990s. Technology Education emerged as the successor to Industrial Arts. Its mission was conceived to be that of providing technological literacy to students as a component of their basic education [9]. In the mid-1980s, Industrial Arts teachers received inservice education sponsored by NYSED. A Technology Training Network, formed by NYSED was in existence for several years. Peer teachers delivered information to colleagues primarily about new curriculum initiatives and student activities. The Network model was successful according to teacher evaluations [10]. However, workshop leaders relied on their existing skills; they not receive substantive enhancement in technical content, pedagogy, or leadership.

4 Project Overview

Over a period of three years, the NYSTEN Project will prepare 120 Technology Education mentors with enhanced pedagogical, technical, and leadership skills. Twenty-four regional teams of five mentors each will be assembled to serve all areas of the State. Pedagogical content will focus on issues and strategies relative to access and equity, cooperative learning, authentic assessment, design and problem solving, and relationships among Mathematics, Science, and Technology Education. Technical content will relate to four technical areas: computer-aided drawing and design (CADD), computer control and interfacing, bio-related technology, and electronics. Leadership skills will be enhanced in areas of community involvement and coalition building, and institutionalizing change. These topics emerged as a result of a needs assessment conducted by the State Education Department which surveyed members of the previous Technology Training Network and other leaders of the New York State Technology Education profession.

The NYSTEN Project will build on the success of the Technology Training Network and involve many individuals who have served as Technology Education staff developers in the past. NYSTEN will also include experienced Mathematics and Science educators. To help cultivate a base of schoolwide and community support for program improvement, school/community partners (corporate and parent partners, engineering society members, and school administrators) will join NYSTEN. In addition to the Network membership, the Project will benefit from other knowledgeable specialists. Nationally known experts with specific expertise will contribute to the technical, pedagogical and leadership enhancement of the mentors.

Thirty-two lead mentors will be selected first. They will be individuals who are experienced staff developers and master teachers. Twenty-four of the 32 lead mentors will be middle and high school Technology educators selected for their specific expertise in one of the four technological content areas. A balance will be sought between individuals with middle school and high school teaching experience. These 24 expert Technology teachers will each represent one of the NYSTEN regions, and will later coordinate the efforts of their team. The eight remaining lead mentors will be Mathematics and Science educators selected from among the statewide professional leadership in Mathematics and Science education. These individuals will be conversant with New York State syllabi. They will assist their Technology Education colleagues to identify mathematics and science concepts and skills imbedded within Technology Education activities; to link these concepts and skills to New York State Science and Mathematics syllabi; and to establish connections with existing networks of Mathematics and Science educators. The lead mentors will participate in enhancement workshops, develop project materials, conduct trial workshops for teachers in their regions, and conduct enhancement workshops for additional mentors.

Recommendations for mentors will be solicited from the New York State Mathematics, Science, and Technology Education teachers and supervisors associations; Mathematics, Science, and Technology Education staff at the NYSED; the New York State Congress of Parents and Teachers; the New York State Society of Professional Engineers; corporate industry; and members of a Project Advisory Council. A special effort will be made to assure racial and gender balance. The multicultural NYSTEN Advisory Council will assist in this regard. The NYSTEN mentors will represent the diversity of the State. The staff development network will include 24 teams of five mentors: two Technology educators, one Mathematics educator, one Science educator, and one school/community partner. The full complement of 120 NYSTEN mentors will, in teams, conduct six staff and community development sessions within each of their geographic regions. Four of these regional workshops will be six hours in length and will provide hands-on integrated pedagogical and technical enhancement to New York State middle and high school Technology Education teachers. The mentors will also present two one-half day hands-on awareness workshops to other members of the school and local community to broaden the base of support for improvement of teaching and learning in Technology Education.

Using State-developed curricula, instructional materials provided by mentors and corporate partners, and materials generated by other funded projects, the mentors will develop, field-test, and refine an Implementation and Resource Guide which infuses modern pedagogical techniques into the delivery of Technology Education content. The mentors will work collaboratively with expert consultants in the fields of authentic assessment, equity and access, cooperative learning, and Mathematics/Science/Technology curriculum integration. The eight Mathematics and Science lead mentors will assure that connections are made in the Implementation and Resource Guide and in the enhancement workshops between the technology topics and their mathematics and science underpinnings. The Guide will be used as a resource by mentors when providing regional inservice workshops.

In addition to engaging Mathematics and Science teachers as NYSTEN mentors, the Project will establish liaisons with existing networks of Mathematics and Science teachers. A Sharing Success meeting is planned for lead NYSTEN mentors, representatives of Mathematics and Science staff development networks, and professional association leadership in Mathematics, Science, and Technology Education. The Sharing Success meeting will serve to disseminate Project materials; cultivate relationships among the leadership of the three disciplines; and showcase activities and programs which establish connections among Mathematics, Science, and Technology Education.

The Project will benefit from a significant cost-sharing arrangement with corporate partners, Hofstra University, and the NYSED. A total of $2.7 million has been pledged to support Project activities. Autodesk Inc., Biomechanics Corporation, and Lego Dacta (education division of Lego Systems, Inc. will provide software, instructional materials, and technical assistance to the regional teams. This substantial support will strengthen local districts' commitment to program improvement. The Project will include an electronic networking component. As part of its cost-sharing commitment, the NYSED will contribute on-line accounts, provide staff development, and totally support on-line time usage for mentors and Project staff on its statewide Technology Network Ties (TNT) computer conferencing system. The TNT network offers gateways to the New York State Educational Research Network, INTERNET, and BITNET. This component will provide interactive communication among all mentors and Project staff.

In the final year of the Project, three-person leadership teams from 15 states other than New York will participate in a one-week National Dissemination Workshop designed to disseminate the staff development model. These teams will consist of Technology, Science, and Mathematics teachers, state-level supervisors, or teacher-educators. Upon their return, they will conduct awareness workshops in their home states.

An Advisory Council comprised of Mathematics, Science, and Technology educators and school, community, and corporate representatives will provide guidance to Project staff. Advisory Council members will review the Project design, plans for dissemination and evaluation, workshop content and timetables.

At the conclusion of the Project, the management of the Network will transition to the New York State Staff and Curriculum Development Network (S/CDN), an established mechanism in New York through which consortia of local school districts support staff development efforts. To help prepare mentors for this transition, the Project will include a focus on leadership development in its final phase. Once the Project transitions, mentors will continue to conduct regional workshops within a new structure to be defined by discussions with mentors, Project staff, and S/CDN management (see Fig. 1 for Project Outcomes).

5 Project Goals

The goals of the NYSTEN Project are to:

— Equip a leadership group of mentors with enhanced pedagogical, technical, and leadership skills in order that they might conduct exemplary inservice education programs for Technology Education teachers and other members of the school and local community.
– Make available regional inservice education to all 3200 New York State Technology Education teachers.
– Facilitate the integration of Mathematics, Science, and Technology Education and foster collaboration among teachers from the three disciplines.
– Enhance the mathematical, scientific, and technological capabilities of middle and high school students through Technology Education programs that build cooperative learning skills and draw connections among math, science, and technology.
– Enhance local school and community understanding of Technology Education programs and broaden the base of support for program improvement.
– Establish connections with existing professional and staff development networks in Mathematics and Science education.
– Develop an Implementation and Resource Guide for mentors that provides instructional frameworks which infuse pedagogical advancements into the delivery of up-to-date technical content.
– Establish a dissemination network involving leadership teams from 15 states other than New York.
– Monitor the success of the Project through continual formative assessment and summative evaluation.
– Support current reform efforts leading to systemic change in New York State's education system

6 Attributes of the Staff Development Model

NYSTEN will incorporate the attributes of successful teacher development programs as identified by Loucks-Horsley [11]. These include: collegiality and collaboration; experimentation and risk taking; use of available knowledge bases; participant involvement in appropriate aspects; time to participate and practice; leadership and sustained support; appropriate incentives and rewards; application of knowledge about adult learning and change; integration of individual, school, and district goals; and integration of staff development within the philosophy and structure of the organization.

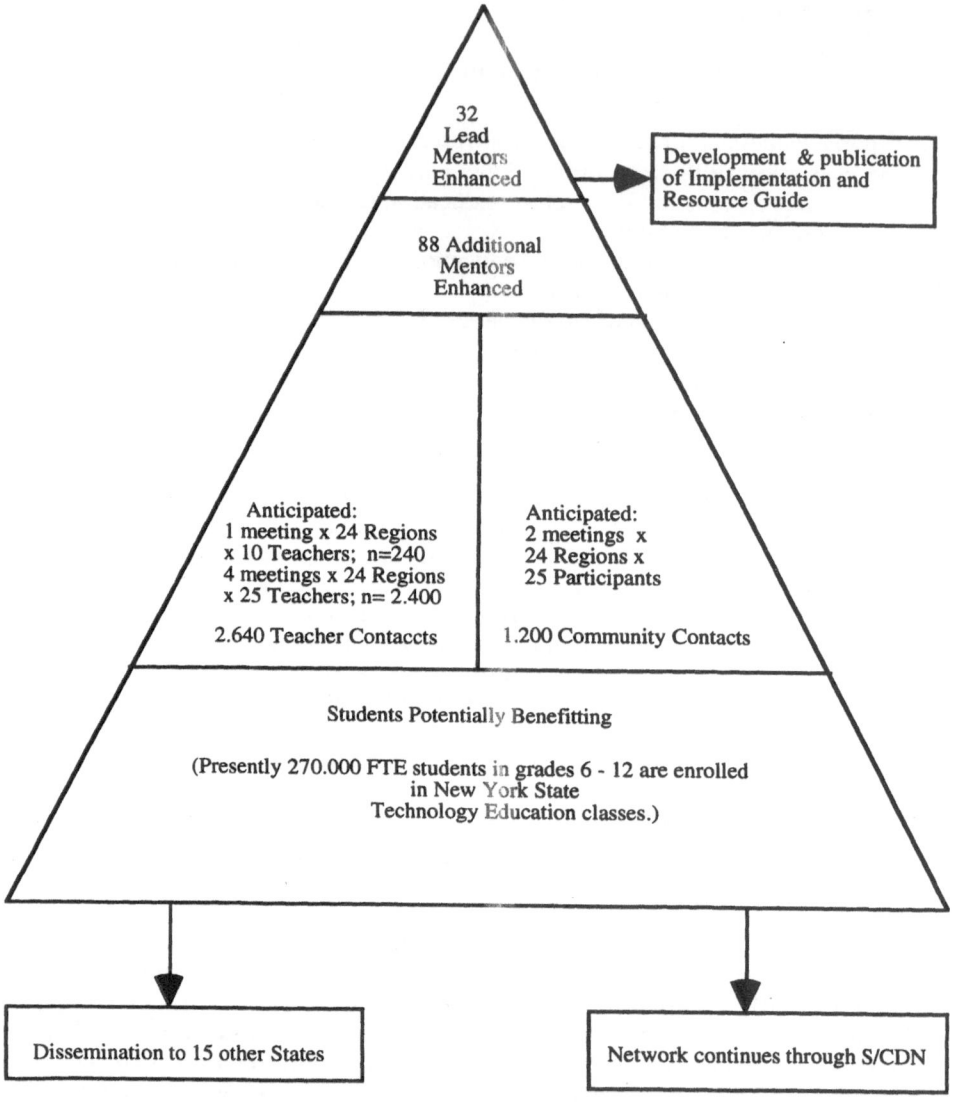

Fig. 1 NYSTEN Anticipated Outcomes: Deliverables and Benefits

7 Implementation and Resource Guide

An Implementation and Resource Guide of about 200 pages will be developed by the lead mentors, with direct support from Project consultants. The Guide will capture the combined efforts of technically expert mentors and pedagogical consultants and blend contemporary pedagogical approaches into the teaching of technologically-based content. Although the Guide will focus on four technical areas (CADD, computer control and interfacing, bio-related technology, and electronics), it will serve as a model for teachers teaching other technical topics as well. The Guide will be used by lead mentors when conducting workshops for additional mentors and by the entire Network of NYSTEN mentors when providing regional workshops for peer teachers.

The Guide will comprise three sections: (1) Inservice Workshop Materials for Mentors; (2) Teaching Resources for Mentors and Teachers; and (3) Leadership and Community Outreach. Expert consultants who will contribute to the pedagogical enhancement of the lead mentors will remain on site while mentors begin to draft the Guide. They will move from group to group as the mentors, clustered in teams related to their areas of technical expertise, develop teaching resource materials for their technical content areas. These materials would provide strategies to integrate mathematics, science, and technology; include cooperative learning, authentic assessment, and design and problem-solving methodologies; and address access and equity issues. Middle and high school mentors will address the specific needs of their students as well as students with special needs. Technical consultants will be available to each group to assure the technical integrity of the Guide.

The Guide will be distributed in draft form for use by lead mentors first with their own students, and then in a set of pilot workshops they will hold for limited numbers of teachers in their regions. The Guide will be revised each year to reflect the experiences of the mentors and the need for additional materials.

The third section of the Guide will be added in the third year, when the focus of the Project is on enhancement of mentor leadership abilities and community outreach. The Guide will be field-tested again during the statewide regional workshops. Revision of the Guide will occur during the summer of that year. The Guide will be disseminated through the Project's National Dissemination Workshop to Mathematics, Science, and Technology Education leaders from 15 states other than New York.

8 Project Workplan

The Project will occur in three phases over a period of three years. During Year I, the Project will focus on the enhancement and preparation of 32 lead mentors and their development of an Implementation and Resource Guide. During Year II, the lead mentors will provide enhancement to 88 additional Network members. In Year III, the full complement of 120 NYSTEN mentors will hold regional workshops statewide for Technology teachers and other school and community members. During this phase, the Project emphasis will be on leadership development, dissemination, and evaluation.

8.1 YEAR I: September 1993-August 1994

During Year I, enhancement in areas of contemporary pedagogy will be offered to the technologically expert lead mentors. Pedagogical enhancement will focus on issues and strategies relative to access and equity; cooperative learning; authentic assessment; design and problem solving; and relationships among Mathematics, Science, and Technology Education. Immediately after participating in the enhancement workshop, the lead mentors, with assistance from on-site expert consultants, will develop the first draft of the Implementation and Resource Guide. The 32 lead mentors will work in four writing groups. Each group will consist of six expert Technology teachers from one of the four technical content areas plus one Mathematics and one Science lead mentor.

8.2 YEAR II: September 1994-August 1995

In Year II, the lead mentors will provide enhancement to the larger body of the NYSTEN mentors. Using the Implementation and Resource Guide, they, along with the consultant experts and Project staff, will conduct inservice education workshops for 88 additional colleagues.

The 24 lead mentors who are Technology teachers will field-test the instructional model and the Implementation and Resource Guide in the content area of their expertise. They will use the materials first with their own students. Then they will each conduct one trial workshop for a small group of peer teachers (8-10) in the region. Formative feedback will be solicited from mentors, peer teachers, and students relative to the effectiveness of the Implementation and Resource Guide and the instructional model. All the 32 lead mentors will be invited to attend a subsequent three-day feedback meeting to discuss initial results and to suggest revisions to the Implementation and Resource Guide and the instructional model.

During the summer, 88 additional NYSTEN mentors will be enhanced. Lead mentors will conduct the enhancement sessions using the instructional model they developed. The NYSTEN Technology, Mathematics, and Science mentors will receive integrated technological and pedagogical enhancement for four weeks. The school/community partners will attend for a one-week session of team building and an overview of Project responsibilities and procedures.

8.3 YEAR III: September 1995-August 1996

In Year III, NYSTEN mentors in 24 regional teams will hold six workshops in each of their local areas. Four of the workshops will be six hours in length and relate to the technological and pedagogical needs of technology teachers. Two half-day workshops will be conducted for other members of the school and local community.

During this phase, the Network mentors will collect evaluation data, hold their final meeting, and arrange to transition Project management to the State Staff and Curriculum Development Network (S/CDN). A National Dissemination Workshop will be convened for leadership teams from 15 states other than New York. Leadership teams will comprise Mathematics, Science, and Technology Educators. They will conduct awareness workshops in their home states upon their return.

A three-day Sharing Success meeting will be convened in the late spring. The meeting will serve to disseminate project results across the Network and to establish collaborative relationships with existing Mathematics and Science teacher networks and professional association leadership from the three disciplines. Mentor enhancement will focus on leadership development, coalescing community support, and sustaining the Network once Project funding ceases. The Implementation and Resource Guide will be revised to reflect feedback gleaned from the regional workshops held during the year. A Leadership section focusing on community outreach and program improvement will be added.

9 Overview of Technical Content

Four technical content areas will be addressed in the enhancement workshops. The topics are those in which teachers expressed high interest in the needs assessment carried out by the NYSED. These areas are computer-aided design and drawing (CADD), computer control and interfacing, bio-related technology, and electronics. Workshops will focus on activities that are low budget and replicable.

Computer-Aided Design and Drawing (CADD): Fundamental student outcomes in Technology Education include the ability to solve problems, utilize creative design techniques, and communicate ideas to others through graphic means. CADD has enabled the modern technologist to design prototypes and develop drawings with great speed, accuracy, and consistency. The Workshop will help teachers understand the effectiveness of a microcomputer-based CADD system in releasing designers, engineers, and drafters from tedious and repetitive tasks and how to use this tool to analyze, review, model and test a design problem through simulation.

Computer Control and Interfacing: Digital control of mechanical systems is an important aspect of modern technology. By using sensors to provide feedback, open-loop digital control systems can be improved to provide more complete control. Teachers will learn how program control and feedback control are achieved in automated systems. They will use modeling and computer equipment to design and build systems that are replicas of automated mechanized systems. Models of automated systems used in homes, transportation, and manufacturing will be designed, built, and operated. Student activities for both middle and high school students will be tried out using modeling systems. Teachers will use a computer interface to control external devices.

Bio-related Technology: Bio-related technology is an emerging area of study within Technology Education. The ITEA National Conceptual Framework for Technology Education identified bio-related technology as one of four major areas of technological process [12]. Bio-related technology involves the practical application of mechanical devices, products, substances, or organisms to improve health or contribute to the harmony between humans and their environment [13]. It includes bioengineering, health care, cultivation of plants and animals, fuel and chemical production, waste management and treatment, and materials applications. Teachers will engage in activities related to ergonomic design, tissue culture, genetic engineering (at a laboratory at SUNY Stony Brook set up with high school students in mind by the Cold Spring Harbor Laboratories), hydroponics,

and bioprocessing. Lead mentors will include middle and high school Science and Technology teachers who have already initiated these activities with their students.
Electronics: Content of the electronic workshops will include fundamental concepts of linear and digital electronics, microprocessors, and applied mathematical relationships. Teachers will work with discrete components and basic microprocessors. Other topics will include sensors, controllers, and output devices. Through hands-on experience with several projects, teachers will read schematic diagrams, apply basic instrumentation techniques, produce printed circuit boards, and wire electronic devices.

10 Overview of Pedagogical Content

Pedagogical instruction will be oriented toward blending contemporary pedagogy into the teaching of technical topics. The focus of the pedagogical enhancement will be on design and problem solving; authentic assessment; cooperative learning; access and equity; and integration of mathematics, science, and technology:
Design and Problem Solving: Design and problem solving is a bridge between pedagogy and content. Design and problem-solving strategies will be melded into instruction in the four technical content areas. The workshop will focus on the integrated use of problem solving, design briefs, modeling, prototyping, illustration, documentation, and presentation. Activities from within the four technical content areas will be approached from a design and problem-solving perspective.
Authentic Assessment: According to the New York State Curriculum and Assessment Council, assessment of student performance should:

- be as authentic as possible, representing real-world tasks and situations
- requiring "higher order" thinking and complex, integrated performance;
- provide multiple ways for students to demonstrate their skill, knowledge, and understanding, including written and oral examinations, performance tasks, projects, portfolios, and structured observations by teachers;
- enable teachers to assess student growth in a cumulative, longitudinal fashion using many kinds of evidence;
- communicate expectations and support student motivation, self-assessment, and continual growth;
- inform instruction and encourage reflective practice;
- be valid and accurate for identifying students' strengths, abilities, and progress, opening up possibilities for encouraging further growth rather than precluding access to future, advanced instruction.

Consultants expert in authentic assessment from New York (Dr. Grant Wiggins) and the United Kingdom (Professor Richard Kimbell) will lead teachers through activities which highlight opportunities for diversified assessment.
Cooperative Learning: Although teachers have traditionally organized students into groups, cooperative learning involves more than just putting

students together and expecting them to learn. A cooperative learning activity has five essential components: (1) Positive interdependence (sinking or swimming as a group); (2) face-to-face interaction (verbal interchanges, oral summarizing, giving and receiving information, elaborating); (3) individual accountability (every member of the group is responsible for learning the material); (4) interpersonal and small group skills (development of conflict management skills, communication skills, and trust); and (5) group processing (giving students time and procedures to analyze how well they are using the necessary social skills) [14]. According to Vygotsky, the intellectual skills children acquire are directly related to how they interact with others in specific problem-solving situations. Children internalize and transfer the kind of help they receive from others and eventually use these to direct their own problem-solving behaviors [15].

Mathematics, Science, and Technology Integration: Studying disciplinary concepts through application adds relevance to the learning experience. The use of design-under-constraint technology activities offers a wealth of opportunities to inculcate mathematics and science concepts.

Often, technology activities (such as bridge building and destruction) are no more than trial and error activities where mathematics and science concepts are serendipitous. This Project will make the math and science concepts explicit to the teachers and help them make connections among syllabi in the three disciplines. For example, one technology activity involves a structural design problem where students are challenged to build an emergency shelter that can be air-dropped to survivors of a plane crash on a mountain top where the temperature is 20° F. The structure must be heated to 50° F by the body heat of five survivors. Teachers will do insulation and heat flow calculations, consider wind and snow load and fresh air exchange, and, in teams, construct and test scale models of different solutions.

Access and Equity: Research has documented the attributes of programs that attract and retain non-traditional students to technical and scientific fields [4; 15]. This workshop will focus on the strategies and techniques that invite the participation of all students in Mathematics, Science, and Technology Education. Often, embedded modes of communication can often be exclusionary. This workshop seeks to highlight teaching practices that need to change to create a more equitable learning environment while introducing new classroom practices and procedures that contribute to greater access for women and minorities to science, mathematics, and technology.

11 Project Materials

Materials used as resources by mentors will include a wealth of K-12 syllabi and student activities developed by the NYSED in Mathematics, Science, and Technology Education. Additionally, mentors will have at their disposal resources developed through prior NSF projects (Integrated MST Activities, James LaPorte and Mark Sanders, Virginia Polytechnic Institute; Fast Plants and Bottle Biology, Paul Williams, University of Wisconsin) and materials contributed by the corporate sector, primarily instructional guides, background materials and software from Autodesk, Biomechanics Corporation, Brookhaven National Laboratory,

General Electric, and Eastman Kodak. Finally, the mentors will draw from materials they themselves have produced and used successfully in prior staff development workshops and with their own classes.

12 Dissemination Plan

In New York State, the Sharing Success meeting held during Year III will serve to disseminate Project materials among the New York State Mathematics, Science and Technology Education leadership. New York State M/S/T professional association representatives on the Advisory Council will disseminate results through professional conferences and existing networks of teachers and supervisors in the three disciplines. The Project Coordinator will publish a quarterly NYSTEN newsletter and disseminate it to Network members. Whereas the electronic mail network will provide immediate interactive communication, the Newsletter will provide a documented history for the Project as well.

National dissemination of Project results will occur largely through the conduct of a one-week National Dissemination Conference held during the final project year. Fifteen three-person leadership teams comprising highly recommended, experienced Mathematics, Science, and Technology educators from states other than New York will be invited to attend the workshop. Letters of commitment have been received from state-level leaders in 13 states who have expressed interest and willingness to recruit participants for such a workshop. The workshop will be conducted by senior Project staff and several NYSTEN mentors. Its focus would be on sharing the project results, with emphasis on the Project model for peer teacher enhancement, the method of integrating modern pedagogy into the delivery of technical content, the development of mentor leadership skills, and the development of community support to sustain quality programs. Workshop participants would conduct two awareness workshops in their home states upon their return.

Presentations by Project senior staff will be made at the annual conferences of the National Science Teachers Association, National Council of Teachers of Mathematics, International Technology Education Association, and Association for Supervision and Curriculum Development. The American Association for the Advancement of Science, through its Chief Education Officer, Dr. F. James Rutherford, has expressed interest in linking NYSTEN to Project 2061. Project results and descriptions will be submitted for publication in professional journals in each of the disciplines within New York State and nationally. Glencoe/McGraw Hill Publishing has expressed serious interest in publishing the Implementation and Resource Guide.

14 Evaluation Activities

The program evaluation will be conducted under the supervision of the Program Evaluator, who will be responsible for developing and/or selecting all evaluation instruments, collecting all data, and preparing evaluation reports. The Program

Evaluator will be assisted by a graduate assistant in collecting and analyzing the data.

The Project evaluation will include three components: monitoring of Project activities and products, including meetings, workshops, and drafts of the Implementation and Resource Guide and related materials; formative evaluation of the drafts of the Guide and the instructional strategies recommended for peer workshops, for school/community leaders workshops, and for middle school and high school student classroom experiences; and a summative evaluation of the Project enhancement activities and the Implementation and Resource Guide. Written interim reports will be prepared for the Principal Investigators at the end of Years I and II and presentations, if requested, will be made to the Advisory Council.

Monitoring will include recordkeeping for attendance at each session, timeliness of submission of written materials, and information (attendance, content, etc.) for required workshops. The formative evaluation will include periodic assessment of the Implementation and Resource Guide to provide guidance to curriculum developers for revisions. Workshop implementation will be evaluated to address issues of instructional strategies, delivery of instruction, and instructional outcomes (both for peers and middle/high school students). The Summative Evaluation will include evaluation of the curriculum development and training process and assessment of the dissemination effectiveness.

15 Transition to the Staff and Curriculum Development Network (S/Cdn)

At the conclusion of the Project, management will transition to the New York Staff and Curriculum Development Network (S/CDN). S/CDN, established in 1985, is composed of representatives of school districts throughout the State. This network, in cooperation with teacher centers, professional associations, and other groups within a particular region and under the direction of a superintendent of schools, works with NYSED staff to organize staff development programs.
Through planning sessions with the Project leadership and members of NYSED, the S/CDN will assume the operational management of the NYSTEN network, support the activities of the mentors, and offer fiscal and logistical support.

16 Information About Collaborators

Mentors: Teacher mentors will be chosen upon recommendation from NYSED staff, professional educational association leadership, and Project Advisory Council members. Mentor teams will reflect gender and cultural diversity. Lead mentors will be expert teachers who have had previous staff development experience and/or are leaders in their respective disciplines. Corporate and parent partners on mentor teams will be individuals who have participated in the NYSED School Quality Review process and those recommended by the New York State Congress of Parents and Teachers, major New York State Corporations, and technical professional associations.

Advisory Council Members: The Project Advisory Council will meet twice yearly during each year of the Project. Advisory Council members will assist in the selection of mentors, review Project plans, provide advice on workshop content and timetables, and strengthen links between NYSTEN and other statewide reform efforts. The NYSTEN Advisory Council will be multicultural and include middle and high school teachers who are leaders in the professional associations in Mathematics, Science, and Technology Education; the New York State Congress of Parents and Teachers; corporate industry; Higher Education; and the NYSED.

17 Summary

In an attempt to supported integrated teaching and learning in Mathematics, Science, and Technology Education, a project has been developed which has been earmarked for $US 1.6M in funding by the National Science Foundation.

The three-year NYSTEN Project will prepare a staff development network of 120 New York State Technology Education mentors with enhanced technological, pedagogical, and leadership skills. Twenty-four teams of five mentors, one for each State Education Department district, will conduct regional staff development workshops throughout the State for all 3200 New York middle and high school Technology Education teachers. The mentors will also present awareness workshops to members of the school and local community, broadening the base of support for improving of teaching and learning in Technology Education. The Network will include Technology, Mathematics, and Science educators and school/community partners as team participants. The Project will promote connections among Mathematics, Science, and Technology Education and support systemic educational reform initiatives in New York. Mentors, assisted by expert consultants, will develop, field-test, and refine an Implementation and Resource Guide which blends contemporary pedagogy into the delivery of Technology Education content. The Guide will be a resource for conducting regional inservice workshops. In the final year, three-person leadership teams from 15 other states will participate in a one-week National Dissemination Workshop. At the conclusion of the Project, Network management will transition to the established New York Staff and Curriculum Development Network.

References

1. New York State Education Department: Technology Education in New York State. Albany, NY, 1989
2. National Curriculum Council: Statutory Orders, Technology. Her Majesty's Stationary Office, London 1989
3. de Vries, Marc: Approaches to Technology Education and the Role of Advanced Technologies: An International Orientation. Springer-Verlag, Heidelberg, Germany, (in press).
4. Gordon, Anthony; Hacker, Michael; and de Vries, Marc (Eds.): Advanced Educational Technology in Technology Education. NATO ASI Series F, Vol. 109. Springer-Verlag, Berlin 1993

5. New York State Basic Educational Data Service. NYSED, Albany, NY 1992 p. 2

6. National Science Foundation: Materials Development, Research, and Informal Science Education Program Announcement. Washington, DC, 1991

7. New York State Education Department: Technology Education in New York State. Albany, NY, 1989

8. Hacker, Michael: Applying Leadership and Strategic Planning Techniques. The Technology Teacher, 49, 4, January 1990, p. 2

9. Summary Report, New York State Education Department. Industrial Arts Futuring Committee. Albany, NY, 1982 p. 3

10. Venezio, Thomas: Technology Training Network Year End Report. Technology Training Network, Albany, NY, 1989 p. 3

11. Loucks-Horsley, S., et al.: Continuing to Learn: A Guidebook for Teacher Development. The Northeast Regional Lab, Boston, Mass. 1987. p. 6

12. Savage, Ernest and Sterry, Leonard: A Conceptual Framework for Technology Education. ITEA, Reston, VA, 1990. p. 11

13. Savage, Ernest. Bo-related Technology. Delmar Publishers, Albany, NY, 1993 p. 11

14. Cast, James: Cooperative Learning Strategies. In: Principles of Engineering. New York State Education Department, Albany, NY, 1991 p. 12

15. Vygotsky, L.: Mind in Society. Harvard University Press, Cambridge, MA, 1978 p. 12

16. Koch, Janice: Lab Coats and Little Girls: The Science Experiences of Women Majoring in Biology and Education at a Private University. Unpublished dissertation, New York University, New York, 1992.

17. Tobias, Sheila: Revitalizing Undergraduate Science: Why Some Things Work and Most Don't. Research Corporation of America, Tuscon, AZ, 1992.

The Role of Universities in the Transition to a Market Economy and in Regional Development

Ivan Hrivnák
Technical University of Kosice
Letna ul. 9, Kosice, 04200, Slovakia

Abstract. The university, as a centre of education, science, and technology in a city and region, must look for the best balance between research, innovation and teaching. The transition from a directed to a market economy is complicated in Slovakia with the structure of our industry, oriented predominantly to heavy machinery and the defense industry. Cassovia Technopolis, the science park of the Technical University of Kosice, contains small companies, composed mainly from university staff. Supporting development in zones of urgent reindustrialisation, research activities at universities, internationalisation of major research facilities, and mobility of students are also discussed.

Keywords. Education, research, science park, reindustrialisation

The Technical University of Kosice is a centre of education, science and technology in the city and region. The university has a wide and deep scientific background due to the highly qualified and skilled professors, lecturers, and assistants in it. Apart from the praxis in the past, now each lecturer must be involved in the university research by capacity not less than 30%. At a time when science and technology advance at an ever accelerating pace, the need for cooperation between scientific communities becomes more evident. Universities respond to this need by promoting communication between their members and by fostering contacts with scientists and specialists from other countries.

One of the most important missions of the University is to provide the highly qualified technical personnel the country needs, and therefore it must look for the best balance between research, innovation and teaching. For this purpose it must strive not only for a close relationship with industry, but for a closer contact with the international scientific circles. For the University it is essential to promote long term technological research since the men that will be responsible for the economy of the region in the next twenty years should be in contact with research of the highest international quality. On the other hand, owing to the high degree of specialization required from today's engineer, it is often impossible for a single university or even for a single country to provide good quality engineering education in the many different fields of engineering and those wishing to be trained at the highest levels needs to cooperate with other institutions like academy of sciences or to study abroad. As a result, the universities should benefit from an influx of students and research scholars from very different cultures, that stimulates and enriches all the academic community.

The main aim of the university is to provide courses and to conduct research which is relevant to a modern society and a changing world. Courses and research in the sciences and technology which have a direct and practical application, requiring that this is of prime importance for the economic progress and social welfare, must be developed. The university should be interested in the advancement of learning and knowledge not just for its own sake but also for the possibility of its application in the interests of society as a whole. Our activities range over a spectrum from engineering, to the physical, environmental and now also social sciences, but all are based on this central philosophy. Our links with industry, commerce and the public services help to ensure that our research and degree programmes are up-to-date. We try to educate men and women for creative and responsible positions in today's world, and to prepare them to be able to respond also to the challenge of tomorrow's problems.

The universities are playing an important role in the development of a region. Slovakia and especially the East-Slovakian region is undergoing a significant change in economy as well as in general life. The transition from directed to a market economy is complicated with the structure of our industry, oriented predominantly to heavy machinery and the defense industry. This region has now the highest rate of unemployment in Slovakia.

What is the main role of the university in such situation. First role is to keep the high level of education which should be - of course - modified or oriented to the region. The university must fulfill not only the recent tasks but - and predominantly - concentrate to the future. That is why we have opened the "Fachhochschule" recently. The university is a centre of science and technology and must help not only in management but also to introduce middle and high technologies into regional economy.

The university should encourage research on the selection, adoption and development of new technologies and on their effects on the volume and structure of employment. These technologies should be most appropriate to the specific conditions of the region.

One way how to introduce new technologies is by means of science parks, technological parks or business innovation centres. Our university settled up a science park named Cassovia Technopolis last year. The science park is a private company – the members are the city of Kosice, some banks, and two other enterprises. The science park has a close link to the manager of the university. Small companies, mainly composed from the university staff are working in the science park. The main intention of the park is to help to restructuralise the industry in this region. Now our university is becoming more aware of the social responsibility to extend knowledge and expertise to society. A concept of service which is quickly and readily adaptable to the changing character of our society and economy was developed in the university.

In the former Czechoslovak Federation, local-level planning even of the most rudimentary form, barely existed. Industrial planning was highly concentrated at the level of Federation and was limited namely to support for large-scale industry and ineffectual plans to redistribute industrial growth to designated growth poles around the Federation.

Beginning in 1991, the main vehicle for industrial policy at the national level became the industrial reconversion programme. It is necessary to withdraw state support from costly and increasingly uncompetitive industries. It is clear that profound changes are needed to revitalise industry. But it is difficult to reach small producers through centrally administrated programmes. That is why it is proposed to set up a found to support development in Zones of Urgent Reindustrialisation (ZUR). In Slovakia, regional and local industrial policy has not reached the level of activism displayed in other industrially developed countries yet. In the optimum case, such an industrial system could be described as being composed of small firms, organized on a local or regional basis, belonging to the same industrial sector, the individual firms tending to specialize in a particular production phase, organized together, and with local institutions, through relationships of both competition and cooperation.

Small-firms can also be acting as vehicles for decentralizing initiative, allowing a much more efficient tailoring of resources, can redress the obvious economic disadvantages that they individually experience in relation to individual large firms. Small firms may specialize, even investing in expensive equipment, in the full knowledge that a large sectorial market is assured.

Small-firms in the science park can benefit from the design, market research, advertising, sales and distribution, finance, staff training providing by the park itself or by the business incubation centre. The role of the university in this process is obvious.

1 Research Activities at Universities

The fundamental research should be carried out principally in the higher education sector. Concentrating fundamental research in the universities offers various advantages, such as the training of undergraduate teaching, the wide range of disciplines and expertises which can cross-fertilize each other, a degree of continuity in research traditions, scope for following curiosity unhindered by short-term pressures and the relative cheapness compared to research in the business or government sectors. Contrary, the universities have difficulties in managing large research programmes and are rather inflexible in ability to react adequately to new scientific developments. Our universities are also too much structured and controlled by established disciplinary (faculty/departmental) interests and this is in contrary to the general statement that the increasingly interdisciplinary nature of research at the frontiers of knowledge do not correspond with traditional scientific disciplines. Under situations in which resources are squeezed faculties have a tendency to fall back on their traditional and central interests the interdisciplinary research require strong central leadership or management.

It is still generally agreed that the peer review system is the best way of reaching a judgement regarding the scientific merits of a piece of work or that a particular line of research will achieve its stated objectives. However, peer review system does have limitations: it does not lead to effective assessments of the practical utility of research, is ineffective when not the disciplinary structure but other divisions in the scientific community (nationality, region, ideology) have great salience and under circumstances in which funding decisions mean choosing between many projects or equally high scientific promise.

In Slovakia, as a country providing a small scientific community, it is often impossible to obtain independent and expert assessments of research in a specialised area.

In research of small countries, internationalisation has to play an important role. The internationalisation of major research facilities is a potentially important means of cost-sharing, and the more intimate scientific contact between the two or more research communities ought in addition to stimulate competition and quality. Mobility of students, research trainers, and staff between countries, and thus between different scientific cultures, contributes vitally to research quality.

In science policy discussions there has been a long-standing concern with the transfer of knowledge from knowledge-producing institutions like universities, to knowledge-using institutions like firms or manufacturing industry. The effectiveness in university-industry links is regarded as characteristics of our higher education system. It was believed that knowledge flowed in one direction and that the fundamental test was whether or not industry was able to gain access to the knowledge stored/produced in the university. Now different kinds of firms typified by quite different processes of innovation, having different levels of research sophistication, with quite different problems of access to expertise, of marketing and of manufacture have quite different expectations of higher educational institutions. Universities can make several contributions to industry, through their department of technology transfer, like the formation of new companies, assistance to small growing companies, collaboration with large science-based firms, and assistance to nature and possibly declining industries.

To sum up, at present Slovakia is entering a period of radical transformation of economic and R and D systems. This is a unique experiment which we must face and it is not possible to follow the development of educational and science systems in countries where these systems were developing concurrently.

Using Advanced Technology for Teaching, Learning, and Assessment

Richard A. Kimbell
University of London
Goldsmiths' College
Technology Education Research
New Cross, London SE14 6NW, United Kingdom

Abstract. One of the keys to the success in technological activities lies in the ability of the child to access information as required for their task, but there is a real conundrum here. It is well documented that in design and technology it is impossible to prescribe in advance what information will be required for a task. (See CNAA 1980, DES 1981, SEC 1985, Hicks 1983). The position is put well by Hicks, who points out that:

> 'teaching facts is one thing....teaching pupils in such a way that they can apply facts is another....but providing learning opportunities which encourage pupils to use information naturally when handling uncertainty is a challenge of a different kind'.

Keywords. Advanced technology, teaching, learning, technological capabilities

This paper provides three examples from the APU assessment survey (UK: 1985-1991) that demonstrate the difficulty of pupils seeking information naturally as part of a design and technology task. And the conventional solution to this problem is for teachers to spend lots of individual tutorial time making sure all pupils are kept on track. This is very time consuming and is also destructive of autonomous action by the child, which is a critical element of capability.

Consequently, the Technology Education challenge to 'Information Technology' is to provide support to pupils in this position; and to all pupils - from age 5 upwards. It needs to provide a vast range of information at a range of levels of complexity, and it needs to provide it in a functionally accessible format, i. e. in a form in which it is needed. Ease of access is the key, and the software needs to be designed so that access can be made through user-nominted pathways. The information must be user-driven or it is useless.

My research unit is currently working with several software development houses to produce systems that begin to approach this principle of user-driven information. And we are working with all ages from children in primary classrooms to adults. I shall outline the principles and the approach used in the design of these systems. They are all interactive systems based on the idea that we can customise generic software tools for particular user groups and purposes. They have all been developed by working with children in classrooms - and the evidence suggests that we can begin to approach the challenge provided by Hicks, and develop user-driven information systems.

We are not computer fanatics - fascinated with the systems for their own sake. Our only measure of success is the extent to which the systems we are developing enable children to operate more effectively in their design & technology projects. Information stored on a disk is useless, dead data until it is liberated by children who need it. This liberation process - rather than the information itself - holds the key to effective software design.

Before addressing the question of how advanced technology can support teaching and learning, it is necessary first to be clear about where it is leading. We must be clear about the goal of the teaching before we can debate its methodology and this then relegates into third place the question of how advanced technology can support this teaching and learning process. We cannot start this paper with a discussion of what computers can do - and then see how this might help us; rather we should first ask what we want them to do. We are committed therefore to a three stage debate;

1. Outlining the goal; the nature of technological capability,
2. Examining the teaching and learning imperatives that flow from it, and only then...
3. Exploring how advanced technology can support the process.

Technological Capability

Much of the history of technology in schools can be summarised as a dispute about the balance to be struck between contrasted views of technology; is it an activity or is it a body of knowledge in the physical sciences?[1] And if it is a bit of both, how do they interact? Increasingly over the last ten years the concept of active technological capability has been recognised as the fundamental goal of technology in schools. It involves a doing capability, requiring pupils to see the world not as a set of fixed realities, but rather as a setting in which human beings struggle endlessly to improve their lot. Technology is about identifying needs that

---

[1]   There is not room here to debate in detail the changing priorities that have influenced the emergence of technology. For a detailed account of these see Penfold 1988, and for a brief summary see Kimbell 1991.

can be satisfied - or equally about exploiting opportunities that arise - and intervening to transform the world in a way that results in "improvement".

The basic premise of design and technology activity is that, using materials tools and systems, human beings can intervene to modify and improve their environment. (APU 1987)

A central issue in the development of capability therefore concerns the relationship between the activity and the resources of knowledge and skill that are needed to pursue it effectively. Pupils cannot pursue any activity without knowledge and skill - but they are not the central purpose of the activity. They are the means to an end - not the end itself. The UK National Curriculum now presents a classic analysis of this dilemma. Pupil capability is defined and assessed in active terms (• investigating• developing• making• evaluating) whilst the teaching programme details the body of knowledge and skills to be imparted (electronics, materials, energy systems etc. etc.). There is a tension between what is to be taught and what is assessed, for the real test of capability is that pupils can make use of the knowledge and skill they have acquired. Teachers therefore have to steer a delicate course; providing pupils with the resources without inhibiting their ability to act autonomously in using them on real technological tasks.

However, a 'capability' view of technology raises at least two other interesting questions, which have resonated around amongst practitioners for a number of years. The first concerns the concept of 'improvement' which must be seen as problematic. 'Improvement for whom' is a key question, for any technological outcome will impact on different people in different ways. A new by-pass that relieves the clog of traffic through a village will typically be opposed by those who resent the despoiling of yet more acres of open country and by the shop keepers who envisage a significant loss of trade. Technology is typically not about the cool objective exercise of scientific principles, it is inescapably entangled in the messy social, ethical, political and financial world. Technological decisions impact on all aspects of peoples lives and we should not be surprised when the values that underlie decisions are questioned[2] .

And a further concern is that it is widely recognised to be difficult to put a ring fence around technology - to know what is and what is not technological activity. Designing and producing a new bed or an improved electronic security system is widely seen as technological, but what about wallpaper design or haute cuisine? Countless hours have been spent in the UK arguing about whether food products are technological or not. If technology in schools is defined in capability terms

---

[2]   A recent manifestation of this complexity is seen in the 'total design' movement which requires designers to see all the consequences of their decisions instead of just the intended ones. The increasing number of 'total design' courses in higher education typically involve students in philosophical, anthropological and political study as well as the more practical study of business, design and manufacturing. They also typically develop a 'green' or 'sustainable' flavour.

(rather than by an arbitrary delineation of a body of knowledge) I can see no sensible way of drawing a line that excludes such products. Our concern should be to highlight the commonality of the activity - regardless of the medium through which it operates.

To summarise therefore, we may assert - with a limited degree of confidence - the following principles that might be taken collectively to describe the goal of technological capability.

– Pupils must become actively capable of designing and developing products & systems, this involves pupils acquiring knowledge and skills, but in a way that encourages their autonomous, active use.
– Pupils must recognise that all design is done for a client - who has a set of values that define the parameters of how their design outcome is to perform and they must equally recognise that others (users/ retailers/ manufacturers / bystanders) may have a different set of values for the same product
– Pupils must come to recognise the breadth of technological activity (bottle-tops to buggies via bras) and recognise the common ground that exists across this wide domain

Given this rudimentary analysis of the goals towards which we might be seeking to help pupils progress, what does it tell us about the teaching and learning priorities that allow us to help pupils to realise a state of technological capability?

Teaching and Learning in Technology

Typical teaching approaches in technology have presented it as a 'problem solving' activity that progresses through a number of sequential steps.

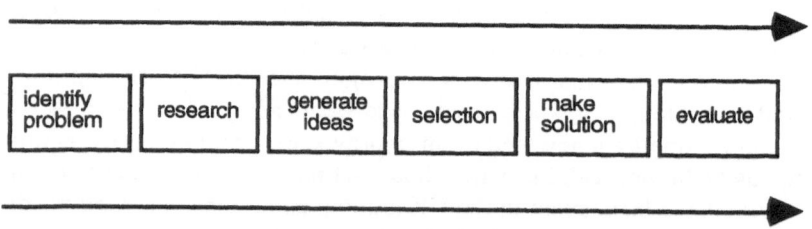

Innumerable variants on this basic idea can be found in the literature and one of the most detailed is in the Curriculum Matters series. (DES 1987), in which there are 15 steps from "the problem" to "the solution".

The steps include such things as 'write design brief', 'collect data', 'model ideas' etc. The difficulty with these linear models, as I have attempted to explain elsewhere (SEC 1986) and (APU 1987) is that it does not make sense to say that evaluation (for example) only happens at the end of the process, or that ideas are only necessary at a particular point. One has constantly to be evaluating, and constantly having ideas that demand such evaluation.

The models seek to impose order on a messy, confusing and essentially interactive process and the danger is that by imposing order they also impose a degree of rigidity and hoop-jumping that destroys the creative essence of the process.

It is not difficult to see why this came about and the roots of the problem lie in the initial attempts of the Schools Council project to assess performance in the activity.

"In seeking to assess a student's attainment across such a wide range of behaviours, ..(we).. need to identify and define the main elements of behaviour within a design situation. These elements are presented as educational objectives and are shown in relation to each other in the design process illustrated...." (Schools Council 1975) (my italics)

The behaviours have become objectives and in the assessment world the next logical step is to ask what evidence is acceptable as proof of the existence of these behaviours. The evidence has to be concrete to be acceptable (written down or drawn or modelled) so investigation as an activity becomes an investigation folder and active design thinking becomes a folio of drawings. The evaluation report at the end of the exercise is the only direct evidence of evaluative activity and therefore becomes synonymous with it. The process has become a series of products.

The progressively more detailed attempts to describe design and technology on this model (eg. in Curriculum Matters 9), conspire to create a minutely detailed series of products (The Brief, The Specification) that at best constrain the activity and at worst strangle it.

In confronting this problem, my research team[3] sought to re-establish the preeminence of the activity by recognising that all work in Design and Technology results from the interplay of thought and action - what is going on in the minds of students and what they are doing with tools materials to confront the reality of their emerging ideas (see APU 1987).

When engaged in a task, ideas (or images) are inevitably hazy if they remain forever in the mind and this inhibits their further development. By dragging them out into the light of day as sketches, notes, models or the spoken word, we not only encourage the originator to sharpen up some of the areas of uncertainty, but moreover lay them open to public scrutiny in a way that is impossible with internal images. The act of expression pushes ideas forward. By the same token the additional clarity that this throws on the idea enables the originator to think

---

[3] For the Assessment of Performance Unit (APU) between 1985-91, at Goldsmiths' College; University of London.

more deeply about it, which further extends the possibilities of the idea. Concrete expression (by whatever means) is therefore not merely something that allows us to see the designers ideas, it is something without which the designer is unable to be clear what the ideas are.

The means of expression often change through this iterative process, for whilst quick, soft material modelling or sketching is ideal for knocking around hazy ideas, more disciplined and detailed means of expression are required to impose clarity on increasingly complex and detailed thoughts.

".. we use expressive models to describe and predict how our ideas are developing. A sketch....a technical lego construction....a sculptors macquette...a stress/strain diagram....a computer simulation.....a prototype... ..an architectural plan....   All these are 'models' that help us to describe and predict how our ideas will work in reality. The more highly developed our modelling capability is, the more descriptive and predictive our models can be." (APU 1987)

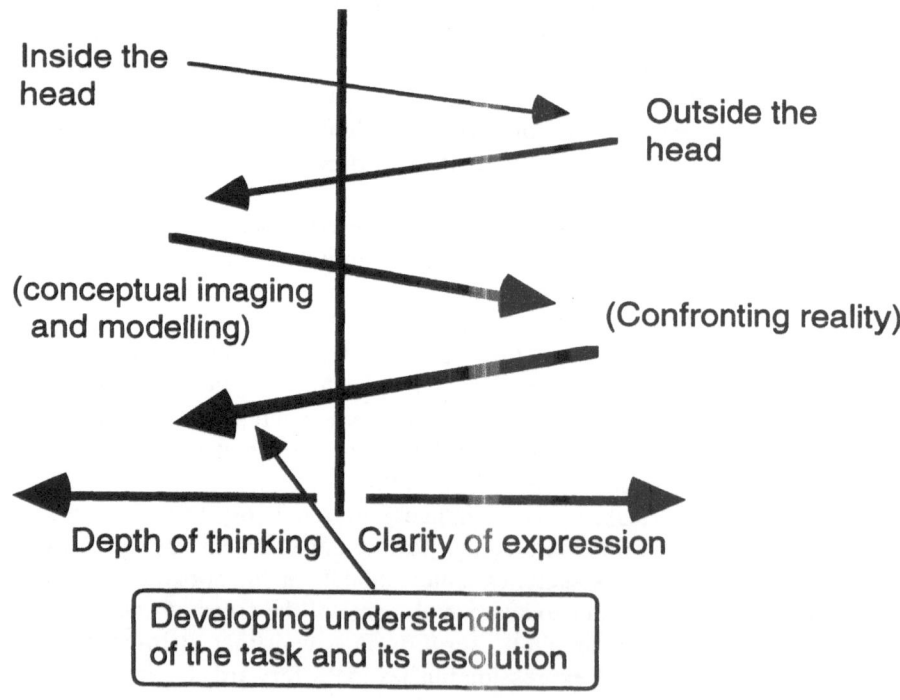

Rather than describing design and technology as a set of pre-ordered behaviours, this model allows us to distinguish between concrete activities (taking a photograph, drawing a diagram, constructing a model) which are the expression of thought, and the intention that drives it (to investigate something, or evaluate something). These broad guiding intentions change through the lifespan of a project as one moves progressively from the identification to the resolution of the task, but often there will be dual or even multiple intentions behind any one piece of activity. As an idea is developed, it must be evaluated, which may lead to a new line of investigation, or even a rethink of the original task. On this model, the whole process is an organic and dynamic entity, not a sterile set of hoops demanding a particular set of behaviours at particular times.

Interestingly, the APU Science team - despite the inherent rigidity of the model they were using to describe scientific endeavour - were drawn to a very dynamic view of 'problem solving' in science.

"...it became apparent very quickly that .... thinking and doing were interdependent activities. Whilst carrying out the investigations, children were obviously refining their approach to the problem and developing a more complete understanding of it at the same time as developing an appropriate strategy for its solution. This dynamic aspect of the children's problem solving activity seemed to be as important as any other observable outcome." (APU 1989)

In the broader context of need-driven tasks in design and technology, the importance of recognising the dynamic interdependence of thought and action is impossible to overstate. For too long, curriculum practice and assessment procedure has been dominated by static, behaviour-demanding perceptions of the process.

The Information Gap

One of the keys to the success in pursuing technological activities as outlined here lies in the ability of the child to access information as required for their task. But there is a real conundrum here. It is well documented that in design and technology it is impossible to prescribe in advance what information will be required for a task. Ultimately this question resolves itself into a debate about what it is necessary to know before one can design and make things, and there have been plenty of warnings sounded about the dangers of being too prescriptive and heavy handed.

When there is a body of received knowledge to be acquired before speculation and imagination can be given free reign, then curiosity and enthusiasm will surely be quenched....It is most important not to equate intellectual rigour with excessive reliance upon the committing to memory of large quantities of factual information. (Dainton 1968)

More recently, and in the specific context of the development of technology in schools in the UK, the former Senior Staff Inspector for technology gets to the heart of the matter;

Teaching facts is one thing; teaching pupils in such a way that they can apply facts is another; but providing learning opportunities which encourage pupils to use information naturally when handling uncertainty, in a manner which results in capability, is a challenge of a different kind. (Hicks 1983)

The difficulty in dealing with 'knowledge' in technology is to know what it is that you need to know. One task needs a quite different set of knowledge to another task. If I am to design a bivouac tent for mountaineering, I need to know about loads, structures, and temperature induced fatigue (in materials as well as in humans); if I need to design a lighting system I may need to know about low voltage electricity and switching systems. Moreover, it is not until I am half way into the tent task that I realise I need to know about the fixing conditions on rock faces, or the sheer load that can be borne by double stitching, or how the friction coefficient of the fabric changes with temperature. And if such information is not readily researchable, I need to devise a way of finding these things out.

When embarking upon a new design, the package of knowledge and skills necessary for the success of the venture will emerge as the design progresses, and so the need to acquire knowledge and skills (and sometimes extend the boundary of knowledge and devise new skills) becomes a clear requirement for the designer (CNAA/SCUE 1985)

The designer does not need to know all about everything so much as to know what to find out, what form the knowledge should take, and what depth of knowledge is required for a particular purpose (DES 1981).

For pupils to be effective in technology they need a cavalier approach to the access of information. They must at times be scientists (setting up experiments to find things out), at times they must be social scientists (devising opinion questionnaires), at times they must be good researchers (able to hunt out knowledge from books/databases/technical specifications) and - perhaps most critical of all - they must at all times be good at asking the right questions of the right people.

It is for these reasons that technology courses have been very cautious about trying to predetermine the body of knowledge that is a necessary prerequisite of capability in technology. Almost every syllabus statement produced in the last ten years will have bold disclaimers ".....it is just not possible to define exactly what one will be required to know about in advance of the activity.." (SEC 1985). And typically they then go on to outline the attitudes pupils need towards gathering information and the strategies they need to learn to handle these "designerly ways of knowing". These strategies are always then presented in terms of liberal and flexible views of the nature and role of knowledge and emphasise the role of the teacher in supporting pupils in pursuing task-related information for themselves.

The recognition that new knowledge and skills are needed in order to continue is provoked by the questions that arise in their speculations, and the crucial role of the teacher at this point is in helping pupils to recognise and address these questions. The 'need to know' is the bridge which gives pupils access into the universe of external knowledge and skill and motivates them to proceed beyond their existing capabilities and resources (APU 1987).

The mark of capability in technology is not established by measuring how much information a pupil holds, but by seeing how effective they are in seeking it out in response to their task. And whilst the reasoning behind this development has been entirely driven by educational concerns, this is an area in which employers have wholeheartedly endorsed the development. There are few employment situations in which young people can simply apply what they already know. Far more frequently they need to be imaginative and resourceful in adapting and extending their knowledge to the immediate circumstances in which they find themselves.

So here we are at the crux of the issue - the development of technological capability requires ready access to information, and advanced technology - Information Technology - ought to be the vehicle that satisfies this need. But can it measure up?

How Advanced Technology Can Support Teaching and Learning in Technology

The Technology Education challenge to 'Information Technology' is to provide support to pupils in their design and development activities; and to all pupils - from age 5 upwards. It needs to provide a vast range of information at a range of levels of complexity, and it needs to provide it in a functionally accessible format, i.e. in a form in which it is needed. Ease of access is the key, and the software needs to be designed so that access can be made through user-nominted pathways. The information must be user-driven. Let me describe the problem.

A student is working on a design task:

Cooking operations typically need to be timed and cooker timers that are built into cookers are often appallingly designed - difficult to see and to set especially for elderly users. The student is designing a free standing timer that is broadly cylindrical and in two parts. It is operated by twisting the top part on the bottom part - essential 'dialling' a time period. As the period expires (using a mechanical clock-work mechanism) it sounds an alarm.

The pupil (age 15) has got to the point where the broad form of the product is resolved, as are the internal systems. She is beginning to specify the kinds of materials and joining systems she hopes to use for the product. She is aware of the problem of hand-grip for the elderly and of the fact that kitchen environments abound with water, oil and other slippery ingredients. She is determined that the twisting action should not be made more difficult by having a slippery surface to the upper section of the cylindrical form. So she specifies her priority for the quality of the materials she needs .... "Grippy stuff ".

This might not be the most sophisticated specification but it is absolutely typical of pupils when they are designing and it clearly demonstrates the problem of access to information. She does not need to know that plastics come in two forms -thermoplastic and thermo-set; she does not need to know about the effect of different iron/carbon combinations on steel - she needs to know about materials that are "grippy".

No materials science database that I know of will supply this information for her. A range of answers do exist that might help her - but she will never retrieve the information from a conventional database using her own language. Such databases are typically written by materials scientists who structure their information according to the structure of their discipline rather than in terms of the form in which the information might be sought. Our pupil of course needs the information structured in a quite different way.

There is absolutely no reason why a database could not be structured around the functional behaviour of materials. Such a database would be able to respond to requests for materials that were.....

"grippy....bendy.....stretchy....or...cold".

Using very simple keywords as their starting point, pupils could be drawn into such a database, progressively deepening the sophistication of their questions in response to the information provided by the database.

The need (especially for young pupils) is for more than a database - it is an expert system that is required. A system that is able to diagnose the level of sophistication of the user and provide information at that level. And moreover to draw the student into the data so that they progressively see the possibilities of the information that is held therein.

The problem with the typical materials database is that it is so poorly structured that you need to know so much about materials before it is any use. You effectively need to know the answer before you can ask the question. The need is for systems that can develop understanding - not for systems that have understanding as a prerequisite of their use.

The problem I have outlined here is not restricted to the matter simply of choosing and using materials. It covers all kinds of information that pupils need to resolve their design tasks. I have merely chosen the "materials choice" issue because it starkly demonstrates the problem.

In my research unit[4] we are currently working with several software development houses to produce systems that begin to approach this principle of

---

[4]   In 1990 I founded the Technology Education Research Unit at Goldsmiths College; University of London.

user-driven information. And we are working with all ages of user - from children in primary classrooms up to adults. The focus of our work lies at the interface between the creative process and information and this is an ideal medium for knowledge-based systems (KBS technology). In the design activity, the process of optimisation and final selection can be supported through such KBS technology in ways that are impossible with conventional text books or traditional databases. Moreover, a good interactive system will be able to enhance and to some degree replace the intensive personal tutor support that is typically devoted to this activity.

One of our current projects concerns the development of just such a system for supporting pupils in the classroom with information on materials and production processes. Whilst developing methods of interacting with a body of knowledge, the project will develop a KBS shell which will give dynamic practical information to support the creative process and enhance the problem solving activity. Ultimately we believe that the CDROM disc will have a KBS shell capable of use with any body of knowledge which needs to be integrated into the creative decision-making process.

The system interface will be double ended in that at one level it will allow students to operate from the functional properties ("grippyness") of raw materials and progressively consider the outcomes that might be achieved with them using a range of production processes. But it will also work back the other way, taking finished products and dismantling them to the point where the initial thinking about materials and production becomes apparent.

The evidence from our preliminary trials of the prototypes suggests that we can begin to approach the challenge provided by Hicks. We can....provide learning opportunities which encourage pupils to use information naturally when handling uncertainty, in a manner which results in capability.

The tool we are using is advanced KBS technology, but the key to its success is an understanding of teaching and learning, and a recognition that the technology must be the servant of the pupil not the other way round. The key is user-driven information systems.

We are not computer fanatics - fascinated with the systems for their own sake. Our only measure of success is the extent to which the systems we are developing enable children to operate more effectively in their technology projects. Information stored on a disk is useless dead data until it is liberated by children who need it. The liberation process - rather than the information itself - holds the key to effective software design.

References

1. Assessment of Performance Unit (APU): Design & Technological Activity: A framework for assessment. HMSO 1987
2. Assessment of Performance Unit (APU): Science at age 13. HMSO 1989

3. CNAA/SCUE Council for National Academic Awards/Standing Conference on University Entrance: 'A' level Design & Technology: the identification of a core syllabus CNAA. 1985

4. Dainton Sir FS: Enquiry into the flow of candidates in science and technology into higher education. Comand paper 3541. HMSO1968

5. Department of Education and Science (DES) Understanding Design and Technology. HMSO 1981

6. Department of Education & Science (DES): Craft Design & Technology from 5-16;Curriculum Matters 9. HMSO 1987

7. Hicks, G.: Another step forward for design & technology. In: APU newsletter, 4, Autumn 1983

8. Kimbell, R. A.: Tackling Technological Tasks. In: Practical Science. Woolnough, B. (ed.). Open Univ Press 1991

9. Penfold, J.: Craft Design and Technology: Past, Present and Future. Trentham books 1988

10. Secondary Examinations Council (SEC): Craft Design & Technology GCSE: A guide for teachers. Open Univ Press 1986

11. Schools' Council: Education through Design & Craft. Schools Council 1975

Collaboration Between Educational Institutions and the World of Work: Future Directions

1 Introduction

In countries throughout the world, there is a growing interest in collaboration between education and the world of work, and the formation of school-industry links. These have the potential to enrich the school curriculum and greatly enhance the quality of science and technology teaching. A common trait of successful school-industry collaborations is that they are mutually beneficial to all parties. This symbiotic feature is essential for the continuation of partnerships because the needs of each organization are addressed. It is also important for both members of the partnership to contribute in a significant manner so that they have ownership of the programs being implemented. Through such collaboration, communities of practice can be established which will increase opportunities for students and teachers to have authentic experiences that narrow the gap between school and the adult world of work. This report provides a brief overview of types of school-industry cooperation with illustrative, examples from different countries, together with a discussion of related issues and recommendations.

2 Types of School-Industry Cooperation

2.1 Experiental

2.1.1 For Students

The largest numbers of school-industry cooperative activities are those that are designed to provide enrichment activities for students and as a context for the application of material contained in the curriculum. In some countries this activity is encouraged by the government or by industrial companies and professional bodies; in others, the initiative lies mainly with the school and teacher. Examples of school-industry cooperation to provide students with work-based experiences can be found in many countries.

Although government support for school-industry links in the former Czechoslovakia has been withdrawn, it is still compulsory for students in the Czech and Slovak Republics to engage in industrial work experience, typically two or three weeks per year.

In Germany all students at the age of 14 spend three weeks full-time in industry or in trade learning about the world of work. After this experience, the students select the educational path that will lead to their chosen occupation. Individual teachers make arrangements with local business and industry for student placements. After completing the experiences, students are required to report the results of their activity to the class. In all regions of Germany there are committees concerned with schools and the economy that work together on subjects related to technology and the economy.

In Turkey, vocational students can follow two paths that involve cooperative school-industry activity. Those students who complete eight years of school can then choose to spend in each week three days in school and two days in industry. Those completing eleven years can choose to spend two years full time in industry. Both of these paths lead to a technician qualification.

In France, for Colléges students between eleven and fifteen years, there are opportunities for short periods of work experience; however, these appear to be primarily for students with lower academic ability.

In the UK, many students at the age of 15+ spend one or two weeks working in industry in order that they make experience first-hand the deeds and demands of the world of work. Where possible this experience is intended to extend and reinforce the material studied in school. Aspects of this approach can also be seen in primary schools, for example, Seebrook Primary School designed and made ceramic products in conjunction with major area manufacturers.There is a longstanding vocational education tradition of "day-release" courses for young people working in industry so they may attend college one day a week. At the undergrate level in the UK and in the Irish Republic, these are "sandwich courses" which allow students to spend time in college and industry. The extent to which the industrial periods of typically 6 months or 1 year are integrated into the academic course varies, but all students are visited in industry by their university tutors.

Although it is not part of the standard curriculum for all students, many U.S. high school students participate in internships for various periods of time. During these internships the students learn about careers in a variety of public and private work settings. Some U.S. high schools require internships for graduation. Some internships involve evaluations by the supervisor at work as well as self-evaluation by the student. As part of their experience, the students are involved in learning the organizational structure and other characteristics of the work environment. Similarly, many U.S. colleges and universities have programs that enable students to earn college credit for cooperative experience in business and industry.

In New York State in the U.S., innovative school-industry collaboration is successfully operating in a number of high schools. For example, at Sachem High School an exciting program involves CYBEX Corporation, a manufacturer of exercise bicycles. Students in engineering, marketing, and advertising classes are briefed about new prototype products. They then help with Beta testing of the products, conduct consumer acceptance studies, and develop advertising videos and newspaper advertisements. The students' work is then presented to company representatives and alliance members.

2.1.2 For Teachers

In several countries cooperative activity between school and industry has enabled teachers to spend time in industry to facilitate their continuing education and to provide opportunity to develop context-based teaching materials for use in school. Thus, in the UK, the Teacher Placement Scheme places teachers in local business or industry and encourages companies to send personnel to work with students in schools. Specifically, the reciprocal school-industry partnership nurtured by the (British) Chemical Industries Association Centre encourage visits by students and teachers to industrial sites as well as advising visitors from industry (who, incidentally, can be role models) on their presentations within schools. Also, the UK Engineering Council's Neighbourhood Engineer scheme enables thousands of professional engineers (many recently retired) to help teachers present some awareness of the relation between technology, industry, work and the national economy to pupils in 2500 schools. In Germany courses are offered by industry for the teachers of technical subjects who are sent by their schools. Recent programs in the State of Oregon in the U.S. have provided opportunities for high school teachers to work in business and industry to learn about "high performance" workplace practices.

2.2 Curricular Material Development

Industry and related associations have developed materials and resources that can be used to supplement the curriculum in schools. In the UK, industry associations, such as the construction, engineering, chemical, and banking associations, have worked in cooperation with educators to develop educational materials for a wide variety of educational topics associated with their industry. Thus, within the industries related to chemistry and chemical engineering, some idea of the extensive generation of resource packages and projects is given (for the approximate ages indicated) by the following: Problem-Solving with Industry, Chemistry Plus, Exciting Science and Engineering (problem-solving and active learning, 7-14); Making Use of Science and Technology (13-16); Salters Institute of Industrial Chemistry (topic-based A-level units, 16-18).

The New York State Education Department, in collaboration with the Department of Technology and Society of the State University of New York at Stony Brook, has developed a set of case studies that are used in a new "Principles of Engineering" high school course. Many of the case studies were developed with support from industry.based foundations and personnel from various companies. A set of energy case studies was developed with funding from New York State Power Authority. The NEC America Foundation is currently funding and providing assistance with a new set of case studies that deals with "Designing Technology for People with Disabilities". All these case studies deal with the design of technological systems for solving problems in the world of work.

Recent reports in the U.S. and the UK (SCANS and the National Council for Vocational Qualifications within the UK) have described the need for national standards for education that prepare students for productivity and fulfillment in the world of work. There are well-recognized qualifications, such as the Higher National Diploma and the Business and Technology Education Council (BTEC) awards that, typically, incorporate an industrial placement of 1 year within an overall 3-4 years.

In the UK industry and education cooperate to develop occupationally specific National Vocational Qualifications (NVQ). These are divided into units and state precisely what students must achieve to gain the qualification. These Qs and general NVQs focus on both vocational skills and the general transferable skills and they require the student to demonstrate knowledge and skills that underpin a broad occupational area.

In Germany, national standards for general and vocational education are established by a conference of the secretaries of education from the German states. The standards for vocational education are established by the national government with the cooperation of chambers of business and industry, and the trade unions.

2.4 Resource Sharing

School-industry cooperation is often organized to allow the sharing of resources between schools and the broader community, the world of work. Such sharing can involve personnel, problems, facilities, or equipment.

Students spend time working with industry on solving problems posed by industry. These problems are real and, when successful, are applied by the company. The industry role is to supply not only resources but also elements of appropriate expertise from within the workforce.

Some schools in the UK hold "mini-enterprise weeks" where all students in a grade work on projects with industrial representatives. The work involves all subject areas and a wide variety of industry activity.

Biomechanics, a U.S. company, had a need to develop a workbook for their new ergonomics software called "Mannequin". The company's educational director worked with teachers from a number of high schools to test and develop a set of design activities. Students from other high schools then field-tested the newly developed workbook.

3 Issues and Recommendations

The relationship between the goals of educational institutions and the goals of business and industry is complex. The various levels of education, by age and type, have different needs at different times and, of course, their aims are by no means confined to ensuring successful assimilation of students into business and industry. Similarly, business and industry have a wide range of objectives, depended on the nature, focus and timetable of each endeavor. These may include recruitment of employees, presentation of industry as the wealth creator for a caring society, influencing public perception of pollution risks and hazards, even some altruison. Such variation makes the matching of goals difficult, and helps explain why studies such as those carried out by Her Majesty's Inspectorate of Schools (HMI) in England show considerable mismatch between the objectives of participants in school-industry links. The situation described above does, however, have a valuable corollary; studies of school-industry projects have shown that projects generally have consistent and sympathetic goals held by both parties.

The following issues and recommendations provide insight into possible paths of exploration that can lead to successful school-industry projects.

3.1 Transferability Across Cultural and Subject Boundaries

Intimate interaction between school and industry may not be an absolute prerequisite for industrial and economic success in all cultures; in Japan, for example, there is relatively little such interaction. Cultural differences should not be underrated. By the way of example, the high public esteem of the professional engineer in some countries (such as the professional elite graduates of the long-established Grandes Écoles in France) is not replicated in others. However, in industrial countries, it is generally accepted that an awareness of industry should be introduced as part of early school life, and that collaboration between schools, business, and industry can contribute to the goals of each. How much can we learn from experiences in different countries? Can successful programs be adapted and transferred across cultures and subject areas?

Recommendations. Educational policy makers in countries with changing economies can benefit from an awareness of programs of technological education, such as the programs under development in New York State in the U.S.

It is likely that the concept of teaching resource packages that are carefully constructed by teams from industry, schools and universities covering substantial parts of the curriculum (of which the UK and Germany have good examples) could be extended to other countries. However, since the particular industries should be ones that have been seen and visited by local students, such material may have to be created in its cultural context rather than merely translated.

Industrial displays such as the three-day events for small groups of 14 and 15 year-olds and their teachers to visit a series of short displays at universities have been successfully organized throughout the UK by the Institute of Physics ("Physics at Work") and the Royal Society of Chemistry ("Chemistry at Work"). Such events, in which ten or twelve local companies each expend considerable effort (aided by teachers) to compose 25 minute presentations to illustrate a scientific concept, might well be extended to other technologies and other countries.

At the undergraduate level, the sandwich system, with students spending alternate periods in industry and in college, already operates internationally. UK sandwich students of chemical engineering and other disciplines often spend a six-month or one-year industrial period in France or Germany; such an experience might be valuable for students in eastern or central European countries.

Finally, and more generally, most school-industry links enable industry to influence education; perhaps industry could benefit from educational influence.

3.2 Matching Aims of Education and Industry

Industry of today and tomorrow requires creative students who can solve complex and interdisciplinary problems. Educational programs that encourage students to work in a multi-dimensional and multi-disciplinary manner can help develop such students. Unfortunately, current educational practice in most countries appears to be failing to meet this challenge.

Recommendations. Teachers will be more able to help their students prepare for work if the teachers themselves increase their awareness of the current nature of industry and its role in society.

Educational methods should be adapted or developed to maximize the potential of school-industry links. Such methods should include opportunities for multi-disciplinary and multi-dimensional approaches to learning.

New educational technology should be exploited to ensure the most effective development and delivery of educational programs.

A continuing program of research and development should be established to bridge the gaps between educational research, teachers, professors, and the world of industry.

Regular programs of scientific meetings should be established to disseminate and stimulate educational and industrial research to support collaborative school-industry activity.

3.3 Strategic Planning and Policy

Unless broad based policy and strategic plans are developed and adopted at all levels in both the educational and industrial communities, then the institutionalization of school-industry links in all schools is unlikely. Furthermore, in the absence of the necessary resources to implement these policies and plans, both present and future linkages are vulnerable. The policy, strategic planning and necessary resource commitments can help bring about a paradigm shift that will enable all constituencies to view school-industry collaboration as contributing to student, community, and economic well-being.

Recommendations. Specific commitments should be made by all the parties involved in school-industry programs. Though the maintance of these commitments, all participants can develop a sense of ownership in the collaborative effort.

School-industry programs should be designed so that they are mutually beneficial to all participants in the partnership. Developing symbiotic relationships among all the participants should be an important goal of collaborative efforts.

Both intrinsic and extrinsic incentives are needed to ensure that participants in school-industry projects are motivated to make positive contributions.

Both school and industrial participants should be encouraged to allocate financial and human resources toward the implementations of programs.

Finally, in some countries industrial companies recognise the enlightened self-interest of substantial time and financial contributions to forging links with schools even without explicit state support; such examples might be followed elsewhere.

Characteristics of Advanced Educational Technology

We would like to emphasize that Advanced Educational Technology should be seen more as an advanced instructional technology for effective learning than as an advanced technology itself. Following advanced does not in this connection necessary mean modern technology-based technology. AET can or cannot be based on powerful modern technologies but it is only one perspective into it. In order to be an advanced educational technology the technology must contain some of the essential outside the technology arising characteristics. In the following a short description of the most important characteristics will be shortly described. In defining of them the recent research results in educational research and the papers presented in the workshop have served as a good framework.

AET and Needs of the Learner. Sound and learning environment should be in agreement with the widely and well-articulated (See e.g. Kath's paper in this volume) learning goals. It should support the development of important characteristics in students repertoire such as self-regulated, responsible, flexible, communicative and co-operative behaviour in the learner. This means that the advanced technology environment ought to have built in specific tutoring and guiding tools for achieving those goals.

The role of AET can be to guide in the direction of learning a subject. It can be prepared to ask questions, to exhibit some examples, to make explanations and to remind necessary information, show problems, to help problem identification and to make analysis.

AET as a Tool for Structuring the Complex Reality. The world is complex and multidimensional and the student reflects, (re)structures and constructs his/her own reality when interacting with it. In order to be a significant part of a powerful learning environment AET should be capable to transmit models, frames and perspectives about the reality. This is supposed to enhance student's opportunities to put hooks into the complex world so that the essential structures will gradually be processed, articulated and understood.

The object of the AET is very complex for the learners. Apprehension of the complexity of the AET needs guidance by the tutor. The complexity has something to do with the number of elements which can be identified in the system, and with number of ways in which they are related; but it is a matter of choice how many elements one wish distinguish.

The increasing of the number of things and concepts increases the complexity of relations and frame generated in the mind of the students. Complex situations help to be carried out within the limitations set by the capacity of students' brain. These limitations should be considered while preparing AET tools.

AET as a Medium for Transmitting the Structural Aspects of Knowledge. One of the main function of AET is to store information and knowledge, that can be later transformed, updated and retrieved. This knowledge can be prepared doing research into the domain of expert tutors by the educators acting as knowledge engineers.

When interacting with the world and some of its phenomena we are testing our theories and hypothesis with the consequencies following out of our actions. Advanced educational technologies can be powerful tools in that if it models, simplifies and offers tools for knowledge structuring and elaboration. When interacting with the system the students can develop meaningful conceptual understandings about the existing phenomena, which enlarges the capabilities for further learning and understanding. As good examples and candidates for the prototypes are recent computer-based system dynamic software and other powerful learning environments, which can simulate reality. The interactive nature of the learning environment is natural condition and characteristic of advanced educational technologies.

AET tools can be tutors themselves for learners to learn how to use AET interactively. The interactive character of the tool can reflect experts approach to teaching.

AET as a Tool for Promoting Contemporary Pedagogy. Because advanced educational technology is mostly based on recent developments of modern technology seeing it solely from technological point of view limits essentially its possibilities in effective and developing learning. As a consequence of recent learning research results one can argue that if the implementations of AET cannot tie the learning goal into context and realistic situations where the learning object is situated there is a danger that the concepts and principles will not be transferred and through that as parts of learners' knowledge structure. Situational cognitive aspects and followingly central aspects of cognitive apprenticeship should be able to implement in AET.

Simultaneous Character of AET. Simultaneous characteristics is important in networks while making decisions, solving problems and finding solutions. The computer supported co-operative work activities such as designing, desicion making and communication with each others are also the subjects of AET.

Advanced Educational Technologies Provide Individual Tutoring. Clearly the most powerful form of instruction involves personal interaction between an individual student and the teacher. Unfortunately, one-on-one instruction is neither practically nor financially feasible. Advanced educational technologies possess the potential to provide the individual tutoring that approaches the quality of one-on-one instruction.

The power of advanced educational technologies to provide individual tutoring lies in their ability to assess student learning, model desired performance, and provide individualized feedback and assistance. Together, these attributes comprise the primary components of a potentially powerful instructional method called *cognitive apprenticeship*. As described in several papers presented at this conference, cognitive apprenticeship is an instructional method that promotes learning through strategies such as teacher modelling and coaching. Student success is ensured through scaffolding techniques, clear articulation by the teacher, and reflection by the student. In addition, this method encourages student exploration through multiple domains in situations that have personal relevance to students. By designing advanced educational technologies around contemporary pedagogies such as cognitive apprenticeship, the effectiveness and efficiency of the educational process can hopefully be enhanced.

One of the ways that advanced educational technologies support individual tutoring is through their **ability to collect, transform, update, and retrieve data**. Through their information processing capabilities, advanced educational technologies can assess student's learning gains, identify misconceptions, and determine the degree of performance fluency during the completion of various tasks. For example, intelligent tutoring systems (ITSs) have been developed that can monitor student thinking and performance. Designed to support learning in complex domains such as electronic troubleshooting, medical diagnosis, and financial decision making, intelligent tutoring systems can collect student performance data on a wide range of variables and compare those data to existing student performance models. The ultimate goal of these advanced educational technologies is to provide immediate feedback to both the student and the instructor regarding the progress of students toward educational goals.

A second way that advanced educational technologies support individual tutoring is through their **ability to model desired performances for students**. Through the years, educational research and practice have demonstrated the importance of modelling as a strategy for learning enhancement. Apprentices work closely with their master to observe first hand the practices of their trade. Athletes spend countless hours viewing video tapes of world class athletes as they perform in their special fields. Primary school children observe and replicate the handwriting techniques shown by their teachers.

Although observation is a powerful form of learning, it is difficult for instructors to model some types of performance (e.g., actions that happen too fast or procedures that are difficult to see). Advanced educational technologies are able to slow down reality to allow students to view procedural and physical sequences in steps. For example, programs have been developed that model the sequences students can follow to solve geometric and algebraic problems. Other programs utilize multimedia technologies to allow students to view video images of technological processes in slow motion and in single frame displays. This capability is especially useful for intricate actions and precise manipulations. Advanced educational technologies also allow students to manipulate and control reality by zooming in and out of moving images that depict model performances.

This allows students to see actions that are too small to observe first hand or occur in tight settings that prevent students from direct viewing.

A third way that advanced educational technologies support individual tutoring is through their **ability to provide individualized feedback and assistance**. With the extensive information processing capabilities of advanced educational technologies, they are able to maintain an extensive record of student's past and present performances. Student actions and even their lines of reasoning during problem solving can be tracked and evaluated. Based on these "real time" assessment capabilities, advanced educational technologies can provide both customized and personalized feedback to students. The feedback can take the form of descriptions of their errors and misconceptions, visual replications of student's performances, and explanations of the corrective actions students should take to resolve the voids in their learning.

Disciplinary, Interdisciplinary and Multi-Dimensional Perspectives

Preamble. Technological literacy is a fundamental prerequisite for effective citizenship in the current era. One of the primary purposes of technology education is to provide instruction and experiences that will assist all learners in the development of technological literacy. Consequently, the primary focus of this paper is upon the provision of experiences in technology education for the general education of all, from the early primary school through adulthood.

While the discussion centers on the provision of experiences in technology education for learners during the years of required schooling, many of the principles involved are also applicable to technological education in other settings. Apprenticeship programs, technical programs, and engineering programs are built upon similar foundations, though their purposes are different. In a few instances, attempts are made to provide specific suggestions for the provision of technical programs at such levels; in other cases, the reader is left to generalize from our suggestions as seems appropriate.

Disciplinarity and Technology. Inter-disciplinarity and Multi-disciplinarity. It is important to distinguish between inter-disciplinary and multi-disciplinary educational approaches. Inter-disciplinary approaches emphasize the inter-relationships between disciplines as these are applied to the solution of the problem at hand. In contrast, multi-disciplinary approaches simply enter the problem via the appropriate windows of the respective disciplines to access the information needed to deal with the problem, without concern for integration of the conceptual and procedural knowledge.

Technology as Integrated Multi-dimensionality. Technological problems cannot be looked at as consisting of a number of disciplines, integrated or otherwise, rather they have a number of dimensions. So, for example, when a power station is being designed the social, environmental, legal and technical dimensions of the design must all be taken into account. In doing this sometimes it will be neccessary to call upon discipline knowledge and procedures, for example in working out the technical details of voltage regulation. However at other times it will not be a relevant way of approaching the problem; the legislation will need to be addressed, but it may be through a more pragmatic way than afforded by the discipline of law. Ethical issues related to environmental pollution, inhumane working conditions, or the use of non-renewable resources would similarly not require the approach of moral philosophy.

Technology as Problem Solving. Technology is an example of the problem solving process. For instance, technology may be viewed as a way of meeting human needs by designing and making appropriate products. In some cases, technology is also viewed as a result of the problem solving process as the accumulated knowledge of processes and procedures becomes generally recognized and applied. Such designing and making involves taking into account a variety of functional, legal, aesthetic and environmental characteristics that an artefact must satisfy. These characteristics, which are the dimensions of the problem, should be represented in a specification and the task for the problem solving is to satisfy the specification, where it may contain elements which are in conflict, e.g., low cost and legal obligations.

Projects and Small Group Activities. Projects, as they are discussed in this report, are group activities rather than individual activities. They are typically pursued by a group of individuals working together in intensive experiences of one day or more or over a relatively long term (at least several weeks to as much as several months or years). (See Wild's paper.). Most projects are assigned, either by an instructor or an employer, but groups occasionally select their own projects; groups nearly always are involved in defining and restructuring their projects as their work goes forward. In his paper, Stern pointed out the importance of problem finding and self-initiated and self-managed activity.

Problem Solving. Industry as a Model. Authenticity is the rationale for the use of industry as a model of technological activity. McCormick argued for a technological community of practice, while Duby suggested that we have a lot to learn from the culture of industry. (We realize that there are some problems with this model, which we deal with in the later section on culture.) This model implies group and organizational problem solving. Bayazit's research on collaborative design in the studio, for example, supports the importance of this kind of problem solving. The group problem solving model may be used whether or not there is a formal organizational structure in place. Organizational problem solving not only stresses interpersonal aspects but also organizational aspects. These latter aspects occur where there are roles and formal relationships for the individuals and the group. The traditional hierarchical relationships in organizations are not the only kinds of relationships that exist between individuals within and among groups. Modern industrial organizations, such as automobile manufacturers, are now adopting cooperative design methods (concurrent engineering) that have different relationships among the individual designers than has been traditional. (See Buresch's paper.) Total quality management and other quality assurance procedures are other industrial examples of group problem solving situations.

Group Problem Solving. Not only does industry require roles within group problem solving, but educational research shows that group problem solving is more successful when students adopt various roles (Healy, Pozzi and Hoyles, 1992). We must therefore encourage the development of group problem solving within organizational contexts that give students the opportunity to experience problem solving in a variety of roles. This experience should include authority relationships which may result in group decisions being overruled by someone in 'authority,' as a simulation of one situation that occurs in some organizational contexts. (McCormick gives a spectrum of school-industry links that include simulation-type activites within school at one end, and work experience in industry at the other.) Equally, students need experiences with group problem solving in a range of other contexts, such as community groups.

The importance of roles, and the associated knowledge and skills that are brought to bear in the workplace, should not overshadow the fact that it is individuals who fulfill the roles and therefore more than professional knowledge is available to solve problems. This fact emphasizes the importance of personal knowledge in contrast to professional knowledge. Although it is recognized that professional knowledge has a personal component, here we have in mind personal knowledge that comes from the experience and interests outside the work environment. Thus the mechanical engineer may bring an interest in music to the problem in hand. Stern's account of creativity in companies shows how unofficial activity is an important factor in producing successful and new responses to problems.

Group problem solving within an organizational structure poses a particular problem in the school setting. (McCormick pointed out Scribner's analysis of the difference between in-school and out-of-school cultures.) Nevertheless, there are aspects of group problem solving that can be taught in schools and we consider these in the next section.

Teaching and Learning of Group Problem Solving in Schools and Colleges. There are many examples of such activity in education that show that it is quite possible to involve students in 'realistic' and to some extent authentic activity. For example, primary students were involved in producing salad cress for sale at a school event. Four classes set up competing companies, but within each company (class) they formed groups to carry out the functions of the various parts of the company: marketing, advertising, growing, packaging etc. Each week one representative of the group attended a board meeting where the decisions were made and interface issues sorted out. This encourages the formation of roles, and encouraged both competitive and co-operative group work, all within a commercial setting. As McCormick notes, in such commercially based activity it is important to point out to students that there are motives other than profit that companies can aspire to, and these should be included in some kinds of activities. (This relates to our reservations about using industry as the sole model for activity, which we will deal with later.)

In dealing with complex problems that have a high degree of multi-dimensionality, using the idea of concurrent learning advocated by Liao in his engineering principles course, it is important to be aware of the fact that this may present too complex a picture for students to deal with. Not only do they have to understand the implications of each dimension, which in itself may require considerable conceptual learning, but they have to integrate the dimensions in the solution. In an industrial context each dimension may be the province of a single expert, or sub-group of experts. In schools and colleges the roles of expert are typically taken by novices, each of whom is usually no better off than his or her peer. (Mature students may bring some aspects of expertise, depending upon the level of the problem.) It is possible to arrange teaching inputs so that individuals take particular roles within a group and these individuals are then responsible for informing the group. This occured in a project to produce a meal for an airline flight, where specific teaching inputs on, for example, food preservation, or microwave reheating, were given. One individual from each of the competing groups attended one of the sessions on the specialist areas, and then had the specialist role in informing the group and feeding in the necessary ideas appropriate to the overall task. Teachers should, in any case, utilize any expertise students bring to the learning situation. A more profound issue of how students are assessed in this kind of group work that relies upon collaborative effort, remains an issue for us. Although methods for carrying out such assessment exist (See Wild's paper), there are usually constraints on assessment systems that only take account of individual achievement.

Types of Problem Solving Various definitions of technological activity emphasize particular kinds of problem solving or other activity. Indeed our statement on technology as a problem-solving process emphasised one approach, that of designing and making. Johnson, in his paper on problem solving cited his other work on fault-finding in electronic circuits, whereas Bayazit was concerned with designing (not including making). This drew our attention to the fact that, whatever the overall task (designing, making, fault-finding), there were at least two types of problem solving that we were concerned with: analytic (including investigative and experimental) and divergent (including design and construction or making). We also realize that within a single kind of activity, such as design, there will be analytic and divergent phases. Much of the concern in traditional school and college problem solving has been with analytic methods and approaches. While this remains important we were concerned with the encouragement and support of divergent problem solving. In design, for example, it is standard for teachers to require students to produce several designs to encourage creative thought, and prevent a student fixing immediately upon a single solution. Not only do teachers often fail to explain this to students (McCormick's point about making the processes of problem solving visible.), but they may not give them any techniques to encourage alternative designs. Techniques such as morphological analysis can help, as can various word associations. However, these methods must all be taught, for students will not just pick up creative techniques by themselves, although some will be more creative than others. Merely taking a multi-dimensional approach to a problem, and using individuals who have different roles, may in itself stimulate creative ideas as students try to resolve the different aspects. Whatever approach or techniques are used, it is important to make clear to students the specific kinds of problem solving that they are being asked to undertake, so that they can build up their own approaches to problem solving. This personal approach is particularly important when the significance of personal knowledge in problem solving is recognized. The confidence to use personal knowledge is taken as a sign that an individual is able to solve multi-dimensional problems.

Issues in Problem Solving. We have already noted the fact that students typically act as novices when their counterparts in industry are experts, and that in education we focus upon individual and not group assessment. Neither of these poses intractable difficulties, although there remain the differences in school and outside school cultures that will always prevent educational institutions from reproducing truely authentic group problem-solving experiences. A much more profound issue for us was the exclusive use of industry as the model for meaningful activity. This relates to a number of concerns we had, in particular the importance of local culture and of the human dimension of technological acitivity. We turn to this issue now.

Culture. The industrial model is an obvious one for representing and involving students in the culture of society. But it has some serious problems in offering a relevant and humanizing approach to technology. While the rationale for using industry as a model is related to the development of programs that provide an authentic view of industry, it is important to note that 'culture' is much larger and more inclusive than 'industry.'

Social and general cultural contexts may be more appropriate arenas for finding alternative models for the design of programs of technology education. Technology-culture interactions facilitate or limit the participation of individuals in terms of their access to tools and means of production. So, for example, in the case of a rural area where employment is unlikely to be in manufacturing industry, but rather in tourism, then the industrial model will not reflect the local culture and may not be appropriate as the main basis for the technology curriculum. Further it may be that if unemployment is a major issue in the area, creating opportunities and challenges may be a more productive way of approaching technological activity. Haché and Sharpe outlined this kind of context in their account of technological activity in rural and economically disadvantaged areas of developed and developing countries throughout the world.

The fundamental values held by individuals in a culture need to be reflected in technology education programs. These individual and cultural values are often complex, reflecting views toward industry and other social institutions.

Such considerations led us to consider other contexts for technological activity, in particular environmental issues. These represent multi-dimensional problem solving that are every bit as demanding as that found in industry, but they are set in quite a different context. For many students these issues may be more urgent and indeed more motivating. There is evidence that, whereas industry is not seen as attractive to students, young people are acutely aware of and interested in environmental issues. The context for dealing with environmental issues has a number of levels that make it particularly attractive for its use in technology education. At the personal level students can look at their own behaviour through, for example, uses of energy, use of resources, or treatment of waste. These kinds of topics can be dealt with at the level of the local community and indeed the national and international communities. Both official and unofficial groups are often involved. The purpose of dealing with environmental issues is to deal with the quality of life, and this is not just a matter of considering the effects of industry (for example) on the natural environment, but the development of compromises to provide employment and improve the 'made' environment, while at the same time minimizing the long-term impact on the environment. This may of course entail an understanding of industrial and technical processes and systems. It will inevitably mean that appropriate technology will be a focus, something often ignored in the industrial setting where commercial success is the main criterion.

Another aspect of the importance of culture was our concern that problem solving processes, particularly those that have an organizational dimension, was to question the extent to which they were transferable. The most obvious transfer issue arises when technologies are transferred from one industry to another. However, in an age of multi-national companies, the transfer of problem-solving strategies by such companies across international boundaries presents an important issue. The emergence of Skoda into the world market, using the management and production process techniques from VW (See Kunz' paper) is an example of this situation. Increasingly, the pervasiveness of technological artifacts and the international production and marketing of them forces a single view of technological processes upon the world. (This is related to the larger issue of technological transfer.) Science educators have searched in vain for a 'local science', which reflects the local culture and economic conditions. Appropriate technology offers a way of considering 'local technology' not just in the kinds of artifacts that might be appropriate to the local conditions, but also those that are created through processes that are similarly appropriate. In that sense we would truly have situated cognition.

References

1. Healy, L., Pozzi, S., Hoyles, C. (1992) Computers in group settings: doing and learning mathematics. In: R. McCormick, P. Murphy, M. Harrison Teaching and Learning Technology. London: Addison-Wesley

List of Participants

Jacqueline Ancess, Dr.
Teachers College/Columbia
University
West 120 th St. Box 110
New York City, NY 10027
USA
Tel.: + 10-212-678-4193

Fatih C. Babalik, Dr.-Ing.
Professor
Uludag University
Faculty of Engineering
Gorukle-Bursa, 16059
Turkey
Tel.: + 9024-42-8019

Joao Dias Baptista, Dr.
University of Minho
Institute of Education
Campus de Gualtar
Braga, 4700
Portugal
Tel.: + 351-53-604241

Nigan Bayazit, Dr.
Professor
Istanbul Technical University
Department of Architecture
Istanbul Taksim, 80191
Turkey
Tel.: + 901- 243-3100/224

Jozef Belák, Dipl.-Ing.
Ministry of Economy of the Slovak
Republic
Department for Technical Policy
Mierova 19
Bratislava, 827 15
Slovakia
Tel.: + 427-299-830-9

Dietrich Blandow, Dr.
Professor
Eindhoven University of
Technology
Department W and M
Den Dolch 2 Postbus 513
Eindhoven, 5600
The Netherlands
Tel.: + 49-361-667643

Lev Bukowsky, Dr.RN
Professor
University of P. J. Safarik, Kosice
Department Computer Science
Jesenna 5
Kosice, 041 54
Slovakia
Tel.: + 42-95-27034

Jürgen Buresch, Dr.
BMW AG
Dept. of Development of Human
Resources
Petuelring 130
München , D-80807
Germany
Tel.: + 49-89-3895-5206

Carlos A. V. Costa, Dr.
University of Porto
Department of Chemistry
Engineering
Rua dos Bragas
Porto Codex, 4099
Portugal
Tel.: + 351-2-2007505

Roseanne DeFabio
New York State Education Dept.
Education, Curriculum &
Assessment Team #2
NYS Education Dept. Room 674
Albany, NY 12234
USA
Tel.: + 518-473-4698

Marc de Vries, Dr.
Eindhoven University of
Technology
Dept. of Philosophy & Social
Sciences
Den Dolch 2 P. O. Box 513
Eindhoven, 5600 MB
The Netherlands
Tel.: + 31-40-474629

Jean-Jacques Duby
UAP Assurances
Scientific Direction
Tour ASSUR-Cedex 14
Paris La Defense, F-92083
France
Tel.: + 33-1-4774-1291

Vaclav Dufala, Dr.
Air Force Academy
Dept. of Economics
Rambova 7
Kosice, 5121
Slovakia
Tel.: + 42-95-35175

Michael J. Dyrenfurth, Dr.
Professor
University of Missouri-Columbia
Dept. of Practical Arts and Vocat.
Techn. Education
105 London Hall
Columbia, MO 65211
USA
Tel.: + 314-882-2782

Jorma Eino Enkenberg, Dr.
University of Joensuu
Faculty of Education
BOX 111
Joensuu, FIN- 80101
Finland
Tel.: + 358-73-1512307

Kenneth L. Fisher, Dr.
Bolton Institute of Higher Education
Chadwick Street
Bolton BL2 1JW
United Kingdom
Tel.: + 44-204-28851

Anthony Gordon
Saginaw Public Schools
Averill Career Opportunity Center
2102 Weiss Street
Saginaw, MI 48602
USA
Tel.: + 1-517-797-4836

George Joseph Haché, Dr.
Memorial University of
Newfoundland
Faculty of Education
Prince Phillip Drive
St. John's, A1B 3X8
Canada
Tel.: + 709-737-7630

Michael Hacker
New York State Education Dept.
One Commerce Plaza Room 1619
Albany, NY 12234
USA
Tel.: + 518-474-3954

Anne Halliday
Psychological Society of Ireland
13 Adelaide Road
Dublin 2
Republic of Ireland
Tel.: + 353-1-783916

Daniel L. Householder, Dr.
Professor
Texas A & M University
Department of EHRD
615 Harrington Tower
College Station, TX 77843-3256
USA
Tel.: + 409-845-2436

Ivan Hrivnak, Dr.
Professor
Technical University of Kosice
Letna ul.9
Kosice, 04200
Slovakia
Tel.: + 42-95-399 087

Scott D. Johnson, Dr.
University of Illinois
Dept. of Vocational and Technical
Education
1310 South Sixth Street
Champaign, IL 61820
USA
Tel.: + 217-333-0807

Derry W. Jones
Professor
University of Bradford
Chemistry and Chemical
Technology
Bradford West BD7 1DP
United Kingdom
Tel.: + 274-733-466-3804

Fritz Kath, Dr.
Institute of Education in the Field of
Vocation and Commerce
University of Hamburg
Sedanstr. 19
Hamburg 13, D-20146
Germany
Tel.: + 49-40-4123-3733

Richard Anthony Kimbell, Dr.
Professor
University of London
Goldsmiths' College
Technology Education Research
New Cross
London SE14 6NW
United Kingdom
Tel.: + 44-81-694-2510

Peter Kunz
Skoda Car Plant
Mlada Boleslav, 293 60
Czech Republic
Tel.: + 42-326-51-6614

Zuzana Ladzianska, Dr. RN
Academy Istropolitana
P. O. Box 92
Bratislava 42, 840 02
Slovakia
Tel.: + 42-7-0901701472

Kati Langer
WOCATE
Schlösserstraße 9
Erfurt, D-99084
Germany
Tel.: + 49-361-5621082

Milos Lansky, Dr. RN
Charles University of Prague
Pedagogical Faculty
M. D. Rettigove 4
Prague 1, 116 39
Czech Republic
Tel.: + 42-2-298751

Anton Lavrin, Dr.
Technical University of Kosice
Dept. of Production Processes
Control
B. Nemcovej 3
Kosice, 4167
Slovakia
Tel.: + 42-95-39772

Francoise Le Guet Tully
Cote d' Azur Observatory
CERGA-URA
BP 229
Nice Cedex 4, F-6304
France
Tel.: + 33-92-003043

Thomas T. Liao, Dr.
Professor
State University of New York at
Stony Brook
Department of Technology and
Society
Engineering Building, Room 210
Stony Brook, NY 11794-2250
USA
Tel.: + 516-632-8767

E. Sebastian Loew
South Bank University
Marketing Services
103 Borough Road
London SE1 0AA
United Kingdom
Tel.: + 44-71-8156707

Maria Malevri
Assistant Programme Specialist,
STE
UNESCO
7 Place de Fontenoy
F-75700 Paris
France
Tel.: + 33-1-568-10-00

Robert McCormick, Dr.
The Open University
Centre for Technology Education
Walton Hall
Milton Keynes MK7 6AA
United Kingdom
Tel.: + 44-908-653771

Matthias Metzing
WOCATE
Schlösserstraße 9
Erfurt, D-99084
Germany
Tel.: + 49-361-5621082

Voitech Molnar, Dr.
Professor
Slovak Technical University
Rector's Office
Nám. Slobody 17
Bratislava, 81243
Slovakia
Tel.: + 42- 7- 537-40

Frantisek Mosna, Dr.-Ing.
Professor
Charles University of Prague
Rettigove 4
Prague 1, 11639
Czech Republic
Tel.: + 42-2-298751

Peter O'Hagan
James Brindley High School
St. Michael's Road
Stoke-on-Trent ST6 6JT
United Kingdom
Tel.: + 782-837-381

Jozef Pastier, Dr.
Professor
Slovak Ministry of Economy
Nierova 19
Bratislava, 827 15
Slovakia
Tel.: + 564-71 kl.442

Albert Ch. Paulsen
Roskilde University
IMFUFA
P. O. Box 260
Roskilde, DK-4000
Denmark
Tel.: + 45-46-757711

Tomas Sabol, Dr.
Technical University of Kosice
Dept. of Cybernetics and Artificial
Intelligence
Letna 9
Kosice, 041 20
Slovakia
Tel.: + 42-95-53574

Jakub Serych, Ing.
Sec. Highschool
Telecommunication
Department of Computer
Technology
Panska 3
Praha 1, 11000
Czech Republic
Tel.: + 42-2-224656/32

Dennis B. Sharpe, Dr.
Memorial University of
Newfoundland
Faculty of Education
Prince Phillip Drive
St. John's, A1B 3X8
Canada
Tel.: + 709-737-7549

Colin Shields
Bolton Institute of Higher Education
School of Education and Health
Chadwick Street
Bolton BL2 1JW
United Kingdom
Tel.: + 44-204-28851

Juraj Sinay, Dr.-Ing
Professor
Technical University of Kosice
Dept. of Transport Systems
Letna 9
Kosice, 04187
Slovakia
Tel.: + 42-95-34805

Sam Stern, Dr.
Professor
Oregon State University
School of Education
Education Hall
Corvallis, OR 97331
USA
Tel.: + 503-737-6392

Corinne Stevenson
Whitemore High School
Porlock Avenue
Harrow HA2 0AD
United Kingdom
Tel.: + 44-81-864-7688

Ervin Szücs, Dr.
Professor
Eötvös University
Department of General Technology
Rákóczi ut. 5
Budapest, H-1088
Hungary
Tel.: + 36-1-2668643

Walter E. Theuerkauf, Dr.-Ing
Professor
University of Hildesheim
Institute of Applied Electrical
Engineering and Technology
Education
Kreuzstraße 8
Hildesheim, D-31134
Germany
Tel.: + 49-5121-304-446/7

Detlef Wahl
WOCATE
Schlösserstraße 9
Erfurt, D-99084
Germany
Tel.: + 49-361-5621082

Dieter Wild, Dipl.-Phys.
Professor (em)
Meiendorfer Str. 74 c
Hamburg, D-22145
Germany
Tel.: + 49-40-6784490

Frank J. Worzala
Professor
University of Wisconsin-Madison
Dept. of Materials Science and
Engineering
1509 University Avenue
Madison, WI 53706-1595
USA
Tel.: + 608-262-1821

George Wybouw, Dr.
University of Moncton
Faculty of Administration
Moncton N.B., E1C 5R7
Canada
Tel.: + 506-858-4233

Subject Index

NATO ASI Series F

NATO ASI Series F

Including Special Programmes on Sensory Systems for Robotic Control (ROB) and on Advanced Educational Technology (AET)

NATO ASI Series F

Including Special Programmes on Sensory Systems for Robotic Control (ROB) and on Advanced Educational Technology (AET)

NATO ASI Series F

NATO ASI Series F